Public Speaking *for* Personal Success

Fourth Edition

Public Speaking
for
Personal Success

Michael S. Hanna   James W. Gibson

University of South Alabama   *University of Missouri, Columbia*

Boston, Massachusetts   Burr Ridge, Illinios   Dubuque, Iowa
Madison, Wisconsin   New York, New York   San Francisco, California   St. Louis, Missouri

McGraw·Hill

A Division of The McGraw·Hill Companies

PUBLIC SPEAKING FOR PERSONAL SUCCESS

4 5 6 7 8 9 10   FGRFGR   9 9 8

ISBN 0-697-20144-9
        0-697-24960-3 (AIE)

Developmental Editor   *Mary E. Rossa*
Production Editor   *Karen A. Pluemer*
Designer   *Kristyn A. Kalnes*
Art Editor   *Brenda A. Ernzen*
Photo Editor   *Laura Fuller*
Permissions Coordinator   *Pat Barth*
Visuals/Design Freelance Specialist   *Mary L. Christianson*

Library of Congress Catalog Card Number: 94-70378

http:\\www.mhhe.com

This book is dedicated to the memory of Sol Newman, Jr. and the memory of Franklin H. Knower.

Brief Contents

Contents

PART 2

Designing the Speech   61

Chapter 4

Selecting and Narrowing Your Topic   63

Chapter 5

Audience Analysis   89

Chapter 6

Supporting Ideas with Argument and Evidence   109

Chapter 7

Gathering Supporting Materials and Using the Library   135

PART 3

Organizing the Speech   167

Chapter 8

Organizing the Body of the Speech   169

Chapter 9

Outlining the Speech   193

Preface

Public Speaking for Personal Success is written for students enrolled in a first public speaking course. We have tried to present a blend of theory and practice that students and teachers will enjoy. Our research and experience convince us that this approach works best in the classroom.

This fourth edition is very nearly a new work—updated, refined, and reorganized, with new illustrations and more and better examples. The changes reflect our continuing effort to keep the work fresh, timely, and consistent with how the basic public speaking course is taught in most American colleges and universities. But we have not abandoned the elements of the book that have made it successful.

A direct relationship exists between verbal ability, especially in one-to-many settings, and personal success. How we perceive others depends, in large measure, upon how others talk. A person who projects an articulate and competent image is believed to be articulate and competent. We make decisions about that person based upon that belief. We turn to articulate and competent people for help and for leadership. So it is that these people tend to succeed in their endeavors.

The title of this book is intended to convey the book's applicability. People encounter many occasions every day in which they must organize their ideas and present them to others. The skills involved in these pursuits can be learned and practiced. And the effort spent in learning and practicing is a solid investment.

People learn to give speeches most easily when they see how the ideas they are studying actually apply. For this reason, the book includes a large number of carefully developed examples and illustrations. Many of the examples have been drawn from the classroom so that students can relate to them and perceive them as models of performance levels that are achievable with practice. Many examples from business and professional settings have been included as well to show how the ideas and skills taught in a public speaking course apply throughout a person's life.

SPECIFIC FEATURES

The chapter sequence and materials in this book have been carefully designed to fit public speaking classes as they are generally taught today. Decisions about how to revise and upgrade this fourth edition have all been driven by a desire to keep the book fresh and current.

Content Features

Chapter 1, "Introduction"

People develop communication skills most easily when they understand the communication process and where public speaking fits into that process. This introductory chapter presents a useful model of communication that shows how public speaking fits into the larger process and how it is set apart from other forms of communication. Public speakers also must assume certain ethical responsibilities. This chapter describes how public speaking requires ethical choices and how those choices are tied to personal success.

Chapter 2, "Planning the First Speech"

Many speech teachers ask students to prepare and deliver a speech early in the term. The students need plenty of information, and they need it fast. This chapter provides that information in an overview of the steps in preparing a speech.

Public speaking often produces anxiety in the student speaker. This chapter provides assurance that feelings of anxiety are normal and that they can be both controlled and used to advantage. The chapter also identifies the most common errors of beginning speech students and explains how to plan and prepare to avoid these errors.

Chapter 3, "Listening"

Material on listening is presented early in the book because many people tend to be poor listeners. This chapter includes a clear discussion of the listening process and focuses on how speakers can use their knowledge of listening to help audiences listen to—and remember—the ideas in a speech.

Chapter 4, "Selecting and Narrowing Your Topic"

Beginning speakers often try to include far too much in a speech. In this chapter, students learn how to select and narrow a topic so that it is based on what they know, appeals to their audiences, is appropriate to the speaking occasion, and falls within the time constraints of the speech.

Chapter 5, "Audience Analysis"

Successful speakers adapt to the audience and to the setting. In this chapter, students learn how audience perceptions and expectations affect their speaking objectives. They also learn how to conduct an appropriate and useful audience analysis, both within the classroom and in broader and less directly accessible situations. This chapter has been completely revised to render it more stimulating and much easier to read and use.

Chapter 6, "Supporting Ideas with Argument and Evidence"

This thoroughly revised chapter provides a firm foundation in the uses of argument and evidence, the basis of successful speech making. In clear and simple terms, and with many examples, the chapter discusses how to analyze and produce inductive and deductive arguments and how to use arguments from sign, cause, and analogy. Aristotle's artistic proofs—*ethos, pathos,* and *logos*—provide the organizational structure for the chapter. Students learn to develop and use all the basic types of evidence: testimony, definition and explanation, statistics, and examples.

Chapter 7, "Gathering Supporting Materials and Using the Library"

As technology advances, gathering information becomes easier. This completely rewritten chapter discusses the most commonly available technology for finding supporting materials, as well as interpersonal interviewing and correspondence skills. The various departments of a modern library are described, along with helpful suggestions about how to use each one. The chapter also discusses computerized database services and networks, how to perform CD-ROM searches, how to evaluate gathered materials, and how to take notes and develop a working bibliography.

Chapter 8, "Organizing the Body of the Speech"

This chapter describes how to use all of the most common organizational patterns taught in public speaking classes: time, space, problem to solution, causal order, topical divisions, and the motivated sequence. In addition, students learn how to build and use transitions, signposts, and internal summaries to help listeners follow their ideas. This chapter has been revised to include many more examples and illustrations, most of them new.

Chapter 9, "Outlining the Speech"

This new chapter includes the best ideas from earlier editions of *Public Speaking for Personal Success* and adds many new explanations and examples. Students learn how to use outlining to plan and develop a speech, and how to develop and use effective speaking outlines.

Chapter 10, "Beginning and Ending a Speech"

This chapter describes the purposes of speech introductions and conclusions and the most effective strategies for developing them. The chapter is full of new and interesting examples and ideas that students can use to frame a speech.

Chapter 11, "Language: The Key to Successful Speaking"

The language we use creates the reality we experience. Thus, language is the most powerful tool that speakers have to accomplish their speaking goals. This chapter explains how thought and language are related, shows how language creates emotional affect, and recommends simple techniques for using language that increase a speaker's success.

Chapter 12, "Supporting Ideas Visually"

This chapter examines how to design and develop visual supporting materials that are cost effective, that are convenient to use, and that powerfully support the ideas of a speech. The chapter also describes some of the technological advances that have simplified making visual materials and sharply reduced their costs.

Chapter 13, "Delivery"

Effective delivery involves using the voice and the body to convey a message to listeners. This chapter describes how to choose the right method of delivery, pay attention to characteristics of the speaking voice (rate, pitch, and volume), and monitor nonverbal messages (gestures, eye contact, personal appearance, and behavior).

Chapter 14, "Informative Speaking"

This chapter describes the different types of informative speeches (definition, demonstration, description, and explanation) and provides guidelines for successful informative speaking. Students learn how to generate attention and interest and deliver a simple, credible, memorable informative speech.

Chapter 15, "Persuasive Speaking"

Persuasive speaking may be the highest form of the speaker's art. So important is it that the ancient Greeks included it among the three essential subjects of any educated person. In the intervening years, scholars have never stopped studying how one person can influence others. Accordingly, this chapter is longer than the others and is comprised of materials from that vast body of knowledge called "rhetoric" that are deemed important for a first course in public speaking. Students who apply the materials in this chapter will be able to give effective and compelling persuasive speeches.

Chapter 16, "Speeches for Special Occasions"

This is the chapter students turn to when called upon to make special occasion speeches, which are organized into three broad categories: speeches of praise and tribute, inspirational speeches, and speeches for the sake of humor. Regardless of the context—a speech of introduction at the Rotary Club, a keynote speech, a tribute on the occasion of someone's retirement—special occasion speeches carry special challenges. The problems and their solutions are described and illustrated in detail, with many examples, in this chapter.

Learning Aids

Chapter Opening Pedagogy

Each chapter has been designed to give students the clearest possible impression of what lies within, and why. The **Chapter Outline** includes three levels of headings and shows students at a glance how the chapter is organized and what it includes. The **Chapter Objectives** point to the most important themes in a chapter and call out the behaviors that a student should be able to exhibit after having studied the chapter carefully. These objectives also serve as a basis for study and review because they tell students what materials in each chapter are important to know and understand.

End-of-Chapter Pedagogy

Several helpful learning tools follow each chapter. These include a carefully worded **Summary** of the chapter's key ideas. The **Key Terms** are each defined in the chapter and again in the glossary and are the essential concepts that students should retain. **Application Questions** ask students to apply what they have learned to real-life situations. They encourage students to practice both analytical and performance skills introduced in the chapters. A keyed **Self-Test for Review** is followed by a brief, annotated bibliography of **Suggested Readings.** Chapter 2 includes a **Sample Speech** that illustrates beyond the text examples what has been described in the chapter.

Profiles

Profiles within most chapters feature well-known people illustrating ideas presented in the text. These will help students to understand the relevance of the public speaking course to the world outside the classroom. For example, students will read comments from Colin Powell on extemporaneous speaking, entrepreneur Guy Kawasaki on being audience-centered, former Congresswoman Barbara Jordan on words, and President Bill Clinton on effective listening.

End-of-Book Pedagogy

Readers will find the end-of-book material especially helpful. In the **Sample Speeches** in Appendix A, teaching value and topic interest were the most important criteria in the selection process. Students need to be exposed to various levels of speaker experience. Therefore, the appendix includes speeches by Vernon Jordan, Jr. and Mario Cuomo, individuals whose success has been based partly on their ability to speak effectively, as well as speeches by students, whose only training had been the basic public speaking class. Between these extremes are speeches by more experienced student speakers and by working men and women who speak occasionally. This presentation of a range of speaker experience shows that growth in public speaking ability is a process, that practice pays off in the form of greater and greater success. Five of the sample speeches include marginal notations that point out strengths, limitations, and particular points of interest in these speeches.

Appendix B, **How to Handle Nervousness,** is designed to help offset the fears and anxieties of many beginning speech students. Its discussions of why nervousness occurs and what to do about it will help students to constructively channel their fears.

Appendix C is a unique **Troubleshooting Guide.** Here, students are able to find answers to questions in their own terms. The guide is organized around the questions most commonly asked by students. For example, the questions might be, "What should I support with a visual aid?" In the troubleshooting guide, under the general heading "Visual Aids," students find one or more questions similar to the one being asked and a page reference to text material that answers the question. Previous users have indicated that the troubleshooting guide gives them wider access to the text by providing a different approach to classifying information.

Appendix D, **Possible Speech Topics,** lists several hundred potential speech topics. Such a list is also likely to trigger the generation of a variety of related ideas that would be suitable speech topics.

The **Glossary** is a compilation of every key term used in the text, defined in exactly the same language that appears in the text, and often expanded beyond the text definition. The **Index** provides further access to the materials discussed in the book.

Thus, like the body of the text, the pedagogical materials in this book have been designed with the student in mind. The overriding concern has been on how to help students to acquire the knowledge, skills, and abilities of public speaking. *Public Speaking for Personal Success* should be much more than a textbook gathering dust on a shelf after one term of use. It will provide public speaking guidance long after students have completed the course. Personal success is, after all, a lifetime adventure.

ACKNOWLEDGMENTS

The following reviewers have provided valuable suggestions for the fourth edition of our work. We are grateful and want to express our sincere appreciation for their contributions:

John Bee, *University of Akron*
Robert Dunbar, *City College of San Francisco*
Beth Ellis, *Ball State University*
Anne Holmquest, *Augsburg College*
Michael Ingram, *Whitworth College*
Patti Kalanquin, *William Rainey Harper College*
John Meyer, *University of Southern Mississippi*
Barbara Mollberg, *Rochester Community College*
John Muchmore, *William Rainey Harper College*
Lawrence Rifkind, *Georgia State University*
Ann Scroggie, *Santa Fe Community College*
Wayne Silver, *Mohegan Community College*
Todd Thomas, *Indiana University–Bloomington*
Beth Waggenspack, *Virginia Poly Institute and State University*
John Williams, *California State University–Sacramento*

We again express our gratitude to the reviewers of the first three editions of our text:

Martha Atkins, *Iowa State University;* Phil Backlund, *Central Washington University;* David Branco, *University of Nebraska–Omaha;* Larry Caillouet, *Western Kentucky University;* Isaac Catt, *California State University–Chico;* Martha Cooper, *Northern Illinois University;* Roseanne Dawson, *University of Southern Colorado;* Elizabeth Faries, *Western Illinois University;* Suzanne Fitch, *Southwest Texas State University;* James Floyd, *Central Missouri State University;* Thurman Garner, *University of Georgia;* Kathleen German, *Miami University;* Dennis Gouran, *Pennsylvania State University;* Gail Hankins, *North Carolina State University;* Susan A. Hellweg, *San Diego State University;* Kelly Huff, *University of South Alabama;* Larry Hugenberg, *Youngstown State University;* Diane Ivy, *North Carolina State University;* Robert

Jackson, *Ball State University;* Fred Jandt, *California State University–San Bernardino;* Lcdr. Keith Maynard, *U.S. Naval Academy;* Linda Medaris, *Central Missouri State University;* Kathleen Morgenstern, *California State University–Fresno;* Mark Morman, *Southern Utah State College;* Greg Olson, *Marquette University;* Patricia Palm, *Mankato State University;* Mary Pelias, *Southern Illinois University;* Robert L. Phillips, *Longview Community College;* Steve Rendahl, *University of North Dakota;* Michael Schliessman, *South Dakota State University;* Larry Schnoor, *Mankato State University;* Bill Seiler, *University of Nebraska;* Paul Shaffer, *Austin Peay State University;* Mark Shilstone, *University of Missouri;* Lee Snyder, *Kearney State University;* James Stewart, *Tennessee Technological University;* Cathy Thomas, *Morehead State University;* Susan Thomas, *University of Illinois;* Nancy Wendt, *California State University–Sacramento;* Donald Wolfarth, *University of Wisconsin– Eau Claire.*

Authors don't write books. Authors write manuscripts. When the manuscript arrives at the publishing house, editors turn them into books. The really great books have all been worked upon by really great editors. So we want to thank, especially, Mary Rossa, who had to put up with our fits of passionate defensiveness, and Mary Monner, whose magic hands touch every sentence in this edition.

We also wish to acknowledge Michelle Campbell, Karen Pluemer, Kristyn Kalnes, Laura Fuller, Brenda Ernzen, and Pat Barth. They comprise the remainder of the book team that turned our manuscript into the beautiful book you are holding in your hands.

Mike Hanna
Jim Gibson

PART 1

Speaking and Listening

© David Brownell/The Image Bank

Introduction

OUTLINE

OBJECTIVES

After reading this chapter, you should be able to:

1. *Name* three areas of your life in which public speaking skills can contribute to your success, and *explain* how improved speaking skills can make those contributions.
2. *Explain* how a course in public speaking requires self-disclosure.
3. *Differentiate* among ethical, unethical, and ethically neutral speaking behaviors, and *provide* examples of each.
4. *Explain* what a model is, and *specify* the defining features of a process model of communication.
5. *Identify, define,* and *explain* the following elements in the process model of communication: physical and emotional context, source/encoder, channels, verbal and nonverbal messages, decoder/receiver, physical and psychological noise, and feedback.
6. *Name* and *explain* the three features that set public speaking apart from other forms of communication.

© David Young-Wolff/PhotoEdit

*I*n this chapter, you learn how skill in public speaking can contribute to your personal and professional success. The chapter also discusses the ethical responsibilities inherent in public speaking skills: You must know what you are talking about, reject fraud and deception, measure your limits carefully and honestly, know and understand your position on controversial issues, and adopt a standard of honor. Building public speaking skills depends on understanding the communication process, and the chapter shows how models help in this understanding. The chapter concludes with a discussion of how public speaking is part of the larger communication process, set apart from other forms by three features: structure, formality, and anxiety. An understanding of these characteristics will help you to be a more effective public speaker.

Congratulations. Your decision to take this public speaking course was wise. People who know how to communicate typically have greater success than those who do not. They know how to share knowledge, to persuade, to motivate. They seem to have control of their lives. They are "can-do" people who are trusted and sought out by others.

In this course, you will learn how to get your ideas across, how to inform and persuade an audience, how to stimulate and motivate people. These skills affect every aspect of your life because public speaking does not occur only in a large hall. Public speaking skills are relevant in small groups or whenever you are trying to persuade. Some are relevant for one-on-one discussions with a colleague or even for when you are talking on the telephone.

Wherever people are communicating effectively, you will find one or more of the skills taught in this course. People who seem successful, who sell themselves and their ideas to others, who exercise power, and who have influence know how to use the techniques that you will practice day after day in this course.

In contrast, people who do not seem successful, who do not think they need to practice or learn how to communicate better, probably are not seen as good speakers. They do not seem to have much self-confidence or to exercise much "clout." They may have a reputation for being dull and boring.

The old cliché "You can't sell a product until you sell yourself first" is true. A person's public speaking skills and personal success are clearly related. Self-confidence gives you the basis for projecting the image you want. That image determines how others perceive you and how much confidence they invest in you. As you increase your public speaking skills, you will gain self-confidence. In turn, this strengthened image will cause other people to place greater confidence in you.[1]

PUBLIC SPEAKING FOR PERSONAL SUCCESS

Public speaking skills can help you to attain personal success in three areas; (1) in your private life, (2) in your professional life, and (3) in your public life outside work.

Your private life can be powerfully affected by increased self-confidence in your ability to express yourself. To illustrate, one student tried three times to give a speech in

STEPHEN COVEY

In his book *Principle-Centered Leadership*, Stephen Covey, who is chairman of the Covey Leadership Center and the nonprofit Institute for Principle-Centered Leadership, encourages readers to approach public speaking as they would approach learning a sport, an instrument, or how to draw: practice. Covey stresses that no one should be afraid to be a "beginner." He explains:

Effective communication requires skills, and skill development takes practice. A person cannot improve his tennis game merely by reading tennis books or watching great tennis players. He must get out on the court and practice what he has read or seen, progressing slowly through different levels of proficiency.

Source: Stephen Covey, Principle-Centered Leadership *(New York: Fireside, 1991), 113–114. Photo courtesy of Stephen Covey. Covey Leadership Center.*

his first public speaking class. He was so nervous and unsettled that he just could not push himself through the classroom door when his name appeared on the speaking schedule. His avoidance behavior also extended to other important areas of his life. He reported having difficulty meeting people. He once made an appointment for a job interview but could not make himself go to it. He had a difficult time asking women for dates and found criticism nearly intolerable. He seldom asked for help, even when he was lost, preferring to wander aimlessly until he found his way. He said that blaming others and expressing anger were strategies he used to hold people away.

Even so, this student finally completed his public speaking course. In a brief "exit essay" for use in helping other students, he wrote:

> *I can't believe it. A year ago, even three months ago, I would never have thought it possible to get through this course. Each time I got through a speech, I felt like I'd done something impossible. In time, as I learned how to do it, I began to feel easier I sure wasn't wonderful, but I sure feel wonderful now.*

His experience is a testimonial to the value a public speaking course can have in your private life.

In addition to affecting your private life, public speaking skills can have a tremendous impact on a developing career. Effective presenters tend to become visible people. Visibility generates opportunities. Public speaking skills call attention to the speaker's thinking and reasoning, to the quality of the speaker's thought. They advertise without bragging. They lend credibility. They make it possible to contribute reserves of energy and knowledge in many different settings. Generally, people who are perceived as more powerful become more powerful.[2]

To illustrate, two graduates entered a large paper company in the same month, right out of college. One student learned to apply the public speaking skills she learned in college to a variety of business contexts, and she could really persuade. The other student, a young man, had equal intelligence but lacked communication skills. The woman used her public speaking skills every day; the man avoided such opportunities. After six years, the woman was in a high-ranking management development position, while the man's climb up the corporate ladder was nowhere near as rapid. In a letter to her former public speaking teacher, the woman wrote:

I volunteered to give an update speech concerning a quality committee I am a part of. (I would never have considered it before your course.) I gave the speech. I was hardly nervous, and since you weren't there, I'll have to tell you, I was great. I was the only speaker who didn't hang on the podium; I went into the audience. I used no notes—only the overheads I'd made. I used the techniques you taught in Public Speaking.

There were about two hundred people in attendance, and over the next few days, it seemed that at least half of them complimented me. The vice president in charge of technology congratulated me and asked my supervisor for details about my career.

It was fun and rewarding. I have the invaluable lessons you teach about speaking to thank.[3]

Public speaking skills can have a big impact on public life away from work, too. Numerous social groups provide opportunities to speak. For example, PTA, Kiwanis, and Women Executives Forum meetings all provide opportunities to contribute what you know—and to practice speaking skills. Church activities or community garden club activities also involve public speaking skills. In these contexts and countless others, if you can make an effective presentation, your ability to make a contribution to others increases. As you gain recognition and respect, your ideas take on greater persuasive force.[4]

THE PUBLIC SPEAKING COURSE

In a public speaking course, you learn to present yourself and your ideas in a public setting by building on the commonsense knowledge you already possess. For example, if you think about it for a moment, you already know about what constitutes effective speech making. You can tell when a speaker holds your attention or successfully meets your criteria for a good speech. You also know when a speech does not go anywhere, lacks focus, or seems shallow and unsupported. This understanding of what constitutes an effective or ineffective speech allows you to apply effective public speaking techniques while choosing to eliminate common public speaking errors.

In a public speaking course, your commonsense knowledge works hand in hand with personal self-disclosure—talking about your beliefs and about objects, people, and events in your world. While the course will draw on your knowledge and experience, it also will ask you to tie new information to what you already know. Personal experience, however, is the basis on which you build your public speaking skills.

Public speaking instructors are valuable learning resources. They organize and develop interesting exercises and assignments, all aimed at helping you to develop a clearer

Social groups provide numerous opportunities to speak.

© 1994 Tara C. Patty

sense of purpose, organization, and style. Your instructor will be glad to answer your questions and, more importantly, to provide comments and suggestions about your classroom presentations. Make a point of getting to know your instructor.

This book will help you, too. It includes many examples drawn from students and from consulting experience. In some cases, the illustrations have been invented. Yet, each one tries to *show* you as well as tell you how to improve your speech making. Even so, effective public speaking requires hard work.

You will make important choices throughout this course. For example, it is up to you to prepare thoroughly, or less so. You can choose to practice often and carefully, or less so. You can expose yourself to speaking opportunities, or you can avoid them. If you work hard, you will finish the course with a new sense of what you can do and with new, powerful, and useful speaking skills. Your success, however, is up to you. A little extra effort will yield rewards far beyond this course—rewards that will improve the quality of the rest of your life.

PUBLIC SPEAKING AND ETHICS

Public speaking that influences others implies certain ethical questions. **Ethics** refers to the study of moral values, of rightness or wrongness. Is it right to influence another person's behavior? Are right and wrong absolutely opposite? Or do they range along a continuum of behavioral choices? Do a speaker's worthy goals ever justify the means used to achieve them? When you set out to change attitudes or behaviors, when you inspire people to adopt a new course of action, your motives come into question.

Credibility refers to the degree to which listeners believe in you, the speaker. To illustrate, suppose you lie to someone, and as a result, she makes a decision she would not otherwise have made. Suppose further that, as a result of the lie, you gain a benefit while she loses. Your listener is likely to decide that you cannot be believed or trusted.

Unfortunately, ethical decisions are rarely black and white. In fact, you may be most tempted as a speaker to use questionable methods of communication when you think that the change you are advocating will benefit your audience. Richard Johannesen identified some basic ethical issues that every speaker should consider:[5]

Can ethical standards be flexible, or must they be absolute?

Is it okay to follow a minimum standard, or must we always shoot for the highest possible ethical level?

Do the ends justify the means? Are questionable persuasive techniques permissible when a worthwhile goal can be achieved?

Is it ever permissible to lie? What constitutes a lie?

Is it ever permissible to create intentional ambiguity—to cloud an issue?

Is television advertising that clouds the truth in vagueness and ambiguity unethical?

Is propaganda ethical? Is persuasion propaganda? Is, then, persuasion ethical?

Is name-calling ethical?

Is the masculine assumption in language adequate to describe the hopes and dreams of both men and women?

Is there an ethic involved in matters of taste?

Thus, as a speaker, you may occasionally be tempted to use statistics based on questionable research, to use a quotation out of context, or to make an emotional appeal when the decision requires logical decision making. Think through your choices carefully. The powerful techniques that you will learn in this course carry with them certain ethical responsibilities.

Because public speaking can influence others, and because public speaking always takes a listener's time and energy, you have an obligation to be prepared every time you speak. This means that you have an ethical responsibility to know your subject, to examine the evidence, and to develop solid and sensible arguments.

Throughout this course, try to imagine giving your presentations to an important decision-making group. Prepare each speech as if you were to talk with a group of powerful business, political, and religious leaders. Assume that your classroom audience has the same motives as any other important group. Prepare thoroughly—it's your best guarantee of success.

Your ethical responsibility as a speaker includes preserving your listeners' choices. Your listeners have a right to complete and accurate information that allows them to choose freely among alternatives. Thus, you have the same obligation to your listeners that, for example, a used-car sales representative would have toward you if you were in the used-car market. Suppose that you find a late-model Pontiac that you really like but the used-car sales representative knows that the car's transmission is about to fall apart. That piece of information probably would influence your decision about buying the car. You have a right to know, and the used-car sales representative has an ethical obligation to tell you. Similarly, your listeners have a right to know all the critical information related to a decision you want them to make. As a general rule, you would be wise to provide it.

Ethics in public speaking reflect time-honored standards of appropriate behavior:

Play it straight. Do not try to deceive.

Do not try to keep critical information from your audience.

Test your evidence carefully.

Avoid exaggeration.

Present information as accurately and honestly as possible.

Know what you are talking about.

Learn how to measure your limits.

Reflect on your position on controversial issues, and have clear reasons for your points of view.

Take care that you do not dishonor yourself or anyone else.

Value human diversity.

Table 1.1 lists additional guidelines.

Table 1.1

ETHICS IN PUBLIC SPEAKING

SPEECH BEHAVIORS GENERALLY CONSIDERED UNETHICAL

A public speaker should not:
    falsify or invent evidence.
    distort evidence.
    deliberately use specious or deceptive reasoning to persuade.
    deceive listeners about purpose or intention.

SPEECH BEHAVIORS GENERALLY CONSIDERED ETHICAL

A public speaker may comfortably:
    support ideas that result from reflective thinking and systematic study.
    reject an idea that seems doubtful because of logical analysis or evidence.

SPEECH BEHAVIORS GENERALLY CONSIDERED ETHICALLY NEUTRAL

Ethically neutral behavior includes:
    purposefully arousing listeners' emotions.
    calling names.
    appealing to listeners' psychological needs.
    making an appeal based on personal prestige.
    appealing to majority opinion.
    appealing to an authority.

THE PROCESS OF COMMUNICATION

Public speaking is part of the overall communication process—the process of message exchange through which people express themselves and share their understanding. Public speaking typically involves communicating in a one-to-many setting, with speakers usually structuring that setting. That is, speakers assume primary responsibility for the communication event. Each component part of the public speaking setting, however, has an impact on the overall event. The section that follows describes certain communication models to help you understand the communication process and how public speaking fits into that overall process.

A PROCESS MODEL OF COMMUNICATION

One of the main reasons why people have difficulty communicating in a public speaking situation is that their conception of the communication process is wrong. They think that communication is like water flowing through a pipe. They believe that, once they send their message on its way, the message, like water in the pipe, eventually reaches its destination. Moreover, although they know there may be kinks and bends in the pipe, they have great faith that, when the message arrives at its destination, it will match the one they sent.

This conception of the communication process is based on a one-way, linear model. A **model** is a physical representation of an object or process. Models may take the form of drawings or three-dimensional forms, or they may be written explanations. Unfortunately, the linear model of communication is too simple. It does not take into account the many variables that can cause trouble when people try to communicate.

A **process model,** on the other hand, shows that communication is a dynamic, interactive phenomenon (see figure 1.1). Communication flows two ways, it happens in a context, and people act on each other simultaneously.

Each of the following component parts of the process model can greatly affect a public speaking situation: context, source/encoder, channels, messages, decoder/receiver, noise, and feedback. A thorough understanding of these components will improve your overall speaking and listening effectiveness.

CONTEXT

Communication always occurs in a context. **Context** refers to the physical, social, psychological, and temporal environment in which communication takes place. Context plays an important part in communication success because it controls how people experience an event. To illustrate, communication behavior at a

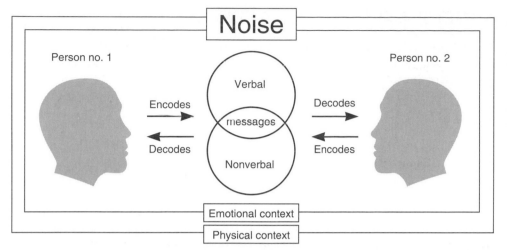

Figure **1.1**

A process model of communication. Communication flows in two directions, it happens in a context, and people act on each other simultaneously.

Context always makes a difference in the choices a speaker makes.

© John Neubauer

pep rally differs from communication behavior in a courtroom. The contexts of these differing events inform and control the different behaviors.

Context can also influence a person's ability to listen, or to be heard, or even to care. If a lecture hall is too warm or stuffy, for example, even the most motivated students will have difficulty concentrating on the lecture. **Physical context** refers to the physical and temporal surroundings in which a communication event occurs. **Emotional context** refers to the social and psychological portion of the communication event.

SOURCE/ENCODER (SPEAKER)

The speaker is both a **source** and a **receiver** of information. The speaker gets an idea and then translates it into **codes** that allow the idea to take shape and to have substance. Thus, another term for speaker is **source/encoder.**

CHANNELS

The speaker or source/encoder sends the shape and substance of ideas through channels to listeners. **Channels** are the means of transmission, the vehicles through which messages are sent. The shape and substance of those messages include both verbal and nonverbal meanings. Thus, in public speaking, *channels* refer to sound waves (your words traveling through the air) and light waves (the visual messages presented by your gestures and posture). As another example, in the communication event in which one person writes a letter to another, the letter assumes written language, and the channels are ink on paper. In figure 1.1, the channels are shown as arrows that carry what is encoded and decoded.

MESSAGES

Whatever information a speaker sends through channels is called a **message.** Messages in public speaking occur verbally as spoken words and nonverbally as visual and auditory signals. There are both intended and unintended messages. For example, sometimes, messages are sent accidentally. Once information is in a channel, however, it can be interpreted, and so it is called a message.

Messages rarely occur one at a time. Rather, verbal and nonverbal messages tend to combine into talk "packages." For example, in a public speaking situation, the messages include both words and such nonverbal messages as posture, gesture, facial expression, eye contact, tone of voice, and clearness of articulation. Listeners use *how* speakers say things to interpret *what* speakers have said. Read the sentences that follow aloud. Stress the boldfaced word in each, and notice how the stress pattern changes the meaning of the sentences.

- *You* can say that again.
- You *can* say that again.
- You can *say* that again.
- You can say *that* again.
- You can say that *again.*

DECODER/RECEIVER (LISTENER)

The listener is also called the **decoder/receiver.** The process of drawing information from communication channels and then interpreting it is called **decoding.** People do not always decode skillfully, which can create obvious communication problems. Even native speakers of a language do not share identical experiences or definitions. Moreover, a source/encoder might use a form of nonverbal emphasis that confuses the decoder/receiver. Put another way, the messages you send may not be the ones your audience members decode and receive.

Table 1.2

EXAMPLES OF PHYSICAL AND
PSYCHOLOGICAL NOISE

PHYSICAL NOISE	PSYCHOLOGICAL NOISE
Just as the professor writes a key statistics formula on the chalkboard, the lights go out. You cannot read the formula.	A speaker uses very strong language to describe his feelings about your favorite political candidate. You resent it and begin to think of ways to respond to the speaker. Thus focused, you miss what the speaker says next.
Just as your friend begins to tell you how to get to her house, static in the phone line keeps you from understanding the directions.	You respond with a strong emotion when your friend tells you about her illness. It shows on your face. She takes your response to mean that you do not want to hear about the illness, so she changes the subject.

NOISE

Anything that interferes with the fidelity of message exchange between two people is called **noise**. Noise that occurs in the channels is called **physical noise.** Noise that occurs inside people is called **psychological noise.** See table 1.2 for examples.

FEEDBACK

Feedback refers to messages that listeners send to speakers. Feedback allows people to correct and control errors in how they understand and interpret each other. In the process model of communication shown in figure 1.1 (p. 11), feedback takes the form of arrowheads. To illustrate, assume that you are trying to explain a difficult concept to one of your friends. His puzzled look tells you that he is having a difficult time understanding you, so you repeat yourself and give an example. In this case, the listener's puzzled look is a nonverbal message that you decode and receive. Instantaneously, you adapt to this feedback by repeating yourself and giving an example.

PUBLIC SPEAKING AS COMMUNICATION

The communication process model in figure 1.1 can be used to describe all kinds of communication events. What, then, makes public speaking unique? Both conversation and public speaking require you to organize your ideas, state them clearly, and establish and

maintain a relationship with the other people involved. Three characteristics, however, set public speaking apart from other forms of communication: (1) the structure of the event, (2) the level of formality, and (3) the degree of anxiety involved.

STRUCTURE

A public speech is highly structured. The parts of a good speech join smoothly together and are designed to form a single entity with a specific purpose, clearly identified arguments, and relevant supporting evidence.[6] Careful planning creates a structure that can be laid out and developed within certain time constraints. The listeners rarely talk, depending, instead, on the speaker to have organized ideas that they can follow and grasp easily. A good speech is designed to draw upon and harness the power held by listeners.

In contrast, a conversation rarely flows so smoothly. One speaker interrupts the other, sometimes introducing entirely new and unrelated topics. People begin, stammer, begin again. Arguments are rarely presented in a reasoned structure. Rather, people say what they think, talk around their ideas, and inject bits and pieces of evidence as they exchange information with each other. Over time, the arguments may emerge, but often, they are not specifically and clearly stated. Instead, the participants just seem to understand that they have reached an agreement without ever having stated what it is.

FORMALITY

When people join an audience, they expect the speaker to take control and to develop ideas critically and fully. In addition, listeners demand certain standards of behavior from speakers that would not apply to casual conversations. For example, speakers must usually adhere to more careful standards of grammar and usage and of appropriate dress than might be expected in casual conversations. When a minister walks to the pulpit, congregation members expect a certain level of formality that they would not require of the same person at a backyard cookout. As another example, President William Jefferson Clinton's inaugural address required greater formality than did Bill Clinton's dinner conversation that evening.

All audiences expect public speakers to conform to standards of formality that might not apply in other circumstances. Your success as a speaker depends, in part, on your ability to make those adaptations and adjustments.

ANXIETY

Anxiety is the third feature that separates public address from casual conversation. Anxiety levels in conversations are usually comfortably low. During a public speaking situation, however, tensions often rise above the comfort level. Even the most experienced speakers may develop high levels of anxiety both before and during a speech. Listeners, too, feel greater anxiety in a public speaking situation than they do in a conversation. For example, when you listen to an important classroom lecture, you probably experience a higher level of anxiety than when you are discussing the same material with your friends after class.

TEXT GOAL AND OVERVIEW

As you read this book, you will examine important features of the communication process that apply to every communication situation. You will also identify those features that are especially important in the public speaking situation. The goal is that you will identify and learn to use the skills that will make you an effective public speaker. Books can explain things, as can your instructor. However, only you can practice. If you want to become a better speaker, you must practice by speaking early and often.

Many public speaking teachers like to have their students speaking right away. Your teacher may assign you to give a brief speech early in the term. Chapter 2, "Planning the First Speech," provides an overview of what to do and what to avoid. You learn a little about choosing a subject and purpose, and a lot about what you can do to manage any communication anxiety you may feel.

An understanding of how people listen and of some of the common problems they have when they are trying to listen can strengthen both your listening and speaking skills. Chapter 3, "Listening," explains how to work with the most common listening problems. By inference, and by applying the ideas in this chapter as you plan and deliver your speeches, you learn how to adapt to listeners' needs.

A speech that is focused on a single, clear, and limited topic marks the difference between a presentation by a skilled professional speaker and that of an amateur. In chapter 4, "Selecting and Narrowing Your Topic," you learn how to select exciting ideas for your speeches and how to focus your speeches on a single goal. You also learn how to test your ideas to discover if they are right for a particular group.

Chapter 5, "Audience Analysis," carries the idea of how to adapt to listeners much further. Through audience analysis, you learn to estimate what listeners already know about your subject and to adapt features of your speech to a specific group of listeners.

Chapter 6, "Supporting Ideas with Argument and Evidence," shows you how evidence and argumentation determine whether or not your ideas seem credible to others. Successful speaking depends greatly on how you formulate your ideas and arguments and on how you support your positions with proof and evidence.

In chapter 7, "Gathering Supporting Materials and Using the Library," you learn how to gather materials for a speech. All kinds of sources are available to you. You are surrounded by experts. You can write away for information. With your computer, you can access all kinds of information easily and quickly. Of course, you can also use the local and university libraries. Almost everything known in the world is available to you if you know how to gather it.

Chapter 8, "Organizing the Body of the Speech," tells you how to organize the information you gather. You learn how the organizing process clarifies and strengthens ideas and what you can do to double-check the completeness and accuracy of your speech plan. You also learn how to help your listeners follow and remember your ideas.

Chapter 9, "Outlining the Speech," shows you how to develop two kinds of outlines. A full-sentence planning outline helps you to study the structure of a speech for accuracy and completeness. Are the ideas related to each other appropriately? Are they developed fully? Are they supported adequately? A speaking outline provides notes, including key words and phrases, reminders, marginal notes, and indications where your visual program fits into the speech, to use as you make your presentation.

Chapter 10, "Beginning and Ending a Speech," identifies the purposes and types of a speech introduction and conclusion. Getting off to a good start and ending well can be the difference between a successful speech and one that does not succeed.

The language you choose can determine whether your speech is great or only mediocre. Language controls the images you create in other people and determines whether or not people understand you. Language also dictates the persuasive strength of your speech. Chapter 11, "Language: The Key to Successful Speaking," shows you how to use language well. There is no substitute for careful choice of language.

In chapter 12, "Supporting Ideas Visually," you learn when to use visual supporting materials, what to support with visual aids, how to select the visual medium most likely to help you achieve your speaking goals, and how to design and use two-dimensional visual aids.

Chapter 13, "Delivery," focuses on both the verbal and nonverbal aspects of effective delivery. You learn about how different delivery methods, vocal control, and your nonverbal messages, such as your gestures, eye contact, and personal appearance and behavior, affect how listeners perceive you and your message.

After you work through chapter 14, "Informative Speaking," your speeches will be clearer, simpler, and more concrete and specific than you ever thought possible. You will understand how to get your ideas across, and your speech making will show it.

Chapter 15, "Persuasive Speaking," teaches you how to influence the attitudes, beliefs, and behaviors of listeners. Persuasion works when you and your message are credible and when your message appeals to both the rational and emotional needs of listeners. You will find very powerful tools in this chapter.

Although you may not deliver many special occasion speeches in your public speaking course, much of your life after college will involve such speech making. In chapter 16, "Speeches for Special Occasions," you learn how to plan and present speeches of praise or tribute, inspirational speeches, and speeches for the sake of humor. This chapter will be useful long after you graduate.

This text tries to teach by example, with current and relevant tables and illustrations in every chapter. In addition, a number of annotated sample speeches have been collected into appendix A at the end of the book. The editorial and critical comments found in the margins of these speeches show you at a glance what the speakers were trying to do and whether or not they were successful. Use the sample speeches for models as you plan your own.

If you have a problem or a question about how to prepare, plan, or deliver a speech, or how to understand or adapt to your listeners, turn to appendix C, the "Troubleshooting Guide" at the end of the book. There you will find references to particular passages in the text that give time-tested and research-based advice.

Summary

Your lifetime will offer many opportunities to speak in public. But even if you never give another speech in your life after this course, your study will pay you valuable dividends.

Improved public speaking skills increase your personal power, and along with that, your ethical responsibilities. However, if you prepare carefully, strive to meet standards of honesty and accuracy, build arguments on sound evidence, and realistically assess your strengths and weaknesses, you will find that you can use the power of public speaking to make important contributions that less skillful people cannot hope to make.

You already have a basic idea of what constitutes a good speech, but you may need help in expanding on and structuring that knowledge. Begin by thinking of the communication process and of public speaking as two-way phenomena. The components of the process (context, source/encoder, channels, messages, decoder/receiver, noise, and feedback) can each play an important part in your overall speaking success.

Public speaking is generally more formal and more carefully structured than other forms of talk and often produces greater anxiety. Yet, your overall speaking effectiveness is likely to improve with practice.

Key Terms

Channels	Ethics	Process model
Code	Feedback	Psychological noise
Context	Message	Receiver
Credibility	Model	Source
Decoder/receiver	Noise	Source/encoder
Decoding	Physical context	
Emotional context	Physical noise	

Application Questions

1. If you were going to develop an original communication model, would you develop a linear model? A process model? What elements would you include? Why? With a few of your classmates, develop a communication model that represents the public speaking situation.

2. In your opinion, who are the greatest speakers of the twentieth century? What criteria help you to judge possible candidates? Would you include Adolf Hitler? Winston Churchill? Jesse Jackson? President Bill Clinton? Why or why not? Would you include Oprah Winfrey? Hillary Rodham Clinton? With two or three of your classmates, develop a list of the twentieth century's greatest speakers. Compare your list to those of other groups of classmates. Are the lists similar? Did the groups use similar criteria?

3. Name two successful people. What measures of success do you apply when making this decision? Have you ever heard either of these people give a speech? With a classmate, create a list of three or four successful people who you know. Then ask these people about their public speaking experiences. How often do they speak in public? Do they find it useful? Report your findings to the class.

Self-Test for Review

1. Name three areas of your life in which public speaking skills can contribute to your success.

   a. _____

   b. _____

   c. _____

2. Public speaking requires self-disclosure. Place a check mark ✓ next to each of the following statements that explains why.

   _____ a. Speech making requires you to talk about your beliefs, and about the things, people, and events in your life.

   _____ b. Anyone who has ever listened to a speech knows if it is a good speech.

   _____ c. When you make an argument, you display your thinking.

3. Mark the following as either E (ethical), U (unethical), or N (ethically neutral).

   _____ a. Falsifying evidence

   _____ b. Rejecting ideas that seem doubtful because of a lack of evidence

   _____ c. Appealing to a listener's psychological needs

   _____ d. Deceiving listeners about your purposes and intentions, even when it is for their own good

4. Match the following terms and definitions.

_____ a. Source/encoder   1. Any sign, symbol, or combination of signs or symbols that function as stimuli for a receiver

_____ b. Channels   2. Any source of interference or distortion in message exchange

_____ c. Decoder/receiver   3. The location of an idea; the originator of a message

_____ d. Messages   4. Messages sent from receiver to source for correction and control of error

_____ e. Context   5. The physical, social, psychological, and temporal environment in which a communication event occurs

_____ f. Feedback   6. The means of transmission; vehicle through which messages are sent

_____ g. Noise   7. The mechanism or agent that translates messages into meaningful, comprehensible units

5. Name three features that set public speaking apart from other forms of communication.

   a. _____
   b. _____
   c. _____,

Answers: 1. a. Private life. b. Professional life. c. Public life outside work. 2. a. c. 3. a. U. b. E. c. N. d. U. 4. a. 3. b. 6. c. 7. d. 1. e. 5. f. 4. g. 2. 5. a. Structure of the event. b. Level of formality. c. Degree of anxiety.

Suggested Readings

Foss, Sonja K., Karen A. Foss, and Robert Trapp. *Contemporary Perspectives on Rhetoric.* Prospect Heights, Ill.: Waveland Press, 1985. This one book constitutes your best source for insights into the thinking of I. A. Richards, Richard M. Weaver, Stephen Toulmin, Chaim Perelman, Ernesto Grassi, Kenneth Burke, Michel Foucault, and Jürgen Habermas—the dominating figures in modern rhetorical thinking.

Littlejohn, Stephen W. *Theories of Human Communication.* 4th ed. Belmont, Calif.: Wadsworth, 1992. This book is a rich source of facts and ideas, and it is a virtual annotated bibliography of important research and theory about meaning, information processing, language use, and conflict.

Rybacki, Karyn, and Donald Rybacki. *Communication Criticism: Approaches and Genres.* Belmont, Calif.: Wadsworth, 1991. This book will help you to become a much more discriminating consumer of communication. This is not an easy read, but is well worth the struggle if you want to improve your performance skills since it also shows how discriminating listeners are likely to receive your ideas.

Planning the First Speech

OBJECTIVES

After reading this chapter, you should be able to:

1. *Specify* five reasons why people give speeches.
2. *Explain* why so many teachers give a first speaking assignment early in the term.
3. *Define* and *explain* communication anxiety.
4. *Name* and *explain* the six most common mistakes that people make in public speaking.
5. *Identify* and *explain* each of the following steps in developing a speech:
   - Select a topic.
   - Determine the purpose.
   - Organize the ideas.
   - Build support for the ideas.
   - Practice carefully.
6. *Define* and *differentiate* among general purpose, specific purpose, and thesis statements.
7. *Define* and *explain* the term *extemporaneous speaking*.
8. *List* five suggestions for practicing public speaking.

© *Bob Daemmrich/The Image Works, Inc.*

*P*ublic speaking happens because people need to express themselves, to inform others, to persuade people, to entertain, or to fulfill an obligation at a ceremonial function. Thus, public speaking pervades our lives.

Speech teachers commonly assign a formal speech early in the term to encourage immediate practice and to diagnose any possible speaking problems that might require special attention. Given the short notice, students sometimes feel anxious about this first speech assignment. General, unexplained anxiety, also known as *communication apprehension,* is common.

Most communication apprehension disappears if you make the situation as predictable as possible. You do this by avoiding common public speaking mistakes and by planning your first speaking assignment carefully: Select a topic you know well; focus on a single, clear goal; organize the speech carefully; support the speech adequately; and practice carefully. This chapter tells you how.

Early in your public speaking course, your professor may say: "Beginning next time, I'd like you to give a brief speech to the class." Some students look forward to their first assigned speaking experience, while others can take it or leave it. Some students, however, dread this first assignment.

In any case, students often want and need help in preparing for their first speech. This chapter provides that help by presenting in an abbreviated form much of what is described in greater detail in later chapters. Your first speech will succeed if you take the time to think it through and if you invest a little energy in practicing it.

WHY WE SPEAK

Public speaking happens all around us every day. Have you ever wondered why? Why do so many people give so many speeches of so many kinds so often? Generally, we give speeches for five reasons: (1) to express ourselves, (2) to inform others, (3) to persuade people to think or act, (4) to entertain or to strike a lighter note, and (5) to fulfill certain ceremonial functions.

TO EXPRESS OURSELVES

People often speak in public to express themselves, to make their feelings and attitudes known. For, example, local citizens may stand up at a town council meeting to request that a traffic light be installed at an intersection near where they live, or parents may speak at a PTA meeting to oppose extending the teaching day. In both of these examples, the general purpose of self-expression shares importance with other public speaking goals. That is, the citizens' request for a traffic light and the parents' opposition to the extended school day almost certainly involve both informative and persuasive public speaking goals as well.

TO INFORM

When we speak to inform, we seek to add to the general storehouse of knowledge that an audience already possesses. Instructors do this when they explain a concept or give an example. You do this on a less formal level when you tell your friend how to find your home.

Teachers often make simple **informative speeches** the first assignment. For example, students may be asked to make a brief speech (usually about three minutes long) in which they introduce their personal hero or in which they teach the audience. One student may talk about how a grandparent was personally inspiring, while another may teach the class how to change the oil in a car, while still another may explain how to judge a good horse from one that is not so good. In each case, the goal is to expand listeners' general store of knowledge. Example 2.1 shows the text of a three-minute informative speech about a personal hero.

EXAMPLE 2.1	INFORMATIVE SPEECH ABOUT A PERSONAL HERO
INTRODUCTION	**INTRODUCTION**
Greeting, name, topic	Good morning. My name is Martin Rousso. I'm a political science major in my second year. *My personal hero has always been the classical Greek philosopher, Aristotle.*
Brief history	Aristotle lived 62 years, from 384 to 322 B.C. He was a member of Plato's academy for twenty years, and he was Alexander the Great's teacher. He founded a school in Athens
Transition to first main idea	called the Lyceum. But these are not my reasons for honoring him. Aristotle was the greatest thinker of his time, and his influence has never diminished.
BODY	**BODY**
First main idea	Aristotle was the greatest thinker of his time—perhaps of all time. But he was not a writer. He was a teacher. What we know of his thinking comes in the form of notes that he made for his lectures. They weren't really edited into texts until some time in the first century by
Details	a Roman named Andronicus.
Supporting evidence for the idea that Aristotle was a great thinker	But what lectures they must have been. And what a far-reaching mind. Aristotle taught philosophy, science, logic, physics, biology, psychology, metaphysics, ethics, politics, poetics, and rhetoric. In each of these fields, his influence lasted for centuries. Even today, in the textbook for this course, you'll find references to Aristotle.
Second main idea	So Aristotle was, I think, the ultimate role model. I'd love to be like him. If it sounds conceited, nevertheless, I'd like to have fame and fortune, and to gain these things as a result of my good works and the quality of my thought. That's what Aristotle did. He was
Support for second main idea	famous and wealthy even in his own time, and his contribution to western thought has lasted more than two thousand years.
CONCLUSION	**CONCLUSION**
	You can meet Aristotle in nearly every department on our campus. He is there, in the textbooks, on the walls, and in the excitement that the teachers have for the long tradition of western thought.
Summary	Aristotle was the greatest thinker of his time or any time, and a personal role model for me. There's no doubt about it. He is my personal hero.
Kicker	Thank you.

TO PERSUADE

Persuasion means the process of influence—that is, trying to change attitudes, beliefs, and behaviors. Obviously, persuasion figures heavily in public speech making. Every political campaign address, every television commercial, seeks to persuade. Every time you make a request or try to prevent an event from occurring, you seek to persuade.

A **persuasive speech** always seeks changes in people's attitudes and behaviors. Your first speech assignment probably will not include a persuasive goal, since the tasks involved demand a fairly sophisticated understanding of human motives. However, you will likely give one or more speeches to persuade later in the course.

TO ENTERTAIN

If you invite friends to your home for a social event, people say that you are "entertaining." In public speaking, a **speech to entertain** holds audience attention agreeably, diverts, or amuses. After-dinner speeches illustrate this purpose because after-dinner speakers generally seek to relax and entertain their listeners.

People often have difficulty designing and delivering speeches to entertain. Such speeches require a light touch and excellent timing skills.

FOR CEREMONIAL FUNCTIONS

More often than you can possibly foresee, people will ask you to give speeches for ceremonial purposes: "Will you introduce the speaker today?" "Would you make the toast before dinner?" "Will you speak at my father's funeral?" "Will you give the valedictory address?" "Will you make a few remarks after the luncheon?"

Each of these examples illustrates a ceremonial function that ordinary people have to fulfill regularly. Because such speeches are so common, students are often asked to begin their classroom speaking experience by making such a speech.

THE FIRST SPEAKING ASSIGNMENT

Your first speaking assignment may come within the first two weeks of your course. Many students approach the assignment eagerly. Others view it with dread. Many students seem, merely, confused. "What should I do now?" they ask. This chapter will help you to prepare for that assignment.

If you understand the purpose of the first assignment, you are more likely to do well. Speech teachers generally have two goals in mind when they assign the first speech: (1) They want to encourage their students into the speaking situation as soon as possible to provide the students with practice and experience, and (2) they want to find out how they can help their students—whether any students will require special instruction for particular speaking problems.

With regard to the first goal, if you want to learn a new skill, no substitute has ever been found for practice. The sooner you practice, and the more often, the better. Thus, the sooner you start giving speeches, the sooner you will feel competent in this role.

With regard to the second goal, an early speaking assignment also helps instructors to diagnose any speaking problems that may need special attention. For example, stuttering, lisping, and other speech problems may show up during the first speeches. Speech teachers can help—either directly or by referring students to a specialist. Some students may speak so softly that even nearby listeners cannot hear them. Speech teachers want to

work on helping these students to speak up. Or some students may fidget or have fallen
into the habit of jamming their hands deep into their pockets. They will require special instruction in how to use the whole body in public speaking. They need to learn that gestures reinforce the meanings of words and tell listeners how to interpret what the speaker
wants to say. These kinds of speaking problems can be eradicated when the teacher has a
little advance warning and enough time to plan to treat them. Early speaking assignments
give speech instructors this needed time.

COMMUNICATION APPREHENSION

The word *anxiety* refers to a generalized state of apprehension: distress or worry caused
by perceived or anticipated danger or misfortune. When you experience feelings of dread,
similar to fear, and cannot put a finger on why you are experiencing these feelings, you
are said to be anxious. You may experience a more specific type of anxiety—**communication apprehension**—when in a communication situation you do not fully understand.[1]

A few people become apprehensive and anxious as their first speaking assignment
approaches. This is normal and expected. You do not know much about the audience or
about what your teacher expects of you. You do not know how well your speech will be
received. Perhaps you do not feel as prepared as you would like. Do not let such feelings

Table 2.1

TIPS FOR REDUCING COMMUNICATION
APPREHENSION

1. Choose a topic you feel knowledgeable about.
2. Choose a topic that interests you.
3. Focus your speech by developing a clear thesis statement.
4. Feel organized by being organized. Carefully outline your main points and subpoints using key words.
5. Prepare an engaging introduction and an effective conclusion.
6. Practice your speech ahead of time.
7. Visualize yourself speaking successfully and translating your emotional tension into a lively and energetic performance.
8. During your speech, don't rush. Act confident. Wait to begin until you feel comfortable.
9. Focus on the friendly and attentive members of the audience.
10. Speak slowly, clearly, and loud enough to be heard throughout the room.

throw you. Every speech teacher is familiar with the communication apprehension experienced by some speech students and knows how to help you work through it. Table 2.1 presents tips for reducing communication apprehension.

Students with communication apprehension may become extremely anxious and nervous. If you are one of these students, be sure to read appendix B, which discusses at length how to handle your nervousness.

MOST COMMON MISTAKES OF BEGINNING SPEECH STUDENTS

Beginning speech students make mistakes. Table 2.2 lists the most common mistakes people make in public speaking. As you think about these mistakes, you will discover two things: First, they all work together as a system. If you make a change for the better in one area, you automatically improve all the rest. Second, each of these mistakes is easy to fix.

Table 2.2 should provide some guidance as you plan your first speech. For example, the table shows that one of the most common public speaking mistakes is that the purpose of the speech is not clear. The listener cannot figure out what the speaker wants. The solution is to know what you want from your listeners and then make that clear to them. This level of specificity and clarity not only eliminates confusion and uncertainty, it also helps to alleviate communication apprehension.

Table 2.2

MOST COMMON MISTAKES
IN PUBLIC SPEAKING

1. *Purpose of speech is not clear.* "I can't figure out what the speaker wants from me."
2. *Speech is not relevant to listeners.* "I can't figure out why I should listen to this speech."
3. *Speech is badly organized.* "I can't follow the logic from one point to another."
4. *Speech includes unimportant or irrelevant detail.* "I can't process all the technical and meaningless details."
5. *Speech does not contain sufficient supporting materials.* "I'd be more interested and more convinced if these ideas were backed up with stories, examples, and other evidence."
6. *Delivery is boring.* "I can't pay attention to monotonous voice, sloppy speech, and listless posture and gestures. This speaker doesn't seem to care — why should I?"

PLANNING YOUR FIRST SPEAKING ASSIGNMENT

Follow these step-by-step suggestions as you plan your first speaking assignment. Learn them well. They will serve you every time you approach the task of giving a speech.

SELECT A TOPIC

You began this course with an enormous amount of knowledge. Draw on that knowledge. Choose a topic that interests you and that you know well. Sort through your life experiences for the moments and activities that bring you greatest pleasure. These are the topics you know well. The following questions should help you find a topic:

1. What is your favorite recreational activity?
2. What has been your most interesting experience since you began college?
3. What kind of job do you have? What kind of job did you have during the summer? What kind of job do you wish to have after graduation?
4. What is the most important event in your life?
5. What is the most unusual feature of the neighborhood where you grew up? That you live in?
6. Who is the most unusual, most outstanding, most interesting, most important, most powerful person you have ever met?

The questions on page 28 usually help good topic ideas to pop into mind. Choose a topic that you can tie to your audience's interests and needs. Put your listeners at the center of your concerns. You know your topic well. The question is, what difference does the topic make to your listeners? For example:

1. How, if at all, can listeners use this information?
2. Does this topic make a difference to listeners that they do not know about?
3. Can you tie your subject to a topic listeners already care about?

To illustrate, a young woman was earning money for college by working on a farm during the summer. For her first speech, in response to the assignment "Teach the class something about yourself in five minutes," she decided to talk about her farm experiences. Her problem was to find a way to relate farm work to an audience in an urban university. She put a little "you can do it, too" spin on her speech when she delivered it to her class. Her speech is presented in example 2.2.

DETERMINE THE PURPOSE

Your speech will succeed if audience members respond by giving you what you want. If they do not, the speech fails to achieve its purpose. What do you want? What is the purpose of your speech?

A general response to this critical question will not guarantee your success. For example, neither "I want to inform my audience" nor "I want to persuade my audience" goes far enough in determining the purpose of a speech. In addition to these general statements of purpose, you need a specific purpose and a thesis statement.

A **general purpose** is the broad intention that motivates a speech—for example, to inform, to persuade, or to entertain. A **specific purpose** is the particular action goal of the speech, what you want from the audience as a result of your speech. The **thesis statement** in the introduction of a speech gives the most important point or purpose of the speech. Table 2.3 compares and contrasts these three aspects of a speech.

Notice that the specific purpose statements in table 2.3 focus on listener behaviors. Speeches are more effective when the speaker has a particular listener behavior in mind. Once you know what behaviors you want from your audience, everything else in the speech seems to fall into place. For example, if your specific purpose is for your listeners to be able to trace the rise and fall of Russian communism, your speech will need to be both specific and memorable. Thus, determining your specific purpose and thesis statement requires more concentrated effort than any other part of your preparation. The examples in table 2.4 illustrate this.

The importance of formulating a general purpose, specific purpose, and thesis statements cannot be overemphasized. Your speech must be focused on a single, clearly identified goal, and your listeners must know what that goal is for your speech to be effective. As with every other important idea in this chapter, this is discussed in more detail in a later chapter. If you want to read further, of course, you can turn to chapter 4, "Selecting and Narrowing Your Topic," right now.

EXAMPLE 2.2	INFORMATIVE SPEECH TO TEACH LISTENERS SOMETHING ABOUT YOURSELF
INTRODUCTION	**INTRODUCTION**
Greeting, name, qualifications to give the speech	Good morning, class. My name is Litisha Bechtold. I grew up on a farm in Missouri, and I've been helping to put myself through college by working as a farm hand right here in south Alabama.
Topic	*(Mild laughter. Litisha paused while it happened.)* I thought that might amuse you. But it's serious business to me. I want to assure you that you can do anything you set out to do. But more than that, *I want to tell you what an*
Thesis	*interesting job I have. As far as I'm concerned, farm work is a job made in heaven.*
Transition and preview	My job has three distinct advantages over most of the summer jobs I know about. It gets me outside. It lets me work with nature. And it makes me feel good about myself.
BODY	**BODY**
First main idea	If you want to spend time close to God, spend time on a farm. Every day seems a God-given gift. Each day I get up, go outside, face whatever weather the day may bring, and know that I am right to believe in God.
Illustration in support of first main idea	You have to believe you're close to heaven when you help a calf get born. I did that last summer. I was riding the fences when I heard this pitiful crying from over in a draw. I went over there and found a heifer down on the ground with a half-born calf. The calf was dry, and I knew there wasn't time to go for help. It was up to me. So I pulled on that calf for all I was worth, and nothing happened. Finally, I tied a rope around the calf's head and forelegs, tied the other to the pommel of my saddle, and pulled the calf out of the cow with horse power. It seemed like a miracle to see that little momma take care of that calf. And I knew I had saved both their lives.
Restatement of the key idea, which serves as a transition to the next main idea	
Second main idea	Every day it's something new. Every day I go out on the farm and solve some kind of a problem. And the more I do it, the better I feel about myself as a person.
Supporting materials for second main idea	Working as a farm hand gives me a sense of self-worth like no other job I've ever had. For example, when I first went to the farm, I was lazy. I couldn't see myself doing any kind of physical labor. Now I'm very proud of the fact that I can milk twelve cows before breakfast. I'm proud that I helped scoop thirty thousand bushels of oats into a storage bin last summer. I feel a good sense of accomplishment that I learned how to plow a straight furrow and that I can toss a bale of hay up to the wagon. These are jobs usually done by men, but I can do them. And they pay me for it—enough to help pay for college.
Internal summary that serves as a transition	If you're ever lucky enough to get an outside job like mine, I guarantee you that you'll end up with a richer faith in God and a stronger sense of confidence in yourself.
CONCLUSION	**CONCLUSION**
Summary	In summary, my summer job as a farm hand gets me out-of-doors. The result is that I see nature in all her moods, and I've learned to believe that God makes all that happen. I feel good that I have had a part to play, and I feel good about myself. What more could you ask from a summer job?
Kicker	Thank you.

Table 2.3

COMPARISONS OF GENERAL PURPOSE, SPECIFIC PURPOSE,
AND THESIS STATEMENTS

GENERAL PURPOSE	SPECIFIC PURPOSE	THESIS STATEMENT
"I want to inform my listeners about something they don't already know." (Inform)	*What do you want listeners to know?* "I want my listeners to know how to make gun powder."	"You can make gun powder from materials you have in your home or can easily get."
"I want to alter what my listeners feel or believe." (Persuade)	*What do you want listeners to feel or believe?* "I want the listeners to believe they should not wait for the newest technology to come out before they buy a computer."	"It makes no sense to wait until the newest technology comes out before you buy a computer."
"I want to get the listeners to do something." (Persuade)	*What do you want listeners to do?* "I want my listeners to contribute at least one hour's salary each month to the United Way."	"I'd like you to pledge one hour's salary each month to the United Way by filling out this pledge card."
"I want to amuse or relax my listeners." (Entertain)	*What pleasant or amusing experience do you want listeners to have?* "I want my listeners to experience happy anticipation."	"I know you're going to enjoy your stay here at the Grand Hotel."
"I want my listeners to believe something." (Persuade)	*What do you want listeners to believe?* "I want my listeners to believe that, while both are terrible economic problems, inflation is worse than depression."	"Nothing could be worse for America than unbridled inflation."

Table 2.4

FOCUSING ON DESIRED LISTENER BEHAVIOR

General Purpose	Specific Purpose	Thesis Statement
"I want my listeners to know something." (Inform)	*What do you want listeners to know?* (Put it in terms of observable behavior.) "I want my listeners to be able to trace the rise and fall of Russian communism from 1917 to 1992."	"The Russian revolution lasted seventy-five years."
"I want my listeners to understand something." (Inform)	*What do you want listeners to understand?* (You cannot see understanding. Put it in terms of observable behavior.) "I want my listeners to be able to explain the root causes of the warfare in Yugoslavia."	"The warfare in Yugoslavia has its roots in two closely related things: race and religion."
"I want my listeners to support federal aid to Russia." (Persuade)	*What do you want listeners to do?* (What does "support" mean in terms of observable listener behavior?) "I want my listeners to sign this petition that I will send to our senators and representatives."	"Ladies and gentlemen, Russia needs your help and your support."

ORGANIZE THE IDEAS

Once you have selected the topic and determined the purpose of your speech, you can begin to think through what you will say and how you will say it. The organizational skills you develop in this course will help you to develop and clarify your thinking. The most critical part of effective organizing involves deciding what you want from your listeners, since this will help to suggest the type of organizational pattern you use in the speech. If your goal is persuasive, for example, you need an organizational pattern that will help you to persuade effectively. If you want to inform, then the subject matter itself may suggest an organizational pattern. Ask yourself: "With my goal in mind, what is a sensible way of pulling my ideas together?"

In general, every successful speech has three parts: an introduction, a body, and a conclusion. An **introduction** is the first part of a speech. Its purpose is to get audience attention, to state the speaker's intention, and to prepare listeners for what is coming. The **body of the speech** is the major portion of the speech. In this part, you develop and support

COLIN POWELL

Americans watched nervously as captured American fliers were paraded across the television. The Allied air attack that was to have lasted twenty-four hours was a week old.

General Colin Powell, then Chairman of the Joint Chiefs of Staff, needed to calm the American people during his January 23, 1991 Pentagon news conference. He began his speech by describing the broad Allied plan for the execution of the Gulf War. According to Powell's biographer, Howard Means, Powell's voice then became strangely reassuring in its sternness and lack of overt passion as he told the reporters and the nation watching on television:

Our strategy for going after this army is very, very simple. First we are going to cut it off, and then we are going to kill it.

When biographer Howard Means asked Powell if these words were off-the-cuff, Powell responded:

People like to focus on that line, but the more important part of that was what I said before that line. It was the windup to that. So I knew what the line was, and I already had it in my mind. I had sort of shared it with my folks around here to get a sanity check, but it was not that extemporaneous. It was *given* extemporaneously, but the thought was not an extemporaneous thought. I'd thought of it beforehand, about twelve hours beforehand.

Powell reminds us that extemporaneous delivery requires careful planning.

Source: Howard Means, Colin Powell: Soldier-Statesman—Statesman-Soldier *(New York: Donald I. Fine, 1992), 278–79. Photo AP/Wide World Photos*

the main ideas and arguments. The **conclusion** ends the speech and focuses listeners' thoughts and feelings on the speech's main idea. A simple axiom for remembering the purposes of the three parts of a speech is: "Tell them what you're going to tell them, tell them, and then tell them what you've told them."

How you organize the body of the speech depends on what you want to accomplish and on your chosen topic. Organizing the introduction and conclusion is less complicated. You may wish to turn to chapter 8, "Organizing the Body of the Speech," to read further about organizing your ideas.

Your goal in the first speech is likely to be informative. What are the natural divisions of the topic? For example, in a speech in which you are to introduce the main speaker at a Kiwanis luncheon, the natural divisions of the topic are:

- The speaker's qualifications
- The speaker's credentials in the area of expertise
- The reasons why the audience should listen to the speaker

EXAMPLE **2.3**	**BRIEF SPEECH OF INTRODUCTION**
INTRODUCTION	**INTRODUCTION**
Greeting	Good morning, ladies and gentlemen.
Your name	My name is Ellen Cambridge, and I am a student here at Colorado State College.
Thesis	It is my privilege and pleasure to introduce Mr. William McKinley, our keynote speaker.
BODY	**BODY**
Qualifications	I have known Bill McKinley for the past twelve years. I have worked for him as one of his employees, and I have worked with him as a colleague on three environmental protection projects. I can assure you that Mr. McKinley has clear and firm ideas about how we should protect our environment.
Credentials	Bill has a bachelor's, a master's, and a doctor's degree in the areas of marine geology and microbiology. He has written two college textbooks on these subjects, and he has published more than fifty scholarly articles in the area. But you probably know him best as the author of the popular book *Save the Earth Now, or Never.*
Reasons to listen	I know that you are concerned about the quality of our own environment here in Colorado. That's the focus of this conference. I am pleased that this is also what Bill McKinley wants to talk about.
CONCLUSION Summary	**CONCLUSION** So, it's my pleasure and privilege to introduce my friend and our keynote speaker.
Kicker	Ladies and gentlemen, may I present Mr. Bill McKinley?

Example 2.3 is a brief speech of introduction. Notice the simple one-two-three sequence in the introduction and the one-two punch in the conclusion. While these introductory and concluding patterns are not elegant, they serve many speakers well.

Planning and organizing a speech does not mean writing out or memorizing a speech. Writing and memorizing approaches generally create more problems for a beginning speaker than they solve. If you write out a speech manuscript and then read the manuscript to your listeners, you are likely to bore them silly. If you memorize and then recite your speech, you almost certainly will lose contact with your listeners. You also might lose your place and then feel foolish and embarrassed because you cannot remember what you wanted to say next. Instead of either writing or memorizing, give the speech extemporaneously.

Extemporaneous refers to a style of delivery that uses careful preparation and notes, but not memorization or a manuscript. Extemporaneous style fosters real contact with listeners and allows you the flexibility to work with and be influenced by listeners' needs.

Suppose you decide to give a simple informative speech about the 1975 Apollo-Soyuz Test Project, a joint space mission. What are the subject's natural divisions? The following possibilities spring to mind:

- Apollo launch
- Soyuz launch
- Docking
- First meeting in space between a Russian and an American

Or you might prefer a different approach. For example:

- Reasons for the joint mission
- Benefits from the joint mission

Example 2.4 shows how one student developed this speech in response to the first formal speaking assignment in her public speaking class. The assignment was to teach something. Do you think her speech was well organized around the natural topics her subject presented?

As you may have determined after reading example 2.4, the student lost her focus: She was not sure what she wanted from her listeners. In the end, her speech seems to be more persuasive than informative. After rethinking what she wanted from her listeners, she reorganized her speech as shown in example 2.5. The student's revised outline follows a natural division of topics. The argument moves in a single direction and has a single purpose. Had she delivered the speech she outlined here, her listeners would have followed more easily.

BUILD SUPPORT FOR THE IDEAS

Each main idea in a speech must seem credible to your listeners. Beyond that, you will often want listeners to identify emotionally with what you are saying. To establish credibility and emotional identification with your listeners, you need to build support for your ideas. **Supporting material** includes any verbal or nonverbal material you use to develop your credibility or to win acceptance for your speech. If you claim, as Ellen Cambridge did in her speech introducing keynote speaker Bill McKinley (see example 2.3), that a speaker has clear ideas and a firm position, your listeners are likely to ask themselves how you know that. You need to back up your claim, perhaps by listing the speaker's credentials, providing an example, or quoting the speaker.

Examine each of the example speeches in this chapter to see if you can strengthen the supporting materials. (To read more about how to support your ideas, turn to chapter 6, "Supporting Ideas with Argument and Evidence.")

EXAMPLE 2.4	INFORMATIVE SPEECH ABOUT THE APOLLO-SOYUZ TEST PROJECT
INTRODUCTION Greeting and name Topic Importance	**INTRODUCTION** Good afternoon, ladies and gentlemen. My name is Junko Hamada, and I'm a physics major here at the university. I've always been interested in space research, and I thought you might be, too. Today, I want to tell you about a very important moment in the history of space research that happened in 1975, the year that I was born. In all the years before or since the Apollo-Soyuz Test Project, not a single incidence of collaboration between the two countries has captured imaginations like this one.
BODY Background First main idea	**BODY** The story actually began in the first years of the 1960s, when President Kennedy committed the United States to a space race. From that moment, for fifteen years, the super powers Russia and the United States competed. The first hint that they could cooperate came in 1972, when the two countries announced that they would jointly put a research mission into space. Russia and the United States proved a long time ago that they could cooperate.
Supporting materials for the main idea that the two countries could cooperate	On July 15, 1975, Apollo and Soyuz blasted into orbit. On July 17, two days later, the two spacecraft met in space, docked, and opened their hatches to each other. The Russian commander, Aleksei A. Leonov, extended his hand and said in English, "Glad to see you." The American commander, Thomas P. Stafford, replied in Russian. The two shook hands through the hatches, then traded gifts. The Americans entered the Russian spaceship first.
A bit out of focus; not directly relevant to the main idea	Can you imagine what that must have seemed like to these men? Their countries were involved in the heart of the cold war. They had been taught for thirty years and more to distrust each other. Then here they were, on live television, shaking hands in a symbolic cooperation that must have thrilled everyone watching. All this happened the day I was born.
Support for the main idea	For two days, the six crew members—three Russian and three American—shared meals. They worked on scientific experiments together. Then, on July 19, the men exchanged gifts, said their good-bys, and separated. They flew together for two orbits after that, making pictures of the Sun and of Earth, and then returned to their separate bases.
Second main idea	What were the benefits, if any? In retrospect, that mission didn't have much scientific impact. And as far as I know, the two nations never flew a joint mission again. But it seems to me that this event, perhaps more than any other, might have—should have—marked the beginnings of the end of the cold war. If Americans and Russians could cooperate in space, they might be able to cooperate on the ground.
	It didn't happen that way. America and Russia were bitter competitors until the collapse of communism and the Yeltsin-Clinton summit in 1993. But it might have been different.
CONCLUSION Summary Kicker	**CONCLUSION** So what have we seen? Something wonderful happened the year I was born. Russia and the United States cooperated in scientific and space research. It might have been the start of the end of the cold war, but it wasn't. Can we learn from the outcome that, where international politics is concerned, cooperation is better than competition? I hope so.

EXAMPLE 2.5   REORGANIZED SAMPLE SPEECH TO INFORM

Subject: The Apollo-Soyuz joint space mission

Specific purpose: I want my listeners to be able to explain how the Apollo-Soyuz mission was a lost opportunity to end the cold war.

Thesis: America and Russia missed a chance in 1975 to end the cold war.

I.   Main idea: The United States and Russia were blinded by competing ideologies.
    A. Economic ideology marked a difference.
    B. Ideology about world domination marked a difference.
    C. The arms race illustrated ideological competition.
    D. The space race illustrated ideological competition.

II.   Main idea: The Apollo-Soyuz mission proved that competition didn't have to exist between Russia and the United States.
    A. They cooperated in space research.
    B. Their cooperation was successful.
    C. It had worldwide television coverage without damage to either country.
    D. It proved that the two peoples could work together.

III. Main idea: The two countries could have continued to cooperate on other projects.

PRACTICE CAREFULLY

Nothing substitutes for practice if you want your speech to achieve its purpose. The following five pointers, which are based on both research and experience, will help you to feel prepared to give your speech and will help to make your speech interesting and relevant to your listeners. By following these pointers, you will avoid the most common mistakes in public speaking, and you will feel more confident and more successful than you might have thought possible.

1. Distribute your practice over many brief sessions, rather than spending the same amount of time in only one session.
2. Keep your practice sessions brief. Two or three run-throughs each time ought to do the trick.
3. Practice in different contexts and settings—in an empty classroom, in your living room, under a tree on campus. Go through the speech as you walk from one class to another.
4. If you have visual aids, practice using them in advance. Touch every switch, flip every chart that you plan to use during the speech. Work the bugs out of your visual aids during practice sessions, not during your speech.
5. Use your notes to remind you of key ideas, but do not read a manuscript, and do not try to memorize your speech.

The following is an example of a short student speech. While not perfect, it is a realistic model for you to aim at. You now have the background for giving a speech of this quality or even better. You are on your way to becoming a successful public speaker!

Sample Speech

"RECYCLING IS EVERYBODY'S BUSINESS"

Speech by Smed Wallis, Student, University of Missouri

Common-ground statement to establish rapport

Practical illustrations to show audience members personal involvement in the topic

Most of us don't give much thought to the items we have in our everyday trash that just won't go away. Oh, sure, we know that some soda bottles and plastic wrap may be around for awhile, but I don't think we really appreciate how serious this problem is.

Let me tell you about some of the daily products that you and I discard. Remember, most of these will still be in our landfills when you and I are dead. Here's a list: Disposable diapers; plastic soda bottles; plastic and paper, cups, and trays; paints; housecleaners; and personal care items. That's a pretty imposing list. But don't take my word for it. The Environmental Protection Agency says we have a crisis of pollution on our hands, and **you and I are the polluters.**

Reasons why the audience should be concerned with the topic

We have developed a "throw-away" mentality. We don't want to be bothered by items, so we just toss them in the trash barrel, leaving them for someone else to handle. But guess where they go. They go to a landfill because they can't be burned or otherwise destroyed. Once in the landfill, they just lie there. No, they don't decay because most of them are not biodegradable. They are there today, they will be there tomorrow, next year, and for the rest of our lives. That plastic cup you tossed away yesterday will be in the landfill long after you are gone!

Some practical cases to show the magnitude of the problem

That's only part of the problem. We not only have too many products that are not environmentally friendly, we are running out of places to put them. The number of landfills is shrinking as some fill up and communities oppose starting new landfills. Remember the story about the barge of garbage that floated from city to city for several months because no one wanted to allow its contents in their environment? We are starting to face that kind of situation with our landfills. Cities are shipping their garbage and waste to other states because they are running out of space.

Illustrations without documented proof

On a more practical level, have you driven along a stretch of interstate highway recently? You may have noticed signs that said the next mile or miles were dedicated to cleaner highways through cleanup by a local service organization. Do you know what they pick up? Discarded food containers, plastic wrappers, and bottles. If you've ever driven past one of these groups during their collection efforts, I'm sure you have been as amazed as I when you have seen the amount of "trash" (unrecyclable in most cases) that they can collect in only a mile or two of highway. That's a little more evidence of our "throw-away mentality."

You may see that we face a truly serious problem. But what can each of us do to help keep our environment healthy?

We can begin by using products that are environmentally friendly. That means new mothers and fathers can use cloth diapers instead of the nonrecyclable plastic diapers. We can use recycled paper. Look at the sacks you receive at your grocery store. Are they marked "recyclable"? If not, insist on sacks that carry that mark. And don't settle for a plastic bag to carry home your purchase. It may seem like a small matter, but when you begin to add all the choices that people make together, it is a huge decision-making process. If you don't think before you buy or make a choice on these environmental problems, you're only contributing more to our already staggering problem.

An outline of possible remedial steps for the concerned listener

When you buy personal care items at the drugstore or discount store, look to see if they are water based. If they are, you're buying a product that can be recycled.

Be a careful shopper. Buy items which are packaged in recyclable cartons. It only takes a few moments. It is your way of being sure that the world you and I enjoy will be here for our children.

Responsible major corporations are more and more active in the recycling movement. Corporations like McDonalds now package some of their products in recyclable containers. But until they place all their sandwiches, french fries, pies, and drinks in containers which will "break down," all these manufacturers are helping to destroy our environment. We focus a lot on the fast food industry. But the paints, polyethylene, and treated paper that live for centuries just pile up in our landfills and are our legacy to our children.

Please become responsible. We've succeeded in eliminating some of our environmental pollution by switching our cars from leaded to unleaded fuel. Let's cooperate in making the annual Earth Day a commitment to a better way of dealing with the pollution you and I create.

Living responsibly is not a large difficulty. You don't want other people tossing trash into your yard, car, or apartment. Think of it this way. When you use plastics and nonrecyclable items, you are leaving your trash for your neighbor, your children, and your grandchildren.

A call for listeners to consider the impact of their acts on the lives of others

Is that your heritage? Are you proud? Your answer is just like mine, NO! So stop and think before you buy and before you discard. Let's force the manufacturers and sellers to become more responsible through our behavior as consumers. Remember, if we don't buy it, they won't make it.

Reprinted by permission of the author.

Summary

People speak to express themselves, to inform, to persuade, to entertain, and to fulfill certain ceremonial functions. These general purposes of speech determine the choices you make as you approach your first assigned speech.

Speech teachers often assign their students the task of preparing and delivering a brief speech early in the term. They do this because they want to encourage immediate practice and to diagnose any student speaking problems that may warrant special attention. But early assignments may cause student concerns, such as communication apprehension. These concerns are largely unwarranted, however, since audiences tend to welcome and to like speakers.

Careful preparation and wise practice eliminate the most common public speaking mistakes and thus assure greater speaking success than you may have thought possible. Choose a topic that you know well and that you can tie to your audience's interests and needs. Determine a specific action goal for the speech and state it in terms your listeners cannot miss. Organize your ideas into an introduction, a body, and a conclusion. Each main idea must have enough supporting material to establish your credibility and to promote acceptance in your listeners. Back up your statements. Then practice carefully. If you do, your first speaking experience should be a pleasant and productive initiation into the world of public speaking.

Key Terms

Body of the speech	General purpose	Specific purpose
Communication	Informative speech	Speech to entertain
apprehension	Introduction	Supporting material
Conclusion	Persuasive speech	Thesis statement
Extemporaneous style		

Application Questions

1. If people did not engage in public speaking, what effect would this have on society? Would society be better or worse? How and why?
2. Can you recall listening to a speaker who did not consider the audience? What effect did this have on the presentation and on the audience? Remember how you felt as you listened. Would you have responded differently to the speech if the speaker had understood the speaking situation better?
3. Go to a speech on campus or in your community—for example, a classroom lecture or church sermon. Listen for evidence that the speaker is really trying to connect with the listeners. What speaker behaviors make you think that the speaker cares—or does not care—about the listeners? Record your observations and bring them to class. Be prepared to discuss how you can apply what you have learned from this exercise to your own speech making.

Self-Test for Review

1. Name five reasons why people give speeches.

   a. _____

   b. _____

   c. _____

   d. _____

   e. _____

2. Why do so many speech teachers make early term speaking assignments? _____
   _____

3. Match each statement in the left-hand column with the number of the entry in the right-hand column that best describes the statement.

   _____ a. "I want my listeners to know how to make gun powder."

   _____ b. "I want to change what my listeners believe."

   _____ c. "I'd like you to pledge one hour's salary each month."

   _____ d. "I want my listeners to believe they should buy a computer now."

   _____ e. "The time has come for you to buy a computer."

   _____ f. "I want my listeners to believe that inflation is worse than depression."

   _____ g. "Nothing is worse for a nation than unchecked inflation."

   1. General purpose

   2. Specific purpose

   3. Thesis statement

4. Match each statement in the left-hand column with the number of the entry in the right-hand column that best describes why the listener is having a problem.

   _____ a. "I can't pay attention. This speaker doesn't seem to care about what she's saying."

   _____ b. "I can't tell what this speaker wants from me."

   _____ c. "I doubt this argument."

   _____ d. "I'm lost in all this jumbled up detail."

   _____ e. "I can't follow this argument."

   _____ f. "What does this speech have to do with me?"

   1. Purpose not clear
   2. Speech not relevant
   3. Irrelevant or unimportant details
   4. Not enough support
   5. Boring delivery
   6. Speech badly organized

5. Mark the following statements: 1 = Good advice about practicing

   2 = Bad advice about practicing

   _____ a. All you really need to do is run through the speech one time.

   _____ b. Keep your practice sessions brief.

   _____ c. Always practice in the same place.

   _____ d. Practice using your visual aids.

   _____ e. Write out your speech and read from your manuscript.

Suggested Readings

Hopf, Tim, and Joe Ayers. "Coping with Public Speaking Anxiety: An Examination of Various Combinations of Systematic Desensitization, Skills Training, and Visualization." *Journal of Applied Communication Research* 20 (May 1992): 184–98. Speech teachers have studied public speaking anxiety for a long time and have used several different approaches to helping their students deal with the problem. This essay compares and contrasts the most popular methods and evaluates their effectiveness. It is not easy reading, but is worth the effort.

Johnston, Deirdre D. *The Art and Science of Persuasion.* Dubuque, Iowa: Brown & Benchmark, 1994. This is a good resource for understanding the persuasion process as a listener-centered phenomenon. It is well written and thorough.

Rybacki, Karyn, and Donald Rybacki. *Communication Criticism: Approaches and Genres.* Belmont, Calif.: Wadsworth, 1991. This first-level textbook will teach you how to listen to others' speeches and how to evaluate your own. It provides many examples and a good foundation in several approaches to speech criticism.

Listening

OBJECTIVES

After reading this chapter, you should be able to:

1. *Draw* and *label* a model of the listening process, and *describe* the four internal elements of this process.
2. *Name* and *explain* two ways in which problems with sensing develop.
3. *Name* and *explain* four problems with attending.
4. *Define* and *explain* the process of understanding.
5. *Discuss* how remembering problems affect the listening process.
6. *Describe* five steps to developing your personal listening skills.
7. *Identify* and *explain* how a speaker can help an audience to listen more effectively.

© Bob Daemmrich/Stock Boston

*W*e spend many of our waking hours listening to the variety of sounds around us. We may hear music, the noise of traffic, the conversation of friends, or the barking of a dog late at night. Each receives varying amounts of our attention because our listening effectiveness fluctuates according to how well we sense, attend to, understand, and remember what we hear.

This chapter describes the listening process and identifies the most common listening problems. It explains how to develop your personal listening skills, but its focus is primarily on how, as a speaker, you can help your audience to listen more effectively. Most audience members do not acknowledge any personal responsibility for listening well. If you want them to get your message, you have to help them.

More than half of human communication behavior is listening. It is the primary way we gain information and receive impressions. Most people are not efficient or effective listeners because they lack certain listening skills, but they can choose to improve their listening behavior.

The fact that most people are not effective listeners creates an interesting challenge for public speakers. If you want your speech to be received by audience members, you have to help them listen more effectively. You can do that by studying the most common listening problems and then compensating for the effects of those problems.

A MODEL OF THE LISTENING PROCESS

Figure 3.1 presents a useful model of the listening process. It helps to identify the areas in which most listening problems occur and also suggests various speaker behaviors that will help audience members to listen more effectively.

As indicated by the model, the listening process goes on inside an individual, but always within a context (represented by the outer box in figure 3.1). As defined in chapter 1, *context* refers to the physical, social, psychological, and temporal environment in which communication takes place.

The inner box in figure 3.1 represents one individual listener in a particular context and shows the four internal elements of the listening process: (1) sensing, (2) attending, (3) understanding, and (4) remembering. Both the context and the listener determine how effectively the listener performs in these four listening tasks. These listening process elements are also the areas in which listening breakdowns are most likely.

SENSING

The first element of the listening process in called **sensing,** which is receiving stimuli through the senses. People can hear us, see us, touch us. If we are close enough, they can smell us. When we see people, talk to them, and then shake their hands, we are sensing them. Through these senses, we internally process information about our world.

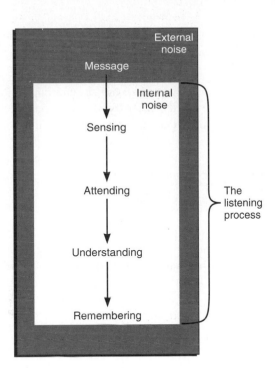

Figure **3.1**

Components of the
listening process.

ATTENDING

The second listening task is **attending.** Attending is the process of selecting and then focusing on certain stimuli. Because we are continually bombarded with billions of stimuli, we cannot process them all. We select some and ignore others.

UNDERSTANDING

Understanding, the third element of the listening model, means interpreting and evaluating what comes in through our senses. If your close friend explains how to assemble the parts of a small toy and you are able to complete the assembly yourself, you understand the message. You must be able to understand (have a shared meaning) as you sense and attend. If you do not understand, then listening fails, and the communication process breaks down.

REMEMBERING

For many, **remembering** is the hardest part of listening. Remembering means bringing back to consciousness those things that are stored in our minds. For example:

"I know you. Your name is June. I met you at the boat races near Madison last August."

"When he talked, he regularly mentioned how important it is to wear seat belts."

"The professor said that the Korean War began in 1950."

Remembering is easy for some people and difficult for others. Some people have no trouble remembering names, while dates or numbers are easy for others. Remembering is critical for using information we have heard previously. It is so important that no learning could occur if we did not have the capacity to remember. We would make the same mistakes over and over.

LISTENING PROBLEMS

Each of the four elements of the listening process—sensing, attending, understanding, and remembering—can cause problems in a public speaking setting. As you study these problems in greater detail, you will begin to see ways of improving your own listening behavior. You will also begin to understand how your choices as a public speaker can make a difference to your audience.

SENSING PROBLEMS

Problems with sensing are the result of either (1) damage to the sensory system or (2) noise. Damage to the sensory system may involve, for example, hearing and vision losses. People who cannot hear well may adjust by using a hearing aid or by sitting closer to the speaker. Someone who cannot see well may buy glasses to correct the problem. These simple choices are the responsibility of the listener.

People also may not be able to see or hear you well due to **noise,** which is any source of interference or distortion in message exchange. For example, outside sounds coming from open windows may make it more difficult for listeners to hear you, or poorly planned seating arrangements may make it more difficult for listeners to see you. In these situations, listeners must depend on you, as the speaker, to help them get the message.

ATTENDING PROBLEMS

Listeners are more likely to have problems with attention than with sensing, primarily because attention problems are more universal and more subtle. Four primary problems in attending are: (1) selective perception, (2) poor attention habits, (3) attitudes and needs that interfere with attention, and (4) low message intensity.

Selective Perception

When you choose to focus on one idea or one person to the exclusion of others, you are engaging in **selective perception.** Your experiences and interests cause you to listen carefully to some ideas and to ignore others. For example, when you choose to listen to a discussion of political matters but tune out financial affairs, you are making a choice about what you perceive is interesting and useful to you. Similarly, your experiences and interests may encourage you to listen to a speaker or to think about some other matter.

Poor Attention Habits

Listeners generally have poor attention habits: Some listeners fake attention, others avoid hard listening, while some listen just for facts. You know this from your own experience as a student. Sometimes, you pretend to be listening to your instructor. Instead, you are thinking mainly about what you are going to do on the weekend. If a speaker is discussing a topic that you find difficult to understand, you may totally avoid listening, or you may only listen for whatever facts you can pick up.

Life is full of examples where you center your mind on an issue that is very important to you but unrelated to the subject the speaker wants you to hear. It is often easier to think about what clothes you are going to wear on a date or how you are going to stretch your money to make it to the end of the month than it is to pay attention to a message. Speakers agree that one of the main problems they face is people who act as if they are listening but who actually are focused on something else.

Attitudes and Needs That Interfere with Attending

You decide to listen to a message based on your attitude toward the subject. For example, if you have strong feelings about AIDS, abortion, or gays in the military, you are not likely to listen carefully to speakers who present arguments that oppose your point of view. If you do not respect the person who is talking, you probably will not pay close attention either. Negative attitudes decrease the likelihood that you will listen.

On the other hand, positive attitudes increase the chances that you will listen to a message. You pay attention to listeners who support your positions.

In addition to attitudes, needs sometimes prevent listeners from paying attention to a speaker. Abraham Maslow's model of human needs was one of the earliest and is still among the clearest explanations of what motivates human beings to behave.[1] He identified a hierarchy, or ladder, of human needs that he believed gives rise to all human behavior (see figure 3.2). According to Maslow, the needs at the bottom of the hierarchy must be satisfied before a person becomes concerned with satisfying any higher-level needs. Thus, physiological needs must be taken care of before security and safety needs become a focus.

These needs can reduce listener effectiveness during a speech. For example, listeners might be too hungry or too sleepy to pay attention. Similarly, a speech that stimulates listeners' insecurity without providing any resolution creates a difficult listening problem. Or individuals may hold a self-concept that prevents them from paying attention to a speaker's appeal. For example, students occasionally believe that they "can't do math." They avoid taking courses in mathematics, which sets up a self-fulfilling prophesy. Low self-esteem regarding math abilities would certainly influence these students' attitudes about a speaker's argument that all students should be required to pass at least two courses in statistics.

Figure **3.2**

Maslow's hierarchy of needs.

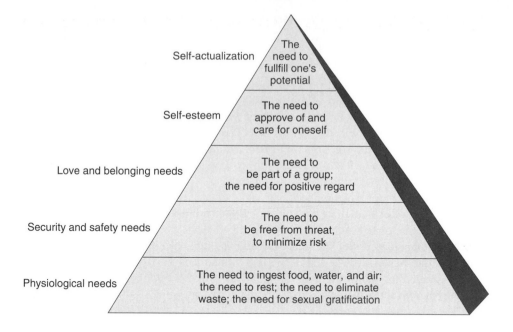

Self-actualization — The need to fullfill one's potential

Self-esteem — The need to approve of and care for oneself

Love and belonging needs — The need to be part of a group; the need for positive regard

Security and safety needs — The need to be free from threat, to minimize risk

Physiological needs — The need to ingest food, water, and air; the need to rest; the need to eliminate waste; the need for sexual gratification

Low Message Intensity

Low message intensity describes a speech in which the speaker talks in a monotone, stresses nothing, and plods on at the same rate and pitch. Such speakers are said to be "flat." Most people find such low-intensity messages impossible to listen to. Speakers who do not seem interested in their own words also lack message intensity, which makes it very hard for listeners to give the speakers' ideas much credibility.

On the other hand, some speakers stress nearly everything as "important." When speakers emphasize everything, nothing seems important. Listeners cannot identify the significant ideas. Ironically, the stress-every-idea approach often results in low message intensity.

UNDERSTANDING PROBLEMS

Understanding means that listeners draw in their own minds roughly the same picture the speaker describes. It involves **shared meaning:** Both speaker and listeners have a similar perception of a word, person, place, or thing. Often, however, speakers and listeners do not achieve a state of shared meaning. The following examples demonstrate possible misunderstandings:

1. A retired businessperson describing a stock purchase: "That stock is an attractive investment." An attractive investment for a retired businessperson provides a substantial amount of income with little or no risk, which may not be at all attractive

Table 3.1

SAMPLE MISUNDERSTANDINGS

WHAT THEY SAID	WHAT YOU HEARD
1. "You need to be flexible in your approach."	Don't take a stand on anything.
2. "The Cardinals are an inexperienced team."	The Cardinals are a pushover this year.
3. "The only sensible weight-control program is to eat less."	You have to starve yourself to lose weight.
4. "Regular studying is the best way to get good grades."	Bookworms get the high marks.

for individuals who want their money to grow. Young investors are often willing to take a few risks in exchange for substantial growth of their money. Unless the person hearing this message is retired, misunderstandings are likely.

2. A football coach describing the team's chances for a successful season: "Our team will be competitive this year." Many coaches use the term *competitive* to mean that the team will put up a good fight but probably will not win many games. Sports fans know that such a message is the "kiss of death" for the season. Unless the person hearing this message is an avid sports fan, however, misunderstandings are likely.

3. A realtor describing a home to first-time buyers: "That house is a gem; it's a cozy first home. You'll love it." Unless listeners are sophisticated in real estate purchases, they may interpret the realtor's description as an endorsement of the appropriateness of their selection. To realtors, however, the description "a cozy first home" often means that the house is small and in need of considerable repair. The dream of owning a home also may obscure listeners' understanding that this house needs a great deal of work and financial investment.

4. A salesperson explaining the advantages of a purchase to a newly married couple: "If you're on a budget, this microwave is the perfect buy at only pennies a day." "Only pennies a day" sounds attractive to anyone considering a purchase. But one hundred pennies a day translates into $365 per year. Does the speaker mean the same thing in presenting an object as inexpensive as you do when you consider the object's total cost? A $350 purchase may be costly to you, but if you do not understand that "pennies a day" means that much money, you have an expensive misunderstanding.

Understanding occurs only when both parties get the same meaning from the language. The previous examples demonstrate how speakers often send "coded" messages that only semi-experts in the field would clearly understand. Speakers must use language that is not "coded" but that is clear to both informed and relatively uninformed listeners. Table 3.1 presents additional cases of misunderstanding and illustrates that what the speaker said is not necessarily what you, as a listener, heard.

REMEMBERING PROBLEMS

How quickly we forget! The rate of human forgetfulness remains one of the most striking findings from behavioral research and is among the most carefully studied.[2] At least one well-respected researcher estimated that we forget 80 percent of the details we hear within twenty-four hours.

Why do we have so much trouble remembering? We pay attention to and remember what seems important to us and what we care about, as long as we find a way to put the information into our long-range memory banks. But we cannot seem to remember many things that people tell us. For example, students do not always remember important points of class lectures, even when they know that those points are likely to show up on a final examination. Unfortunately, most listening audiences do not even have exams to motivate them to remember.

DEVELOPING YOUR PERSONAL LISTENING SKILLS

Enhancing your personal listening skills requires (1) concentrating on the message and the speaker, (2) identifying with the speaker, (3) reacting to the speaker, (4) staying objective about the speaker's message, and (5) working hard at remembering.

CONCENTRATE ON THE MESSAGE AND THE SPEAKER

It is not easy to be an effective listener. Determine right away that you intend to listen and then concentrate your mind on the message. Decide that you will "stay on track" and not allow yourself to wander to another subject. Make better listening your personal goal, and remind yourself of this goal every time you find yourself in a listening situation.

IDENTIFY WITH THE SPEAKER

Try to empathize with the speaker. **Empathy** involves placing yourself in the physical or mental state of another and includes the ability to identify with the other person and to respond appropriately (as the other person perceives appropriate). Empathic listening means that you suspend your personal judgment and listen to ideas from the speaker's point of view. How does the speaker feel about the subject? What are the reasons for this feeling? Thinking briefly about the speaker's needs instead of your own will give you a different outlook. Consider ideas from both your standpoint and from that of the speaker. This approach will help to reduce the blocks to good listening and will help you to hear and understand the speaker and the speaker's ideas.

PRESIDENT BILL CLINTON

During the 1992 Presidential Candidate Debate held in Richmond, Virginia, Bill Clinton practiced effective listening by concentrating on, identifying with, and reacting to the audience of everyday citizens and their questions. In an interview, Clinton recalled his thoughts going into the debate:

You know, it's not easy to listen to people anytime. It's a lot easier to be a good talker than a good listener. But in that format, with all that pressure, with one hundred million people watching, it's probably even harder to be a good lis-

tener. And one thing I thought about going into that debate was that these are real people; it doesn't matter whether they're for Bush or Perot or for me, these are people who are out there living with the consequences of America today, and I have to listen to them. And I'm going to try to respond to them. I can give my speech, but respond to them.

Source: Jack Germond and Jules Witcover, Mad As Hell: Revolt at the Ballot Box, 1992 *(New York: Politics Today, 1993), 13–14. Photo © Timothy Murphy/The Image Bank*

REACT TO THE SPEAKER

Get and give feedback. Effective listeners are involved. In a conversational setting, you react to the words of others by verbally agreeing or disagreeing. They also give you feedback when you talk. Those same principles apply in a public setting. Nonverbal reactions, such as nodding, smiling, or shaking your head, give speakers an indication of how you feel about their ideas. *Paraphrasing,* which is putting another's ideas into your own words, is an excellent way to check your understanding of the speaker's message. The speaker may say, "Procrastination is at the root of most of the problems the average college student faces." A paraphrase of that statement might be, "I must stop putting things off, or I'll have more problems." If you cannot paraphrase what the speaker is saying, use nonverbal signals to show the speaker that the message is not clear. Shake your head or move your hands to show that you do not understand and that you want some clarification.

BE OBJECTIVE ABOUT THE SPEAKER'S MESSAGE

Suspend your mental sets. You can listen more effectively if you are willing to think consciously about your attitudes and notions and try to set them aside. You may have strong feelings about several subjects. Your position is important, but be willing to listen to the other side. Your interest in the subject should aid, not interfere, with your reception of the message. Ask yourself:

- What has this speaker said?
- What is the major point?
- How clearly and well is it supported?

Listeners communicate a lot to speakers by giving feedback. What can you infer about these listeners from the photograph?

© Billy E. Barnes/Stock Boston

As you listen to the speaker, do not mentally debate each idea you hear. Try to listen with an open mind and judge the statements on their own merits. Avoid jumping to conclusions. Hear all sides, and then you can make a reasonable judgment. If you try to *summarize* the speaker's ideas in your own mind, you will have a clearer idea of the speaker's position and how it ties together with yours.

A genuine effort to understand the major ideas you hear helps you to grasp the idea and to become more effective as a listener. Tell yourself that each listening situation has promise. Open your mind to new ideas.

WORK HARD AT REMEMBERING

The best way to commit a speaker's ideas to your short-term memory involves:

1. Taking brief notes. Use key words so that you will not miss any ideas and will be able to recall the information later. Try to use the speaker's organization in organizing your notes.
2. Consciously striving to set aside any distractions that tend to "jump out" in your mind during the message.
3. Putting aside your personal motives so that you are not mentally arguing with the speaker.

If you want to keep information in your "long-term storage," you need to practice. After twenty-four hours, go over your notes about a speaker's message. Review them again after a week, a month, and after six months. Write down all that you can remember and then compare this information with your notes from the listening event. You will be surprised by how much of the material you have retained.

Table 3.2

STEPS TO BETTER LISTENING

1. Focus on the speaker.
2. Suspend your attitude toward the speaker and the subject.
3. Keep an open mind.
4. Establish common ground with the speaker.
5. Be an active listener—stay awake and alert.
6. Look interested.
7. Take notes.
8. Remove interferences.
9. Try to improve your attention span.

In addition to the ones already described here, table 3.2 offers several additional ideas on how to become a better listener.

HELPING THE AUDIENCE TO LISTEN MORE EFFECTIVELY

Speakers can encourage good listening. At its best, listening is a shared activity in which the speaker offers clear, exciting ideas and listeners receive the material from the speaker's point of view and remember it. As a speaker, if you increase the listening effectiveness of audience members, you are much more likely to accomplish your goal. Listeners need all the help you can give them to sense, attend to, understand, and remember your message. Listeners also need help in empathizing (identifying) with the speaker and the message.

PROBLEMS WITH SENSING

As a speaker, you can do a lot to compensate for problems with sensing, but only if you train yourself to think about those problems. For example, to help correct for listeners' visual impairments, be sure that the lighting is adequate and that you are standing or sitting in the light. You also might want to use a good visual aids package.

As a speaker in a setting where there is external noise, ask someone to see about the source of the noise and to try to correct it. For example, if someone is mowing a lawn nearby, the individual could be asked to move to a different side of the building while you are speaking. Or you could close the windows or the door.

Occasionally, some audience members talk so loudly that the speaker cannot be heard:

During her comments to the city council on rezoning her residential area to light commercial business, Erica was distracted several times by the loud talking of several other opponents who sat near the back of the room. They seemed to be in

Listeners can find it difficult to pay attention if the speaker does not help them.

© Bob Daemmrich/Stock Boston

agreement with her, but their voices were so loud and their comments so constant, other people had trouble hearing her. Twice she was so flustered by the noise, she lost her train of thought.

Politely ask noisy audience members for quiet. Or specifically ask the talkers to control themselves: "I'd appreciate it if you'd give me a chance to make my statement. It's hard for me to think when you're speaking so loudly, and I know some others can't hear." Other times, a simple request to the talkers, such as, "Please hold it down now so we can get our business managed, OK?" will do the job.

The best overall advice for beginning speakers who want to compensate for the sensory impairments of audience members is to speak up, slow down, and repeat yourself. If you speak loudly enough to be heard, are sure that you are talking slowly enough to be understood, and repeat your message several times, you will help listeners to overcome a variety of sensing problems.

PROBLEMS WITH ATTENDING

For listeners to pay attention to your message, you need to give them *reasons to listen*. People listen to ideas that they see tied to their lives. They need to know why it is worthwhile for them to attend to your words. Simply put, they must understand what is in it for them. Providing your listeners with reasons to listen will depend to some extent on how wisely and accurately you analyze your audience (see chapter 5, "Audience Analysis").

Listeners will also be more likely to attend to your message if you are *a credible speaker*. If you act and sound like you understand your subject and your mission, people are more likely to listen to you. Credibility does much to control the communication situation. People are more likely to listen to a speaker who:

- Acts energetic and interested.
- Speaks confidently.
- Has good command of the subject.
- Supports ideas with examples and evidence.
- Is well organized.

PROBLEMS WITH UNDERSTANDING

People understand ideas better if you put the ideas into a familiar framework or if the ideas deal with strong listener needs and wants. Again, this requires accurate audience analysis (see chapter 5, "Audience Analysis").

For example, assume that an audience is composed of factory workers, most of whom never went to college. If a politician tries to persuade this group using examples from the banking industry, the speech might fail because the listeners lack a familiar framework into which they can place the speaker's arguments. A wiser politician would use examples from the factory life that the audience members live every working day.

Similarly, an idea that bears on listeners' needs and wants will seem easier for listeners to understand than an idea that has no relationship to them. The same audience of factory workers would have little basis for listening to, paying attention to, or remembering a speech about economics theory, but they would have no trouble understanding and remembering a talk about changes in the way their pay would be calculated.

The setting also affects an idea's attractiveness and listeners' desire to understand. Consider the differences in the following listening settings:

1. Spring break on the beach in Florida
2. Student government meeting where a tuition increase is the topic for discussion
3. A rally to demonstrate opposition to the death penalty
4. A debate in the U.S. Senate on the right to filibuster
5. Japanese-American talks on ways to correct the trade imbalance

For example, as a speaker in a spring break setting, you would need to know that what is interesting to some students on their spring break may not be appealing to others. Some students may want to talk or listen, while others may seek only swimming and enjoyment. The spring break setting makes listener understanding of your message questionable.

The attitudes people bring to a situation and the location where they hear the message also affect understanding. For example, in a student government meeting, a message opposing a tuition increase probably would be understood and accepted by most listeners, but the tuition increase might also be appealing to some listeners if it could be tied to additional student benefits. The well-informed student government representatives also should understand the rationale for the proposal and could understand both sides of the issue.

Each setting has different circumstances and should be analyzed individually. What effect will the setting likely have on listener attention and attitudes? Account for listener characteristics. These elements are the keys to listener understanding.

In addition to the setting, the speaker can greatly influence listener understanding. A speaker who is brief and well organized is easier for people to follow. Listeners are also likely to be more interested if the speaker uses vivid language, descriptions, or examples. For example, President Bill Clinton developed a national reputation when he delivered the keynote speech at the 1988 Democratic National Convention. His listeners became bored as he droned on for close to an hour. He would have helped convention delegates and the national television audience if he had been brief and if he had been more animated and used more examples. His fame, nationally, became one of a "long-winded convention speaker," a distinction he joked about for nearly four years.

As a speaker, make it easy for listeners to know when important ideas are coming. Such cuing devices as, "My second point is . . ." or "The best example of this situation I know is . . ." help listeners to know what is important.

Also, use the simplest language possible. For example, use the word *everywhere* instead of *ubiquitous*. A few of your listeners might understand that a synonym for *ubiquitous* is *everywhere,* but you are risking using language that could be misunderstood. Send simple words to deliver your message. The ideas can be impressive without the language being overwhelming. The language in Lincoln's Gettysburg Address is simple, but the message is profound.

Finally, keep your message full of examples and illustrations. Many listeners reason from examples. Their ears "perk up" when they hear the words *for example* because they know that the material is much more likely to be interesting and concrete.

PROBLEMS WITH REMEMBERING

People work hard at trying to remember ideas and names, but sometimes, the material simply will not stay in their minds. In general, people forget what they hear rather quickly, unless there are compelling reasons for them to retain it.

As a speaker, what can you do to help your audience remember your ideas? Listeners retain material that is (1) useful and of interest, (2) striking or out of the ordinary, (3) organized, and (4) visual.[3] These four elements, which are basic to effective communication, are also the ones that make the material more memorable. You can help your audience to remember your ideas more easily if you incorporate these elements into your talk.

Another point to remember is that people retain material best if they understand it the first time they hear it. Responsibility for this lies primarily with the speaker.

Repetition also helps listeners to remember. Repeat every important idea more than once, and provide the repetition through more than one channel. For example, use a visual aid or tell a story that highlights the point. In your summary, state the point still again.

Associating your ideas with something important or emotionally involving to your listeners is another technique for helping listeners to remember. This is a matter of identification and empathy. Tie your idea to a story. Develop a metaphor that will help listeners to associate your idea with something they know. Put your idea into a context that listeners care about. Even a touch of humor can help audience members to remember. For example, in a speech about southern hospitality, one student taught her classroom audience to treat everyone as though they were special. "Don't try to make them feel at home," she said. "If they wanted to feel at home, they would have stayed at home."

PROBLEMS WITH EMPATHY

Listeners often find it hard to empathize, to identify mentally or physically, with the speaker. They may not agree with the speaker's position, or the message might not be consistent with what listeners believe.

As a speaker, this does not mean that you have to give up your ideas or your controversial position. It does mean, however, that you must find ways to present your position so that it is more likely to be accepted by your listeners. That calls for careful audience analysis and an understanding of where listeners stand on the issues you support. Then you can polish your message and your argument. Develop clear ideas and present them with a variety of easily understood examples so that listeners can follow each portion of your message. This can make the difference in whether listeners tune you in or tune you out.

Empathy also involves feedback. Most listeners are unwilling to interrupt a speaker, believing that such behavior is rude. Thus, as the speaker, you must pay attention to the nonverbal messages that listeners send while you are speaking. For example, listeners may nod, smile, frown, or touch their ear to indicate that they cannot hear you. These messages may be the most accurate feedback you will receive from your audience. Watch your listeners and react to their behavior. Use their feedback to help you focus your message and to create listener empathy.

Occasionally, you may not be sure what some of the nonverbal messages from listeners mean. Ask questions if it appears that audience members are confused. You could say, "You seem to be confused about that last idea. Would you like me to repeat and explain it?" No one is likely to be offended. Do not allow poor use of feedback to result in a listening breakdown where listeners have lost all feelings of empathy with the speaker.

Another way to help your listeners identify with you is to know your subject well. Fill your speech with well-reasoned arguments and evidence. Stay calm. Clearly indicate what audience members should expect to gain from your speech. If you have nothing attractive to offer listeners, you may want to ask yourself why you are speaking to them.

In an effort to create ongoing empathy with your listeners, *ask them to think about your ideas after you finish speaking*. Indicate what you want them to take away and remember. If you leave them with "memorable nuggets," they will think about how your message is important to them.

Summary

Because most people are not efficient or effective listeners, if you, as a speaker, want audience members to get your message, you will have to help them to listen.

The four elements of the listening process are: (1) sensing, (2) attending, (3) understanding, and (4) remembering. How effectively the listener performs in these four listening tasks depends on the context, the speaker, and the listener. These four areas are also the ones in which listener breakdowns are most likely.

Listening problems include (1) problems with sensing due to noise or damage to the sensory system; (2) attending problems, such as selective perception, poor attention habits, attitudes and needs that interfere with attention, and low message intensity; (3) understanding problems, which involve speakers and listeners not achieving a state of shared meaning; and (4) remembering problems. Listeners forget most of what they hear.

Enhancing your personal listening skills requires (1) concentrating on the message and the speaker, (2) identifying with the speaker, (3) reacting to the speaker, (4) staying objective about the speaker's message, and (5) working hard at remembering.

As a speaker, you need to help listeners to listen more effectively so that they can sense, attend to, understand, and remember your message. To compensate for listeners' sensory impairments, speak up, slow down, and repeat yourself. Attending problems are best addressed by giving audience members reasons to listen. People will understand your ideas better if you put the ideas into a familiar framework or if the ideas deal with strong listener needs and wants. The setting, listeners' attitudes, and the speaker also affect listener understanding. Help listeners to remember your message by making your ideas useful or interesting, striking, organized, and visual. Repetition of main ideas and association of ideas with something important or emotionally involving to listeners are additional techniques for helping listeners to remember. Help listeners to empathize with you and your message by tailoring your presentation to your specific audience, encouraging feedback, and knowing your subject well.

Key Terms

Attending	Remembering	Shared meaning
Empathy	Selective perception	Understanding
Noise	Sensing	

Application Questions

1. How important is feedback to you when you speak? Do you change what you say when you see how listeners react? How accurate is your perception of listeners' responses?
2. Some people believe that they can listen only part of the time and still receive all of the message. How true do you think this statement may be? How does your answer apply to your role as a listener?
3. What steps can a speaker take to help listeners attend to and remember a speech? Who is most responsible for reception of a message? Why?

Self-Test for Review

1. List the four internal elements of the listening process, as identified in the model in figure 3.1.

   a. _____

   b. _____

   c. _____

   d. _____

Mark each of the following as either true (T) or false (F).

2. To sense is to select and give attention to selected stimuli.   T   F

3. For many people, attending is the hardest part of the listening process.   T   F

4. A primary problem in attending involves selective perception.   T   F

5. When you say that a speaker is "flat," you are referring to the speaker's intensity level.   T   F

6. Empathic listening means that you listen to ideas from the speaker's perspective.
   T   F

7. Note taking interferes with good listening.   T   F

8. A credible speaker increases the likelihood that audiences will pay attention.
   T   F

Answers: 1. a. sensing, b. attending, c. understanding, d. remembering. 2. F. 3. F. 4. T. 5. T. 6. T. 7. F. 8. T.

Suggested Readings

Wolff, Florence I., and Nadine C. Marsnik. *Perceptive Listening.* 2d ed. Orlando, FL.: Harcourt Brace Jovanovich, 1992. This book is written for all levels: students, businesspeople, and professionals. It is a very practically oriented and easily read work that stresses contemporary applications, the values of listening, and general guides for rapid improvement in listening skills.

Wolvin, Andrew, and Carolyn Gwynn Coakley. *Listening.* 4th ed. Dubuque, IA: Brown & Benchmark Publishers, 1992. This is probably the most comprehensive study of listening behavior available today. It combines all the relevant research findings and discusses, at length, the elements of the listening process. This is must reading for anyone interested in listening.

PART 2

Designing the Speech

© Bob Daemmrich/The Image Works, Inc.

CHAPTER 4

Selecting and Narrowing Your Topic

OBJECTIVES

After reading this chapter, you should be able to:

1. *Name* and *explain* four criteria that should affect your topic selection.
2. *Describe* four techniques for generating speech topics that are based on what you know.
3. *Explain* several brainstorming techniques for generating speech topics.
4. *Describe* the four sequential steps for narrowing a speech topic.
5. *Define* the term *thesis statement*, *write* a thesis statement from a specific purpose, and use four questions to test the phrasing of the thesis statement.

© *Chuck Mason/The Image Bank*

*P*ublic speakers must be able to select and narrow a speech topic so that it will be appropriate for the occasion, fit within time constraints, meet audience expectations and abilities, and be consistent with their own intellectual limits. To discover many potential speech topics, brainstorm, search your personal knowledge, examine your personal library, and look through your personal calendar. Then narrow the topic and bring it into focus.

You can narrow a speech topic by turning a general purpose (inform, persuade, entertain) into a specific purpose that tells what single, observable goal you want listeners to accomplish. Then you are ready to develop and test a thesis statement. Selecting and narrowing a speech topic may be the most difficult and most important part of speech preparation.

Many students have trouble selecting and narrowing a topic for a speech. They say things like, "I just don't have anything to say," and "There's nothing for me to talk about that would fit this assignment." Nearly everyone has such feelings at one time or another. They want to do well. They want to impress their listeners, to inform or persuade them. Intuitively, however, they know that these goals will not be achieved if they do not find and focus on a topic that their listeners will see as important and relevant. While no one has ever written a surefire formula for selecting the perfect topic, this chapter suggests guidelines for topic selection and focus.

SELECTING A TOPIC

The number of possible speech topics is limitless. For example, the first *A*-page of the *Random House College Dictionary* lists the following ten possible topics, among many others:

AA, Alcoholics Anonymous

AAA, Amateur Athletic Association

AAAL, American Academy of Arts and Letters

Aachen, a city in Germany

Aalto, a Finnish architect and furniture designer

AAM, air to air missile

Aar, a river in central Switzerland

Aaron, the brother of Moses

ABA, American Bar Association

Abacus, a device for making arithmetic calculations

Not counting the appendices that list signs and symbols, colleges and universities, and English masculine and feminine names, and that also include a basic manual of writing

This lineman can talk with anyone about his job because he knows it well. Always choose a topic you know well.

© Kay Chernush/The Image Bank

style—every entry of which would make an interesting speech topic—this dictionary has 1,543 pages of words and definitions. Simple multiplication tells you that this one book includes more than fifteen thousand potential speech topics.

Appendix D, "Possible Speech Topics," lists several hundred potential speech topics. Such a list is also likely to trigger the generation of a variety of related ideas that would be suitable for a speech.

What you need, then, is a method for finding a topic that is right for you, right for your audience, right for the occasion, and right for the time constraints on your speech.

Select wisely. Focus on what you already know and on what seems relevant and important to your listeners. A worthwhile, important, and interesting topic will sustain you as you plan for, research, and organize your ideas. It will also motivate your audience members to listen to your speech. Few speakers and listeners can sustain interest in or focus their attention on a topic that they do not consider worthwhile.

Four factors should affect your topic selection. Select a topic that (1) you are knowledgeable about, (2) is interesting and appealing to your listeners, (3) fits the occasion, and (4) can be discussed within the time constraints of your speech.

SELECT A TOPIC BASED ON WHAT YOU KNOW

Your speech topics should be based on what you know. Never talk about a subject you do not know well. This does not mean that you have to be an expert on the subject. Rather, you should select topics about which you already have information. The following four techniques for generating topics can provide you with countless ideas: (1) Brainstorm your ideas, (2) search your personal storehouse of knowledge, (3) examine your personal library, and (4) look through your personal calendar or daybook.

Table 4.1

A LIST OF TOPICS BY POSSIBLE CATEGORIES

WHO	WHAT	WHEN	WHERE	WHY	HOW
Minister	Guns	Exam time	Home	To make war	Submarines surface.
Tenants	Airplanes	Spring	New York	For peace	Wine is aged.
Cops	Stereos	Evening	France	To study	Experience affects behavior.
Military	Music	Birthday	Superdome	For profit	Rumors are spread.
Friends	Income tax	Rainy days	The office	To learn	Exams are failed.
Models	Television	Vacation	Library	To pray	Exercise works.
Athletes	Classes	February 14	The park	For health	The body burns food.
Dentists	Books	Mardi Gras	The Mall	For pleasure	
Students	Vocabulary	Martin Luther King Day	Downtown	To remember	

Brainstorm Your Ideas

Brainstorming is a timed procedure for generating a large number of ideas quickly. You can brainstorm alone or with other people. Before brainstorming for a speech topic, sit down with a blank sheet of paper and draw six columns—labeled *who, what, when, where, why,* and *how.* Then begin to write down whatever enters your head about each category. A few of the entries may seen unrelated and confusing. Others may seem to have potential. Do not jump to conclusions too soon. Avoid judging your work until later. Ideas that do not seem to hold much promise at first have a way of becoming more attractive as you play with them.

To illustrate, select one of the entries in the first column in table 4.1. Randomly draw lines that connect this entry to an entry in the second column, and the second-column entry to an entry in the third column. For example,

Who	**What**	**When**	**Where**	**Why**	**How**
friends	music	birthday			

This exercise reveals an interesting, relevant speech topic, one that even suggests the main ideas: What can you do to celebrate a birthday? You can invite friends to play or to listen to music. Looking at the remaining categories further sparks the imagination: Where can you stage this celebration? The park might be a good place.

Try using different categories in your brainstorming. For example, you might want to replace *who, what, when, where, why,* and *how* with *people, places, phenomena,* and *events.* Or you might find speech topics by brainstorming about *things,* or *characteristics,* or *processes,* or *problems.* Free your imagination and list as many things as you can under each category, staying within a given time limit. Choose different categories and do the exercise again. If you are still not satisfied, try it yet again. The method works.

Table 4.2

A STUDENT'S LIST OF POSSIBLE SPEECH TOPICS

PEOPLE	PLACES	PHENOMENA	EVENTS
President Clinton	Mobile	Rain	Vacations
President Bush	Alabama	Sleet	Holidays
Jerry Allan Bush	Mississippi	Snow	Fourth of July
Richard Wagner	Georgia	Wind	Christmas
Pablo Picasso	Louisiana	Hurricane	New Year
Artists	Baton Rouge	Tornado	Chinese New Year
Matisse	New Orleans	Earthquake	Year of the Boar
Mondrian	Mississippi River	Sunshine	Year of the Cock
Grandma Moses	Missouri River	Winter	Year of the Rabbit
Albrecht Dürer	Nile River	Spring	Rabbit hunting
Salvador Dali	Egypt	Fall	Dove hunting
Leonardo	Pyramids	Summer	Deer hunting
Writers	Mediterranean Sea	Evening shadows	Sports events
Philosophers	Black Sea	Morning light	World Series
Scientists	Pacific Ocean	Sea breezes	Super Bowl
Soldiers	Atlantic Ocean	Scent of roses	Kentucky Derby
Grant	Gulf of Mexico		White-water canoeing
Lee			Camping
Colin Powell			Fishing
Rambo			

Table 4.2 shows four lists that a student made in just ten minutes. As this student brainstormed, his lists began to suggest additional ideas. For example, when he wrote *"Pablo Picasso,"* he began to think about artists, so he listed other artists' names as well. Your lists will suggest additional topics to you, too. That is how brainstorming works.

For fun, draw random lines through the lists in table 4.2 to see if any speech topics pop out. For example, what if Pablo Picasso were alive and went to Georgia for a vacation? What would this influential twentieth-century artist find interesting or useful?

Another type of brainstorming involves developing a visual pattern to help identify possible speech topics. Figure 4.1 displays one such pattern, developed by a student. In three minutes, the student generated a large number of possible speech topics from his own knowledge and experience. Try using the lines of analysis that he followed—work, study, recreation, other interests (in this student's case, computing)—to see how far you can develop such a pattern.

As you think about your choice of speech topics, adapt to what you know. Each of the entries in tables 4.1 and 4.2 and in figure 4.1 provokes the imagination. Each suggests not just one speech topic, but many. In fact, the potential number of good speech topics is mind boggling.

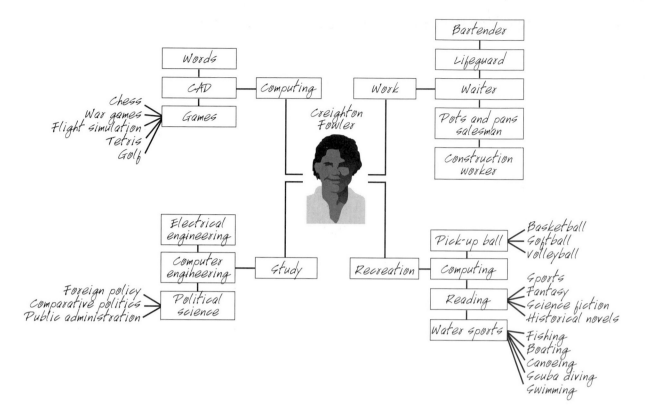

Figure **4.1**

One student's brainstorm pattern about himself.

Search Your Personal Storehouse of Knowledge

Another technique for selecting a speech topic involves tapping into your personal storehouse of knowledge. What do you know about? You know more about certain things than anyone in your audience. To interest your listeners, take advantage of your personal strengths.

What do you care about? What circumstances produce strong emotions in you? Each item you identify in response to these questions could serve as a speech topic. For example, you might really like jazz music. You might be afraid of the water. You might find computer games irresistible. You might hate bigotry in any form. Present your unique perspective in these areas.

Examine Your Personal Library

Selecting a speech topic is also easier when you examine your personal library. Look at the books, magazines, catalogs, and other reading materials you have collected. What do you read, both as part of your academic effort and for fun? Do you subscribe to a computer magazine? Do you read mystery novels? Do you find Civil War history especially fascinating? Are you interested enough in garden ponds to own a book on the subject? Have you purchased a magazine about cooking or painting? Have you ever lost yourself in a photo album? Items in your personal library suggest hundreds of excellent speech topics. What you read reflects what you find interesting.

Look Through Your Personal Calendar or Daybook

What do you do with your time? What do you get invited to do? What do you choose not to do? How you spend your time often describes your areas of interest and expertise and may suggest possible speech topics. Many people mark their commitments in an appointment book, in a diary, or on a wall-hung calendar. These resources can help you to figure out what you do for fun and profit and what you might feel comfortable speaking about.

To illustrate, one student shared her appointment book with her speech class. For September 28th, she had written:

8:15	Breakfast w/Jane. Jag Room.
9:00	Meet Jack. Studio.
4:15	Work out w/Whitney.
8:00	Meet w/CA 275 group.
10:30	Crash?

What this student did on September 28th suggests a number of possible speech topics for her, as shown in table 4.3.

SELECT A TOPIC THAT WILL APPEAL TO YOUR AUDIENCE

As you think about what you will say in your speech, try to adapt to your audience: (1) Does the age, gender, or experience of audience members suggest or eliminate any topics? (2) Do the social, religious, political, or economic feelings of listeners suggest or eliminate any topics? (3) Does the geographical locale suggest or eliminate any topics? These types of questions help you to form a demographic profile of your audience (see chapter 5, "Audience Analysis") and can assist you in selecting and focusing your topic.

For example, suppose your topic is *hot rod*. According to the dictionary, *hot rod* is "a slang term used to name a car, especially an old one, whose engine has been altered or replaced for increased speed, and whose chassis and body are often radically modified."[1] Given this topic, ask yourself questions regarding your listener's age, gender, and experience; social, religious, political, and economic feelings; and geographical locale.

This analysis indicates, for example, that you should focus your topic differently for an audience of young adults (say, ages nineteen to twenty-three) than for an audience of older adults (say ages fifty to sixty). A fifty-five-year-old today would have been in school during the 1950s and 1960s. Hot rods were commonplace in those days but looked different and performed much less efficiently than current-day hot rods.

Similarly, audience gender mix and geographic locale could influence your approach to the topic *hot rods*. In her highly readable book *You Just Don't Understand: Women and Men in Conversation*, Deborah Tannen identified significant gender differences in how men and women use words, in how they argue, in how they use gossip, in how they listen, and in attitudes and interactive styles surrounding issues of dominance and control.[2] All of these gender differences will affect how you, as a member of one gender, focus on your

Table 4.3

POSSIBLE TOPICS DRAWN FROM APPOINTMENT BOOK

ENTRY		POSSIBLE TOPICS
8:15	Breakfast w/Jane. Jag Room	Keeping weight off at the university Memorable breakfasts that aren't based on food Starting each day with pleasure Institutional architecture that serves a purpose
9:00	Meet Jack. Studio.	Learning from your friends Music as a part-time job How frequent, brief practice sessions work better than one long session The music department's need for new pianos Dates you can afford
4:15	Work out w/Whitney.	Ending your workday with a workout Forty-five minutes to better health Your body, your mind—Training yourself to learn The weight room as a woman's world
8:00	Meet w/CA 275 group.	How to work with volunteers Separating the people from the problem Task groups are everywhere What one person can do to set the tone of a meeting How to set an agenda and make it work
10:30	Crash?	Treating yourself to a rest The best way to study for an exam Water beds—the best beds How to sleep in a noisy place

speech topic *hot rods,* and how audience members of both your gender and the opposite gender will interpret and react to your *hot rod* speech. In the same way, a rural audience might have different needs from an urban audience. Thus, the rural audience might prefer a speech on the merits of four-wheel-drive pickup trucks instead of one about hot rods. Or they might prefer a speech on how to "soup up" a pickup truck and turn it into a hot rod.

Chapter 5, "Audience Analysis," discusses this matter of adapting speech topics to the audience in greater detail.

SELECT A TOPIC THAT FITS THE OCCASION

In a speech, the occasion comprises the context component in the communication process model (see chapter 1). The **occasion** is the particular time, place, and purpose of a speaking event. Two questions about the occasion influence topic selection: (1) Does the occasion suggest a topic? and (2) Does the occasion eliminate any topics?

Table 4.4

FIVE POSSIBLE SPEECH TOPICS FOR FOOTBALL BANQUET

1. *Great moments in the season*—A speech about four of the season's emotional or action highlights
2. *A coach is more than a coach*—A speech about the nurturing that successful coaches always extend to their players
3. *Football as preparation for life after school*—A speech about the benefits derived from participation in team sports
4. *Fourth and goal to go*—An inspirational speech about determination and courage
5. *Practice makes perfect*—A speech about being all that you can be

For example, suppose the coach asks you to make a few remarks at the annual city-wide football banquet. Does the occasion suggest a topic? A football banquet is held for specific reasons, including to honor the players, to acknowledge the coaches and supporting staff, to make the parents feel good about their sons playing the game, and to shower credit on school administrators and on the local population who support the citywide athletic program. Possible speech topics seem to jump from the list of purposes, as shown in table 4.4.

Asking the second question about the occasion can prove equally fruitful. Does the occasion eliminate any topics? Would the football banquet audience want to hear

BARBARA JORDAN

Early in her career, Barbara Jordan, one of the first African-Americans elected to the U.S. Congress, knew she had the power to reach people with her speeches, but she did not know why. In her biography, she describes the bewilderment she felt after presenting a speech as a candidate for the state legislature.

At the conclusion of my speech, the audience stood up and applauded. That was the first standing ovation I had ever received, and it occurred to me right then that the question was: Why are all these people standing? They hadn't stood for the others. I needed to know whether they were standing because I was the only black, or the only woman, or sounded different, or had said such fantastic things about state reform. I didn't know what had really turned them on, what had given them the spark. And I needed to know so that I could keep doing it throughout the campaign. There they were, all on their feet just cheering and cheering.

Later in her career, Jordan learned why she received ovations. The audience was "interested in her words." Jordan, as a speaker, knew "how to project the passion and compassion which let you bring your audience into where you were."

Source: Barbara Jordan and Shelby Hearon, Barbara Jordan: A Self-Portrait *(New York: Doubleday & Company, 1979), 113, 267. Photo © Terry Ashe/Liaison International*

about the evils of a school funding system that spends more money on sports in one year than it does on music, theater, and the arts in ten years? Probably not.

As another example, assume that you have been assigned to give a speech to inform. Following your teacher's advice, you decide to talk about some aspect of your job, which is applying chemicals to residential buildings for the Orkin Company. Your speech to inform could be about termites, termite control, how to apply chemicals, or the need for termite control in your geographical region. You could also talk about the people you have met, the homes you have been in, how people maintain or do not maintain their places, or how home maintenance relates to insect infestation. Any of these topics would be interesting and relevant to your classroom audience and would be appropriate for the occasion.

However, talking about the various accidental and sometimes embarrassing invasions of privacy that tend to be routine in your world of work would *not* be appropriate for this occasion. The assignment is to inform. The context involves a college classroom. The occasion is a round of assigned practice speeches. The humorous potential involved in accidental invasions of privacy would be a better topic for a speech to entertain.

SELECT A TOPIC THAT FITS THE TIME CONSTRAINTS OF YOUR SPEECH

As in the previous section, suppose that you have been invited to make a few remarks at the citywide football banquet. Also suppose that you have been asked to limit your presentation to five minutes. Does the five-minute time constraint suggest a topic? How about: "Five minutes to halftime," a speech about ways students can make the best use of their remaining high school days?

The five-minute time constraint also eliminates topics. In five minutes, you cannot discuss the nature of the universe, the nature of team sports, or even the nature of football. Limit and focus your ideas to fit in the time available. For example, you might be able to talk about how a second-string end came into the game in the fourth quarter, caught a desperation pass, and made the winning touchdown and then argue that, in life as in football, ordinary people can make extraordinary contributions.

NARROWING THE TOPIC

Once you discover a topic that suits you and that seems relevant and appropriate to the audience, the occasion, and the time constraints, you are ready to begin the real work of speech making. More speeches fail because they lack focus than for any other reason. To narrow and focus your ideas, follow the four steps in this sequence: (1) Specify the general purpose of the speech, (2) determine the specific purpose of the speech, and then (3) develop the thesis statement. Once you have done that, (4) test the thesis statement.

SPECIFY THE GENERAL PURPOSE

As you read in chapter 2, "Planning the First Speech," the **general purpose** of a speech is the intention that motivates the speech. A speech can have three general purposes: (1) to inform (2) to persuade, and (3) to entertain. Your classroom experience probably will not include a speech to entertain.

If your general purpose is to inform, then in your mind, you must become a teacher. Your purpose is to convey information to your audience. Emphasize simplicity, clarity, accuracy, and interest.

If your general purpose is to persuade, then in your mind, you must become an advocate or salesperson. Your purpose goes beyond merely transmitting information to the listeners. You want to *change* the listeners, perhaps so that they believe what you believe, develop a different attitude, or act in a specific and observable way. In a speech to persuade, you must determine what change you are trying to get from your listeners.

Almost always, your class assignments will specify the general purpose of the speech. Outside the classroom, you will not have that luxury, but table 4.5 may help in making the determination.

Speeches, like photographs, fail to communicate when they are out of focus. If you feel frustrated looking at this picture, you get a sense of how important it is to listeners that you work hard to focus your speech.

Table 4.5

OBJECTIVES FOR THE THREE GENERAL PURPOSES OF SPEECHES

The general purpose of your speech is . . .

TO INFORM	TO PERSUADE	TO ENTERTAIN
if what you want from your audience is . . .		
To know	To believe	To amuse
To understand	To value	To delight
To discriminate	To want	To charm
To comprehend	To hope	To please
To discern	To request	To laugh
To perceive	To urge	To smile
To conclude	To demand	
	To feel	
	To act	

DETERMINE THE SPECIFIC PURPOSE

Most college speaking assignments have a time limit of about five minutes. In that short amount of time, you will not be able to cover everything on your topic. Thus, once you have specified a general purpose for your speech, boil it down to size and focus you can manage within your time constraints. Determine the **specific purpose,** the particular action goal of your speech. Think in terms of **observable behavior** (any behavior that you can see or hear). What observable behavior do you want from your listeners?[3]

One student speaker decided to talk about the annual on-campus blood drive that was about to begin. She had worked as a volunteer in that drive for two years. She had her topic area. In addition, she knew that she wanted to get her classmates involved. Thus, her general purpose was to persuade:

Topic: The annual on-campus blood drive

General purpose: To persuade

Now the student had to determine a specific purpose for her speech. She needed to specify a single, observable behavior she would like from audience members. The key is to include your audience in your thinking. Think about what you want from the audience, not merely what you want. She wrote, "After giving this speech, I want my listeners to give blood in the on-campus blood drive." Her effort to focus and narrow her idea resulted in a relevant and interesting topic with a specific purpose that she could manage within the assignment's three-minute time limit:

Topic: The annual on-campus blood drive

General purpose: To persuade

Specific purpose: To persuade my listeners to give blood during the blood drive this week

This student's speech is presented in example 4.1.

Table 4.6 compares and contrasts general and specific purposes for speeches on a variety of topics. These examples highlight a clarity problem. For example, after reading the specific purposes, do you know in every case what the speakers want of their listeners? Any confusion results from the lack of a single, clear, *observable* goal. Table 4.7 shows examples of unclear specific purposes and how they can be improved so that they are observable. Notice how the improved versions point to action that you can see or hear. Such goals are specific. They say exactly what you want from your listeners.

Five guidelines help you to develop clear and specific purpose statements:

1. **Write a complete sentence, not a sentence fragment.** Sentence fragments may pinpoint the speech topic but do little to indicate the general or specific purpose of a speech (see table 4.8).
2. **Write a sentence that includes the audience and a specific behavior you want from the audience.** In the examples in table 4.8, the sentences mention a specific behavior that the speaker wants from the audience. Notice that the sentence format is: "I want my audience (or listeners) to . . . ." This format can help you to finish the sentence with specifics. Say what you want your listeners to do or to be able to do, as shown in table 4.9.
3. **Avoid judgmental statements and figures of speech.** Judgmental statements and figures of speech (metaphors, similes, analogies, personification, and so on) create confusion in a purpose statement and often seem trite. In addition, they usually do not specify an action goal. The examples in table 4.10 demonstrate this.

EXAMPLE 4.1   **ANNUAL ON-CAMPUS BLOOD DRIVE SPEECH**

I thought you might like to meet a friend of mine this morning. He can't be with us here in the classroom, although I am sure he would rather be here than in his hospital room. Tommy is nine. He's a bright kid who is interested, more than anything else, in becoming an astronaut. And he has a good chance, too—even though he has something called *pre-leukemia.* He has intelligence, curiosity, wit, and charm, and amazing self-possession for a nine-year-old.

Tommy has enormous brown eyes that seem to look beyond you. He smiles quickly and often. He seems at ease with people of every age. He is full of fun, and he is full of hope. What he doesn't have, and what he needs most, is your help. He needs blood, lots of it. And that can only come from people.

And not only Tommy. There are many people who need blood in this community every day, and there is only one place where they can get it.

Today, in the University Center, they're having a blood drive. They've come here, to our campus, because they know that a college campus is the best place to find a large number of healthy adults who have more blood than they need, and more caring and concern for their fellow man than anywhere else.

They've come here knowing that all they have to do to get help for Tommy is to ask you. They know that you've been helpful in the past. In fact, last year at this time, you gave about half the blood that they collected, citywide, in their whole campaign. In doing that, you gave back the lives, for a while, at least, to over a hundred patients who needed your help.

And now they're asking for your help again. I am asking for your help, too, for my friend Tommy. He needs you. He really, really needs you, and he knows you'll help. Will you walk with me, right now, over to the University Center—for Tommy and for yourself?

---

4. **Be sure that your specific purpose sentence includes only one goal.** A specific purpose statement that includes more than one goal tends to confuse both the speaker and listeners. Supporting materials are likely to go in two directions. Determine if your specific purpose statement includes more than one idea by looking for connecting terms, such as *and, but, however,* and for connecting punctuation, such as a comma. These often indicate that a sentence contains two or more ideas. See table 4.11 for examples.

5. **Specify a goal your listeners can give you.** Speakers' ambitions may reach beyond what they can accomplish. Seek an achievable goal. Otherwise, you simply cannot succeed. Look at the examples in table 4.12. Audience members can give the response requested in the last example. They can write a letter. The speaker is clear about what listeners should do.

After you write down the specific goal you want from your audience, test it against the checklist in table 4.13. If your answer to any of the checklist questions is "no," you would be wise to go back and fix the problem.

Table 4.6

COMPARING TOPICS, GENERAL PURPOSES, AND SPECIFIC PURPOSES

TOPIC	GENERAL PURPOSE	SPECIFIC PURPOSE
Music as a part time job	To inform	"I want my listeners to know how they can use what they love to do as a part-time job."
Ending your workday with a workout	To persuade	"I want my listeners to use the gym."
How to work with volunteers	To inform	"I want my listeners to know three things about working successfully with volunteers."
Treating yourself to rest	To persuade	"I want my listeners to get at least eight hours of bed rest each day."

Table 4.7

MAKING THE SPECIFIC PURPOSE OBSERVABLE

EVALUATION	SPECIFIC PURPOSE
Not specific	"I want my listeners to know how they can use what they love to do as a part-time job."
Better	"I want my listeners *to specify at least three ways* they can use what they love to do in a part-time job."
Not specific	"I want my listeners to know three things about working successfully with volunteers."
Better	"I want my listeners *to specify three ways* to help volunteer workers succeed."
Not specific	"I want my listeners to participate in the blood drive."
Better	"I want my listeners *to give blood* at the University Center this afternoon."
Not specific	"I want my listeners to use the gym."
Better	"I want my listeners *to sustain an elevated heart rate* for at least thirty minutes."

USING COMPLETE SENTENCES, NOT FRAGMENTS

EVALUATION	SPECIFIC PURPOSE
Fragment	Violins and fiddles
Sentence	"I want my audience to be able to specify the differences between violins and fiddles."
Fragment	The larva of the butterfly
Sentence	"I want my listeners to be able to explain the process of metamorphosis."
Fragment	The speech mechanism
Sentence	"I want my listeners to be able to list the parts of the speech mechanism that are contained in the mouth."

INCLUDING THE AUDIENCE AND SPECIFYING LISTENER BEHAVIOR

EVALUATION	SPECIFIC PURPOSE
Not specific	"I want my audience to know about the French origins of many English words."
Problem	This statement does not specify what the speaker wants the audience to do.
Better	"I want my audience to be able to explain how French words, such as *parliament, sermon, scarlet, chair, conversation, logic,* and hundreds more, came into the English language at the time of the Norman Conquest."
Not specific	"I want to inform my audience about how the word *crucifix* came into English."
Problem	The statement does not specify an action goal for listeners.
Better	"I want my audience to be able to explain how the term *crucifix* came into English."
Not specific	"I want my audience to agree that the university should change to the semester system."
Problem	Agreement cannot be observed. What does the speaker want audience members to do? The speaker must work to achieve clarity and specificity, or listeners are not likely to figure it out.
Better	"I want my listeners to vote in the upcoming Student Government Association referendum on the proposed switch to the semester system."

Table 4.10

AVOIDING JUDGMENTAL STATEMENTS AND FIGURES
OF SPEECH

EVALUATION	SPECIFIC PURPOSE
Judgmental	"I want my listeners to believe that the Student Government Association president is a jerk."
Problem	Although the judgment tells what the speaker thinks, it does not specify what the speaker wants from listeners. Also, the statement would be clearer if the speaker had written an observable action.
Better	"I want my listeners to sign this petition to recall the Student Government Association president."
Judgmental	"I want my audience to know that the Greek-letter system on campus is corrupt and should be abolished."
Problem	"Know" seems misleading. The speaker probably means "believe." Even so, the statement does not specify what the speaker wants from the audience. Notice, also, that the statement includes two goals, neither of which is an action goal. The word *and* gives the clue.
Better	"I want my listeners to believe that the Greek-letter system on campus should be abolished."
Problem	Although the focus is better in this attempt, and although belief is a legitimate persuasive goal, what does belief look like? The goal is not observable, so developing the speech will be more difficult.
Still Better	"I want my listeners to join the Student Coalition for a Greek-Free Campus."
Trite Use of Metaphor	"I want my listeners to know that the movement on campus to abolish our football team is *dead as a doornail*."
Better	"I want my listeners to be able to describe the status of the Abolish Football movement on campus."

Table 4.11

INCLUDING ONLY ONE GOAL

EVALUATION	SPECIFIC PURPOSE
Two Goals	"I want my listeners to agree with me that they should support student theater productions on campus, and buy a ticket to next week's play."
Better	"I want my listeners to believe that they should support student theater productions on campus."
Still Better	"I want each of my listeners to purchase a ticket to next week's student theater production."
Two Ideas	"I want my audience to know *and* believe . . ."
Three Ideas	"I want my listeners to know *and* believe *and* act . . ."
Better	"I want my audience to explain . . ."
Still Better	"I want my listeners *to be able to define* each term in the model."

Table 4.12

SPECIFYING AN ACHIEVABLE GOAL

EVALUATION	SPECIFIC PURPOSE
Overambitious	"The university library should be expanded."
Problem	Who can do this? Can the audience do this? Can the listeners expand the library? A student group could not. The Board of Regents could. Check to see if the goal lies beyond what audience members can give. Specify an achievable goal. What does *expand* mean? More money? More space? More books?
Much Better	"I want my listeners to write to the university president to ask that the library's undergraduate collection be enlarged."

Table 4.13

SPECIFIC PURPOSE CHECKLIST

1. Does the specific purpose fulfill the assignment? (For example, if the assignment is to inform, are you trying to persuade?)
2. Is the specific purpose focused on the audience? (Does the purpose statement name and include the listeners?)
3. Does the specific purpose specify something for audience members to do? (Does it name an observable action—even if you do not plan to call for the action ["After this speech, I want my audience to be able to . . ."]?)
4. Is the specific purpose within listeners' capability? (They may not be able to change the system, but they can contribute to the cause, vote, sign a petition, make phone calls, and so on.)
5. Does the specific purpose matter to listeners? (Think about the listeners' perspective. What will they consider relevant and important?)
6. Is the specific purpose too trivial for listeners? (Topics that diminish anyone in the audience only give offense. A speech on how to wash the clothes, or how to sweep a room, or the best kind of paper clip tend to put listeners down.)
7. Is the specific purpose too technical for listeners? (How to run a regression analysis, what's wrong with today's camera lenses, how to select the right bandwidth for your multimedia application, and celestial navigation in the south Atlantic may all seem overwhelming to your listeners.)
8. Can the specific purpose be accomplished within the time limits of the assignment? (You could not teach listeners how to play jazz music on a sax in one six-minute classroom speech. You could not even teach them how to finger the sax in that length of time. However, you might be able to teach them how to vibrate the reed.)

DEVELOP THE THESIS STATEMENT

The **thesis statement** is made in the introduction of a speech and gives the most important point or purpose of the speech. Think of a specific purpose statement as planning. Think of the thesis statement as something you say *while you are giving the speech.* Table 4.14 illustrates the difference.

Specific purpose statements point to the planning a speaker has to do to accomplish the speaking goal. For example, if you wish to teach listeners how to make gunpowder, you need to discover, and then tell the audience, what materials to use, in what proportions, and where to find them. These considerations suggest the main ideas of the body of the speech. In the actual introduction, give your thesis statement: "You can make gunpowder from materials you have in your home or that you can get easily." Point to the main idea you are trying to get across.

Table 4.14

SPECIFIC PURPOSES AND SAMPLE THESIS STATEMENTS

SPECIFIC PURPOSE	THESIS STATEMENT
"I want my listeners to vote in this afternoon's Student Government Association election."	"You must vote in the Student Government Association election this afternoon."
"I want my listeners to think of buying a computer as they think of buying a car."	"Now is the time to buy your first computer."
"I want my listeners to write Representative Calahan in support of his handgun legislation."	"Representative Calahan wants to hear from you."
"I want my audience to make two changes in essay exam procedures: (1) provide a clear and accurate study guide and (2) return a hypothetical 'A' answer with each student paper."	"Two valuable improvements in essay exam procedures will help your students without inconveniencing you."
"I want my audience to be able to describe how to make gunpowder."	"You can make gunpowder from materials you have in your home or that you can get easily."

TEST THE THESIS STATEMENT

Good speakers test the phrasing when they plan a thesis statement. Beginning speakers, however, often have difficulty with this task. Do not worry if you are one of these students. If you have a single, observable goal in mind, your thesis will come into focus as you work on developing the body of your speech. If you have developed the body and still cannot state the thesis, your speech is probably out of focus. Double-check that your main ideas all drive toward the single, observable goal you have written down.

Four questions you can use to test the phrasing of your thesis statement are:

1. Is the statement expressed in one, simple, declarative sentence? (It should not be a question.)
2. Does the statement summarize the purpose and main ideas of the speech?
3. Does the statement specify or at least clearly imply what you want listeners to remember after the speech?
4. Is the statement free of judgmental and figurative language?

The sample thesis sentences in table 4.15 illustrate the problems implied in each of these questions and show how to improve them. Each of the "Better" examples tells, in one sentence, the speaker's main idea, focuses listeners' attention on this main idea, and prepares listeners for what is coming in the rest of the speech.

Table 4.15

IMPROVING THESIS STATEMENTS

EVALUATION	THESIS STATEMENT
Wrong	"How much should you pay for a personal computer?"
Problem	The question might work as an attention-getting device in the introduction, but it does not carry any information. The main thrust of the speech is not clear. What the speaker wants from listeners cannot be determined from a question.
Better	"You can get a computer for about $1,000 that will run every kind of business software."
Wrong	"Federal government entitlements are wrecking our economy."
Problems	This claim is too general. An audience would not know what to do with it. There is no indication that the speaker has the audience in mind. What action goal, if any, does this statement point to?
Better	"Write to your congressperson and ask for a bill to end all farm subsidies above $25,000."
Wrong	"This is a good time for entrepreneurship."
Problems	This statement hides the main idea from listeners. Also, it does not suggest or imply any observable behavior.
Better	"This is a good time to borrow venture capital."
Wrong	"I want you to be able to explain how well built the new fine arts building is."
Problem	The goal is not clear. Listeners know that the speaker is asking them to learn, but what? What does the speaker want them to take away from the speech? Even such a direct sentence can confuse listeners.
Worse	"The new fine arts building is built like a battleship."
Problem	The figurative language seems trite, and the metaphor does not fit the situation. It raises the confusing question: Why would anyone build a building like a battleship?
Better	"The new fine arts building has an earthquake-proof foundation."

Summary

There are millions of good speech topics, and you already know about thousands of them. Selecting a topic is not so difficult. Rather, the problem lies in selecting a topic that you are knowledgeable about, that relates to the audience, that fits the occasion, and that can be discussed within the given time constraints. Bringing the topic into focus around a clear action goal is the second part of the challenge.

Your speech topics should be based on what you know. Brainstorm ideas, search your personal storehouse of knowledge, look through your personal library, and examine your appointment calendar. The demographic makeup of the audience also often suggests and eliminates topics, as does the occasion and time constraints. All of these sources help you to locate a topic that you know and can care about.

What remains, then, is the task of narrowing the topic down to manageable limits. Begin with the general purpose of the speech. Do you want to inform, to persuade, or to entertain? This information tells you the mind-set that will help you most. For example, if your general purpose is to inform, the most helpful mind-set is that of a teacher. If your general purpose is to persuade, then in your mind, you must become an advocate or salesperson.

Regardless of the general purpose, the easiest and best way to determine the specific purpose of a speech is to think in terms of audience behavior. What single, observable behavior do you want from listeners? Guidelines for developing clear and specific purpose statements include writing a complete sentence that includes the audience and a specific behavior you want from the audience, avoiding judgmental statements and figures of speech, and specifying only one goal, a goal that listeners can achieve. When your specific purpose is stated in terms of one observable goal, everything else about speech making seems to fall into place. Know your specific purpose and know your audience, and you will know what you must do in the rest of the speech.

A specific purpose statement is part of speech planning, whereas a thesis statement is stated during the actual speech. State the thesis in the introduction as part of your effort to prepare listeners for what is coming. The thesis statement should be one, simple, declarative sentence, *not* a question. It should summarize the purpose and main ideas of the speech, as well as specify or clearly imply what you want listeners to remember after the speech. The thesis statement also should be free of judgmental and figurative language.

Key Terms

Brainstorming	Observable behavior	Specific purpose
General purpose	Occasion	Thesis statement

Application Questions

1. Either alone, or preferably with one or more of your classmates, attend a speech on campus or in your community. Try to determine if the speaker has a clear purpose in mind. What is the topic? What is the specific purpose? Does the speaker have a thesis statement? How do you assess the quality of the speech? Do you think that the quality and effectiveness of the speech has anything to do with the speaker's focus? In your opinion, are the speech topic and focus appropriate to the audience and occasion? If not, why not? What changes could you suggest?

2. Visit the courthouse in your community or county during a jury trial. As you listen to the proceedings, can you identify how the bits and pieces of evidence and argument fit together? Can you infer how they relate to the attorney's specific purpose?

3. Drive down one of the busier commercial streets in your community. Let the things you see stimulate your thinking. Have a friend riding with you write down every possible speech topic that occurs to you as a result of this trip (or you can do this yourself after you park the car). What insight, if any, does this excursion generate in you about the number of potential speech topics?

Self-Test for Review

1. List four guidelines for selecting a topic.

    a. _____
    b. _____
    c. _____
    d. _____

2. Which of the following items influence whether a speech topic is appropriate to an audience or an occasion? (Check the correct answer.)

    _____ a. The occasion.
    _____ b. The weather.
    _____ c. The time limits.
    _____ d. The clothes you are wearing.
    _____ e. Features of the audience.
    _____ f. Your personal knowledge.

3. An old friend of your parents is offering you unsolicited advice about your speech class. Which of the following is *good* advice? Place a "✓" mark next to each piece of good advice.

    _____ a. "Ask the person who invited you to speak what she wants you to talk about. Talk about that subject no matter what. Otherwise, you're bound to miss the audience."

    _____ b. "It's okay to wing it sometimes, if you aren't sure what you're talking about. Most of the time the listeners won't know your subject anyway."

_____ c. "A good way to find a topic is to search through your own library. You are what you read, you know!"

_____ d. "If you keep a daybook or diary, you'll have no difficulty finding a topic. All you have to do is look at that to see how you spend your time. With some thinking, you'll locate a lot of speech subjects there."

_____ e. "You can develop about one main idea per minute, so if you have a ten-minute time limit for your speech, you can introduce and develop about ten main ideas."

_____ f. "You always have to have at least two main ideas. Remember the rule about outlining? If you have an *A,* you must have a *B.*"

_____ g. "It's not wise to have more than one specific purpose for a speech."

4. Match each statement on the left with the stage of speech planning on the right to which it applies.

_____ a. Think in terms of observable behavior.

_____ b. Inform, persuade, or entertain.

_____ c. Be sure that your statement points to the main idea you are trying to get across.

_____ d. Does the statement summarize the purpose and main ideas of the speech?

_____ e. Write down the intention that motivates the speech.

_____ f. Write a complete sentence, not a sentence fragment.

_____ g. Check to see if the statement expresses one, simple idea in a declarative sentence.

_____ h. Make this statement in the introduction, while you are giving the speech.

1. Specifying the general purpose

2. Determining the specific purpose.

3. Developing and testing a thesis statement

5. Which of the following is the *best* definition of a *thesis statement?* (Circle the correct response.)

a. A statement in the introduction of a speech that specifies the most important point

b. A statement designed during the planning stages of the speech that tells what you want from listeners

c. A general goal for a speech

d. A specific purpose statement that tells what the speech is all about

6. Write an appropriate thesis statement for each of the following specific purposes.

a. "I want my listeners to vote in the Student Government Association elections tomorrow."

a. _____
   _____
   _____

b. "I want my listeners to sign this petition in support of abolishing the foreign language requirement."

b. _____
   _____
   _____

c. "I want my listeners to be able to describe how it is possible for a sailboat to sail upwind."

c. _____
   _____
   _____

7. List the four questions you can use to test a thesis statement. Then use these
questions to check the thesis statements you wrote for question 6.

a. _____

b. _____

c. _____

d. _____

Answers: 1. Adapt to the occasion, to the audience, to time constraints, to what you know. 2. a, c, e, f. 3. c, d, g. 4. a, 2, b, 1, c, 3, d, 3, e, 1, f, 2, g, 3, h, 3. 5. a. 6. a. "Exercise your right to vote tomorrow." "Vote in the Student Government Association elections tomorrow." b. "We must work together to abolish this unnecessary, arbitrary, and harmful requirement." "I'm going ask you to put your name on a petition that would abolish the foreign language requirement." c. "The laws of physics make it possible for a sailboat to move upwind." "Sailboats really do move against the wind." 7. Is the statement expressed in one, simple, declarative sentence? Does the statement summarize the purpose and main ideas of the speech? Does the statement specify or imply what you want listeners to remember after the speech? Is the statement free of judgmental and figurative language?

Suggested Readings

Brigance, William Norwood. *Speech Composition.* New York: Appleton-Century-Crofts, 1937, 1953. This old chestnut is still one of the best sources of help on speech making. See chapter 3, "The Speech Purpose," pp. 52–65.

Freeley, Austin J. *Argumentation and Debate: Critical Thinking for Reasoned Decision Making.* 8th ed. Belmont, Calif.: Wadsworth, 1993. This is another classic work. The first edition appeared in 1961. Acceptance for this work has lasted through eight editions because it is so helpful. See, especially, chapters 3, 4, and 5, "Stating the Controversy," "Analyzing the Controversy," and "Exploring the Controversy." If you understand these chapters, you will never have a question about how to focus a speech idea.

Warnick, Barbara, and Edward S. Inch. *Critical Thinking and Communication: The Use of Reason in Argument.* 2d ed. New York: Macmillan, 1994. This text is extremely useful for help in focusing ideas.

CHAPTER 5

Audience Analysis

OBJECTIVES

After reading this chapter, you should be able to:

1. *Explain* the nature of an audience.
2. *Describe* the three elements of the audience setting and how these elements affect your role as a speaker.
3. *Explain* how audience perceptions and expectations affect your speaking objectives.
4. *Describe* the two methods of conducting an audience analysis: direct-access audience analysis and inferential audience analysis.
5. *Define* demographic profile, and *explain* how demographic characteristics can affect how audience members feel about and react to your speech.
6. *Develop* a demographic profile of your audience.
7. *Perform* an audience analysis using the information gained through a demographic profile.

© Michael Dwyer/Stock Boston

Your success as a public speaker depends on how well you relate to your listeners. By developing a demographic profile, you learn listeners' characteristics, such as their age, gender, and socioeconomic status. This information makes it possible for you to infer their needs and perceptions accurately and to predict how they are likely to react to your speech. Your audience analysis also helps you to estimate what the audience already knows about your subject, suggests how to adapt features of your speech to a specific group of listeners, and predicts what kind of speech will have a maximum effect on an audience. This chapter discusses the process of audience analysis and examines those kinds of analyses that will help you to achieve a higher level of success with your target audience.

The president and chancellor of a large midwestern university recently failed to analyze their audiences well. Both individuals are well educated, have national reputations in their fields, and receive large salaries for managing educational and financial operations. When the university agreed to provide each of them with a car at school expense, both of them bought expensive cars for business use.

Soon, the media got wind of the purchases and publicized the "extravagance" of the two officials:

> *If you have a kid attending MU, or if you are going to have one attending, or if you pay taxes in the state of Missouri, you are part owner of two brand new Buick Park Avenue Ultra automobiles costing $26,154 and $28,250—more than many people earn in a year.*
>
> *But try to lay a claim on your part of those automobiles, and MU campus security will probably haul you off to jail.*
>
> *You are also paying for the $150,000-per-year salaries of the real owners of the luxury cars—university president George Russell and Columbia chancellor Charles Kiesler. You are paying for their houses on university property, which probably aren't dumps, that they don't have to pay to live in, and housekeepers, country club memberships, entertainment allowances, and retirement annuities for each of them. Kiesler also got a $50,000 signing bonus. . . .*
>
> *MU has paid big bucks to land two high-profile players in the educational world. . . . Tuition at MU rose 14.6 percent last year and will rise 47 percent over five years to pay for these benefits along with capital improvements, program updates, and raises for the faculty.*[1]

One of the university officials said that he needed to project the proper "image" and that the expensive car helped him do that. When he appeared before the House Appropriations Committee to request state funding for the school, the university president defended the purchase and said that the car was part of his contract, that he had no intention of changing his mind, and that he could not be bothered by articles in the newspaper.

The state attorney general then entered the picture by noting that the university officials' cars violated the fuel efficiency laws for state-bought cars. The average miles per gallon of the luxury cars was four miles under the minimum required by the state for cars purchased with state money. The public was angry. Radio and television headlined the story. The university officials were the butt of jokes around the state. "How," people asked, "can you ask us to pay more for higher education when you live like kings?"

In their responses to all the criticism, the university chancellor and president did not exhibit any sensitivity to or concern for their audience. They did not bother to think about how people would see their decisions. They did not consider how unwise it is to ask for more money while spending a large amount on yourself. In other words, they failed to engage in adequate audience analysis.

Audience analysis is the process by which a speaker tries to identify and understand the major characteristics of a group of listeners. One important facet of audience analysis is **demographic analysis.** *Demography* is the statistical study of a population's vital characteristics, including income, marital status, age, sex, and socioeconomic status. Demographic information allows you to make educated predictions about the responses of listeners. Demographic analysis of your audience before you speak increases the chances that your listeners will respond according to your plan.

The audience is central to the aim of your message. Audience members, however, are not all alike and often have different opinions on the same subject. For example, some people may believe that it is all right for university officials to spend that much state money on a new car. Others may believe that a new car is only an expensive status symbol.

Before you talk to an audience, try to discover how audience members feel about your topic, how much they know, and what things are likely to affect them. Your listeners are different people, with differences you have to determine to be successful. You will not usually have the chance to directly question your listeners about their feelings, information, and so forth. Instead, you must operate *inferentially,* which means that you must make educated guesses about audience characteristics. The university officials discussed here clearly did not bother to analyze their statewide audience inferentially. They simply ignored them!

THE NATURE OF THE AUDIENCE

Even though the word *audience* describes a group, an **audience** is a collection of individual, unique human beings. Audience members have particular characteristics. They make their own decisions. They want you, as a speaker, to consider their personal opinions and priorities. You cannot and should not treat audience members as if they were all alike. To be successful, you must respect the interests of each individual audience member.

However, you also cannot talk with each of them individually. You must determine which subgroups exist within the audience. After you have identified the subgroups, you can anticipate their probable reactions. The value of audience analysis is that you adapt your materials to your listeners.

THE AUDIENCE SETTING

As a speaker, one of your key concerns is the **audience setting,** your speaking environment. Early audience analysis should involve looking at the three elements that make up the audience setting: (1) *when* you plan to speak, (2) *where* you will be speaking, and (3) the *events that precede and follow* your appearance. Let us see how these three elements affect your role as speaker.

WHEN YOU SPEAK

Audience attention is higher at some times of the day than at others. For example, after-dinner or after-lunch speakers face a formidable challenge: Listeners are tired, their stomachs are full, and they have a tendency to doze off. Even if your speech is sparkling, listeners may let their minds wander because of the time of day. Speakers who must make their presentations just before a meal face listeners who are distracted because their stomachs are empty and their tempers are short. Speakers with midmorning engagements on a Tuesday or Wednesday, however, are much more likely to get their audience's attention. These are times when listeners are alert, have a good energy level, and usually are not thinking about Friday and the upcoming weekend.

The time of year when you speak also can have an effect on listener response. It is hard to be attentive when you are drowning in sweat during the summer or chilled to the bone during winter. Speakers usually cannot change the time of day or time of year of a speech. However, they can consider how these factors may affect audience attention and interest.

WHERE YOU SPEAK

Where will you be presenting your speech? Will it be in a large auditorium with a public address system? Will you be talking in a gym with poor acoustics? What types of audience adjustments will be necessary if you are speaking in a quiet church or synagogue? Even speaking in a classroom has its own set of challenges: Students might be making noise in the hall, or campus maintenance could be mowing the grass outside the classroom. If you are speaking outside and audience members have to stand, you need to remember that their legs will tire soon. If you are speaking inside and audience members have to sit on hard, wooden chairs, they will get restless in a hurry.

In all of these cases, where you speak may demand that you make adjustments so that you do not lose listener attention. For example, if you know there will be a high level of noise, think about how you can eliminate as much of it as possible. Or if the problem cannot be reduced, determine how you want to overcome it.

EVENTS SURROUNDING YOUR SPEECH

The events surrounding your speech affect your listeners and your chances for success. For example, in a classroom setting, if you are the first speaker, your classmates are interested in how you will manage the situation. You set the tone for the rest of the speeches that day. Or if you are one of the last speakers, the audience reaction to you will be affected by the three or four people who went ahead of you.

You have probably been to a public gathering where one of the speakers was especially good. Speakers who follow that person are especially challenged to maintain the "standard of excellence" that has now been set. Listeners are conditioned to expect good performances from everyone who comes later. Speakers usually rise to the challenge and succeed.

You cannot always predict what events will affect your speech. Remember, though, that whatever happens before you talk will affect how listeners react to you.

Where you speak, when you speak, and the setting that contains and surrounds the speech all affect your success as a speaker.

(top) UPI/Bettmann
(bottom) © Nancy J. Pierce/Photo Researchers, Inc.

AUDIENCE PERCEPTIONS AND EXPECTATIONS

How do audience members feel about you? What is their image of you? Do you have *credibility?* If your listeners view you as friendly, well informed, and interested in them, they are more likely to accept what you say. Audience analysis helps you to accurately estimate the audience's perception and expectations of you. When you know how they feel about you, you can make better communication choices.

How do audience members feel about themselves? How much do they know about your topic? Make sure that your presentation does not aim over or under their heads. If you simply assume that they know as much or feel the same way you do about a particular subject, you may be in trouble.

To illustrate, one student spoke about how to take better pictures on a summer vacation. He brought a camera with him and pointed out the important features. His speech concentrated on the importance of depth of field, shutter speed, and selective focus. He explained, at length, how these features related to each other. They were the major elements, he said, in making sure that a picture would turn out properly. Audience members were confused. They did not understand the difference between a 2.0 and a 2.8 f stop. So they did not see how aperture related to shutter speed. Since that information came early in the speech, most of the listeners tuned the speaker out. His information was new, and he did not prepare his listeners for it. One student said, "He sure may know his photography, but he doesn't know how to explain it. I was lost after he asked if I'd like to take better pictures." This student speaker failed to evaluate the knowledge base of his listeners, and they tuned him out. If he had been more careful in his audience analysis, he probably would have succeeded.

Another question that you should ask yourself is, how do audience members view the occasion? What do they expect from the speaking situation? What standards of taste do they embrace? Listeners tend to apply different standards to various situations. For example, audience members at a luncheon meeting of the local Rotary International expect their speakers to be dressed formally. A speaker dressed in jeans and a T-shirt would find communicating with the Rotary audience difficult.

After you have researched answers to these types of questions, you will know more about your audience members and will have a clearer sense of how they will respond to your message. Center your message on audience members and the information they already have. Success in speaking means that you adjust your comments to listeners by making inferences about their knowledge, attitudes, and beliefs and that you then show listeners that you are aware of them. Table 5.1 summarizes the various elements that affect audience analysis.

Speaking is an audience-centered process. To be successful, you need to know the image that listeners have of you, themselves, and the occasion. Table 5.2 is a checklist of audience-related factors to help you find the answers you need to craft a message that will be adapted to your audience.

Table 5.1

ELEMENTS THAT AFFECT AUDIENCE ANALYSIS

1. Time of day
2. Location of speech
3. What precedes and follows your speech
4. Audience expectations
5. Listener attitudes and perceptions
6. Collective audience feeling

Table 5.2

CHECKLIST OF AUDIENCE-RELATED FACTORS

How Do Audience Members See You?

1. Do they think that you are interested in them?
2. What do they believe you have in common with them?
3. Do they believe that you are qualified to talk to them?
4. Why do they think that you are speaking to them?
5. Do they see you as trustworthy?

How Do Audience Members See Themselves?

1. Are they open to new ideas?
2. Do they know much about the subject?
3. Have they had previous experience with this subject?
4. What kind of attitudes do they have toward this subject?

How Do Audience Members View the Occasion?

1. Will the physical setting help you to reach your goal?
2. Is your message consistent with what listeners expect on this occasion?

CONDUCTING AN AUDIENCE ANALYSIS

There are two methods of conducting an audience analysis, and the choice of method depends on your access to the audience you plan to address. When you have direct access to an audience—like, for example, your classroom audience—you can gather information about the audience by simply asking questions, listening to discussions, conducting interviews, and asking audience members to fill out questionnaires. This is called **direct-access audience analysis.** When you do not have direct access to your audience, your audience analysis must be inferential. **Inferential audience analysis** involves making educated guesses that are based on what is already known about the audience.

DIRECT-ACCESS AUDIENCE ANALYSIS

Immediate audiences are those groups that you, as a speaker, can contact directly for analysis. Because you have direct access to these people, you can explore several areas that will help you to be more effective in speaking to them. The kinds of questions you ask should be tied to the topic you have chosen and the purpose of your presentation.

When you speak in class, you are talking to an immediate audience and therefore have a unique opportunity to engage in audience analysis. The people in your classroom will be the same throughout the course. You can ask them questions. Through discussions, you can determine their attitudes, goals, interests, and preferences. Always seize opportunities to get information directly from these future listeners.

Even though your classmates are a "captive" audience, since attendance is usually required and they do not feel free to leave whenever they choose, that does not mean that their needs can be ignored. Each of them has needs, wants, and information, just like an audience in the outside world. They have different points of view that you, as a speaker, need to take into account. A class speech is a kind of lab experiment: The people and the topic are real, as will be audience reactions.

Immediate audiences are not just found in classrooms. For example, if you are a member of the local chamber of commerce and the program committee asks you to talk about an upcoming event at its next meeting, you can get direct information about audience members. They are the people you see and work with every day. They are an immediate audience, just like your college class audience.

One way to begin analysis of your immediate audience is to ask people questions about your topic in an interview. First, work at obtaining general information about audience reaction to your topic. Table 5.3 lists typical questions and responses.

While the general information presented in table 5.3 is useful, you also need more specific information that will help you to adjust your organization and ideas. Try developing a short questionnaire. You then will have a standard approach for getting detailed information from all your listeners. Table 5.4 shows sample types of questions you could use. Example 5.1 shows a sample questionnaire that you might want to ask an immediate audience to complete if you have decided to present a speech on the security of the U.S. banking system.

Interviews and questionnaires are important information-gathering tools that will give you a much better grasp of your audience's level of understanding for and feelings about your topic. Do not overlook the chance to get information directly from an immediate audience. It gives you a head start to success.

The classroom audience *is* an audience.

© *James L. Shaffer*

Table 5.3

DETERMINING AUDIENCE REACTION TO YOUR TOPIC

WHAT YOU SHOULD ASK	WHAT ANSWERS YOU CAN EXPECT
Ask: What kind of information do listeners have on my topic?	1. No information 2. Have heard about the topic but know very little 3. Moderately informed 4. Know a lot about the topic
Ask: How important is this topic to my audience?	1. Boring, boring, boring 2. Do not care much about the topic 3. Could be important but depends on how you develop the topic 4. Very important issue
Ask: How do audience members feel about this topic?	1. Have strong negative feelings 2. Do not care either way 3. Are anxious to hear someone talk about the topic

Table 5.4

ADVANTAGES AND DISADVANTAGES OF DIFFERENT TYPES
OF QUESTIONNAIRE ITEMS

TYPE OF QUESTION	EXAMPLES	ADVANTAGES/DISADVANTAGES
Forced choice	"Do you know the size of the national debt?" [Yes or No] "Is Somalia in Asia?" [Yes or No]	Limits the type of answer. Gives information but very little detail.
Scale item	"How worried are you about getting AIDS?" [Very worried, somewhat worried, uncertain, not very worried, unconcerned] "The income tax system in the United States is unfair." [Strongly agree, agree somewhat, neutral, disagree slightly, disagree strongly]	Shows the strength of feeling and the nature of attitude. Questions must be written carefully to avoid creating bias in the answers.
Open-response item	"What do you think should be done with Social Security?" "How do you believe we can become a more energy-efficient country?"	Gives a great deal of information. Some of the information may not be useful.

EXAMPLE 5.1   SAMPLE QUESTIONNAIRE FOR TOPIC: THE SECURITY OF THE U.S. BANKING SYSTEM

1. Do you know how secure your money is in a national bank?

    ___ Yes ___ No ___ Not sure
2. Can you estimate how many U.S. banks failed last year?

    ___ Yes ___ No ___ Not sure
3. Are U.S. banks more secure than banks in other countries?

    ___ Yes ___ No ___ Not sure
4. How much money was lost as the result of bank failures last year?

    A huge amount _____\ ____\ Very little
5. To what extent is the public aware of the crisis in the U.S. banking system?

    Not at all _____\ _____\ ____\ Quite aware
6. How do you think the federal government should become more involved in the security of U.S. banks? _____

    _____

    _____

Audience analysis may involve talking with individual representatives of the target group.

© *Lorraine Rorke/The Image Works, Inc.*

INFERENTIAL AUDIENCE ANALYSIS

Analyzing your audience directly with interviews and questionnaires gives you fairly accurate information about what your audience knows and feels. Sometimes, though, you do not see your audience until a few minutes before your speech begins. In these situations, you have to make an educated guess about audience characteristics. This process is called *inferential* audience analysis because audience characteristics are *inferred* from information already known about the audience. An inference is an educated guess.

When you lack firsthand information about your listeners, you can conduct an inferential audience analysis by using one or more of the following three methods:

1. Ask the person who invited you to speak to describe the audience.
2. Ask some members of the audience to help you estimate the crucial characteristics of the rest of the group.
3. Ask people who have spoken to this audience before to describe the audience.

These methods substitute the information you get from others for direct gathering of data. Then you must make careful, educated guesses (inferences) about the characteristics and attitudes of audience members. This analysis will present you with a clearer picture of your listeners and how they will likely respond to your topic selection and presentation.

But how do you make educated inferences about your audience? You can do it best by describing the audience in terms of a demographic profile.

AUDIENCE DEMOGRAPHY

A **demographic profile** is the description of an audience that results from analysis of statistical data that describe audience members' vital and social features, such as age, gender, and socioeconomic status. These demographic characteristics may affect how audience members feel about and react to your speech. Knowing some of the demographic characteristics of your audience will allow you to make educated inferences about their attitudes and information. Table 5.5 lists sample demographic categories. More detailed discussion of these categories follows.

GENDER

Although for many years, gender was a reasonably accurate predictor of the attitudes and knowledge of listeners, it is less certain today. Activities, occupations, and other areas that traditionally were male dominated now include nearly as many women as men. Two-income families are becoming the norm, with more women actively involved in the workplace than ever before. Both men and women now have equal access to participation in sports activities, and coverage of women's sports events is increasing. Women are now more fairly represented in governorships, state legislatures, the U.S. Supreme Court, the presidential cabinet, and the U.S. Congress. Both sexes have interests in public affairs, education, financial matters, and health issues, to name only a few. The convenient gender-biased niches of information and attitudes that were once assumed are no longer valid.

Still, the interests of women and men remain somewhat different. Overall, women tend to be more interested in matters of fashion and nurturing, while men generally tend to be more interested in mechanical and athletic activities. Also, as mentioned in chapter 4, "Selecting and Narrowing Your Topic," gender differences in how men and women use words, argue, use gossip, and listen, and in their attitudes and interactive styles surrounding issues of dominance and control, are still significant. However, the many exceptions to these statements require that the entire matter of interests and preferences based on gender be approached with extreme care. Rather, the challenge lies in presenting a subject that is interesting to and appropriate for your audience without making gender an issue.

AGE

The chronological age range of audience members often offers a reasonably accurate idea of their interests. As people grow older they tend to become more politically conservative. They also tend to be more concerned with health-care matters. They typically have more money than younger people because of a longer time in the work force. Their interests reflect their age. People over age fifty tend to be less interested in fast cars and popular music and more concerned with getting and keeping resources. Younger audiences tend to be more concerned about crime, healthy lifestyles, and world peace. They want to

Table 5.5

SAMPLE DEMOGRAPHIC CATEGORIES

DEMOGRAPHIC CATEGORY	WHAT IT MEANS
1. Gender	How many of your listeners are women? How many are men? What is the "mix" of the audience? What effect, if any, will gender have on your topic choice and presentation?
2. Age	How old are your listeners? What is the range of ages? How is age distributed (many young, a few old, some young, some old, some middle-aged)?
3. Educational level	Are your listeners high school graduates? How many have completed college? Do they have a special type of educational background, such as engineering, music, physics or medicine?
4. Political affiliation	Are your listeners primarily members of one political party? Do they represent all elements of the political spectrum? How strongly do they hold their political views?
5. Socioeconomic status	Are your listeners wealthy? Do they have social status? How many live in a socially disadvantaged situation? Is theirs a minority or a majority economic and social situation?
6. Religious affiliation	Do your audience members hold a particular religious belief? How strong is their religious commitment? Do they support all the policies of their denomination?
7. Race	What is the racial composition of your listeners? Does one race predominate? Does audience racial composition have an effect on your subject development?
8. Occupation	In what field do your listeners work? How much experience do they possess? Are they white-collar or blue-collar workers? Is their work related to their level of education?
9. Organizational memberships	Are your listeners members of a professional, social, or service organization? Are they "joiners"? What does their membership tell you about their interests and feelings?

find a job that they like and that pays well. They want to know ways to enjoy themselves and how to make the lives of their children promising. People under age thirty in the 1990s are generally interested in leisure activities, skeptical of politicians, and horrified at the national debt. Age-based information like this helps you to choose interesting topics and to adapt your speech to your listeners.

EDUCATIONAL LEVEL

What interested you when you finished high school is different from what appeals to you now. For example, when you visit with friends who did not go to college, you soon discover that their current interests are often different from yours. Part of that difference is the result of your education.

College graduates are more likely to vote, read more books and magazines, and attend and know more about cultural events and activities. They are community leaders, are interested in their government, and have higher incomes than people without college educations. While there are exceptions, these generalizations tend to describe people whose education goes beyond high school.

If you know the educational level of your listeners, you can craft a message that they will understand and accept. An audience of college English teachers might not be any more interested in writing poetry than a group of high school students, but because of their educational level, you would need to approach the subject in a different way. The same principle applies if you talk to an audience of architects about your interests in city planning. That presentation would be much different from the city planning talk you give to road maintenance workers. The road crew probably would be less interested in your message than the architects.

Attained educational level is not a reliable indicator of intelligence. However, lesser educated people tend to have a narrower range of interests. Effective speakers adapt to their listeners' educational level and focus on listeners' concerns and interests.

POLITICAL AFFILIATION

Political stereotypes abound. Members of the Republican party are said to be conservative, wealthy, older Americans, while Democrats are believed to be young liberals who want to spend other people's money. If you are a member of either of these two political parties, you will probably argue that the descriptions are simplistic and wrong. There are conservative, wealthy Democrats who are over sixty. Similarly, there are young Republicans who have little wealth and a fairly liberal ideology.

Do not use the political affiliations of your audience members to jump to conclusions about their attitudes or information. Instead, combine political choice with other demographic factors for a more accurate and complete picture.

SOCIOECONOMIC STATUS

Socioeconomic status involves issues ranging from income level to geographical location. Low-income people have different attitudes and wants than high-income individuals.

GUY KAWASAKI

What do you as a public speaker have in common with McDonald's? Guy Kawasaki, entrepreneur, marketing consultant, and columnist for *Macworld Magazine* maintains that you must know your audience if you are to be successful. In this excerpt taken from his book *Selling the Dream*, Kawasaki explains the importance of being audience-centered:

Knowing your audience helps to make your presentation interesting and relevant. It means understanding as much as you can about your audience before the presentation: their age, gender, income level, current interest in your cause, and their hot buttons.

Imagine the difference in a presentation to single parents versus senior citizens, or environmentalists versus corporate executives. We've all sat through presentations in which the speaker didn't know his audience. We all ended up bored and resentful.

Take a cue from McDonald's. Before it opens a new franchise, it makes sure that there are people to eat its food and young people to employ. Burger King may be even smarter—it seems to follow McDonald's around so that it can avoid the expense of market research. The point is that McDonald's knows its audience before it sells a franchise in an area.

Source: Guy Kawasaki, Selling the Dream *(New York: HarperCollins Publishers, 1991), 96. Photo courtesy of Guy Kawasaki*

A middle-class group has a different agenda of interests and information than other elements in the spectrum of society. Consider, for example, the differences in the following groups:

- Wealthy blacks in major U.S. cities
- Poor chicanos in rural Florida
- Middle-income whites in the metropolitan Midwest
- Reservation-dwelling Native Americans in the Southwest

These groups have obviously different wants and needs. For some, income increases are of primary importance. For others, basic needs like food and heat are the major concerns. And these groups are typical of only a few of the many different socioeconomic audiences that you, as a speaker, may encounter.

Geographic location is another socioeconomic issue that reflects great differences in people. Rural listeners generally are more concerned about weather changes than are metropolitan residents. People in New England tend to prefer fresh seafood, while those in the Southwest tend to like the spicy food of the Spanish tradition. An audience of people from Great Britain would know immediately the meaning of a "VAT" or value-added tax. Most U.S. citizens, on the other hand, would require a lengthy explanation of this national sales tax equivalent. Knowing the income, location, and status of your listeners is critical to developing an appealing and effective message.

RELIGIOUS AFFILIATION

Speakers must be sensitive to the religious preferences of their audiences. Avoid any topics or developments that raise questions or that stereotype any religious denomination. Check your calendar before you speak. Is this day of special religious importance to some or all of the audience members? For example, if you have many Jewish audience members, remember that Christmas is not a holiday for them as it is for Christians. You will please them if you mention Hanukkah when you speak of events in the month of December.

Remember that your audience may have diverse religious beliefs. Do not offend listeners by ignoring those deeply held commitments. Instead, use your audience analysis to make your statements and remarks more appealing to them:

> **Weak:** "It's a pleasure to talk with you today about the most important book in the history of the human race. I'm referring to the New Testament. It can change your life just like it did mine."

> **Stronger:** "Let me explain what I mean when I refer to major works that have changed history. I have in mind such books as the Old Testament, the New Testament, the Koran, and the Vedas. All those religious books tell us how we can live better lives with our neighbors and our God. They have a common theme: Love and respect your fellow man."

RACE

Ethnic identification often influences what attitudes and points of view people hold, and what they are likely to know and think about issues. For example, Hispanics, who are the fastest growing ethnic minority group in America, might have different views from whites on the question of whether English should be the only official language in America. Thus, if you wanted to speak about this issue, knowing the racial composition of your listeners would be important demographic information to have prior to your presentation.

OCCUPATION

Engineers have specialized information that is different from that of short-order cooks. Farmers know about animal behavior in ways that veterinarians may never have dreamt. The bank teller knows how to count money carefully, the loan officer learns what to look for in an application form, and the police officer listens to alibis that stretch even a generous imagination. All of these occupations have a set of basic information. What and how much we know depends not only on our formal education but also on the kind of work we do every day.

Knowing how your listeners are employed will begin to tell you what general kinds of information they hold. However, do not assume that everyone in the same general field has the same amount or the same kind of information. For example, the four people described in table 5.6 are all in some way employed in efforts to stop shoplifting. Yet, their actual knowledge of shoplifting and shoplifters varies greatly.

Table 5.6

INFORMATION VARIANCE WITHIN FOUR OCCUPATIONS WITH SIMILAR GOALS

Occupation	Job Description	Job Knowledge
Department store clerk	Observes customers.	Has casual knowledge of some shoplifters. Has seen and stopped a few.
Police officer	Arrests shoplifters.	Knows the patterns of shoplifters. Is professionally trained in detection and arrest.
Criminologist	Explains factors underlying criminal behavior.	Has generally abstract knowledge of shoplifters. Is long on theory, short on practical application.
Insurance salesperson	Sells commercial insurance to department stores.	Knows that shoplifters are a problem but does not know much about techniques or appearances.

Remember that knowledge can vary greatly and is often a result of the person's occupation. Check out your audience in advance and determine which occupations are represented. When you combine that information with other demographic data you have collected, you will have a good picture of your listeners' attitudes and information.

ORGANIZATIONAL MEMBERSHIPS

Your listeners' organizational memberships will tell you much about their interests and the type of information they have. Are they members of the local chamber of commerce? If so, they are probably concerned with the business welfare of the community. Do they belong to the League of Women Voters? If so, they are probably politically aware and active. Audience members may also belong to church groups, community service organizations, or trade groups.

Summary

Your success as a public speaker depends on how well you and your listeners relate to each other. Even though we think of audiences as a group, each audience is a collection of individual, unique human beings with particular characteristics, interests, attitudes, and information. Audience analysis is the process by which speakers try to identify and understand the major characteristics of a group of listeners so as to better adapt their message to the audience.

Audience analysis should involve looking at the three elements that make up the audience setting—your speaking environment: (1) when you plan to speak, (2) where you will be speaking, and (3) the events that precede and follow your appearance. Audience analysis also includes determining what image listeners have of you, themselves, and the occasion. This information helps you to make speaking an audience-centered process.

There are two methods of conducting an audience analysis, and the method of choice depends on your access to the audience you plan to address. In direct-access audience analysis, you go directly to your audience and gather information by asking questions, listening to discussions, conducting interviews, and asking audience members to complete questionnaires.

In inferential audience analysis, you do not have direct access to your audience and must instead rely on alternate sources for information about listeners' characteristics and attitudes. You then make educated inferences about your listeners by describing them in terms of a demographic profile. Demographic characteristics that you might want to explore include gender, age, educational level, political affiliation, socioeconomic status, religious affiliation, race, occupation, and organizational memberships.

Key Terms

Audience

Audience analysis

Audience setting

Demographic analysis

Demographic profile

Direct-access audience
  analysis

Immediate audience

Inferential audience
  analysis

Application Questions

1. Suppose that you have been assigned to speak on the subject of abortion. Working alone, perform an inferential demographic analysis, using your class as the target audience. Use table 5.3 to guide your research. Bring your notes to class. Then, working together as a class, perform a direct-access audience analysis. Compare and contrast your inferences about the audience with the actual findings of direct-access analysis. What were the similarities and differences? Why? Did other class members analyze the classroom audience in the same way you did? How do you account for the differences?

2. With two or three other members of your class, attend a public speaking situation. For example, go to a church or temple and listen to the sermon, or attend a political rally and listen to the key speaker, or attend a PTA meeting or one of the weekly meetings of the Kiwanis or Junior League. Do you think that the principal speaker at this event conducted an audience analysis? Why or why not? Be as specific as you can in discussing these questions with your classmates.

Self-Test for Review

Mark each of the following as either true (T) or false (F).

1. The audience's image of you as a speaker can have a significant effect on the success of your speech.   T   F

2. An audience is a single group and, for speaking purposes, should be treated as a group.   T   F

3. Gender is a reasonably accurate predictor of the attitudes and knowledge of listeners.   T   F

4. Factors that make a difference in how an audience reacts to a message (age, sex, race religion, and so on) are called demographic variables.   T   F

5. How you organize and present your speech may depend on the outcome of your audience analysis.   T   F

6. Inferential audience analysis involves interacting directly with your audience to obtain information.   T   F

7. Organizational memberships and occupation rarely are important demographic variables.   T   F

8. If you have direct access to your audience and want to determine audience attitude and information before a speech, ask audience members to answer scale items and open-response questions on the topic.   T   F

Answers: 1. T, 2. F, 3. F, 4. T, 5. T, 6. F, 7. F, 8. T.

Suggested Readings

Hirsch, E. D., Jr., Joseph F. Kett, and James Trefil. *The Dictionary of Cultural Literacy.* Boston, Mass.: Houghton Mifflin, 1988. This is a compendium of the places, people, and things that most Americans should know. It helps to define the information you and your listeners should share. You will find it useful in understanding and interpreting audience knowledge and attitudes.

Terkel, Studs. *The Great Divide.* New York: Pantheon Books, 1988. This is the latest in a series of works by Terkel that explore the behaviors, attitudes, and work ethics of the American people. Starting with the Pulitzer Prize winning work *The Good War* to the later book *Working,* in which people talk about what they do all day and how they feel about it, Terkel chronicles people like no other writer in contemporary America. For enjoyable and revealing reading, try this book, the others listed by Terkel, and also consider *American Dreams: Lost and Found* and *Division Street: America.* After you have read Terkel, you will understand much about people and why they behave the way they do.

CHAPTER 6

Supporting Ideas with Argument and Evidence

OBJECTIVES

After reading this chapter, you should be able to:

1. *Explain* how to support your ideas with five kinds of argument: (a) inductive argument, (b) deductive argument, (c) argument from sign, (d) argument from cause, and (e) argument from analogy.
2. *Explain* how to test each kind of argument for accuracy and credibility.
3. *Define* the terms *ethos, pathos,* and *logos,* and *explain* how to use each of these kinds of artistic proof.
4. *Describe* and *give examples of* four categories of emotional appeals that can be used in informative and persuasive speeches to influence listeners.
5. *Explain* how syllogisms and enthymemes differ.
6. *Name* and *define* four kinds of evidence: (a) testimony, (b) definition and explanation, (c) statistics, and (d) examples.
7. *Explain* how to evaluate evidence in terms of the competency of the source and the believability, consistency, verifiability, and currency of the evidence itself.

© James L. Shaffer

*S*uccessful speaking depends greatly on how you formulate your ideas and arguments and on how you support your positions with proofs and evidence. In this chapter, you are introduced to the different types of arguments and how these can provide you with structures for presenting your reasoning. You also will learn about artistic proofs, which are elements like speaker credibility and reputation, emotional appeals, and rational appeals, that provide listeners with reasons for supporting your position. The chapter also offers suggestions about effectively using evidence—testimony, definition and explanation, statistics, and examples—to enhance your presentation.

Most of your speech making will involve arguments, such as the following:

It's clear to me that the major television networks don't care about viewers' interests because they keep shifting program times and days around so you can't find the show you want to watch. For example, NBC has moved the day and time for "Seinfeld" three times during one season.

Being a parent puts incredible stress on a marriage. Instead of the usual relationship, suddenly everything usual must be done, but the infant has to be fed, attended, and changed while both parents are tired and barely able to do their normal tasks. The real test of a marriage often comes when the first child is born. People have to develop new coping mechanisms.

Because people often make arguments with little thought about how to render the arguments convincing and compelling, listeners often do not act as a result of them. Making an argument compelling is fairly easy, once you know how, and the effort will pay for itself in many ways. For example, you will be able to provide others with effective arguments about why they should join you for a social event. You will be able to deal more directly with and analyze better the claims the auto salesperson makes about the product you are examining. You will understand how to build arguments that will persuade your friends to join a campus political action group. The next time you think you should get a raise, good arguments—soundly developed and supported—will make an impression on your boss.

SUPPORTING IDEAS WITH ARGUMENT

In speech making, the word *argument* does not refer to when two people disagree strongly and may shout at each other. It does not refer to warnings, commands, or other kinds of directive speech. Instead, it suggests that one person presents a position and supports that stance with various types of reasoning. According to S. Morris Engel, "an **argument** is a piece of reasoning in which one or more statements are offered as support for some other statement."[1]

The statements used for support are called **proofs.** In successful argument, the speaker puts together various items of proof to present a convincing case on one side of an issue. The proofs provide a reason for accepting the speaker's argument.

All good public speaking consists of a speaker first presenting an argument and then following up that argument with proofs. For example:

"It's sensible for us to buy the property on Dauphin Island *because*

(a) It's priced below the assessed value,

(b) It's the only lot that has beach privileges, and

(c) The design is exactly the one we said we wanted."

This type of structure provides the reasons for an audience to accept and understand the message.

Five types of argument are available to public speakers. They are: (1) inductive argument, (2) deductive argument, (3) argument from sign, (4) argument from cause, and (5) argument from analogy.

INDUCTIVE ARGUMENT

Inductive arguments work from a series of individual cases to a conclusion. Induction, then, moves from specifics to a generalization. While you cannot say with certainty that anything will happen, you can, however, use induction to look at cases from the past and to indicate the *probability* of a problem or situation in the present or future. For example:

Case 1: IBM has reduced the size of its work force.
Case 2: General Motors has cut back on its number of employees.
Case 3: United Technologies has permanently laid off many employees.
Case 4: Xerox Corporation has had a large work force reduction.
Generalization: *Major U.S. corporations are downsizing to become profitable.*

Case 1: In 1890, the U.S. center of population was just outside Cincinnati, Ohio.
Case 2: In 1940, the center of population for the United States was in western Indiana.
Case 3: In 1960, the population center of the United States was in west central Illinois.
Case 4: In 1990, the U.S. population center was in southeast Missouri.
Generalization: *The population center of the United States is gradually moving westward.*

In the first example, inductive reasoning indicates that it is highly likely that major U.S. companies are reducing the number of employees to become more efficient. In the second example, inductive reasoning indicates that the U.S. population center is moving westward. These generalizations cannot be made with absolute certainty. But if (1) you choose a sufficient number of cases, (2) those cases are representative, and (3) the generalization comes from the cases, then the conclusion will likely be valid.

Inductive argument is probably the most popular form of reasoning. When you, as a speaker, reason by induction, it allows your listeners to see how you arrived at a particular conclusion. It also is the way most of us arrive at decisions in daily living. We draw conclusions based on occurrences we have observed.

DEDUCTIVE ARGUMENT

Deductive argument follows an opposite sequence from that of inductive argument.
When you reason deductively, you proceed from a general conclusion and identify the
specific instances that establish the conclusion. The following is an example of reasoning
by deduction:

Conclusion: The greatest amount of money spent on advertising comes from
consumer product or service companies (because):

Case 1: The biggest spender is Proctor and Gamble, makers of soap products,
toothpaste, personal care items, and kitchen products. They spent $2.8 billion on
ads in 1989–1990.

Case 2: Philip Morris, the company that owns Kraft-General Foods and Miller Beer
and that manufactures several brands of cigarettes spends nearly as much annually
on ads as Proctor and Gamble.

Case 3: Sears Roebuck spent over $1.5 billion in advertising name brand consumer
products and its own house brands in 1989–1990.[2]

Deductive argument is especially useful when listeners do not know much about the
subject and would not be able to provide the specific cases on their own. The specific
cases or elements of a deductive argument provide all the information needed to arrive at
a certain conclusion.[3]

Table 6.1

FALLIBLE AND INFALLIBLE SIGNS

SIGN	CONCLUSION	QUALITY OF SIGN
1. Ice on the lake	Water temperature is at least 32 degrees or colder.	Infallible
2. They drive a Rolls Royce.	They are wealthy.	Fallible
3. The person took out a key, opened the door, climbed into the car, and drove away.	The car belongs to the person.	Fallible
4. Listeners make eye contact and nod their heads.	Audience members are interested and agree with you.	Fallible

ARGUMENT FROM SIGN

[handwritten: Birds flying south, leaves dins colors, Men raking yard. inicators giving the signs (symptoms) but event has not actually happened.]

When you observe characteristic features or symptoms and then argue that the feature or symptom suggests a state of affairs, you have presented an **argument from sign.** Here are two examples:

There are many dark clouds and lightning.
The weatherman forecast storms for today. *It's going to rain.*

[handwritten: → Assume it will rain because of what we see or feel. these are opposite]

They drive a late-model BMW. They always dress in expensive, hand-tailored clothes.
They live in a mansion in one of the most expensive parts of the city. *They are wealthy people.*

To check your argument's strength or validity, determine if the signs are *infallible*—that is, if they always lead to the conclusion. Infallible signs are rare. The more signs you can introduce, however, the greater the likelihood your argument is sound. In the absence of infallibility, present enough cases so that you and your audience have confidence in your conclusion. Table 6.1 presents examples that show the difference between fallible and infallible signs.

ARGUMENT FROM CAUSE

An **argument from cause** is based on the assumption that something happened because of an earlier event. The following are examples of **effect-to-cause arguments:**

[handwritten: The car is wet]

The ground is wet. There are puddles in the road. It must have rained.

[handwritten: Something happened because of earlier events]

The empty car rolled backward out of its parking place and smashed into a second car parked across the street. The brakes must have failed.

[handwritten: OR the guy worked his car]

Cause-to-effect arguments are demonstrated in these examples:

> I don't feel that I know how to answer many of the questions on the final exam. Because I failed the midterm, I'll probably fail the course.

> The plane I'm supposed to catch at 7:30 is an hour late in Memphis. I'll probably miss my connection in Dallas-Fort Worth.

Valid arguments from cause must meet some tests. Ask the following questions about the arguments:

1. *Is there a real connection between the cause and the effect?* Do not be misled into believing that a result occurred because of something that preceded it. When Aunt Sally comes to visit and it begins to rain, you might say, "You certainly brought bad weather." However, there is no real connection between the visit and the weather change.
2. *Could any other cause produce the observed effect?* Usually, a single cause is not the basis for the observed effect. Instead, the effect probably is the result of several causes. For example, if someone asked you, "Why did you decide to major in economics?" you might say, "Because I liked Econ 101." While that might have been one element in your decision, there probably were others as well. You may have liked some of the faculty in the economics department, job possibilities in economics may have been attractive, and/or your parents may have encouraged you to consider economics as you tried to choose a major. As a speaker, you need to be sure that the causal relationship is strong enough for people to believe it.
3. *Has anything prevented this cause from operating?* A car with an empty gas tank has no fuel, and a driver cannot make the car go by putting the key in the ignition and turning it. When you examine a causal relationship, be sure that nothing (empty gas tank) has prevented a cause (turning the key) from producing the desired effect (starting the car).
4. *Is this cause sufficient to produce the effect?* To your roommate's question: "Why didn't you read the history assignment?" you might reply: "Because I couldn't get to the library tonight." Is this enough of a cause to prevent reading the history assignment? Maybe yes, and maybe no. Be sure that the cause is sufficient to produce the effect before you accept or present an argument.

ARGUMENT FROM ANALOGY

An **argument from analogy** involves comparing a known and understood set of facts to less well known ones and then arguing that the two sets of facts are similar.[4] For an argument from analogy to be valid, it must satisfy two tests that tie the argument together:

1. Do the points of comparison outweigh the points of difference? Example: "Enlarging the airport in Kansas City would help the city's general economy because enlarging the airports in Dallas and Newark had a positive effect on both cities." For this argument from analogy to be valid, the similarities between the cities mentioned must be shown to be greater than the differences. For example, the cities' economic

bases, sizes, networks of available highways, and transportation requirements are important issues of comparison. The similarities among the cities must outweigh the differences if the argument is to be accepted.

2. Are the points of comparison relevant? The items that are compared may be alike in ways that are not relevant to the argument. Example: "My cousin is as good a basketball player as Shaquille O'Neal. He can run the court just as fast, he can lead the fast break, he's murder on the backboards, and he is a 'franchise' player. He also went to Louisiana State University." The argument from analogy fails in this case, because there is more to being a star basketball player than the characteristics listed. The cousin's athletic prowess does not make him the equivalent of one of the premier NBA centers. Star players must have many other crucial attributes in addition to being able to run the court, control the backboard, and attend LSU.

ARTISTIC PROOFS

As mentioned earlier in the chapter, the statements used to support an argument are called proofs. However, proofs can be more generally defined as *artistic elements* that provide a reason for supporting the argument and cause a change in listeners' attitudes or behaviors. In what may have been the most important book ever written on speech making—the *Rhetoric*—Aristotle identified three categories of **artistic proofs** that speakers can control and use in both informative and persuasive speeches to influence listeners.[5] These categories of artistic proofs are ethos, pathos, and logos.

ETHOS

Ethos is Aristotle's category for the artistic dimension in which reputation and appearance create credibility for the speaker and the message. **Credibility** is the degree to which a receiver (listener) believes in something, and it's central to much of what people attempt in communication. Both the message and the person delivering the message must have believability. The ethos of the speaker creates credibility for both the message and the person.

One category of ethos is reputation. What listeners know about a speaker before the speech affects how listeners react to the speaker's message. The following are examples of the reputation a speaker brings to a public setting.

Good: Paul Portenzo has worked for twenty years as a coal miner, deep underground. He has survived five methane-gas explosions, and he now is the "lead" member of his mining team. He has strong opinions about how to create a safer work environment.

Better: Sam McIlhenny worked in the coal mines for ten years before he took out loans to get a college degree in mechanical engineering. He has been working for the Bureau of Mines as an expert consultant on mine safety for eleven years. He believes that it is possible to make mines safer for workers without bankrupting the mining companies.

Both men in these examples could provide expert testimony on mine safety. McIlhenny, however, has not only the work history as a miner but also practical knowledge and professional experience as a mechanical engineer. While safety is a major concern of both parties, McIlhenny brings more ethos to the speaking situation than Portenzo.

Reputation has other dimensions also, including how smoothly a person speaks, how much eye contact is made with listeners, and how self-confident the person appears. Language can have a major impact on a speaker's reputation. Notice how the wrong use of certain words affects how the message is received in the following examples:

Poor: "Like, I want to tell all of you that Americans aren't very successful at marriage, you know what I mean. The information I found shows that like over 95 percent of the people in this room will get married. But only like about a little more than half of them will stay married to the same person. OK?"

Better: "Americans are one of the most 'marrying' people in the world. More than 95 percent of Americans get married at least once. What's sad is that about half of those marriages end up in divorce. If you think marriage is all songs and roses, ask those 50 percent who found out that it didn't work."

Appearance is another dimension of ethos. For example, personal height is an element of credibility in evaluating the U.S. President. Only Harry Truman, in 1948, was less than 6 feet tall. Most of the chief executives of the United States have been tall. In a public gathering, the president is always looking across or down at other national figures or heads of state, *never up*. Others look up to the president, signifying the respect given to the nation. The president automatically receives respect because of the office, and also commands respect because of physical stature.

Personal grooming and style of dress are additional aspects of appearance that affect ethos. A well-groomed, appropriately dressed speaker who is poised during the presentation, makes effective use of physical movement, and chooses effective language has a high level of ethos.

ANN RICHARDS

Ann Richards, Governor of Texas, is an audience-centered speaker who can communicate with, motivate, and even electrify an audience. Here are a few impressions of Ann Richards as a speaker taken from her recent biography *Storming the Statehouse*:

Ann Richards is . . .

. . . at the head of any class: with her, political oratory is performance art. And since she considers it her job to communicate with people, if they do not understand what she is trying to say, she considers that her fault.

. . . a performer. She feeds off an audience: she gets all these endorphins. And she's not going to leave an audience disappointed.

. . . a great motivator in speeches. When she walks into a room, she's electric. She has presence. She carries herself very well, and she has a very distinctive personality. People respond to that.

Her speeches . . .

. . . had the virtue of strengthening support she already had: they were crucial to sustaining and fanning the enthusiasm people had for Ann Richards, and that enthusiasm was ultimately what made her different from her opponents.

Source: Celia Morris, Storming the Statehouse: Running for Governor with Ann Richards and Dianne Feinstein *(New York: Charles Scribner's Sons, 1992), 32, 47, 55, 296. Photo © Bob Daemmrich/Stock Boston*

PATHOS

Aristotle's second category of proofs—**pathos**—is a less rational dimension than ethos. Pathos refers to emotional appeals. Think of the advertising messages you hear every day that touch on your emotional bonds to other people: "When you care enough to send the very best"; "The diamond anniversary ring: Show her you love her all over again." These appeals are powerful because they touch people's basic emotional needs and create real and powerful reactions in the people who hear them.

Four categories of emotional appeals can be used in both informative and persuasive speeches to influence listeners. The pathos categories are: (1) feelings of fear, (2) feelings of pride, (3) feelings of pity or concern, and (4) feelings of courage.

Feelings of Fear

Feelings of fear are among the most common type of emotional appeal. They can powerfully influence people but also may have a "boomerang" effect when people are highly involved or when the fear level is intense. When a speaker presents material that is highly graphic, too explicit, or too gory, listeners may shift their attention away from the speaker.[6] For example, they may appear disinterested, or their gaze may wander around the room. Moderate-intensity fear appeals work best. The following are examples of fear appeals that fit the "moderate" classification:

There's a direct relationship between cigarette smoking and 90 percent of the lung cancer in American men.

If you drink substantial amounts of alcohol over a period of time, it can damage both the brain and the liver.

In 1990, manufacturing companies in the United States released 4.8 billion pounds of toxic chemicals.[7]

Feelings of Pride

Appeals to feelings of pride stir listeners' emotions. Pride is one of the major reasons schools and colleges hold commencement. Graduation ceremonies give both graduates and their friends and family an opportunity to bask in the pride of accomplishment. The processional "Pomp and Circumstance" speaks volumes about the nature of the occasion. Other examples of appeals to pride include:

We're number 1.

The Lexus won the J. D. Power Award for Automotive Excellence again this year.

My hometown is the best place in the world to grow up.

Feelings of Pity or Concern

Appeals to feelings of pity or concern powerfully affect most people. For example, listeners usually have a "soft spot" for those less fortunate or for someone stricken with a crippling disease. Organizing groups who are willing to donate their time to collect funds for the disabled, the homeless, or the cancer society usually is not difficult. Three examples of this type of appeal are:

Give blood. Give the gift of life.

Help save the children. Only 25 cents a day will feed a starving child in South America.

He's not heavy. He's my brother.

Feelings of Courage

Appeals to feelings of courage call for listeners to show their nerve and determination. Hollywood has used this appeal for years in movies that arouse patriotic feelings, generate help for the threatened, or encourage a determination to do what is right and not necessarily conventional. The following examples of this type of appeal all ask people to "stand tall" and to take the moral and personal high ground, despite the odds or popular opinion to the contrary:

You've got to have the courage to not be afraid to lose.

It's not just a corny saying that you can make a positive out of most any negative if you work hard enough at it. I've always thought of problems as challenges, and this wasn't any different.[8]

It's better to have tried and lost then never to have tried at all.

LOGOS

Aristotle's third category of proofs—**logos**—is attractive to the rational, logical side of human thinking. Speakers who intend to support their position with logos introduce evidence and argument as the building blocks. This kind of proof assumes that, if people are introduced to sound arguments and effective support, they will come to a logical conclusion. Two types of rational appeals are the syllogism and the enthymeme.

Syllogisms

Aristotle described a form of argument, called the **syllogism,** that continues to be used frequently today. A syllogism consists of a major premise, a minor premise, and a conclusion. For example:

All men are mortal. (Major premise)

Socrates is a man. (Minor premise)

Socrates is mortal. (Conclusion)[9]

Different terms are often substituted for major and minor premise. The major premise is also known as the *general case,* and the minor premise is also known as the *specific case.* The following example applies the alternate terminology:

Students admitted into Phi Beta Kappa spend considerable time studying.
   (General case)

Fran is a member of Phi Beta Kappa. (Specific case)

Fran must spend considerable time studying. (Conclusion)

Enthymemes

An **enthymeme** is a syllogism based on probability and in which either the general case or the specific case is usually implicit and may be dropped from the stated argument. Knowing how to tell the difference between an enthymeme and the larger category, syllogism, allows you to construct stronger arguments and to better analyze arguments you hear. Much of modern reasoning omits either the general case or the specific case in drawing the conclusion. For example:

Phi Beta Kappa students spend much time studying, so Fran must be a book worm.
   (General case and conclusion)

Fran is a member of Phi Beta Kappa and must spend considerable time studying.
   (Specific case and conclusion)

Most people do not need to hear all three elements of a syllogism to understand an argument and are satisfied with an enthymeme, a syllogism that typically lacks either the major case or the specific case. This reasoning should be approached carefully, however.

Using Syllogisms and Enthymemes

In employing syllogisms and enthymemes in your arguments, be aware that syllogisms are certain, while enthymemes are *probabilities*. For example, that Socrates is a mortal is a certainty if the major and minor premises are valid. However, it is only probable that Fran spends considerable time studying because it is not definitely known that all Phi Beta Kappas spend much of their time studying. They probably do, but no premise or case claims that with certainty. That is the basic difference between syllogisms and enthymemes.

In daily conversation, you are more likely to hear an enthymeme, but keep in mind that an argument's validity also rests on listeners accepting the probability of the conclusion. If listeners do not accept the probability of the enthymeme, there is no support for the argument.

Be careful in your use of either syllogistic reasoning or the enthymeme. Sometimes, the major premise is not true. In other instances, the specific case does not stand. With either of these problems, your conclusion would be invalid. To test your reasoning, you might want to ask the following questions of your general case, specific case, and conclusion:

1. Is the argument possible?
2. Has the event actually occurred?
3. Is this event likely to happen in the future?
4. Is this a major problem?
5. Is the argument "more or less" true, desirable, profitable, moral, workable, sensible?[10]

If your answers to these questions are "yes," then your arguments are logically sound. Be sure to test your arguments because audiences are unlikely to listen to a speaker whose arguments seem flawed. They must feel confident about the arguments and claims they hear. Your arguments are the foundations for the appeals and the data that you will introduce to "sell" your ideas to listeners, so construct them carefully.

SUPPORTING ARGUMENTS WITH EVIDENCE

When a speech student, who happened to be the starting tight end on the football team, gave his first self-introductory speech, he appeared calm but said, in part;

> When I stand up here, I don't see people. I just see a blur. I guess I'm scared to death. On Saturday afternoon, it doesn't bother me to get out on a field in front of 65,000 people. But the twenty-five here now are something else. I may not look frightened, but if you could see my knees or listen to my heart, you'd know that I'm not comfortable.
>
> Just before a game, some of my teammates get the "butterflies" until their first tackle or block. Well, I wish someone would block or tackle me now. That might get rid of my feelings. It sure would help calm me down, I think.

Most of you think that because I'm 6'3" and weigh 268 that little things like this won't bother me. I'd rather go head-to-head with an All-American center than face you twenty-five people.

This student's listeners believed him because he gave them reasons why he did not enjoy talking to them. He offered **evidence** to support his claim.

Evidence is the basic material of the argument, the data that are used as a base for an argument.[11] Arguments must be supported by evidence that backs up the speaker's claims. Arguments made without the use of evidence are assertions, claims that you are asking others to accept based on your "good word." Instead, build as strong a case for your arguments as possible with the use of powerful and valid evidence.

Several types of evidence are examined here, including testimony, definition and explanation, statistics, and examples. Tests that you can apply to your evidence to determine its appropriateness are also discussed.

TESTIMONY

Testimony involves using the words of another person as evidence for your argument. You can directly quote a person, or you can paraphrase what the person said. Speakers rely on the testimony of experts, on lay testimony, and on personal testimony to support their positions.

Expert Testimony

Testimony from a prominent, qualified individual is called **expert testimony**. The testimony source should be known and acceptable to listeners or else should have some position or some achievement that qualifies this person as an expert in the field. Obviously, you strengthen your speech only if the source of your testimony has special training or experience that makes what the person says valuable.

While discussing the influence of new programs on the television industry, a student speaker talked about the failure of the new television program "You Bet Your Life." He put the matter in perspective by quoting a prominent executive:

Steve Hirsch, president of Camelot, King World Productions, said, "There was concern among advertisers that 'You Bet' would take audience away from our two sustaining shows. This year, there's finally an acknowledgment that 'Wheel' and 'Jeopardy' will be around and strong for many years."[12]

This expert testimony in the form of a direct quote helps to support and make more believable the argument that new programs will not steal viewers from successful shows.

Another student was speaking about the U.S. national deficit problem. She said that the deficit was not the fault of anyone in particular. Then, for emphasis and support, she quoted Ross Perot:

According to Ross Perot, "The people in Washington are fundamentally good, it is the system that is wrong. When an entity owes four trillion dollars and does not drastically alter its way of doing business, now that's crazy. Even worse, one billion dollars is being added to the bill every day, and it is perfectly legal."[13]

Direct quotations bring the force of word-for-word testimony by experts to support your argument. They are one of the most frequently used kinds of supporting information.

Supporting materials that you **paraphrase,** that put the ideas of others in your own words, can be as effective as direct quotations. The key is to give credit to the original source.

One student used paraphrase to tell listeners about ways they and their parents could help reduce the cost of automobile insurance:

> *Let me give you this information. According to an article in a recent issue of* Smart Money, *published by the* Wall Street Journal, *you can reduce your car insurance bill by participating in car pools, by having student drivers who get grades of "B" or better in their classes, and by only allowing your college student drivers to operate your car when they are home. Additionally, if your drivers have completed a course in driver training, and your car has passive restraints (both seat belts and air bags), your premiums will go down. Those are fairly simple ways to save yourself money.*[14]

The words of experts, whether directly quoted or paraphrased, help you to influence others. They are a powerful form of proof, one that most listeners like to hear. We respect experts and are influenced by them. Use expert testimony as a cornerstone support for your ideas.

Lay Testimony

Speakers also often use **lay testimony,** testimony from the "man in the street." This technique usually lends a more realistic tone to the material. It is similar to the person who has seen an event firsthand and provides a description of the situation. In the following example, a student speaker used lay testimony in a speech about farm labor:

> *George Hendrick, who's farmed all his life, is tired of hearing about how tough it is for people who work in offices. He says, "They start work at 8 A.M., earn salaries from $25,000 to $90,000 a year, and have a two week vacation. I start work, milking cows, at 5 A.M. every day. I milk those same cows again at 6 P.M. every night, fifty-two weeks a year. In between, I feed all the cattle, including the sheep, make hay for feed, plant crops, maintain and repair machinery, harvest the yield, and keep records for the IRS. I make about $6,000 a year. Not much, huh? It's below the poverty level. I've invested about $800,000 in equipment and land I farm. That's a return on investment of only .007, less than 1 percent. I'm not an economist, just a farmer, but I think something's wrong here."*

Personal Testimony

Occasionally, you may wish to provide "first-person" testimony to help support your argument. A student speaker in a state that has considerable snowfall told of an experience while traveling further south during spring break:

> *Most of you accustomed to snow would find it hard to believe. If I hadn't been there myself, I'd be suspicious. There were only 4 inches of snow on the ground, but*

This speaker is using testimony by referencing a source that is acceptable to his audience.

© Bob Coyle

everything shut down. They had no snow removal equipment. I watched television, and the newspeople told us to stock up our freezers and stay inside because of the unbelievable conditions. The bridges were ice covered, but there wasn't much snow on the road itself. But people didn't seem to know how to drive. One guy passed me on an ice-covered bridge. I was driving 20, and he must have been going 60 on the ice. Wrecked cars nearly filled the ditches. They called it a blizzard. We'd call it snow flurries here, and it would just be an ordinary day.

When speakers indicate that "I was there; I saw; here were my experiences," the speech becomes a type of eyewitness testimony. Personal presence makes it more believable. The comments enhance speakers' credibility and strength of their arguments.

Applying Standards to Testimony

Do not use the words of other people unless the source seems qualified and the statement makes good sense. Apply standards to testimony to be sure the information will help to support your case. Ask yourself:

- How consistent is the testimony? Does the information correspond to what listeners believe is reality? Is the information consistent within itself? Is it consistent with what we know about the world? Does the speaker get into contradictory positions or statements? If the answer to any of these questions is "yes," look elsewhere for testimony to support your ideas.

- Does the source have preconceived biases? Many people have an ax to grind. Is your source prejudiced or open-minded? Listeners respect a person who sees both sides of the issue more than a prejudiced source.
- Does the testimony agree with other expert? Look for consistency and representativeness in testimony. Everyone does not agree on every issue. However, sources who are at odds with everyone else may have questionable believability or motives. Check to see if your sources are in the mainstream of the field. If they are pioneers in their field, their testimony may be controversial, and you should inform listeners of possible controversy when you introduce your sources' testimony.

Check that your use of testimony meets these basic standards. If it does not, continue to develop it until all the criteria are satisfied.

DEFINITION AND EXPLANATION

Definition and explanation constitute another type of evidence that can be used to support arguments. In particular, definition and explanation are useful for clarifying ideas. For example, what do the words *democracy, communism, fairness,* and *loyalty* mean to you? Is a *freedom fighter* different from a *terrorist?* Or does the difference depend on whose side you are on? Clearly, terms such as these require definition and explanation.

Every important term in your speech should be defined. Avoid using dictionary definitions, if possible. Rather, supply your own "working definition"—how you are using the term in your speech—but do not move outside the scope of a meaning that is accurate and reasonable.

Two kinds of terms need definition: (1) very technical terms or jargon that only a specialist would understand, and (2) familiar terms that we use every day, but that because of their various connotative meanings, convey different things to different people. A student speaker needed to define some terms in a speech she gave to her class. She said: "The Pascagoula raw material upgrade for December showed a negative upgrade of $1.81 per barrel of oil." However, no one in her audience knew that she meant $1.81 per barrel had been lost in December. An engineer from a paper mill gave a talk about problems during the night shift. He said, "Among the sensitivities we must deal with over and over are breakages in the Soft and Pretty line." None of his listeners knew that "sensitivities" were *problems,* or that the "Soft and Pretty line" was the *production line* where toilet paper was manufactured.

STATISTICS

We live in a world filled with statistics. **Statistics** are a shorthand method of summarizing a large number of cases. Use statistics as supporting material to suggest the extent of a problem or to clarify or strengthen some point you want to make.

The use of numbers to support ideas drives our conversations and public speaking. For example, we are told about the comparative income level of engineers and teachers, we hear about a 3.2 percent annual rate of inflation since 1926, and we read that some brokerage firms charge as little as thirty-five dollars to buy one hundred shares of common stock. It is easy to become confused with the wealth of statistical information that dances around us.

People feel more comfortable when they hear ideas that have some statistical support. For that reason, statistics can be powerful supporting material in your speeches. For example, you might present statistics on the comparative cost of new cars, living expenses in the western United States versus the South, or the productivity of the American worker versus the Japanese employee. Here is how you could support the argument that Americans spend more money on movies than other nations:

> According to the Wall Street Journal, *"Americans spent about $18.4 billion to watch movies last year, more than the combined spending of Japanese and European consumers. . . . About 27 percent of the total was spent in movie theaters, and about 24 percent went to watch movies on such pay-television services as Home Box Office."*[15]

In this next example, the speaker uses statistics to support a contention about world energy production. Ask yourself how easily you can remember the figures.

> *Most people think nations in the Middle East are the primary producers of energy. How wrong they are. According to the 1993* World Almanac, *the Soviet Union produced over 27 percent of the world's primary energy in 1990. The United States produced the same percentage, while Saudi Arabia generated a mere 6 percent and Iran contributed only 3 percent of world energy production.*[16] *That means that the United States produced three times as much energy as Saudi Arabia and Iran combined!*

In this case, the speaker may have "overloaded" with statistics, to the point where listeners find it difficult to comprehend all of the information.

As the previous example demonstrates, statistics are powerful supporting material, but you need to follow some guidelines in using them. Guidelines for using statistics include:

1. *Round off complicated statistics.* Say "eight million" instead of "seven million nine hundred and fifty thousand." Rounding off makes statistics easier for audience members to remember. If you do not round off, audience members often become confused and stop listening. When you round off, however, be sure to represent the data accurately by presenting it as the nearest round number.
2. *Use representative statistics.* It is possible to find statistics to support nearly any position imaginable. Work hard to find statistical data that *accurately* presents your argument.

> Some less ethical or less well informed speakers misrepresent data through the use of statistics. For example:

> *The average income of citizens of Centertown is $21,350 per year. That certainly is enough money for them to live on in modest comfort. I can't believe that anyone would argue that they are at the poverty level.*

In this example, the statistics are not representative. Several Centertown citizens have very large incomes, while the bulk of the population earns only $11,000 to $13,000 per year. But those few huge incomes distort the town's *mean income.* The

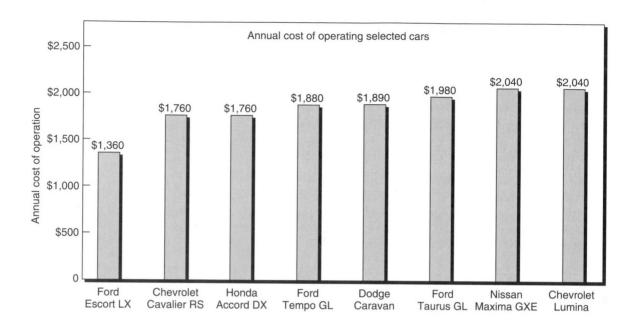

Annual cost of operating selected cars

Figure 6.1

Visual aid to help explain statistics.

mean is the average, and the average Centertown resident certainly is not earning $21,000 per year. Here, the statistics are not representative and mislead listeners.

3. *Explain what the statistics mean to listeners.* An explanation of what the statistics mean to listeners, of how listeners can relate to the statistics, is especially important when you are relaying large numbers. In the following example, the speaker explains and compares the statistics presented so that listeners get a true feeling for the density differences of urban and rural environments:

> *In Washington D.C., the population density is 9,800 persons per square mile. In the state of Wisconsin, the density is 90 people per square mile.[17] This means that there are 108 times as many people living in each square mile of Washington as live per square mile in Wisconsin. When you compare Washington, D.C. to the state of Wisconsin, the nation's capital seems very crowded.*

4. *Use visual aids to help explain the statistics.* A string of sentences using statistics can be confusing. When you are trying, for example, to explain the cost of operating a car, listeners may not always be able to follow your data:

> *Statistics show there's a substantial difference in fuel, tires, and maintenance for different cars. The Ford Escort is the least expensive at $1,360 per year, followed by the Chevrolet Cavalier and the Honda Accord at $1,760. The Ford Tempo will cost the average driver $1,880, only $10 per year less than the Dodge Caravan at $1,890. The more expensive cars for maintenance and operating costs are the Ford Taurus at $1,980, and the Nissan Maxima and the Chevrolet Lumina, both at $2,400 per year.[18]*

This statistical information is much clearer to listeners when presented in conjunction with a visual aid, such as figure 6.1. Make it easy for your audience to understand your statistics by placing them in a visual format whenever possible. See chapter 12, "Supporting Ideas Visually," for specific suggestions about preparing your visuals.

5. *Do not use too many statistics.* While statistics are strong support, include just enough to make your ideas believable. If your speech is overloaded with statistics, listeners become confused and bored with the total presentation. Use statistics sparingly, as you would seasoning in cooking.

6. *Do not use sloppy statistics.* Use statistics only when you are sure that they are truly representative, that they have been generated sensibly, and that they come from reliable sources. Statistics that do not fulfill these requirements are sloppy.

To illustrate the problem of sloppy statistics: One student decided to survey campus students about a proposed tuition increase. She collected data from 1:00 to 2:00 P.M. on Friday, while standing outside the engineering building in the center of campus. The question she asked was: "Do you favor the proposal to increase student tuition charges next year by 10 percent?" During her hour-long survey, eighty-five people responded. Only 10 percent favored the increase, while 75 percent opposed it.

Do you believe that those statistics truly represent the student body? Of the respondents, sixty-one were men, and twenty-four were women. Since women make up 58 percent of the student population, the 28 percent response by females was not representative of the campus gender mix. What is not known about the respondents also affects interpretation of the survey information. For example, what was the major field of study of the respondents? Were most engineering majors? How many of them pay their own tuition, and how many receive complete parental support? What percentage of respondents receive financial aid? Does the response mix represent the institution's ethnic picture?

If the student had asked a few additional questions, the survey would have been more valid. Fewer people might have participated, but the answers would have been much more representative. The data that came from the student's survey give sloppy results. Her only valid claim is that 10 percent of the people she interviewed outside the engineering building on a Friday afternoon supported the tuition increase. Any other conclusions would be unjustified.

EXAMPLES

Examples are another type of evidence that you can use to support the arguments in your speeches. Examples illustrate the idea you are discussing. They give life and color, identify specific situations, and clarify abstractions. When we do not understand an idea or an argument, we ask people to "give me an example." A great deal of our thinking involves reasoning from example because this gives us specific information that is clear and vivid. The different kinds of examples you might use include real examples and hypothetical examples.

Real Examples

A real example is a presentation of something that actually happened. Because it occurred, it emphasizes and clarifies materials for listeners. A real example must be genuine. Listeners need to believe that you are using realistic material.

A student speaker was discussing the extremes that people go to today in filing frivolous lawsuits. To support his argument that almost anything today is fair game for a lawsuit, he cited a brief example:

> *Eric Edmonds—determined to lose weight—went to Humana Hospital Bayside and had his stomach stapled. With staples, surgeons shrank the size of his stomach. But within forty-eight hours after surgery, he snuck out of his room and raided the hospital refrigerator and ate so much he burst his staples. Mr. Edmonds is suing the hospital for a quarter million dollars for failure to keep its refrigerator door locked.*[19]

While most real examples probably are not as amusing as this one, they have in common the fact that they really happened.

Sometimes, a speaker chooses to cite an extended example. Extended examples are more lengthy, but factual, and permit the presentation of considerable detail to make the case more believable. The following extended example offers numerous real-life details that help to support the speaker's presentation:

> *When politicians express concern about their representation in the media, students often seem surprised. Students don't understand why public officials resent the way newspapers and television represent them. Things were much worse, earlier in our national history.*
>
> *For example, Abraham Lincoln's opponents attacked him unmercifully. One piece said, "His presumptive parents were immoral, shiftless, poor white trash. Unscrupulous as a lawyer, he was unprincipled as a politician. He was a man of low morality and his 'inordinate love of the lascivious, of smut,' it was whispered, was 'something akin to lunacy.' "*[20]
>
> *Lincoln was a favorite target in his time, but these things didn't just happen on a national level. If you think candidates for public office today are sensitive about press coverage, consider what happened in California in 1899. There, they passed legislation that prohibited cartoons and caricatures that reflected on their character.*[21] *It was illegal to draw pictures that made fun of the appearance or actions of a public official. Fortunately, the law wasn't enforced, but it gives you an idea of how far things went in the past.*

Because this information is accurate and true, it provides more impact for and clarification of the speaker's ideas.

Search for real examples that will support your ideas. Listeners are more likely to accept your position when you base it on concrete ideas.

Hypothetical Examples

Hypothetical examples are invented by speakers, but can be used to represent reality when actual examples are not available. Hypothetical examples, however, must be believable and must show events as people believe or know them to be. When you use a hypothetical example, follow or precede it, if possible, with information that makes the "invented" example as believable as possible.

The following student speech excerpt made good use of a hypothetical example:

Elisha Van Beek wanted so badly to go to college. But her parents didn't have the money. And four years of undergraduate work, even with the scholarships she'd receive, would force her to borrow over $20,000. She'd wanted so much to work with retarded children, but now her only choice was to work in the local department store, save as much as she could, and hope that someday she could have the dream of going on to the state university. Meanwhile, all those children she could help would have to wait until she earned enough money to start her freshman year. Is that the American dream?

Listeners believe hypothetical, well-constructed examples because they know that these events could occur. In that way, hypothetical examples support and clarify a speaker's ideas. Speakers, however, have the responsibility of informing the audience that an example is hypothetical.

Applying Standards to Examples

Speakers must apply standards to their use of examples. Since it is possible to find an example of almost anything today, listeners may be skeptical. You can defuse their skepticism if you use the following principles in selecting your supporting examples:

1. Examples should be typical. They should represent events or situations that are believable. Avoid the "man bites dog" type of example. Finding a single example of nearly anything is possible, but that does not increase the support for your argument.
2. Examples should be sufficient in number. Do not rely upon a single example to establish your argument. Provide at least two examples to show listeners that you have a common position that is understandable.
3. Examples should be recent. Unless you are talking about historical matters or can show a reason for introducing "old" data, present examples chosen from recent events. Time changes society, and listeners want up-to-date support that recognizes situations of today.

MEETING EVIDENCE STANDARDS

Several types of evidence—testimony, definition and explanation, statistics, and examples—have been discussed in this section. With all of these evidence types, test the evidence to be sure that it meets your standards. Ask the following questions about any evidence you plan to use:

1. Is there enough evidence to make your point believable? Exercise personal judgment here. Include enough high-quality evidence that a reasonable person will decide that your point has been supported convincingly.
2. Is the evidence consistent with what is already known? Listeners are more likely to believe your evidence if it corresponds to what they already believe or know. Such evidence as "a fifty-five pound infant" or a "racoon that dresses itself" clearly does not "match up" with listeners' previous experience. They already know that infants do not weigh that much and that animals do not dress themselves. Introduce evidence that reinforces already acquired information.

3. Can you verify the evidence? Be sure that your evidence agrees with other sources. Select evidence that others can see and determine is valid. If your evidence is not verifiable, your credibility is damaged.

4. Is the source of the evidence competent? This criterion applies to people as well as to publications. Sources who are "degreed," who have an MD, JD, PhD, or EdD, automatically have believability, although listeners want to know, when you refer to "doctor," whether you mean a physician, a veterinarian, or a college teacher. People with recognized reputations in their field are highly credible. Introduce them by demonstrating their level of competency.

    Standards of competency also apply to published sources. Among the widely respected, nationally circulated newspapers are such publications as the *Wall Street Journal,* the *Des Moines Register,* the *Los Angeles Times,* and the *New York Times. Time Magazine, Newsweek,* and *US News & World Report* are weekly magazines that meet the tests of believability.

5. Is the source of the evidence biased or prejudiced? Introduce evidence from impartial sources that do not profit from the information itself. Sources that look at all the information objectively do not reach biased conclusions.

6. Is the evidence current? Sometimes, the situation may call for evidence that shows historical development, but in most cases, your evidence should be fresh and up-to-date. In cases where you are presenting a particular persons's view, remember that that person's position may have changed over time. Use information that honestly shows how the person feels now. The same standard applies to an issue like the national debt as a percentage of the gross national product. Be certain that you present the current picture, as well as perhaps provide a historical perspective.

Appendix A, "Sample Speeches," contains a speech that applies evidence well. The speech, by Amy Olson of Bradley University, uses evidence to prove to listeners that a problem exists in the movement to recycle paper.

Summary

Successful speaking depends greatly on how speakers present and support their ideas and arguments. This chapter examines the different types of arguments, artistic proofs, and evidence.

An argument is a piece of reasoning in which one or more statements are offered as support for some other statement. Inductive arguments work from a series of individual cases to a conclusion, while deductive arguments proceed from a general conclusion and then identify the specific instances that establish the conclusion. Arguments from sign observe that characteristic features or symptoms suggest a state of affairs. An argument from cause is based on the assumption that something happened because of an earlier event. An argument from analogy involves comparing a known and understood set of facts to less well known ones and then arguing that the two sets of facts are similar.

While the statements used to support an argument are called proofs, proofs can also be more generally defined as artistic elements that provide a reason for supporting the speaker's position. Aristotle identified three categories of artistic proofs: ethos, pathos, and logos. Speaker credibility, an essential element in any communication, is an element of ethos. Pathos involves emotional appeals, such as feelings of fear, pride, pity, or concern, and courage. Logos includes two types of rational appeals: the syllogism and the enthymeme.

Effective arguments must be supported by evidence that backs up the speaker's claim. Expert testimony, lay testimony, personal testimony, definitions and explanations, statistics, and real and hypothetical examples are all effective categories of evidence. All evidence should be evaluated in terms of the competency of the source and the believability, consistency, verifiability, and currency of the evidence itself.

Key Terms

Argument	Definition and explanation	Lay testimony
Argument from analogy	Direct quotation	Logos
Argument from cause	Effect-to-cause arguments	Paraphrase
Argument from sign	Enthymeme	Pathos
Artistic proofs	Ethos	Proofs
Cause-to-effect arguments	Evidence	Statistics
Credibility	Examples	Syllogism
Deductive argument	Expert testimony	Testimony
	Inductive argument	

Application Questions

1. Arguments occur all around you. Spend half a day making notes each time you hear or see some examples of argument. Try to classify the arguments as inductive or deductive, or as an argument from cause, sign, or analogy. Compare your notes with your classmates' findings. Based on this informal research, which kinds of arguments seem most common? Why do you suppose that is?

2. Bring to class a magazine that you purchased before reading this chapter. With a group of your classmates, page through the magazine and study the advertisements. You will find that every ad in the magazine makes an argument. Can you classify the arguments you find? Do the advertisers offer any supporting proofs for their arguments? How do the proofs stand up to the tests of evidence?

3. What is your position on the following controversial issues?
   • Euthanasia
   • Assisted suicide
   • Guaranteed minimum annual cash income for every American citizen
   • The next U.S. president being a Republican

How much evidence, and what kinds, would someone have to provide to persuade you to change your mind? What insights does this give you about argumentation?

Self-Test for Review

1. Match the following terms and definitions.

    ____ a. Argument
    ____ b. Inductive argument
    ____ c. Argument from sign
    ____ d. Proofs
    ____ e. Argument from cause
    ____ f. Argument from analogy
    ____ g. Artistic proofs
    ____ h. Credibility
    ____ i. Enthymeme
    ____ j. Evidence

    1. Statements used for support of arguments
    2. "My brother is as good a golfer as Lee Trevino ever was."
    3. Ethos, pathos, logos
    4. Reasoning that a feature or symptom suggests a state of affairs
    5. Reasoning in which one or more statements are offered as support for some other statement
    6. A syllogism based on probability, usually with an implicit premise that has been dropped from the argument
    7. Statements or facts used to support a knowledge claim
    8. Degree to which a listener believes something
    9. Reasoning that something happened because of an earlier event
    10. Reasoning from individual cases to a conclusion

2. "There is ice on the lake. Winter has come early." This is an example of an argument from

    a. sign.
    b. cause.
    c. induction.
    d. analogy.

3. First person: "They say Tabasco sauce in raw oyster sauce kills bacteria." Second person: "Hmm. I always put Tabasco into my sauce. No wonder I never got sick from eating raw oysters." The second statement is

    a. an example of a categorical syllogism.
    b. a logically correct example of argument from sign.
    c. a logically fallacious example of causal reasoning.
    d. a correct example of inductive reasoning.

4. Match each of the testimony examples with the numbered "test" for judging the quality of testimonial evidence that could be applied to identify problems with the testimony.

1. How consistent is the testimony?

2. Does the source have preconceived biases?

3. Does the testimony agree with other expert opinion?

_____ a. "Of course it was hot outside. In New York in January, the average daytime temperature is somewhere near 75 degrees."

_____ b. "It's a well-known fact that the African race just isn't as smart as the Aryan race."

_____ c. "I'm not a doctor, but I play one on TV. So I'm concerned about the common cold. Despite what they may say, one cold tablet has been shown by leading experts to cure the common cold in just seven days."

Answers: 1. a.5, b.10, c.4, d.1, e.9, f.2, g.3, h.8, i.6, j.7. 2.a. 3.c. 4.a.1, b.2, c.3.

Suggested Readings

Fahnestock, Jeanne, and Marie Secor. *A Rhetoric of Argument.* New York: Random House, 1982. This older work is one of the clearest and easiest to follow of the many texts about argumentation. It is written in a question-and-answer format.

Freely, Austin J., *Argumentation and Debate. Critical Thinking for Reasoned Decision Making.* 8th ed. Belmont, Calif.: Wadsworth, 1993. This is one of the standard works in argumentation and is essential for anyone who wants to understand the area.

Nozick, Robert. *The Nature of Rationality.* San Francisco: Laissez Faire Books, 1993. This work is sometimes difficult to read, but it is well worth the effort. The book shows clearly that rational thought is essential to civilization and human progress.

Reinard, John C., *Foundations of Argument: Effective Communication for Critical Thinking.* Dubuque, Iowa: Brown & Benchmark Publishers, 1991. This work is more difficult reading but is well worth the effort for a student who wishes to explore in greater depth the theory and methods of contemporary argumentation.

Warnick, Barbara, and Edward S. Inch. *Critical Thinking and Communication: The Use of Reason in Argument.* 2nd ed. New York: Macmillan, 1994. This thorough work is clearly written and full of illustrations and examples. You will find it both interesting and easy to read.

CHAPTER 7

Gathering Supporting Materials and Using the Library

OBJECTIVES

After reading this chapter, you should be able to:

1. *Explain* how to locate information through interviewing and corresponding with your connections.
2. *Describe* some of the more useful computerized database services available.
3. *Name* and *describe* the ten most important departments in a college or university library, and *explain* what those departments do.
4. *Explain* how to find materials in the library.
5. *Explain* how to use the holdings catalog in your library (card or online).
6. *Describe* how to locate various general and specialized indexes in your library.
7. *Take* adequate notes from materials in the library.
8. *Develop* a working bibliography for a speech.
9. *Use* a card file to organize your ideas for a speech.

© Ulrike Welsch/PhotoEdit

*T*o succeed as a speaker, you must know how to gather supporting materials. This chapter describes how you can use readily available intellectual resources to expand and build upon your good ideas. The process involves (1) using what other people can tell you (through interviews and correspondence), (2) tapping into computerized database services, and (3) becoming familiar with all of the resources at your library.

Because of their wealth of information, libraries tend to overwhelm beginning students. You can manage library complexity by learning to use the holdings catalog in both an online and card format. Generalized and specialized indexes make finding supporting materials on almost any subject easy. Also, librarians can and want to help you.

When you locate the supporting materials you need, you should take notes in a system that works for you and that does not allow for accidental plagiarism. Those notes can then be used to develop a working bibliography, with which you can "play" as you organize ideas for your speech.

While the information in this chapter is useful, practical, and far reaching, the supporting materials in your speeches do not need to adhere slavishly to materials produced by others. Trust your own thinking. Rely on your personal expertise. Use what you already know as the basis for your investigations. Doing so will help to sustain your research interest and also will allow you to draw on your personal library of examples and illustrations that you can relate to listeners in a compelling fashion.

Unfortunately, you cannot always depend entirely on what you know to provide an interesting and appropriate speech topic. Each of us has intellectual limits. Sooner or later, you will need to go beyond your personal fund of knowledge to locate supporting materials for your speech. That is when this chapter, which describes how you can use readily available intellectual resources to expand and build upon your good ideas, will become indispensable.

USING YOUR CONNECTIONS

Gathering information for a speech often means asking questions of people who have specialized information. For example, one student decided to give a speech about early automobiles. She approached her aging grandfather, who had owned an automobile dealership in Boonville, Missouri. His long-term memory was a treasure trove of information. He recounted a story of the time when, as a little boy, he and his father traveled by car from St. Louis, Missouri, across the state to Joplin, Missouri. There were no roads, only wagon tracks that often passed right through a farmer's field. There were no bridges, only fords. There were no filling stations, so they had to carry extra fuel. Tires were not well made, so they had to carry extra tires, inner tubes, and an inner tube repair kit. No motels awaited them along the way, so they had to plan to stop in the towns that might have a hotel or boardinghouse. More often, they asked a nearby farmer for permission to stay in the barn loft. There were no convenient fast-food restaurants at the intersections; they had to carry food. The car's canvas roof leaked, so they got wet when it rained.

Her grandfather's stories seemed more interesting than her original idea for the speech, so the student changed her focus from "early cars" to "early car travel." Because of what she had learned from her grandfather, she was able to go to the library and fill in the gaps. For example, she found out when paved roads finally connected St. Louis and Joplin and when motels began to appear along the highways.

The student's audience listened with rapt attention when she gave her speech. She would not have enjoyed such success if she had not known how to interview her grandfather.

Who do you know? The potential for drawing information from your personal network of family members, friends, acquaintances, coworkers, colleagues, and teachers is enormous.

Take advantage of your connections. For example, your professors are all readily available subject-matter experts. They know how to get information about their professional areas of interest. They know others in their particular area of expertise. They belong to professional associations and interest groups. Most will gladly help you to locate sources of information—people you can interview or write to for information.

Two ways to ask questions of other people are through interviews and correspondence. An **information-gathering interview** is designed to acquire information about a subject, process, or person.[1] It usually involves five planning steps, each of which can determine whether you get the information you need or want. Table 7.1 describes the five steps in planning an information-gathering interview and suggests questions you may want to ask yourself.

Sometimes, personally interviewing your information source is not possible. In these situations, you need written communication skills to correspond with potential sources and to gather information for your speeches.

Possible correspondence sources include interest groups and chambers of commerce. Interest groups register with the local, state, and national governments they wish to influence. The Federal Regulation of Lobbyists Act of 1976 requires all lobbyists to register with the Clerk of the House and the Secretary of the Senate. The names of these registrants are then published quarterly in the *Congressional Record.* For example, the National Tobacco Association registers lobbyists with the federal government because it wants to influence federal legislation that pertains to the tobacco industry. Most interest groups publish literature to support their positions. You can write to virtually any one of these groups and expect to receive information.

If you need information about a product or industry, a local or nearby chamber of commerce will probably be able to help. Every chamber of commerce lists its members. In larger cities and towns, the chamber of commerce may publish an index of manufacturers sorted by product category. To illustrate, the chamber of commerce in Mobile, Alabama, provides an index of its members sorted alphabetically by products. The products range from acids and acoustical panels through coffee, die cutting, inorganic chemicals, jet fuel, metal doors, rubber linings, sails, sawmills, tables, underwear,

Table 7.1

THE FIVE STEPS IN PLANNING AN INFORMATION-GATHERING INTERVIEW

Step 1   Identify where you can go to discover the information necessary to conduct an interview.
- Who is available that knows what you want to learn?
- Will the person be likely to tell you what you want to know?
- What background material will you need?

Step 2   Identify what questions you must ask the person you interview.
- What information do you want to get from this particular person?
- How might you phrase questions that will get at this information without offending the person?

Step 3   Plan how to probe into the answers you receive.
- What questions might you ask to secure *elaboration?* (Examples: "Could you elaborate on that, please?" "Could you tell me more about that?")
- What questions might you ask to secure *clarification?* (Examples: "Could you clarify that for me, please?" "Could you give me an example of that?")

Step 4   Plan how to handle common problems in the interview.
- Reluctant respondent
  "You seem uneasy. Could you tell me why?"
  "Would you like to move somewhere else?"
  Active listening or silence may draw out a reluctant respondent.
- Emotional respondent
  "It's okay to cry. Please go on when you can."
  "We're not in a hurry. Take as much time as you want."
  "Would you rather talk at another time?"
- Hostile respondent
  "You seem angry. Would you tell me about it?"
  "Are you upset? Is anything wrong?"
  "Would you be willing to elaborate on your criticism?"

Step 5   Determine how to validate or verify what you learn in the interview.
- Seek contrasting opinions from other experts.
- Seek alternative interpretations of specific and technical information.
- Consider your source. Was the source biased? competent? forthcoming?

Source: Based on Gerald L. Wilson and H. Lloyd Goodall, Jr., Interviewing in Context *(New York: McGraw-Hill, 1991), 216–40.*

varnishes and paints, vehicle parts, welding equipment, wire cloth, wood products, and yarn. All of these companies can provide you with printed information or correspondence on their industries and products.

Your interview and correspondence connections can help you to obtain information that might not be available in any other way. Do not overlook their potential for giving your speech a unique perspective.

COMPUTERIZED DATABASE SERVICES AND NETWORKS

If you own a computer with a modem, you have access to an almost limitless body of information through easy-to-use information networks. These networks usually charge a fee for their services or may, instead, request membership dues.[2] With access to these amazing and rich resources, you can get free advice from people who use computer equipment like yours, view hundreds of free computer bulletin boards, and save up to 40 percent or more by shopping with your computer. You also have access to information from specialized newsletters and can be involved in electronic banking, investment managing, and bartering. Information networks open doors to vast libraries of information and allow you to play real-time computer games and send and receive all kinds of letters, telexes, and faxes. Table 7.2 lists some of the more popular database services and networks.

To illustrate, The Source, a subscription service, offers its members about twelve hundred features and programs. There is a full range of stock, bond, and commodities information, including an option to have your portfolio automatically updated, as well as economic, political, and trade information. Some corporations use The Source to set up a corporate database system. If you like games, soap operas, traveling, poetry, and talking via computer to other people, you will find offerings to interest you. The most popular categories include: (1) communications, (2) news and information, (3) business-related information and services, (4) personal computing information and services, (5) education and careers, (6) online shopping, (7) computer conferencing, and (8) fun and games. Each of these categories is rich in information. For example, the fun and games category provides airline schedules; a restaurant guide to U.S. and Canadian cities and towns; an up-to-date listing of what is happening in New York; the ability to make reservations for hotels, airlines, car rentals, and tours; and access to movie reviews and a large number of computer games.

Other online databases provide additional attractive services. CompuServe has something for everyone. Are you a pilot? Do you own an aircraft? Do you clip food coupons? Do you want to know the weather in Tokyo? Do you want to know what was in the last issue of *Popular Science?* Do you need emergency health information? Do you dabble in the market and need up-to-the-minute commodity prices? Do you need any information from an online encyclopedia? At $8.95 per month, CompuServe may be right for you.[3]

You can subscribe to any number of encyclopedic databases. General interest databases will let you search through online Yellow Pages across the telephone system or a directory of mail-order catalogs. You can access *Books in Print* from your home computer or a *Magazine Index* to over four hundred popular magazines—including anything you found in *Reader's Guide.* There is an *International Software Directory* and a database that indexes, every day, more than two thousand news stories, articles, book reviews, and so on from fifteen hundred newspapers, magazines, and periodicals. Need to know about a person in a hurry? Call the *Biography Master Index.*

Table 7.2

SOME COMPUTERIZED DATABASE SERVICES AND NETWORKS

America Online, Inc.
8619 Westwood
Center Drive
Vienna, Va 22182
(800)827–5938

AT&T Mail
AT&T EasyLink Services
400 Interpace Parkway
Parsippany, NJ 07054
(800)MAIL 672

BIX
1030 Massachusetts Avenue
Cambridge, MA 02138
(800)227–2983

BRS/After Dark
BRS Information
Technologies
Maxwell Online, Inc.
8000 Westpard Drive
McLean, VA 22102
(800)289–4277

CompuServe, Inc.
P.O. Box 20212
Columbus, OH 43220
(800)848–8199

DASnet
DA Systems, Inc.
Marketing Department
1503 Campbell Avenue
Campbell, CA 95008
(408)559–7434

Data Times
14000 Quail Springs Parkway
Suite 450
Oklahoma City, OK 73134
(800) 642–2525

Delphi
1030 Massachusetts Avenue
Cambridge, MA 02138
(800) 695–4005

DIALCOM
BT North America
2560 North First Street
San Jose, CA 95161–9019
(800)872–7654

Dialog Information
Services, Inc.
3460 Hillview Avenue
Palo Alto, CA 94304
(800)334–2564

Dow Jones News/Retrieval
Dow Jones & Co., Inc.
P.O. Box 300
Princeton, NJ 08543–0300
(800)522–3567

EasyNet
Telebase Systems, Inc.
Suite 600
435 Devon Park Drive
Wayne, PA 19087
(800)220–9553

GE Information
Services (GEnie)
P.O. Box 6403
Rockville, MD 20850–1785
(800)638-9636

This breathtaking array of information resources is constantly changing and growing. But you do not need to own a computer and a modem to access this information. All you need to do is find your way to the library.

USING THE LIBRARY

You cannot find a better intellectual resource than your school or public library. More-over, library skills you learn now will be helpful long after you complete this public speaking course. Libraries hold the world's knowledge—yours for the asking. But you must know what to ask for and how to ask for it.

IQuest
Telebase System, Inc.
Suite 600
435 Devon Park Drive
Wayne, PA 19087
(800)220–9553

Knowledge Index
Dialog Information
Services Inc.
3460 Hillview Avenue
Palo Alto, CA 94303
(800) 334–2564

Lexis and Nexis
Mead Data Central, Inc.
P.O. Box 933
Dayton, OH 45401
(800) 227–4908

MCI Mail
1111 Nineteenth Street NW
Washington, D.C. 20036
(800)444–6245

NewsNet
945 Haverford Road
Bryn Mawr, PA 19010
(800)345–1301

PC–Link
America Online, Inc.
8619 Westwood
Center Drive
Vienna, VA 22182
(800)827–8532

PRODIGY
Prodigy Services Company
445 Hamilton Avenue
White Plains, NY 10601
(800)PRODIGY

Promenade
America Online, Inc.
8619 Westwood Center Drive
Vienna, VA 22182
(800)525–5938

The Source
P.O. Box 586
Mt. Morris, IL 61054
(800)872–0172

SprintMail
US Spring
12490 Sunrise Valley Drive
Reston, VA 22096
(800) 736–1130

USA TODAY Sports Center
Four Seasons Executive Center
Building 9, Terrace Way
Greensboro, NC 27403
(800) 826–9688

The WELL
27 Gate Five Road
Sausalito, CA 94965
(415) 332–4335

FINDING YOUR WAY AROUND THE LIBRARY

Think of a library as you would a department store. When you enter any large department store, you know that you will find such departments as men's clothing, housewares, electronics, cosmetics, and the like. Department stores do not all have the same floor plan, of course, but that rarely stops you from finding what you want. In general, regardless of the department store's name or location, you know what department you need to go to when you want to make a particular purchase.

Libraries resemble each other, too. Some are larger, some are smaller, and they may be organized a bit differently. Even so, most college or university libraries have the following departments: (1) reference, (2) circulation, (3) reserve readings, (4) government documents, (5) serials and periodicals, (6) microform, (7) instructional media, (8) interlibrary loan, (9) database searching, and (10) specialized collections.

Reference Department

The library reference department houses a broad range of reference works that usually are not circulated out of the library. Here you will find general and specialized dictionaries, general and specialized encyclopedias, almanacs, handbooks, college catalogs, directories, telephone books, and many general and specialized bibliographies, abstracts, and indexes.

Students often find encyclopedias especially helpful. Encyclopedias are arranged alphabetically by subject matter and are very easy to use. Look around at the collection in your library. Along with the standard and general encyclopedias (*Britannica* and *Americana*), you will probably find a number of specialized encyclopedias, such as those listed in table 7.3.

The library reference department houses many wonderful treasures. To illustrate, table 7.4 lists just a few of the available materials you might find if you wanted to research the topic *communication* in a typical reference department. Your library probably owns a similar list of resources in any area of interest that you might want to pursue.

Table 7.3

SPECIALIZED ENCYCLOPEDIAS

Animal Life Encyclopedia
Concise Encyclopedia of Western Philosophy and Philosophers
Encyclopedia of Education
Encyclopedia of Philosophy
Encyclopedia of Psychology
Encyclopedia of Religion and Ethics
Groves Dictionary of Music and Musicians
International Encyclopedia of the Social Sciences
McGraw-Hill Encyclopedia of Science and Technology

Clearly, you cannot absorb all of this information without spending time and effort. Go to the reference department at your school or local library. Meet one of the librarians, look around, and get acquainted with the variety of information sources available.

Circulation Department

Employees of the library circulation department typically maintain the library's book-shelves and check out materials that circulate. Most books, of course, circulate, as may records, tapes, CDs, portable computers, computer software, VCRs, and videotapes. The circulation department is usually located near the library's main entrance for convenient check out of materials by library patrons.

Reserve Readings Department

Many instructors place materials "on reserve" for their students. These materials may include library property and/or the instructor's personal property. Reserve materials do not usually circulate for more than an hour or two at a time. Some libraries allow overnight circulation privileges in certain cases.

Most libraries have both temporary and permanent reserve collections. Materials on temporary reserve flow in and out of the department according to the institution's needs. For example, particular courses offered in a given term may require that special materials in the library be placed on temporary reserve for the students in those courses. Institutional and funded research projects also may require that the library place certain materials on temporary reserve.

Permanent reserve materials usually include very rare or valuable materials that the library could not replace. Libraries often house this material in an area called "Rare Books and Materials."

A listing of reserve materials can usually be found at the reserve desk. A librarian at the reserve desk can help you to locate reserved materials and can answer your questions about the reserve readings collection.

Table 7.4

RESOURCES IN THE LIBRARY REFERENCE DEPARTMENT
THAT FOCUS ON COMMUNICATION

DIRECTORIES

Broadcasting & Cable Marketplace
Editor and Publisher International Yearbook
*Gale Directory of Publications and Broadcast
   Media*
Working Press of the Nation
Video Source Book

HANDBOOKS

Copyright Handbook
Handbook of American Popular Culture
NBC Handbook of Pronunciation
Writer's Market

YEARBOOKS AND ALMANACS

Communication Yearbook
Europa World Yearbook
International Television and Video Almanac
Mass Communication Review Yearbook

FILM

*American Film Industry: A Historic
   Dictionary*
Film Review Index
Magill's Survey of Cinema
Motion Picture Guide

BIOGRAPHY

Biography and Genealogy Master Index
*Biographical Dictionary of American
   Journalism*
Biography Index
Dictionary of American Biography
Dictionary of National Biography
Index to Who's Who Books
Journalist Biographies Master Index
*Who's What and Where: A Directory and
   Reference Book on America's Minority
   Journalists*

BOOK REVIEWS

Book Review Index
Book Review Digest
Communication Booknotes

GUIDES

Mass Media Bibliography
Global Guide to Media and Communications
*On the Screen: A Film, Television, and Video
   Research Guide*
*Public Relations in Business, Government
   and Society: A Bibliographic Guide*
Television: A Guide to the Literature

INDEXES AND ABSTRACTS

Business Periodicals Index
Communication Abstracts
Current Index to Journals in Education
Dissertation Abstracts International
Essay and General Literature Index
Humanities Index
Index to Journals in Communication Studies
Index to Legal Periodicals
InfoTrac. General Periodicals Index
The (London) Times Index
Media Review Digest
New York Times Index
Newsbank
Philosopher's Index
Psychological Abstracts
PAIS International in Print
The Readers' Guide to Periodical Literature
Resources in Education
Social Sciences Citation Index
Social Sciences Index
Sociological Abstracts
The Wall Street Journal Index

DICTIONARIES AND ENCYCLOPEDIAS

Broadcast Communications Dictionary
Encyclopedia of American Journalism
*International Encyclopedia of
   Communications*
*Webster's New World Dictionary of Media
   and Communications*

Note: A library-specific version of this table was generated for use in the University of South Alabama Library by the reference section staff.

Table 7.5

BASIC CATEGORIES OF THE SUPERINTENDENT
OF DOCUMENTS CLASSIFICATION SYSTEM

C	Commerce
ED	Education
NS	National Science Foundation
OP	Overseas Private Investment Corporation
P	United States Post Office
PE	Peace Corps
PM	Personnel Management Office
Pr	President of the United States
PrEx	Executive Office of the President
RR	Railroad Retirement Board
S	State Department
SBA	Small Business Administration
SE	Securities and Exchange Commission
SI	Smithsonian Institution
T	Treasury Department
TC	International Trade Commission
TD	Transportation Department
VA	Veterans Administration
X & Y	Congress

Government Documents Department

The government documents department in a library houses publications originating in or issued by federal, state, and local government agencies. Some of these circulate; some do not. This collection may seem daunting and difficult to access because the government has such varied interests, but it is also one of the library's most useful collections. Your library may have part of the collection on CD-ROM. If so, the task of locating materials becomes much easier.

Usually, you will find a brochure in the government documents section that tells you how to use the collection, but you will never learn everything about this wonderful resource. Even the most experienced researchers have to ask the librarians who know the collection well for help. Table 7.5 lists the most important categories and their abbreviations put out by the federal Superintendent of Documents. Each of the agencies listed here publishes numerous books, papers, research reports, abstracts, and other documents. Imagine the wealth of interesting materials you might find.

Serials and Periodicals Department

The library serials and periodicals department will help you find information in newspapers, magazines, and other serial publications. Some of these are bound volumes, while others are stored on microfilm or microfiche. The most recent issues of journals, magazines, and newspapers are stored on racks near or in a reading room. Not all libraries house these materials in one centralized location. Your library may divide the collection according to appropriate subject areas. Ask the librarian at the serials and periodicals information desk about how the department is arranged, and request help with your research if you need it.

Microform Department

The library microform department may be integrated with serials and periodicals or with print materials (especially in subject-divided libraries), or it may be a separate department. Microform materials include back issues of newspapers and magazines and such wonders as the *Library of American Civilization* and the *Library of English Literature.* These materials do not usually circulate, but you can make photocopies. Ask a librarian for help.

Instructional Media Department

The library instructional media department houses a wide variety of audio and visual materials, including records, tape recordings, foreign language lessons, plays, films, 35mm filmstrips, slides, videotapes, and photographic archives. These materials may circulate.

Some libraries only acquire instructional media that are for class-related use. Others acquire entertainment materials. Your library may own both types of holdings.

Interlibrary Loan Department

Even with all the materials available in a single library, serious researchers may have to borrow from more than one library. For example, a PhD dissertation written by a University of Wisconsin student might hold the key to a California-based researcher's problem. Materials of all kinds move from one library to another through the interlibrary loan system.

Before using this service, be sure that your own library does not have the materials you need. Interlibrary loans can be expensive. Also, although materials usually arrive within three to five days of the request, delays are not uncommon.

Database Searching Department

Your library may have a database searching department or division, while other libraries may have a database searching unit within the reference, serials and periodicals, or interlibrary loan departments. This unit provides computer searches in specific subject areas of both the library's holdings and of materials not owned by the library. A search produces citations (with or without abstracts or summaries) of books, articles, and other documents.

Table 7.6

OTHER USEFUL INDEXES ON CD-ROM

NAME	DESCRIPTION OF INDEX
Newsbank	Newspaper articles
InfoTrac	General periodicals index
MLA	Modern Language Association International bibliography of books and articles on the modern languages and literatures
PsycLit	American Psychological Association index to articles and chapters in books
Dissertation Abstracts	Authors, subjects, institutions, and abstracts of doctoral dissertations
Medline	*Index Medicus* lists authors, subjects, and some published medical research
CINAHL	*Cumulative Index to Nursing and Allied Health Literature*

In many libraries, you can do your own database searches. For example, in most college libraries, what used to be a *card catalog* has now become an *online catalog,* housed in a dedicated computer or in the institution's mainframe computer. You go to a menu-driven terminal (located throughout the library) to make your initial search, which is both fun and easy.

You are also likely to find a massive collection of database materials stored on CD-ROM. For example, the Educational Resources Information Center (ERIC) provides access to literature in nearly all education areas. This includes journal articles, research reports, conference papers, and bibliographies, dating back to about 1966. The collection is constantly growing because ERIC updates this database four times each year.

ERIC's database includes such wonders as *Resources in Education* (RIE), a file of document citations that includes research that may never get into print. For example, scholarly papers presented to academic and professional meetings often find their way into the RIE file. *Current Index to Journals in Education,* also an ERIC file, lists article citations from over 750 professional journals.

In addition to ERIC, other library CD-ROM collections may include *Books in Print,* an annotated list of everything published in English in the United States, and *Reader's Guide to Periodical Literature,* which provides a similar list of serial and periodical publications. Table 7.6 lists other indexes that might be on CD-ROM at your library.

Specialized Collections Department

Libraries sometimes develop specialized collections that are often housed in separate facilities. For example, if you have a medical school at your institution, you will almost certainly find a medical or biomedical library. Law schools usually have a law library.

Journalism schools often house a branch of the library specifically for their students. You probably will find a map library that supports your institution's programs in geography and geology. Your institution also may have a religion and theology library.

Find out which specialized collections your library holds and where the collections are kept. Even if your special interest lies outside the medical field, you might need the books, journals, and other materials that support medical research, basic medical sciences, speech pathology, nursing, and other allied health science programs. These specialized collections often include database searching facilities. You can normally use these facilities without charge.

FINDING MATERIALS IN THE LIBRARY

Now that you have some insight into the various library departments and their enormous volume of resources, you must face up to a new challenge: How do you use them? Become familiar with helpful reference tools—the card and online catalogs, the general and specialized indexes, and the librarians—and your life as a student will become easier.

Holdings Catalog: Card and Online

A **holdings catalog** indexes the materials in a given library or collection. The materials are described and classified in such a way that the user can refer to an entry and then easily find the material in the library. Before the days of computers, the holdings catalog was called the **card catalog.** Now you will usually find the holdings in an **online catalog.**

Three typical cards from a card catalog are a subject card (figure 7.1), a title card (figure 7.2), and an author card (figure 7.3). Figure 7.4 shows that an online listing provides the same basic information as the card catalog.

Most public libraries, especially in smaller communities, still use a card catalog. Many college libraries do, too, or are in the process of converting to an online system. So knowing how to use a card catalog is still important.

Card catalogs list authors, titles, and subjects alphabetically—usually in separate catalog sections, although a few libraries intermix all three. If a book is co-authored or listed under more than one subject, you may find several cards for the same work.

Listings by author include the names of authors, editors, compilers, and translators of the work. If you want to know what works by a particular author you may find in the library holdings, go to the author catalog and search by the author's last name.

If you know the title but not the author of a book, consult the title catalog. Entries by title leave off the articles *a, an,* and *the* when they appear as the first word of the title.

The subject catalog may be the most helpful of the three if you know the subject you wish to research. The subject catalog has a card for every work the library owns on a particular subject. You may find it helpful, therefore, to begin your research in the subject catalog. Make certain that you look under all the headings that pertain to your subject. For example, if you want to look up the topic *speaking,* you will not find it listed in the card catalog under that heading. The *Library of Congress Subject Headings Book* would direct you to look under the headings: Debates and debating, Elocution, Extemporaneous speaking, Lectures and lecturing, Oratory, Rhetoric, and Voice. Then, under *Debates and debating,* you will find additional related subjects to explore.

Figure **7.1**

A subject card.

CHINA--HISTORY--20TH CENTURY.

DS
774
.S59   Spence, Jonathan D.
             The gate of heavenly peace : the Chinese and
            their revolution, 1895-1980
            / Jonathan D. Spence. --New York :
            Viking Press, 1981.
              xxii, 465 p. : ill. ; 24 cm.
              Bibliography: p. [423]-444.
              Includes index.

              1. China--History--20th century.
              2. China--History--1861-1912. I. Title

WMA   23 NOV 81   7555180   WIM8sc   81-65264

Figure **7.2**

A title card.

The gate of heavenly peace

DS
774
.S59   Spence, Jonathan D.
             The gate of heavenly peace : the Chinese and
            their revolution, 1895-1980
            / Jonathan D. Spence. --New York :
            Viking Press, 1981.
              xxii, 465 p. : ill. ; 24 cm.
              Bibliography: p. [423]-444.
              Includes index.

              1. China--History--20th century.
              2. China--History--1861-1912. I. Title

WMA   23 NOV 81   7555180   WIM8at   81-65264

149

Figure **7.3**

An author card.

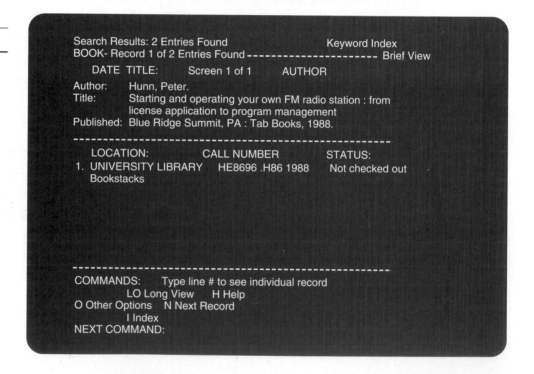

```
DS
774        Spence, Jonathan D.
.S59          The gate of heavenly peace : the Chinese and
           their revolution, 1895-1980
              / Jonathan D. Spence. --New York :
           Viking Press, 1981.
              xxii, 465 p. : ill. ; 24 cm.
              Bibliography: p. [423]-444.
              Includes index.


              1.  China--History--20th century.
              2.  China--History--1861-1912. I. Title

WMA        23 NOV 81      7555180  WIM8at      81-65264
```

Figure **7.4**

A typical online listing.

```
Search Results: 2 Entries Found                    Keyword Index
BOOK- Record 1 of 2 Entries Found ---------------------- Brief View
     DATE TITLE:      Screen 1 of 1      AUTHOR
Author:    Hunn, Peter.
Title:     Starting and operating your own FM radio station : from
           license application to program management
Published: Blue Ridge Summit, PA : Tab Books, 1988.
-----------------------------------------------------------
     LOCATION:           CALL NUMBER         STATUS:
1. UNIVERSITY LIBRARY   HE8696 .H86 1988   Not checked out
   Bookstacks




-----------------------------------------------------------
COMMANDS:     Type line # to see individual record
         LO Long View     H Help
O Other Options   N Next Record
         I Index
NEXT COMMAND:
```

Study the card headings and subheadings carefully. Notice that the subject cards cross-reference other entries in the same catalog system. Other systems used in your library are cross-listed, too. For example, most college libraries include works that are cataloged using both the Dewey decimal and Library of Congress systems. If your library uses both systems, you may have to search before you find what you want. Knowing the general categories in each of these systems is helpful. The older Dewey decimal system is far less precise than the newer Library of Congress system. Table 7.7 compares these two systems side by side.

Table 7.7

COMPARISON OF DEWEY DECIMAL AND LIBRARY
OF CONGRESS SYSTEMS

CATEGORIES IN THE DEWEY DECIMAL SYSTEM		CATEGORIES IN THE LIBRARY OF CONGRESS SYSTEM	
000–099	General works	A	General works—Polygraphy
100–199	Philosophy	B	Philosophy—Religion—Psychology
200–299	Religion	C	Archeology—General biography
300–399	Social sciences	D	History and topography (except America)
400–499	Language	E	America—American history
500–599	Pure science	F	Local history—Latin American history
600–699	Technology	G	Geography—Anthropology—Sports
700–799	The arts	H	Social sciences—Business
800–899	Literature	J	Political science
900–999	History	K	Law
		L	Education
		M	Music
		N	Art—architecture
		P	Language and literature—Drama
		Q	Science
		R	Medicine
		S	Agriculture—Plant and animal husbandry
		T	Technology
		U	Military science
		V	Naval science
		Z	Bibliography and library science

When you find something that interests you in the holdings catalog, write down the complete call number. The call number is located in the upper left-hand corner of the catalog card. In the example in figures 7.1, 7.2, and 7.3, the call number is:

DS
774
.S59

The call number is the book's address in the library. Be sure to record the complete call number, or you will lose much time in the library stacks. To illustrate, merely writing down "DS774" as the call number for the previous example is like saying, "I live on Maple Street. Pick me up at 6:00 P.M." There may be dozens of houses on Maple Street, or hundreds. Similarly, dozens or even hundreds of books may carry the classification number DS774.

Table 7.8

KEYWORD SEARCH OF AN ONLINE CATALOG

Simple Keyword Searches: And, Or, Not	K = cameras This retrieves all records that have this word.
	K = IBM *and* computer This retrieves all records that contain **both** of these words.
	K = wilson *and* organizations This retrieves records with **both** a name and another word. Most online catalogs do not use punctuation or capitalization, but yours may.
	K = dog *or* K9 This retrieves all items that contain **either** word.
	K = hamlet *not* shakespeare. This eliminates undesired records.
Qualifying Search Terms to Fields: Author, Title, Subject Headings	K = johnson.au. and president.ti. This retrieves items with Johnson just in the author field and president just in the title field. Very useful for authors with common names.
	K = blue.ti. This retrieves items only with the word *blue* in the title.
	K = johnson.su. This retrieves only items with Johnson as the subject.
Qualifying Search to Format, Language, Year	K = management and s.fmt. This retrieves all records in a serial format that also have the word *management* in the record.
	K = fellini and f.fmt. This retrieves all films and videotapes that also have the word *Fellini* in the record.
	K = opera and italian and m.fmt. This retrieves Italian operas in a music format, such as scores, records, and CDs.
	K = sartre and fr.la. This retrieves French language materials with the name *Sartre* in the record.
	K = hanna and 1992.yr. This will retrieve records with a 1992 date that have the name Hanna in the record.

Online catalogs provide basically the same information as card catalogs. Because there is no standardized computer-access system, though, you will need to learn the one used in your library. Even so, online catalogs generally have certain features in common. You can usually do a search by author (A = chaucer), by title (T = *canterbury tales),* and by key-words (K = poetry). The keyword search feature has greatly simplified the research process for many students (see table 7.8). Most computer-access systems are menu driven—that is, all you have to do is read what is on the screen and follow simple directions.

Truncation of Search Terms	Some systems will let you use wild cards, such as ?, to reduce the amount of typing necessary to access a record. Hint: Truncate only to the root word to avoid irrelevant records.
	K = tolst? and war.ti. This will pull up records with varied spellings for Tolstoy that also have the word *war* in the title.
	K = wordsworth and 197? This will produce all records that have a date in the 1970s and the name *Wordsworth*.
Stop Words	A number of short, often-used words, such as *a, an, it, no, on, the, to,* and various forms of the verb *to be,* do not work in database searching. A help screen often lists the seventy or more items that qualify as stop words in your catalog.
Qualifying by Position: *Adjacent, Near, With, Same*	Specifying the word order of a keyword search helps to eliminate unwanted records. K = child? abuse The system assumes that you mean *next to* or *on either side,* so it brings up child abuse as well as abuse of children. (*Of* is a stop word, so it is not counted.)
	K = home adj nursing This retrieves records with the words adjacent and in this order (that is, *home nursing*). It excludes records about nursing homes.
	K = writing with manual This brings up all records with the two words *writing* and *manual* in the same sentence.
	K = writing same editing This retrieves records that have the words *writing* and *editing* in the same set of fields. All the subject headings will be pulled up, for example.
Nested Searches	You can accomplish truly sophisticated and magical searches by using parentheses to set off different parts of the search.
	K = (theatre or theater) and history) and (greece or greek) This retrieves records about the theater of Greece and the history of Greece and includes, as well, records bearing the language "Greek theater" and "Greek history," no matter how you spell *theater*. Note: The authors gratefully acknowledge the University of South Alabama Library staff for their help in providing this information.

General and Specialized Indexes

While a holdings catalog is a reference tool for finding information in books, general and specialized indexes are reference tools for accessing information in periodicals. The word **index** refers to any alphabetized listing of names or topics. An index provides access to periodical articles by subject and occasionally by author or title. An index also provides the complete bibliographical information (author, title of article, name of periodical, volume and issue number, date, and pages) needed to locate an article. A general index, such as *Reader's Guide to Periodical Literature,* has a broad focus of interest. In contrast, specialized indexes, such as the *Index to Journals in Communication Studies through 1990,* have a very narrow focus. Indexes are especially useful in forming a working bibliography.

Consult the holdings catalog under the subject "indexes" to see which ones your library owns, or ask a librarian to make suggestions. General and specialized indexes come in a variety of formats. Examine each index to learn how to use it. Learning the system for each index will be well worth your effort.

Before using an index to obtain research sources, find out which serials and periodicals your library owns. Then you will not waste time listing index entries for serials and periodicals that your library does not have. You may not have time to use the interlibrary loan system.

A collection of abstracts is similar to an index. An **abstract** briefly summarizes each item included in its various issues. Like indexes, abstracts and abstract collections have many formats. If you run into trouble, ask a librarian for help in using them.

Librarians

While holdings catalogs and general and specialized indexes are helpful in your research, librarians may be the best resource references in your library. Even so, students often hold back from asking librarians for help—perhaps because they feel foolish or perhaps because they do not want to impose. Librarians, however, take professional pride in helping people learn how to use the library. They can and will save you much time if you simply ask them for help.

GATHERING YOUR RESEARCH MATERIALS

Once you have an idea of where items are located in a library and how to find them, the task of researching a speech becomes much less daunting. In fact, the discovery aspect of research collection can even make the process fun and exciting. Research gathering involves taking notes from the different materials you examine and keeping a working bibliography of the various sources.

HOW TO TAKE NOTES

Use Note Cards or Half-Sheets

The size of the cards you use for note taking depends on your personal preference. Some people prefer small note cards as a way of keeping their notes brief. Others like larger note cards so that they can edit their notes later, directly on the cards. Still others prefer half-sheets of paper. They type the bibliographical data, except page references, on several half-sheets at once, using carbon paper. Then they take longhand notes on one sheet

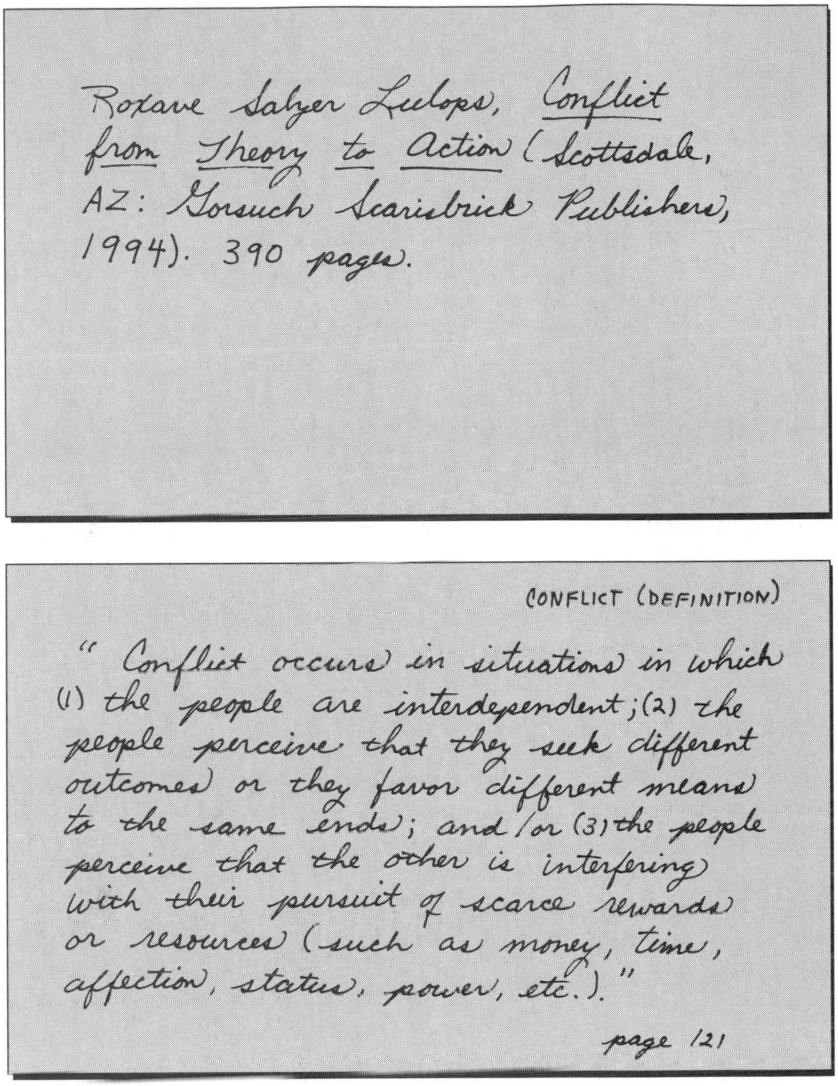

Figure 7.5

Figure **7.5**

Both sides of a note card. Notice that the bibliography side carries the same information that a bibliography card carries. The note side shows how you would enter a direct quotation.

Roxane Salyer Lulops, Conflict from Theory to Action (Scottsdale, AZ: Gorsuch Scarisbrick Publishers, 1994). 390 pages.

CONFLICT (DEFINITION)

" Conflict occurs in situations in which (1) the people are interdependent; (2) the people perceive that they seek different outcomes or they favor different means to the same ends; and /or (3) the people perceive that the other is interfering with their pursuit of scarce rewards or resources (such as money, time, affection, status, power, etc.). "

page 121

at a time. If you elect this method, type in everything except the page number. Then, as you make notes on a particular sheet, write in longhand the appropriate reference page number or numbers on which the information is found.

The kind of notes you take should guide your decision about note card size. Make your selection and then live with it. Make all of your notes that size. Figure 7.5 shows both sides of a note card.

Using a full-size notebook for notes is not recommended. Full sheets invite you to make your notes too lengthy. For example, you might write verbatim what you find. Or you might be tempted to follow the organizational pattern of your source. If you do not

Figure **7.6**

A note card showing direct quotation.

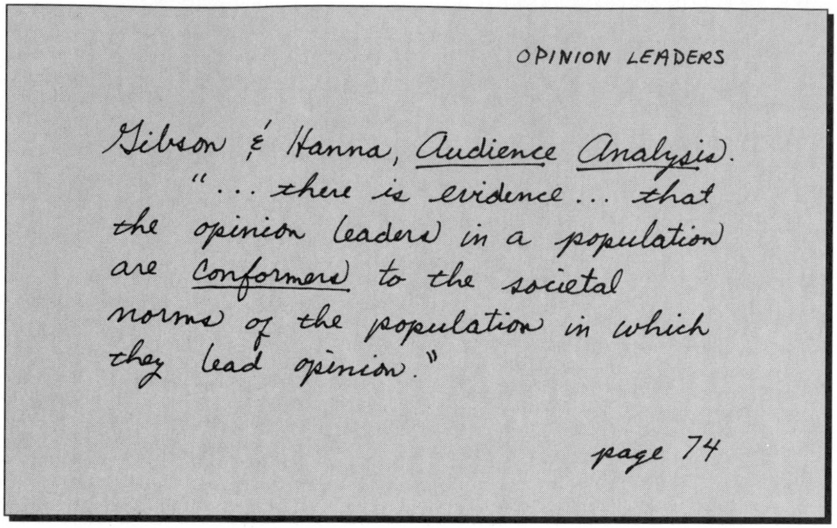

A note card reading:

OPINION LEADERS

Gibson & Hanna, *Audience Analysis*.
"... there is evidence ... that the opinion leaders in a population are *conformers* to the societal norms of the population in which they lead opinion."

page 74

severely limit your notes, you run the risk of accidental **plagiarism,** which is taking the ideas or language of someone else and claiming them as your own.

Establish a Standard Form of Entry

Use a standard form of entry for your note taking. The two most common methods of note taking are direct quotation and paraphrase. As mentioned in chapter 6, "Supporting Ideas with Argument and Evidence," a direct quotation is an exact replication of the original, while a paraphrase is a summary of the original in your own words. Develop a system that clearly shows which method you are using. For example, put quotation marks around all quoted materials, and write "paraphrase" on any card on which you have put the author's ideas into your own words. Figure 7.6 and 7.7 illustrate the differences.

Use One Card Per Entry and One Entry Per Card

Note cards work well because you can shuffle them and rearrange them—but only if you follow the simple rule: one card per entry and one entry per card. The temptation, of course, is to put more than one entry from a single source on one card, thereby reducing the number of times you have to write out the complete bibliographical data. (Using the half-sheet system mentioned earlier, in which bibliographical data are typed on several half-sheets at the same time, helps to eliminate some of the redundancy.) One card per entry, one entry per card also promotes better accuracy in note taking and greatly facilitates organization and outlining.

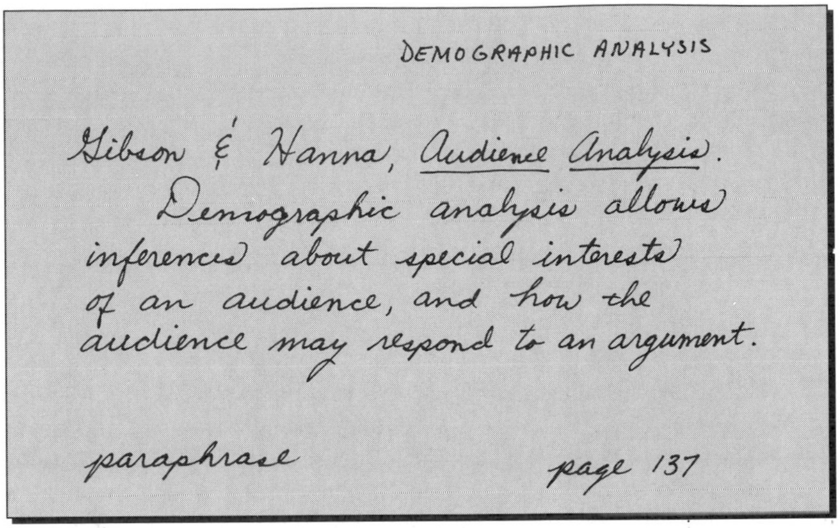

Figure **7.7**

A note card showing paraphrase.

DEMOGRAPHIC ANALYSIS

Gibson & Hanna, Audience Analysis.
Demographic analysis allows
inferences about special interests
of an audience, and how the
audience may respond to an argument.

paraphrase   *page 137*

Take Plenty of Notes

Every scholar learns the wisdom of taking sufficient notes. At some point, you will in-evitably discover that you did not take enough notes and that you cannot remember that bit of information you now need or even where you found it.

One rule of thumb is: If you find it interesting, make a note. This will not slow you down anywhere near as much as the countless hours you may spend searching for the in-formation you once had at your fingertips.

Do Not Plagiarize, Even by Accident

As mentioned earlier, **plagiarism** means taking another person's ideas or language and claiming them as yours. Doing this intentionally is outright stealing. Individuals who pla-giarize risk ruining their careers and their lives.

Most often, plagiarism occurs by accident. Honest, well-intended people use another person's ideas or language but fail to give the other person credit because they simply do not realize what they have done. Even so, there is no excuse for plagiarism.

Crediting your source is a matter of form and style, as well as of integrity. If you do not follow a correct form of entry or if you do not indicate by the way you record infor-mation that the ideas or the language are not your own, you can run into trouble. For ex-ample, some students believe that the correct way to give credit is to include a superscript (footnote or bibliography number) at the end of a paragraph or a page and then include an entry in their notes at the end of the paper. They follow this format whether they are quot-ing materials directly or paraphrasing. The problem is that this approach misleads the reader. Instead, when you quote directly in a paper, set the quotation apart from your own material with quotation marks or indentation. Indicate paraphrased material by writing something like, "In his 1985 essay, John Marshall suggested . . . ." Then include a footnote that indicates where you got the quote or information.

Similarly, when you directly quote or paraphrase materials in your speeches, your wording must show that you are doing so. For example, you might say, "John Marshall once said . . ." or "To paraphrase John Marshall . . . ."

HOW TO DEVELOP A WORKING BIBLIOGRAPHY

Start Early

Once a speech has been assigned and you have identified your topic, begin immediately to compile your research and supporting materials. Starting early gives you time to prepare, to think about your ideas and the materials your research has turned up, and to practice. When you start early enough, you avoid the tensions that accompany every kind of brinkmanship.

To illustrate just one of many problems brought on by procrastination, suppose you decide to talk about government farm subsidies but wait until the last moment to research your ideas. You go to the library, only to discover that three of the most important books you need are already checked out. You realize that you do not have time to recall those books, so you decide to interview a professor. You phone the professor, only to find that she is out of town and will not be returning until the day after you are to give your speech. You phone the local chamber of commerce, hoping to set up an interview, but the individual who can help you is out of his office and does not return your call.

Do not let this become your story, too. If you wish to develop a solid argument, you need solid information. That can take time. Start to gather your information early.

Generate a Preliminary Card File

As you browse through the holdings catalog, or as you are looking at *Reader's Guide* or *Psychological Abstracts,* you are sure to come across materials you may want to use. Make notes as you go of every book or article that seems relevant to your speech topic or that seems interesting to you. Include all the bibliographical information, as well as a brief annotation that will tell you, later, what is in the source. Include the call number if it is a book or the exact location of an article in a journal or magazine, including where in the library you can find the article. Write the information down carefully—then double-check it. Slow down enough to make your notes legible. Remember the rule: one entry per card, one card per entry. Figures 7.8 and 7.9 show two typical cards from a preliminary card file: Figure 7.8 is for a book; figure 7.9 is for a magazine article.

Evaluate Your Materials

In time, you will develop a second sense about the quality of the information you have located. Try to secure the most credible and worthwhile information you can. The better the evidence, the more credible the argument. But do not waste a lot of time checking the

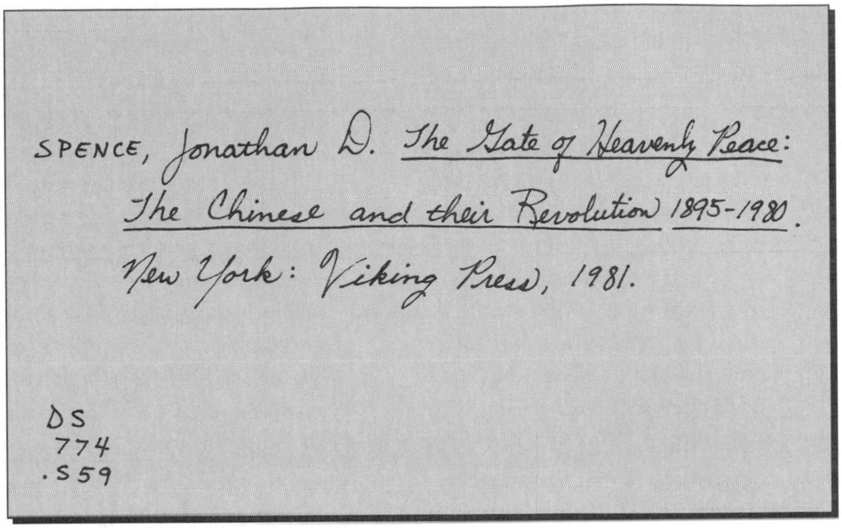

Figure 7.8

Bibliography card for a book.

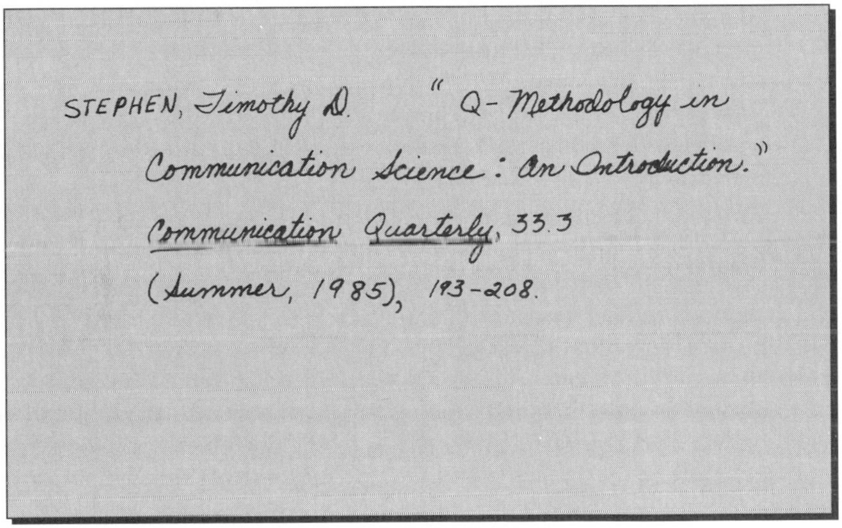

SPENCE, Jonathan D. *The Gate of Heavenly Peace: The Chinese and their Revolution 1895-1980*. New York: Viking Press, 1981.

DS
774
.S59

Figure 7.9

Bibliography card for a magazine article.

STEPHEN, Timothy D. " Q- Methodology in Communication Science : An Introduction." *Communication Quarterly*, 33.3 (Summer, 1985), 193-208.

quality of the materials if the information is not that important to your speech. If it is important, check it. If it is critical, check it with determination. Table 7.9 is a checklist of criteria that may help you to evaluate your sources.

HOW TO USE YOUR CARD FILE

Each note you take can change your outlook on your subject. As you study, new ideas, new connections, new questions pop into mind. Your speech may begin to take shape, but do not make a permanent decision yet. Play with your ideas a bit. The really fun part of speech preparation lies in this critical thinking stage.

Table 7.9

CRITERIA FOR EVALUATING RESOURCE MATERIALS

CRITERIA	DESCRIPTION	WHAT TO LOOK FOR
Primary or secondary?	Primary materials (manuscripts, diaries, newspaper articles, and certain books) have not been edited or altered by anyone other than the first author(s). Secondary materials are characterized by interpretation and evaluation. They often have been changed to reflect the second author's particular viewpoint.	If it is a newspaper clipping or an original manuscript, you probably have found primary material. If the author describes what an earlier author said about a subject, or cites another source to support the argument, you probably have got secondary material. Stay as close to the original source as you can.
Free from bias?	Few works remain completely objective. Authors may slant their material in a way that can damage the evidence and the credibility of your argument. For example, literature published by Green Peace on the subject of open-sea net fishing probably is biased. Taking a biased position is okay, as long as you know that you are doing so.	Look for editorial and evaluative language. Ask yourself if the author seems to be taking a single or one-sided point of view. Ask yourself what the author's cause may be and where the financial interests lie.
Author qualifications	Author qualifications can affect the quality of a source. For an obvious example, professors of communication may not be qualified to write competently about nuclear physics. A less obvious example that makes the point better: You would probably get a second opinion if a doctor recommended that your arm be amputated. If the information is important, the evidence must be solid. The better qualified the source, the more credible the evidence.	Check out the author's employment position. Is the author secretary of state? a professor? a hack writer? You can find a wealth of information in various biographical dictionaries and encyclopedias. If you interview the source, you can usually go by the person's position and the credibility of his or her organization. Professors and others might be willing to provide you with a curriculum vitae (a full description of professional accomplishments and activities).

The final speech assignment in a student's public speaking class was to develop a five- to six-minute speech that argued that someone should do something. The student decided to give a speech arguing that the university needed a new sports arena. He wrote the following thesis: "The university should build a new sports arena." The idea was popular on campus. He found much support for it among his friends on the basketball team and among the coaches. An article about the subject that appeared in the student newspaper also was supportive. The student interviewed the dean of students, who supported the idea. However, one evening after class, the student asked his personal finance professor what she thought about the idea of a new sports arena. She said that she was opposed to the idea and suggested that he look at the costs and benefits. "Examine the annual budgets of the university," she said. The student was surprised when she added: "Each year's budget is placed on permanent reserve in the library. All you have to do is ask."

As the student compared expenditures for different parts of the university across the past five years, the picture that emerged was troubling. The library allocation had not changed. His department's allocation had changed, but only a little. He found unfunded proposals for needed additions and expansions to several buildings. He found postponed requests for new faculty and for instructional equipment. Meanwhile, the athletic program budget had grown at a steady pace.

"Perhaps," the student thought, "the university should spend more money on academics and less on athletics." By the end of the week, he was convinced. He changed his speech focus from "The university should build a new sports arena" to "The university should double its allocation to the library."

This speech student used his research to reach an entirely different conclusion from what he had originally proposed. You can use your card file to take you through the same kind of critical thinking process as he used. First, sketch out your purpose statement, and write a tentative thesis sentence on a blank card. Write possible main ideas for the speech on note cards, one to a card. Lay the main idea cards out in a row and then experiment with arranging your supporting materials below these cards. Then ask yourself:

Do the ideas hang together?

Are they supported fully and completely?

Can I find any new or unusual or unexpected connections among the ideas and supporting materials I have laid out?

Do the ideas and supporting cards drive toward the specific purpose of my speech?

If I use this arrangement of ideas and evidence, will my audience be able to give me the goal I have in mind?

Summary

You can easily learn the skills involved in gathering supporting materials and using the library. And these skills have enormous value. Everything known in the world is available to you when you are willing to invest a little time learning to find it.

Begin by learning to use your connections—your personal network of family members, friends, colleagues, and so on. Information-gathering interviews and correspondence skills will provide you with much helpful information from these sources. Computerized database services and networks can open doors to a vast, rich, and ever-growing array of information resources if you have a computer with a modem.

Still, you cannot find a better intellectual resource than your school library. Libraries have predictable departments: reference, circulation, reserve readings, government documents, serials and periodicals, microform, instructional media, interlibrary loan, database searching, and specialized collections. No matter where these departments reside in your library, you can depend on their enormous volume of resources.

To find materials in the library, you must learn to use helpful reference tools. The holdings catalog indexes the materials in a given library or collection. It may take the form of a card catalog or an online catalog, both of which are easy to use. While a holdings catalog is a reference tool for finding information in books, general and specialized indexes are reference tools for accessing information in periodicals. Finally, librarians may be the best resource references in your library. Do not be afraid to ask for their help.

Research gathering involves taking notes from the different materials you examine and keeping a working bibliography of your various sources. Use note cards or half-sheets for your notes, establish a standard form of entry, use one card per entry and one entry per card, take plenty of notes, and be careful not to plagiarize, even unintentionally. Start early to develop your working bibliography, and begin with a preliminary card file. Evaluate your materials carefully to make sure that your sources are credible. Then use your card file to engage in critical thinking about your purpose statement, thesis, and supporting arguments.

Key Terms

Abstract	Index	Online catalog
Card catalog	Information-gathering	Plagiarism
Holdings catalog	interview	

Application Questions

1. Go to your college library and using the holdings catalog, look up the author *Sidney M. Jourard.* Does your library own anything by this author? Make a bibliography card for each work published in 1964 or 1971. Now, in the titles section, look up a book called *Word Play.* If your library owns this book, write a bibliography card. Now, in the subject catalog, see if your library owns a copy of Fred Kerlinger's book, *Foundations of Behavioral Research.* If so, write a bibliography card. Bring your bibliography cards to class. Compare your cards with those of other students. Are they exactly the same? Would you be able to find the works in the library by using other classmates' bibliography cards?

2. Some students enjoy the game of library hide-and-seek. Try to find answers to the questions that follow by researching in the library. Return to class and compare notes with other students. Where did you find the information? What questions were most difficult to answer? Why? Which ones were easiest to answer? Could you use the computer to help you? Can you draw any insights about using the library from this exercise?

Questions for Library Research:

a. When was *The Book of Mormon* first published?
b. What was in the news on June 6, 1944?
c. Who was Hetty Green?
d. What can you find out about a painting called *Les Demoiselles d'Avignon?*
e. How much money did the ransom note demand for the return of 20-month-old Charles A. Lindbergh, Jr., who was kidnapped in 1932?
f. Why did Truman fire MacArthur? When?
g. What was Marciano's knockout record?
h. What was Margaret Sanger noted for?
i. Who won the gold medal in women's high jump in the 1972 Olympics? How high did she jump? Where was she from?
j. Who was Gerald Ford's vice president?
k. Who directed *One Flew Over the Cuckoo's Nest?* Who played the leading role?
l. Did Ted Turner ever try to buy CBS?
m. What is the current rate of exchange between U.S. dollars and French francs?
n. What is Princess Di's dress size?
o. How fast did the last Triple Crown winner run at Belmont? How far? Which horse came in second?

Self-Test for Review

1. List the five steps involved in planning for an information-gathering interview.

   a. _____
   b. _____
   c. _____
   d. _____
   e. _____

2. What information can you get from The Source?

   _____
   _____

3. Match the following library departments with their descriptions.

   _____ a. Reference

   _____ b. Circulation

   1. Publications originating in or issued by federal, state, and local government agencies
   2. May be part of serials and periodicals department; responsible for storing back issues of newspapers and magazines, *Library of American Civilization,* and so on

_____ c. Reserve readings

_____ d. Government documents

_____ e. Serials and periodicals

_____ f. Microform

_____ g. Instructional media

_____ h. Interlibrary loan

_____ i. Database searching

_____ j. Specialized collections

3. Helps you borrow from more than one library

4. Maintains the library bookshelves and checks out materials

5. Computer searches in specific subject areas

6. Newspapers and magazines, some of which are bound and some of which are stored in microform

7. Biomedical collection, law collection, map collection, and so on

8. Materials set aside for special uses or classes; do not circulate for more than an hour or two at a time

9. Audio and visual materials, films, photographic archives, and so on

10. Location of encyclopedias, almanacs, directories, bibliographies, abstracts, indexes, and other works of general interest

4. Suppose you go to the holdings catalog, look up a book, and find the following call number:

   DS

   774

   S59

   What should you do next?

   a. Write down everything. This is the book's address.
   b. Write down "DS 774" and go to the stacks.
   c. Write down the author's name and the book title.
   d. Ask a librarian for help.

5. How would you go about finding what works by George Lakoff your library owns?

6. How would you find out who wrote the book: *Women, Fire, and Dangerous Things?*

7. Suppose you would like to read something about the connection between language categories and how people think. How would you find such a work?

Suggested Reading

Pournelle, Jerry, and Michael Banks. *Pournelle's PC Communications Bible: The Ultimate Guide to Productivity with a Modem.* Redmond, Wash.: Microsoft Press, 1992. The book title does not seem immodest when you actually hold this incredibly rich resource in your hands. Its 555 pages tell you more than you ever wanted to know about online services, including how to get started and a detailed discussion of the kinds of modems available, along with their strengths and weaknesses. It provides an overview of bulletin board systems and online services. It also names and provides access to all the major E-mail services, the major consumer online services, the major front-end services, and the major database and information-retrieval services.

PART 3

Organizing the Speech

CHAPTER 8

Organizing the Body of the Speech

OUTLINE

OBJECTIVES

After reading this chapter, you should be able to:

1. *Explain* why organization of a speech is important.
2. *Name* and *define* the characteristics of good organization.
3. *Identify, explain,* and *use* the following patterns for organizing a speech: (a) time, (b) space, (c) problem to solution, (d) causal order, (e) topical divisions, and (f) motivated sequence.
4. *Name* and *describe* the five steps of the motivated sequence.
5. *Define* and *use* the following organizational links: transitions, signposts, and internal summaries.

© Michael Hayman/Stock Boston

*T*he better organized you are in developing and presenting your speech ideas, the more effective your message will be. An organized speech also increases the probability that listeners will pay attention to and remember your main points.

In this chapter, you learn how good organization is characterized by a clear and simple format and basic language, emphasis on only a few main points, and reasonable and logical idea development. You also examine different organizational patterns for speeches. Speakers usually organize ideas by time or space; by movement from problem to solution, cause to effect, or effect to cause; according to natural topical divisions; or by following the five steps of the motivated sequence. This chapter also suggests ways of using organizational links, such as transitions, signposts, and internal summaries, to help tie together the major points of your speech.

As mentioned in chapter 2, "Planning the First Speech," every successful speech has three parts: an introduction, a body, and a conclusion. An introduction is the first part of a speech, and its purpose is to get audience attention, to state the speaker's intention, and to prepare listeners for what is coming. The body of the speech is the major portion of the speech, in which you develop and support the main ideas and arguments. The conclusion ends the speech and focuses listeners' thoughts and feelings on the speech's main ideas.

Throughout this chapter, emphasis is on organizing the *body* of the speech. Developing your introductions and conclusions is the focus of chapter 10, "Beginning and Ending a Speech."

> *"Wow! Dr. Feldman's lecture was fantastic this morning! He's really interesting and funny, too. Trouble is, later, I'm never quite sure how to round out my notes. Once I'm out of the lecture, the whole thing seems a blur. Just look at these notes. They're a jumble, and nothing seems to connect."*
>
> *"Yeah, I know," said another student. "I tried to take notes for a while, but I finally gave up. I just couldn't follow that guy. I always had to spend a lot of time figuring out what his point was."*

As Dr. Feldman's two students have implied, unless a speaker can organize ideas clearly and simply so listeners can follow, audience members will give up trying.

WHY ORGANIZATION IS IMPORTANT

Ideas and actions make more sense when they are clear and well organized. Organization in communication is critical. If ideas are in a jumble, how can listeners follow or understand them? Consider the following examples:

Poor: The major ideas about political campaigns that I want to discuss with this class are:

1. Why do we have political campaigns?
2. Barry Goldwater's campaign for president
3. How we should reform campaign financing

PEGGY NOONAN

To succeed as a speaker, you need to convince your audience that what you have to say is important enough to deserve their attention. Peggy Noonan, one of former President Ronald Reagan's most successful speech writers, tells how she learned to catch and *hold* the attention of an audience. Note that one of her first steps was to map out the narrative.

All speech writers have things they think of when they write. I think of being a child in my family at the dinner table, with seven kids and hubbub and parents distracted by worries and responsibilities. Before I would say anything at the table, before I would approach my parents, I

would plan what I would say. I would map out the narrative, sharpen the details, add color, plan momentum. This way I could hold their attention. This way I became a writer.

[Your listeners] are distracted by worries and responsibilities and the demands of daily life, and you have to know that and respect it—and plan the narrative, sharpen the details, and add color and momentum.

Source: Peggy Noonan, What I Saw at the Revolution: A Political Life in the Reagan Era *(New York: Random House, 1990). Photo © Diana Walker/Liaison International*

Better: The major ideas about political campaigns that I want to discuss with this class are:

1. Why do we have political campaigns?
2. How long do the campaigns last?
3. How do we pay for the campaigns?

The "poor" example has three somewhat unrelated points. "Why" we have political campaigns is a totally separate question from the presidential campaign of Barry Goldwater, and the desirability of campaign financing reform is an entirely separate issue that is not connected to the other two points.

The "better" set of major ideas is more logically and sensibly developed. Here, the speaker focuses on related issues. The sequence flows easily from why we have campaigns and their length to how they are financed. A speech like this is easy to follow and understand because the major ideas relate to each other and have a logical sequence.

Research indicates that an organized speech is easier to understand and makes a better impression than a disorganized one.[1] For example, a messy desk makes it more difficult to find the final draft of a term paper. However, if you put the paper in a folder, mark the folder, and place it in a clearly labeled location, you can find it more quickly. In the same way, listeners should not have to work hard to understand your arguments and ideas. Instead, your intentions and the logic of your presentation should be obvious.

When a speaker is well organized and appears to have a clearly determined destination, listeners are more willing and more likely to pay close attention. Good organization also helps listeners pay attention to what is important. It provides a "verbal road map" for audience members so they know where they have been, where they currently are, and where they are going. Since an audience is more likely to remember and understand a message that contains a few, well-supported ideas, a speech with clear and simple organization has an obvious advantage.

CHARACTERISTICS OF GOOD ORGANIZATION

Characteristics of good speech organization are: (1) The organization is clear and simple, (2) only a few main points are introduced, and (3) ideas are developed in a logical sequence.

CLEAR AND SIMPLE

An effectively organized speech has ideas that are easy to follow and simple in their thrust. The ideas point to an unmistakable message direction: One idea follows logically from the other so that listeners are not confused. The following is an example of organization that an audience can follow easily:

I.   Inflation makes your dollar worth less.

II.   Nearly all items cost more when we have high inflation.

This topic has just two main ideas, and the points are clearly stated. Listeners will understand what the speaker intends to say and should be able to follow the message easily.

Another aspect of clear and simple ideas is that the language used to express those ideas should be basic and easy to understand. For example:

I.   Wrestling is a dangerous sport.
   A.   Many wrestlers suffer head injuries.
   B.   Injuries to joints and bones are common.

II.   Children under age twelve should not wrestle competitively.

Here, the speaker uses simple language to make the point that wrestling is dangerous and that, for that reason, young children should not wrestle competitively. It is hard to get lost in this organization because it uses simple words and moves in an uncomplicated way through two major points.

FEW MAIN POINTS

Beginning speakers often try to do too much. They arrange a variety of ideas into a complex structure, and the audience soon wanders away. Audiences listen only if the speaker makes it easy for them to follow a few main points.

EXAMPLE 8.1	POOR AND BETTER STRUCTURES FOR A FIVE-MINUTE SPEECH

POOR	**BODY**
	
	I. Flags have an important place in our history.
	    A. How the American flag was developed
	    B. Betsy Ross produced the first flag.
	    C. Raising the flag at Iwo Jima
	II. Flags create strong personal reactions.
	    A. They stand for values and attitudes.
	       1. The American flag never dips.
	       2. Flag destruction is legal but controversial.

BETTER	**BODY**
	
	I. The flag is important to the United States.
	    A. We can trace American historical developments.
	       1. Betsy Ross made the first flag.
	       2. The number of stars has changed many times.
	    B. The flag reminds us of our heritage.
	       1. Fort Sumter and the flag are the heart of the national anthem.

Consider the outline for a five-minute speech presented in example 8.1. In the "poor" example, the idea behind the message is good, but complicated. The speaker is trying to do too much and has too many sub-ideas. The speech could be made simpler by talking about just a few major historical events involving the American flag since the American Revolution. The second major point and all of its supporting details could be easily dropped, as shown in the "better" alternative. In this outline, the organization is simpler, and unified ideas are easy to follow.

Effective speakers do not discuss five or six main ideas in a five-minute speech. Too many ideas cannot be thoroughly developed in the available time, and the audience probably will forget the first point before the speaker reaches the fifth. Listeners will remember one or two main ideas much more easily than they will five.

LOGICAL DEVELOPMENT

In addition to restricting the number of main points in your speech, you need to develop these main ideas in a reasonable and logical way. In the "better" outline in example 8.1, there is only one main idea, and the supporting ideas contribute clearly to that single point. The subpoints flow from the following statement: "The flag is important to the United States *because,* Each subpoint provides an explanation of *why* the major point is important or true. The supporting ideas should always help to answer the question "why?" They should give listeners reasons to accept and understand the major point. Notice the use of this principle in the outline in example 8.2.

EXAMPLE **8.2** **LOGICAL DEVELOPMENT OF IDEAS**

Specific Purpose: I want my listeners to know some of their rights as taxpayers if they are audited by the IRS.

Thesis Statement: You have important rights in an IRS audit of your tax return.

I. The IRS must conduct taxpayer interviews under specific guidelines.
   A. The agent must explain the audit process and taxpayer rights.
   B. If the taxpayer wants counsel, the interview must be halted until arrangements are made.

II. Levies may be used to collect unpaid taxes.
   A. The IRS must wait for thirty days after notification before seizing property.
   B. The sale proceeds cannot exceed the amount of tax deficiency.

Logical development of your main ideas increases the chance that your ideas will be understood and accepted by the audience. Keep the organizational framework simple: One idea should lead to another as obviously as the "One Way" sign points a direction on a street so that listeners will see where the message is going and find it easy to come along.

ORGANIZING THE BODY OF YOUR SPEECH

The structure of your speech depends, largely, on its content and purpose. There is no single "right" way to organize materials. Ask the following questions about any structure used in a speech:

1. Is this the best pattern for helping me to achieve my purpose?
2. Is this the best pattern for explaining the ideas in my message?
3. Does this pattern keep the material simple and clear?
4. Does this approach support my ideas with good argument?

If you can answer "Yes" to all of these questions, then you have chosen the best organizational pattern for your speech. The most common patterns for structuring speech materials are (1) time, (2) space, (3) problem-to-solution, (4) causal order, (5) topical divisions, or (6) motivated sequence.

TIME

Time refers to the organizational pattern that is based on some sequence of events. Time organizes our ideas from early to late, from the past to the present. A chronology of events is something we all understand. We know that there are sixty minutes in an hour, twenty-four hours in a day, twelve months in a year, and so forth. Speakers who organize materials in a time sequence set the information up on a time line. For example:

The presidential primaries begin first with the caucuses in Iowa. After that, the candidates go to primaries in states such as New Hampshire. Then, after the New

EXAMPLE 8.3

TWO CHRONOLOGICALLY ORGANIZED SPEECH OUTLINES

Outline 1

Specific Purpose: I want my listeners to know the major steps in developing black and white photographic film.

Thesis Statement: You can develop your own pictures at home, without a darkroom, if you're careful and follow these steps.

I. Develop the film in the canister for the time shown on the sheet of paper inside the film box.

II. "Stop" the developing process by using a diluted acid bath.

III. "Fix" the image on the film with liquid "fix."

IV. Wash the film and hang it up to dry, using a light weight to keep it from curling.

Outline 2

Specific Purpose: I want my listeners to know the basic steps in preparing a home garden.

Thesis Statement: Home gardening is easy.

I. First you must prepare the soil.
   A. Till and loosen it for planting.
   B. Rake it smooth and level.
   C. Mark the rows.

II. Next you must plant the seeds.
   A. Draw a three-inch-deep furrow.
   B. Place seeds and fertilizer in the furrow.
   C. Close the furrow.

> *England primaries, they may face the "Super Tuesday" primaries in the South and Midwest. This series of primaries usually ends with the big prize in California, the biggest state in the nation. When they've finished these primaries, the candidates then go to their party convention to nominate a presidential candidate.*

This description of the primary election process organizes the events chronologically, starting with the first primary. The description is organized in the same sequence as the events—day by day, week by week. It is much like the organization we use when we tell a story:

> *First, I went to the garage. While I was there, I talked with the mechanic about the noise in my circulating fan. Then I drove to the dorm and picked up my laundry. Next, I . . .*

In this description, the speaker relates events in the same order as they happened in time.

Example 8.3 shows two examples of outlines organized in chronological order. These outlines are for speeches to inform (see chapter 14, "Informative Speaking"), but

they also could be for speeches to demonstrate. In both of these types of speeches, chronology is an appropriate choice for organization.

By organizing a speech chronologically, you provide listeners with a familiar pattern that they can follow mentally. This helps audience members to keep track of what you have already said and to anticipate where you are going. You are much more likely to hold their attention if they understand your organizational pattern.

SPACE

Speeches also can be organized according to **space,** a pattern of organization that relies on geographical and spatial relationships, such as top to bottom, east to west, front to back, or side to side. The outlines in example 8.4 show the use of spatial relationship in organization.

PROBLEM TO SOLUTION

In public speaking, a **problem-to-solution organizational pattern** identifies a difficulty and then presents a solution that solves the problem. It is especially useful in showing people what is wrong and how the problem can be corrected. All of us use problem-to-solution patterns of organizational thinking daily—in doing dishes, studying for a test, or buying a new pair of shoes.

The first portion of a problem-to-solution organizational pattern involves showing the nature and size of the problem. The second part describes a workable solution.

EXAMPLE 8.4	TWO SPEECH OUTLINES THAT ARE ORGANIZED ACCORDING TO SPATIAL RELATIONSHIPS

Outline 1

Specific Purpose: I want my listeners to know how an architect plans academic buildings.

Thesis Statement: Architects plan the most utilitarian classroom buildings with you in mind.

I. The main function of a building gets first consideration.
   A. Classrooms and workspaces must accommodate the teaching/learning activities that will go on inside them.
   B. Food service and recreational space are placed as far away as possible from the work space.
II. Space for supporting functions must be convenient to the main functional spaces.
   A. Utility space and restrooms must be adjacent to both work space and recreational space.
   B. Storage space must be convenient to other spaces.
   C. Everything must be accessible from a central entry space.

Outline 2

Specific Purpose: I want my listeners to know which is America's most scenic highway.

Thesis Statement: You can take America's most scenic drive without ever leaving U.S. Highway 89.

I. In the north, you see Glacier National Park, Yellowstone National Park, and the Grand Tetons National Park.

II. About midway, you drive into the great canyon lands of America, including Bryce Canyon, Zion Canyon, Lake Powell, and the Grand Canyon.

III. Toward the south, you drive into the Painted Desert, through Oak Creek Canyon and Sedona, and onto the vast Sonoran Desert.

A sample outline for a speech using problem-to-solution organization is shown in example 8.5. A second sample of the problem-to-solution sequence of organization is shown in example 8.6. The speech outline is on the left, and the text of the speech appears on the right.

The problem-to-solution organizational approach is most suitable for persuasive speeches, in which you first identify a problem and then suggest a workable and useful solution. Persuasive speeches are discussed in greater detail in chapter 15, "Persuasive Speaking."

EXAMPLE 8.5 SPEECH OUTLINE WITH PROBLEM-TO-SOLUTION ORGANIZATION

Specific Purpose: I want each of my listeners to contribute fifty dollars to the student scholarship fund.

Thesis Statement: Many students are unable to continue their education because of the high cost of college.

I. College tuition costs are rising at approximately twice the rate of inflation.

II. Increased scholarship money would help to solve the financial problem of tuition for many worthy students.

EXAMPLE 8.6 OUTLINE AND SPEECH USING PROBLEM-TO-SOLUTION ORGANIZATION

Outline:

Specific Purpose: I want my listeners to write their state representatives and ask for support of improved mass transit systems for medium-sized cities.

Thesis Statement: Solving the transport problems of thousands of American cities will reduce pollution and traffic congestion.

I. Traffic jams and air pollution are serious problems in all American cities.

II. The best solution to these problems is the purchase of new buses and new minivans.

Brief Sample Speech

Traffic jams are one of the most serious problems in our major cities. In Chicago, it often takes 2½ hours to drive from the "Loop" to the near west suburbs in bumper-to-bumper traffic. Los Angeles has had a reputation for years of being one of the most traffic-clogged locations in the United States.

One result of all these cars, idling their engines in an urban traffic jam, is the accumulation of smog. We've all heard about the "smog alerts" in Los Angeles. The quality of air in New York, Philadelphia, Denver, Chicago, and even Seattle has been hurt seriously by the high level of traffic.

People must travel to their work in the downtown areas of major cities. But they don't all have to drive. We could improve our transportation systems quickly and cheaply through the purchase of new buses and minivans. Keep the rapid transit systems already in place. Add the buses and minivans to move people to the fast trains that will speed them downtown. If rapid transit is easy to use, people will choose it. In San Francisco, BART, the Bay Area Rapid Transit system, has been extremely popular because it moves people quickly from one urban area to another.

So this is a problem that can be solved. We need to encourage our officials to institute minivans and more bus routes on a trial basis to reduce the number of cars on city highways and to cut down the pollution that results.

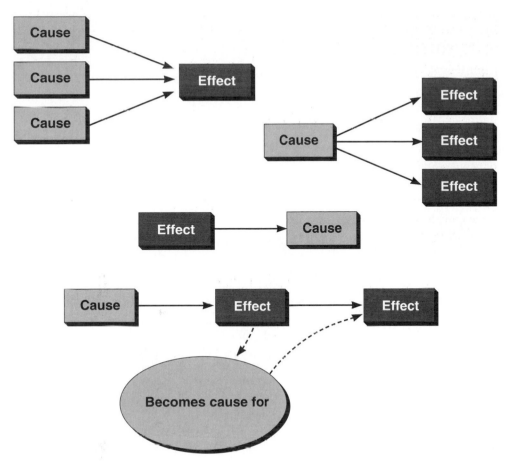

Figure **8.1**

Four variations of causal order pattern.

CAUSAL ORDER

Sometimes, neither time, space, nor problem-to-solution patterns seem applicable approaches for the speech you want to present. A common way of thinking in American culture, and therefore an excellent organizational pattern, is the **causal order pattern.** Figure 8.1 shows some of the possible ways of arranging causal order arguments.

A **cause-to-effect organizational pattern** helps an audience to see that one set of conditions is responsible for a result. People often link conditions with outcomes:

> I haven't gotten much sleep recently, and I caught a chill last night. No wonder I feel a cold coming on.

> People who invest wisely will have a large retirement "nest egg."

With a cause-to-effect pattern, you organize your material so that the cause is explained first and the second main point deals with the effects. A sample outline and speech using this approach is presented in example 8.7.

EXAMPLE **8.7**   SAMPLE OUTLINE AND SPEECH USING
CAUSE-TO-EFFECT ORGANIZATION

Outline

Specific Purpose: I want my listeners to get a flu shot before winter begins.

Thesis Statement: Go to the school clinic or to your family doctor and get a flu shot.

I.   Each winter, millions of people contract viruses through coughs, sneezes, or by breathing the exhaled breath of others.

II. These viruses can cause the flu unless these people have received a shot that makes them resistant to the "bug."

Brief Sample Speech

Millions of people across the country and many in this room will get the flu this winter. You'll get it from the sneezes of others or by breathing in the germs from their coughs. Just by being in a closed area, like a theater or a meeting room, you breathe the air these "sick" people exhale. You then are "at risk" of catching the flu.

Ever wonder why so many people catch the flu in the winter? It's because people are indoors and the temperature outside is so low that the viruses creep inside and thrive. The most casual contact passes the virus from one person to another.

It doesn't have to be this way. You can still have contact with others, but take a simple precaution. Go to the health clinic or your family physician and ask for a flu shot. It's simple and inexpensive. In most cases, people who get flu shots either won't get influenza or they'll have only a mild case. Even a mild case is better than spending a week in bed with a pounding headache and a body that feels like it's under a steamroller.

So go to the clinic or your doctor today. You'll be glad you did when you see the sunken, dark eyes of your friends who didn't bother to get their shots.

An effective alternative to the cause-to-effect pattern is the **effect-to-cause** sequence. With this pattern, you deal with the consequence first and then proceed to the cause. A sample outline and brief speech using effect-to-cause organization is shown in example 8.8.

Both causal patterns—cause-to-effect and effect-to-cause—are common and appropriate for either informative or persuasive speeches (see chapter 14, "Informative Speaking," and chapter 15, "Persuasive Speaking"). Central to both of these causal patterns is the requirement that, if the cause is removed, then the effect is eliminated.

EXAMPLE 8.8   SAMPLE OUTLINE AND SPEECH USING
EFFECT-TO-CAUSE ORGANIZATION

Outline

Specific Purpose: I want my listeners to know the effect that technology has on our society.

Thesis Statement: Advances in technology are seriously damaging the humanity of the world.

I.   Television, computers, airplanes, and satellites have destroyed many of the close relationships between people.

II. Impersonal technology reduces the amount of direct contact people have with friends, relatives, neighbors, and business associates.

Brief Sample Speech

We've become so technologically oriented that, sometimes, we forget we're people. We sit in front of a TV set and just watch. We turn on our radios and "soak up some tunes." People retreat to their computers and let transistors and circuits give them messages. The great reliance we have on technology makes us become more impersonal. We don't need others because we have our computers for entertainment, our TV for news, and our radios to listen to others talk. But we aren't a talking society much anymore.

It's not so necessary for us to talk with our neighbors when we can get the news from television, radio, or on the computer. Why, people ask, should I ask my insurance salesperson about my auto policy when I can get information from my home computer or watch an "infomercial" on TV about buying insurance and saving money?

Let me ask you one question: When you have to have personal attention, how well will that "infomercial" serve you? It can't answer your Sunday call, contact the claims department, or counsel you about any possible rate increase. Consider the kinds of bonds we create when we talk with people. They understand us, and we appreciate them. Think about that the next time you decide to kill time by watching TV or turning on the radio. Make a friend. Talk to someone.

TOPICAL DIVISIONS

Sometimes, the natural **topical divisions** of a subject suggest a method for dividing the topic into manageable units. For example, a speech about the human body might be organized around the various body systems: skeletal, circulatory, respiratory, muscular, nervous, and so on. A speech about football that is organized according to topical divisions might include information on the basic equipment worn by players and the purpose

EXAMPLE 8.9

Example 8.9   SPEECH OUTLINE ORGANIZED BY TOPICAL DIVISIONS

Specific Purpose: I want my listeners to understand the effects that running a marathon has on some key parts of the body.

Thesis Statement: When you run a marathon, certain parts of your body have abnormal needs.

I. Your respiratory system must operate efficiently to provide enough oxygen for your blood and your heart.

II. Your cardiovascular system must pump nearly twice the normal amount of blood to all portions of your body.

III. The muscles of your body burn most of the stored glycogen and require regular liquid replenishment during the race.

of each item. Or, if you wanted to talk about the effects that running a marathon has on the body, your topical divisions organization might resemble the outline in example 8.9.

Figure 8.2 shows another example of topical division. A student first drew the pattern, or "scatter diagram," and then worked from that diagram to create the outline. While neither the diagram nor the outline are perfect, they clearly illustrate organization by topical division.

MOTIVATED SEQUENCE

Alan H. Monroe developed the **motivated sequence,** a pattern for organizing persuasive speeches (see chapter 15, "Persuasive Speaking") during the mid-1930s.[2] This pattern works because it follows a predictable pattern of thinking that is common in American society. The motivated sequence has five sequential steps, as shown in table 8.1.

Attention Step

The attention step is designed to gain the attention of listeners. The response you want from your audience is something like: "I really want to listen to this person." One speaker got listeners' attention with the following:

> *I'll bet that many of you are listening to music using a recording system that is over eleven years old. Compact discs first came on the market in 1983, but many people still listen to music on audiotape. Why should you be interested in CDs? Let me explain how a CD is made and why it gives more realistic sound.*

CDs are not a new topic, but the speaker is attempting to put a novel "spin" on the subject to get listeners' attention. Most people probably do not know how record companies make a compact disc or why a compact disc provides more realistic sound. So their curiosity involves them in the speech and makes them want to listen to the message.

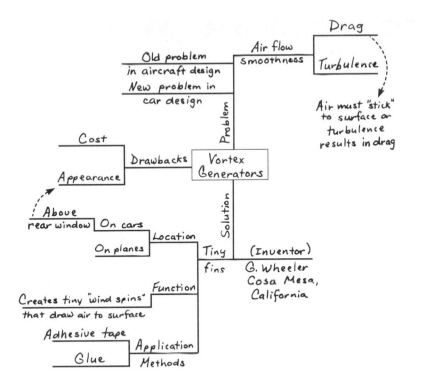

Figure **8.2**

A pattern, later developed into an outline, showing possible divisions of a topic.

VORTEX GENERATORS
Discussion

I. The problem we must solve is called "drag."
   A. Air must "stick" to the surface of a car, or else the turbulence results in "drag."
   B. Drag is an old problem in aircraft design.
   C. Drag is a new problem in automobile design.
II. The solution to drag is called "vortex generators."
   A. Vortex generators were invented by G. Wheeler of Cosa Mesa, California.
   B. Vortex generators are tiny fins that create tiny "wind spins."
   C. Vortex generators are placed above the rear window on a car.
   D. Vortex generators are glued or taped on.
III. Vortex generators do have two important drawbacks.
   A. One drawback is the added cost of the car.
   B. Another drawback is the appearance of the vortex generator.

Table 8.1

SEQUENTIAL STEPS IN THE MOTIVATED SEQUENCE

Step in the Motivated Sequence	Function
1. Attention step	1. Gets the attention of the audience for the speaker and the subject
2. Need step	2. Provides listeners with a reason to listen; may identify and prove that a problem exists
3. Satisfaction step	3. Gives the audience information and solves any proven problems
4. Visualization step	4. Helps listeners to "see" themselves in the situation—solving the problem or performing the action
5. Action step	5. Asks listeners to take the action outlined in the satisfaction and visualization steps

Need Step

The need step describes or defines a problem or demonstrates that the audience has a need for the speech you are about to give. It gives listeners additional reasons to want to listen to you.

One way to develop a need in listeners is to tie your topic to issues that directly affect all of your listeners. For example:

> *Our national debt is out of control! Many of you may think that subject is one that is overexaggerated and overdiscussed. Let me try to describe the size of this problem. While I'm speaking today, the national debt will increase by over five million dollars. Just in these few minutes, the United States will owe as much additional money as five of you will earn in your lifetimes. Five lifetimes of earnings! Doesn't that scare you just a little? Folks, we have a huge problem if we increase our national debt at about a million dollars a minute. That's way over a billion dollars a day. No person or country can afford to live that way. It's your debt, and you have to pay for it!*

Most listeners would not have a problem understanding that a million dollars a minute is a rapid increase and that the United States has a problem when it goes "in the hole" at this rate. Now listeners are prepared for the speaker to tell them more about the details of the problem. Arguments, support, and proofs must follow.

This salesperson uses the motivated sequence developed by Alan H. Monroe. Which step in the sequence do you suppose is being presented here? How can you tell?

© Bob Coyle

When the goal of your speech is to convince an audience of a problem, only the first two steps of the motivated sequence, attention and need, are involved. A speaker who intends to show how the problem can be solved will present the third step: satisfaction.

Satisfaction Step

The purpose of the satisfaction step is to show how the problem described in the need step can be solved. In solving the problem (or satisfying the need), explain that the solution is desirable, fits the problem, and will not create new difficulties. For example:

The easiest way to avoid problems with your car is to have regular maintenance. No, that's not just some game the manufacturer suggests to make more money. An oil change and new filter every five thousand miles keep your valves and cylinders from wearing too much. Those maintenance checks also often show problems about to happen. In our "high-tech cars," the mechanic may see that a belt is wearing, a hose is leaking, or a wiper is worn. Many accidents happen because the power steering fluid has leaked out, the brakes failed for the same reason, or the driver couldn't see the road in the rain.

There's an ad that used to run on TV. The Fram Corporation filmed a spot showing a mechanic holding a Fram filter and saying, "You can pay me now, or you can pay me later." He had just finished talking about regular oil and filter changes. Believe him. An oil and filter change cost about eighteen dollars. A new engine costs between twelve hundred and five thousand dollars. Easy choice!

In this example, listeners learn that the problem of car breakdown can be solved and that they will save money and protect their investment if they have their car serviced regularly.

Visualization Step

The purpose of the visualization step is to get listeners to "see" in their mind's eye the consequences of their choices. For example, if you want listeners to buy a product, they must be able to visualize the pleasure and satisfaction that accompanies this purchase:

Picture yourself in your apartment with that new CD player and the latest disc. You'll hear sharp sounds that are like those in a concert hall. The bass will boom out. The woofer and the tweeter will work in ways you only dreamt. See yourself wrapped in the sounds of your favorite song. Imagine what it would be like to have your favorite vocalist giving you a concert in your apartment. Invite them on a CD. There's nothing closer to music reality.

Action Step

After you have attracted listeners' attention, created and satisfied need, and encouraged listeners to visualize themselves in the situation you describe, you use the action step of the motivated sequence to get listeners to agree with you or to perform the action suggested. The speaker's goal is to get the audience to say, "Yes, I'll do what you suggest," or "I believe you." For example:

After the terrorist bombing of the World Trade Center, we must prevent vans and trucks from entering underground parking garages. We've been an open society for many years, but we're too lax now. It's cost us our security and some innocent human lives. For safety's sake, it's going to cost us some of our freedom of movement.

Like Great Britain, we must make it illegal to park cars or vans near public buildings. We have to take steps to keep international madmen from killing more innocent people. Join in the national crusade to "Stamp Out Terrorism."

During the action step, you should also clarify the action you want listeners to take:

So, plan to go to Augusta, Georgia, in the spring. See the azaleas, the dogwood, the redbud. See the greatest golfers in the world playing in a tournament with the most prestige possible. If you take just one day from your schedule to go to Georgia, you'll walk the Augusta National Golf Club with such greats as Jack Nicklaus, Ben Hogan, Arnold Palmer, and Sam Snead. You can walk the fifteenth hole, where Gene Sarazen scored his incredible double eagle on his way to victory in the Masters.

It's a trip through history. It's a treat to the eye. No one plays here except by invitation. You have that once in a lifetime chance. Yes, tickets cost a hundred dollars, but how much is it worth to see the best in the world? Save two dollars a week for a year, and treat yourself to the greatest tournament in golf in nature's most magnificent setting next April.

I urge you to go to the Masters next year. For anyone remotely interested in golf, this is the ultimate fantasy: "seeing the Masters live." Winning the Masters is so important to pro golfers that the prize money is incidental. It's the pride. Share the pride. See the Masters.

In this example, there is little question about the desired action. If you develop and organize your speech clearly and help listeners to understand what you want them to do, they will be more likely to act on your words.

ORGANIZATIONAL LINKS

The parts of a message need to be tied together in a coherent way. A speech may have only two main points, but the movement from the first to the second must be smooth. The relationship of one point to the other also must be clear. Similarly, the speech introduction must have an obvious relationship to the body of the speech, and the speaker must tie the conclusion to the speech's main ideas. (See chapter 10, "Beginnings and Endings," for more detailed discussion of introductions and conclusions.) If that harmony is missing, the speech sounds wrong. Unity of ideas is essential.

Organizational links tie a speech together and keep listeners headed in the right direction. You can make your ideas more understandable and your organization more effective with the use of the following organizational links: transitions, signposts, and internal summaries.

TRANSITIONS

Transitions are verbal bridges designed to move listeners from consideration of one idea to consideration of the next. They tie major ideas together, focus attention, keep the speech interesting, and weld the various parts of the speech into a single unit. Indeed, the best speeches are characterized as much by effective transitions as they are by strong arguments or emotional appeals.

To use transitions well, you must have a repertory of techniques and types. Otherwise, you risk falling into the habit of saying the same thing over and over. "My next idea is . . ." may be an effective transitional statement once, but if used two or three times, will put listeners to sleep.

Here are examples of different types of transitions:

Besides being slow-moving, cricket *also* is a very complicated sport.

Although some people would argue that history is boring, let me show you how it helps us to understand what the future holds.

Meanwhile, people ignore the slaughter on our highways.

Those are the two main problems. *Now, let's see how they can be solved.*

Finally, look at the three simple techniques you can use in writing a letter of application.

To summarize, we have the three elements for violence in all our major cities.

SIGNPOSTS

Another way to alert listeners to an important point you are about to introduce is through signposts. A **signpost** is a unit of speech that announces or points to some new or important idea. Sometimes, a signpost is merely a number. At other times, it takes the form of a direct question, or it may highlight a key idea. Here are some examples of each type:

Hold onto this idea.

The thing to remember is . . .

The first major objection . . .

The third and final problem . . .

Try to remember this!

How can we best manage this financial crisis?

In a speech with three major points, you might say, for example, *"The first reason we should be interested in ozone depletion is . . ."* As the speech progresses, you could introduce the next points by saying: *"The second problem associated with ozone loss is . . ."* and *"Third, and finally, ozone loss affects us because . . ."* This approach announces the introduction of new ideas and keeps audience members aware of the idea sequence. Signposts make speeches easier to follow and help listeners to identify and remember major ideas.

INTERNAL SUMMARIES

Listeners need to be reminded frequently of the ideas you have discussed. **Internal summaries,** sometimes called mini-summaries, are an effective way of doing that. Internal summaries are often used at the conclusion of a major point in a speech. A speaker might say:

As I said, there are several ways to stop groundwater pollution. First, . . .

So you can see, worker attrition isn't an easy way to slow the growth of government.

For this reason alone, televised football games provide a large source of revenue for athletic departments.

Fire can spread through a house very rapidly. You need to remember that smoke detectors will warn you. Next, . . .

Internal summaries help listeners to keep track of the flow of ideas and the significance of the major points. Listeners' memory spans are short. The internal summary is another useful organizational link that helps to assure that your message is heard, understood, and remembered.

Summary

Effective organization of ideas is critical to successful public speaking. When you are well organized and appear to have a clearly determined destination, listeners are more willing and more likely to pay close attention. In addition, listeners who can follow your message easily will also be able to recall and act upon your major ideas.

A well-organized speech is clear and simple; only a few main points are introduced, and ideas are developed in a logical sequence. A good speaker must be able to select the most appropriate organizational pattern and then place major ideas and supports within that structure. The best-known and most frequently used organizational patterns are time, space, problem to solution, causal order, and topical divisions. A sixth organizational pattern—motivated sequence—works primarily for persuasive speeches and has five steps: (1) attention, (2) need, (3) satisfaction, (4) visualization, and (5) action.

Organizational links, such as transitions, signposts, and internal summaries, offer bridges between ideas, tie a speech together, and point out significant ideas. Effective use of these organizational links helps to assure that your message is heard, understood, and remembered.

Key Terms

Causal order organizational
  pattern
Cause-to-effect
  organizational pattern
Effect-to-cause
  organizational pattern
Internal summaries

Motivated sequence
Organizational links
Problem-to-solution
  organizational pattern
Signposts
Space pattern of
  organization

Time pattern of
  organization
Topical divisions
  organizational pattern
Transitions

Application Questions

1. Describe to a group of friends how to get from home to work. What organizational pattern did you use in your description? Ask your friends to tell you how successful your description seemed. How could you have provided better directions?
2. With a group or the class, identify a course and a professor you particularly enjoy. What are the characteristic elements of organization this professor uses for the course materials? What did you learn from this exercise that you can use in your own speaking?
3. Working with a classmate, select a television commercial that you find attractive. If possible, audiotape or videotape the commercial. Then try to identify how the commercial was organized. That is, does the commercial follow any of the

organizational patterns and strategies described in this chapter? If so, which? Why do you think so? If not, how was the commercial organized? What inferences can you draw from this study? Be prepared to discuss this exercise with your class.

Self-Test for Review

1. A *signpost* is
   a. a major subject heading in an outline.
   b. a unit of speech that announces a new or important idea.
   c. a transition.
   d. a main idea and its subordinate points.
   e. *a* and *d*

2. A *transition* is
   a. a main idea.
   b. a verbalized pause between key ideas.
   c. a signpost.
   d. a bridge between key ideas.

3. List the names of the six major organizational patterns discussed in this chapter.
   a. _____
   b. _____
   c. _____
   d. _____
   e. _____
   f. _____

4. Which organizational patterns are most appropriate for speeches to persuade?

5. "Drive to the second light. Turn left on Wilson Boulevard and go five blocks. You'll come to . . ." is an example of which organizational pattern?

6. Suppose the following problem: You think that things are satisfactory the way they are, but you would like to see a change to create a benefit that is not possible at present. What would be the best way to organize your speech?

Answers: 1. b. 2. d. 3. a. time, b. space, c. problem to solution, d. causal order, e. topical divisions, f. motivated sequence. 4. problem-to-solution pattern and motivated sequence. 5. space. 6. problem-to-solution pattern.

Suggested Readings

Crescimanno, Russell. *Culture, Consciousness, and Beyond: An Introduction*. Washington, D.C.: University Press of America, 1982. This book concentrates primarily on how language structures the mind—how the reality of everyday life is really a social creation. It considers the more intuitive, holistic way of knowing the world that is a function of the right side of the brain. This reference is included here to provide perspective to the idea that, ultimately, organizing ideas for a speech works best when it relates to the perceptual and intellectual needs of listeners.

Welch, Natalie. *"Inspiration* Lets Users Organize, Show Off Their Bright Ideas Faster: Version 4.0 Improves Outlining, Charting." *Macweek,* 9 November 1992, 8. Computer programs to assist speakers in organizing and refining their ideas are now available to the general public. As more sophisticated approaches to the development of ideas spread in the software community, a flow of programs that will assist both the novice and experienced speaker are likely.

CHAPTER 9

Outlining the Speech

OUTLINE

OBJECTIVES

After reading this chapter, you should be able to:

1. *Compare* and *contrast* planning outlines and speaking outlines.
2. *Describe* the steps in developing a planning outline.
3. *Develop* a planning outline.
4. *Describe* the steps in developing a speaking outline.
5. *Develop* a speaking outline.

© *Bob Daemmrich/Stock Boston*

*C*hapter 8, "Organizing the Body of the Speech," examined the types of organizational strategies that would work best for you in a particular situation. This chapter focuses on how to develop and use two tools that simplify the organizing task: (1) planning outlines and (2) speaking outlines.

Outlines are useful tools in planning and delivering a speech. An outline provides a speaker with a framework for idea development. A planning outline helps in determining the most appropriate organizational sequence for presenting a particular topic to a given audience. It is more detailed than the speaking outline because it labels the main parts of the speech, describes subpoints, and shows relationships between major ideas. A speaking outline is helpful when the speaker actually delivers the speech. Much briefer than a planning outline, the speaking outline's only purpose is to provide cues that help the speaker to stay on track during the speech.

Suppose you wanted to drive cross-country to a place you have never been before. Would you start out without referring to a road map? Probably not, because to a large extent, the ease and convenience of your trip depends on the road map's accuracy, clarity, and simplicity. In fact, without a road map, you are likely to get lost.

A carefully developed speech outline is like a road map. The stronger the outline's internal structure, the stronger the speech will be. The more clearly your ideas are related to each other, the more easily listeners will follow them. When your purpose is well focused and your ideas drive toward the purpose, listeners are much more likely to arrive at their final destination—the end of your speech—with an understanding of where they have been and what you would like them to do now.

TYPES OF SPEECH OUTLINES

As mentioned in previous chapters, all speeches should have three major parts: an introduction, a body, and a conclusion. The introduction draws audience attention to the speaker and the speech topic, helps listeners to identify the central idea of the speech, and prepares listeners for what you are about to say. The body of the speech lays out the arguments and evidence that establish and support your thesis statement. The conclusion of the speech summarizes the key ideas and provides listeners with a final, upbeat, motivated impetus to think or act as you want them to do. Each of the three parts of a speech should be outlined.

An **outline** consists of written phrases or sentences that show the structure or arrangement and relationships among ideas. An outline provides you with a framework for developing ideas and a means for double-checking that all ideas are adequately supported and contribute toward your speaking goal. Like a blueprint, an outline shows how the parts fit together and thus is a good tool for planning how the ideas in a speech will relate to each other. Developing an outline helps you to see clearly what supporting materials you need. In addition, any necessary reorganization is easier to see and accomplish using an outline.

A **planning outline** is a working document in which you develop the structure and relationships among your ideas and the evidence that supports them. Many speech teachers ask students to submit a planning outline so that the teachers can compare what students planned against what students presented. Such comparisons help teachers to specify how their students can improve their speeches. Be sure to check whether your speech instructor has any special outline or format requirements.

A **speaking outline** is a very brief outline of the topics you will discuss and is usually derived from the planning outline. Its purpose is to provide you with notes you can refer to as you speak.

DEVELOPING THE PLANNING OUTLINE

The planning outline must be developed before the speaking outline and requires much more time, research, and critical thinking. For that reason, the bulk of this chapter focuses on how to develop a planning outline.

Steps involved in developing a planning outline include: (1) labeling the major parts; (2) using a standard outline format; (3) writing the general purpose, specific purpose, and thesis statement; (4) supporting main ideas with subpoints; (5) following an organizational pattern; (6) using simple sentences and action verbs; (7) planning organizational links; and (8) including supporting evidence and documentation.

Example 9.1 shows a partial planning outline. Supporting materials have been dropped from the outline to highlight the relationships among ideas, but the words *Supporting evidence* indicate where this material was placed in the original outline.

LABEL THE MAJOR PARTS OF THE OUTLINE

Within your outline, label the introduction, the body, and the conclusion as separate parts. This guarantees that you will plan and include all three in your speech. Each part label should appear prominently in your outline. Some instructors want them in the center of the page. Others prefer that they be aligned on the left-hand margin. This chapter assumes a preference for centered part labels. Find out what your instructor prefers and follow that preference consistently.

Introduction

Under the centered label *Introduction,* include such subtitles as *Opening, Thesis statement, Preview,* and *Transition.* Other possible subtitles are *Importance, Definition,* and *Name,* as you will see in some of the examples in this chapter. Which of these labels you include will depend entirely on your speech.

The opening should be designed to draw listeners' attention. A startling statement of opinion, a reference to one of the audience members or to the common experience of the audience, or even the simple greeting: "Good morning, ladies and gentlemen. My name is _____ " will gather listeners' attention. The thesis statement tells listeners what you want from them or what you plan to discuss. The preview—a brief description of your analysis, a hint at the main ideas—is sometimes included to provide a quick overview your listeners will find helpful. A transition is a sentence or two designed to move listeners

EXAMPLE **9.1**

EXAMPLE PLANNING OUTLINE
(This outline is presented by permission of Heather Davis.)

LET WOMEN SERVE AS COMBAT PILOTS

INTRODUCTION

Opening: Good morning, class. My name is Heather Davis. I'm in the Coast Guard. I fly a Coast Guard jet. I'd like to be a combat pilot, but right now I'm not allowed, just because I'm a woman.

Thesis statement: The argument that women pilots should not be allowed to fly combat missions is groundless.

Preview: Opponents argue along four lines of analysis, none of which makes any sense. They say women don't fly as well as men, that women can't handle the stress of dangerous combat missions, that women can't handle exposure to the bloody results of warfare, and that women should not be exposed to rape, torture, and the like, that might result if a woman pilot was downed in enemy territory.

Transition: I'd like you to consider each of these four arguments, one at a time.

BODY

I. **Main idea:** The idea that women don't fly as well as men is groundless. *(because)*
    A. Women pilots take the same training as men. [Supporting evidence]
    B. Women pilots pass the same physical and intellectual tests as men. [Supporting evidence]
    C. Women pilots have fitness ratings that are equal or superior to their male counterparts. [Supporting evidence]

Transition: Given these facts, surely no one can seriously argue that women don't fly as well as men. Maybe that's why we so often hear a second groundless argument.

II. **Main idea:** The argument that women can't handle the stress of dangerous combat missions doesn't make any sense. *(because)*
    A. Women presently fly in dangerous situations that require them to handle high levels of stress. [Supporting evidence]
    B. Women in general are known to handle stress better than men. [Supporting evidence]

Transition: So far, then, we've seen that women fly as well as men and that we can handle stress and danger. See what is happening to the position that women shouldn't be allowed to fly combat? There is a third groundless argument.

III. **Main idea:** The idea that women can't handle exposure to the blood and gore of warfare is silly. *(because)*
    A. Women have been exposed to the blood and gore of warfare since warfare began. [Supporting evidence]
    B. Women have worked successfully in similar circumstances outside of the theatre of war. [Supporting evidence]

EXAMPLE **9.1**   CONTINUED

Transition: It's clear, then, that women pilots can handle the bloody consequences of battle. This argument just doesn't hold up. What about the fourth argument?

IV. **Main idea:** The idea that women should not be exposed to rape, torture, and the like seems irrelevant. *(because)*
   A. No one, regardless of sex, should be exposed to rape, torture, and other forms of violence.
   B. Any downed pilot faces exposure to interpersonal violence. [Supporting evidence]
   C. All combat pilots freely choose exposure to interpersonal violence at the hands of their enemies if they are downed.
   D. Women are fully as capable of making that choice as are men.

CONCLUSION

Summary: In summary, then, it's clear that women should be allowed to fly combat missions. We fly as well as men. We handle stress as well or better than men. We have a long history of exposure to the consequences of battle and a successful record of service in professions where that exposure is commonplace. Finally, the risks of being shot down seem equally awful, regardless of gender. Both men and women have to make choices about whether they will accept those risks. It hasn't anything to do with sex.

Closing: Inevitably, you must come to the conclusion that women pilots should be allowed to fly combat missions. There simply aren't any substantial arguments against the idea.

[Note: This speech was delivered during the spring term of 1993. In mid-May of that year, Defense Secretary Les Aspin ordered the military services to drop restrictions on women flying combat missions.]

smoothly from the introduction to the body of the speech. It might be as simple as, "So, let's consider the first part of the problem we are facing. We don't have enough space to do what we are supposed to do." In this example, the first sentence is the transition, and the second sentence is the first main idea in the body.

Example 9.2 shows a sample introduction outline. Notice how each of the parts has been labeled.

Body

It makes sense to outline the *body* of your speech before you outline the *introduction* and the *conclusion*. The body of the speech includes all the main lines of analysis and all of your supporting evidence and arguments. As long as you have a clear idea of your thesis statement, develop the body outline first. From it, you might be able to draw ideas for the introduction. Certainly, you will need the body outline before you can outline the conclusion.

In this chapter, most of the discussion focuses on guidelines for outlining the body of the speech. You can read more about introductions and conclusions in chapter 10, "Beginning and Ending a Speech."

INTRODUCTION

Opening: As I drove here today, I was struck by the evidence of wealth that surrounds us just before Christmas. People were rushing about doing their last-minute shopping, arms filled with packages. We are told by the Downtown Merchants' Association that this is going to be a record-breaking year in retail sales. But not everyone in this country is so lucky.

Thesis statement: Today, within just a few miles of where we sit, there are people who desperately need our help if they are going to have any Christmas at all.

Preview: I am going to ask you to make a Christmas gift before you leave this room—a gift of caring that will do more good than all of those presents you will place under your own Christmas tree.

Transition: But first, I would like to tell you a true story.

CONCLUSION

Summary: In summary, not everyone will be able to enjoy Christmas this year. But you can help.

I. Nearly one-fifth of the people in Cedar Suburbs are living at or near the poverty level.

II. When income is sufficient only for food and shelter, people can't afford to buy special gifts and decorations.

III. Most of us are not aware that some people living near us lack the finances to celebrate one of our traditional holidays. They can't afford a gift exchange or even a tree.

IV. Often, we fail to realize our own good fortune.

Closing: The next time you think life is rough, pause and consider how you will celebrate this holiday. Ask yourself if the chances you have for gift giving are shared by everyone in the community. Isn't sharing what this season is all about? And will you share?

Conclusion

Under the centered label *Conclusion* in your outline, include such subtitles as *Summary* and *Closing*. The summary is a brief recapitulation of the main ideas that you developed in the speech. The closing is a statement designed to focus listeners' thinking and feelings on what you have said or what you want them to do. Example 9.3 shows a sample conclusion outline.

EXAMPLE **9.4**   A STANDARD OUTLINE SYMBOL AND
INDENTATION PATTERN

INTRODUCTION

Opening

Thesis statement

Transition

BODY

I.   **Main idea**
   A. First subpoint
      1. First sub-subpoint
         a. Supporting evidence
         b. Supporting evidence
      2. Second sub-subpoint
   B. Second subpoint

Transition

II. **Main idea**
   A. First subpoint
      1. First sub-subpoint
         a. Supporting evidence
         b. Supporting evidence
      2. Second sub-subpoint
   B. Second subpoint

Transition

CONCLUSION

Summary

Closing

USE A STANDARD OUTLINE FORMAT

Follow a standard outlining format, like the one used in the examples in this chapter. Separate the body from the introduction and conclusion. Identify the main points of your speech with Roman numerals, the subpoints with capital letters, the sub-subpoints with Arabic numerals, and the supporting evidence with lowercase letters. Indent each level consistently to prevent confusion as you flesh out your ideas. No absolute rule limits the number of subpoints and sub-subpoints you can have, but common sense prescribes not going beyond three or four indentations.

Example 9.4 shows a standard outline symbol and indentation pattern. Notice how indentations suggest the relative importance of particular ideas. Do not indent main ideas. Clarifying and supporting materials are indented according to their significance: The less significant the idea, the greater the indentation. Consistent use of the same outline pattern will eliminate a good deal of confusion.

WRITE THE GENERAL PURPOSE, THE SPECIFIC PURPOSE, AND THE THESIS STATEMENT

To review from chapter 4, "Selecting and Narrowing Your Topic," a general purpose is to inform, to entertain, or to persuade. The specific purpose is what you want to accomplish with your speech—the action goal or the particular response you want from listeners. The thesis statement is the sentence in the speech introduction that states your most important point or purpose. Write these out before you begin to outline the body of the speech. Double-check that the thesis statement does not carry more than one idea and that it implies an action. Refer back to chapter 4 for additional guidelines for developing your general purpose, specific purpose, and thesis statements.

SUPPORT THE THESIS STATEMENT WITH MAIN IDEAS AND SUBPOINTS

Use the *because* **test** to determine that all your main ideas support the thesis statement and that all your subpoints support the main ideas. The *because* **test** is merely a technique to help you identify the appropriate level of subordination. To illustrate, suppose you decide to give a speech that compares commercial television to public television. Your thesis is that public television is far superior in quality to commercial television. You believe the following assertions, but how should you arrange them to be sure they are in the right superior and subordinate relationships? The *because* test asks, "How do you know? *Because* . . ."

> Commercial television program producers seek the largest viewing audience possible.
>
> Commercial television advertisers seek the largest possible audiences.
>
> The larger the television audience, the higher the ratings.
>
> The larger the television audience, the more valuable the commercial time.
>
> Commercial television panders to the lowest common denominator.
>
> The larger the television audience, the more likely that advertisers will sell products.

To arrange these ideas in an outline, first find the statements that are broadest in scope:

> Commercial television panders to the lowest common denominator.
>
> Commercial television program producers seek the largest viewing audience possible.
>
> Commercial television advertisers seek the largest possible audiences.

Place the word *because* after the first statement, indent the next, and then read it all as one sentence. Do the same with the first and third sentences. If the relationships are logical and the sentences make sense, you have found appropriate subordination. If the sentences do not seem to make sense, then rearrange the combinations and try again. Once you have found sentence combinations that appear to reflect the correct superior/subordinate relationships, add the appropriate outline symbols. For example:

Thesis statement: Public television programming is far superior to commercial television. (*because*)

I. **Main idea:** Commercial television panders to the lowest common denominator. *(because)*
    A. Commercial television program producers seek the largest viewing audience possible.
    B. Commercial television advertisers seek the largest possible audiences.

Now try to fit the remaining ideas into this matrix. Remember, the more significant the idea, the farther to the left it goes. The less important and more subordinate the idea, the farther to the right it is indented. Ask yourself: Why do commercial television producers seek the largest possible viewing audience? Because they want to sell commercial time, and the larger the audience, the higher the ratings and the more valuable the commercial time. Why do television advertisers seek the largest possible audiences? *Because* the larger the audience, the more likely that advertisers will sell products. The outline now looks like example 9.5.

CONSISTENTLY FOLLOW AN ORGANIZATIONAL PATTERN

After you have decided what type of organizational pattern would work best for your topic (see chapter 8, "Organizing the Body of the Speech"), you are ready to begin working on the outline for the body of your speech. Your outline should follow the organizational pattern you select.

For example, one student decided to organize her talk about her summer study trip to Paris chronologically. Example 9.6 shows a portion of her planning outline. The student knew that she could not possibly develop her entire outline in the six minutes she was allowed for her speech. To focus her topic, she decided that she could only talk about her idea that six days in France were very busy. She turned this idea into her thesis statement. Example 9.7 shows how she did this. The student's final planning outline is shown in example 9.8.

| EXAMPLE 9.6 | PARTIAL PLANNING OUTLINE ORGANIZED CHRONOLOGICALLY |

Thesis statement: My study abroad trip to Paris was wonderful.

BODY

I.   **Main idea:** Getting to Paris wasn't easy. *(because)*
    A. Jet lag created a problem.
    B. Jet Jazzercise helped.

II. **Main idea:** The six days in France were very busy. *(because)*
    A. The monuments of Paris could take a month.
    B. We traveled to Chartres and Versailles.
    C. We walked our socks off.
    D. The Latin Quarter was a highlight.

III. **Main idea:** The return home was an important part of the trip. *(because)*
    A. Saying good-by to Paris wasn't easy.
    B. Meeting Mr. and Mrs. Harris helped.
    C. Mom and Dad had a surprise "Welcome Home" party for me.

| EXAMPLE 9.7 | REVISION OF EXAMPLE 9.6 PLANNING OUTLINE |

Thesis statement: My study abroad trip to Paris was wonderful.

BODY

I.   ~~**Main idea:** Getting to Paris wasn't easy. *(because)*~~
    ~~A. Jet lag created a problem.~~
    ~~B. Jet Jazzercise helped.~~

II. **Main idea:** The six days in France were very busy. *(because)*
    A. The monuments of Paris could take a month.
    B. We traveled to Chartres and Versailles.
    C. We walked our socks off.
    D. The Latin Quarter was a highlight.

III. ~~**Main idea:** The return home was an important part of the trip. *(because)*~~
    ~~A. Saying good-by to Paris wasn't easy.~~
    ~~B. Meeting Mr. and Mrs. Harris helped.~~
    ~~C. Mom and Dad had a surprise "Welcome Home" party for me.~~

EXAMPLE **9.8**	**FINAL PLANNING OUTLINE**

FINAL PLANNING OUTLINE
(Used with permission of Michelle Rampulla.)

INTRODUCTION

Opening: Good morning. My name is Michelle Rampulla. Last summer, I spent six days in France as part of my summer study program.

Thesis statement: I can tell you for sure that six days in France aren't enough!

Importance: I've never been to a place where it's possible to learn so much so fast.

Transition: Each day was absolutely full of activities and excitement. I only have time to tell you about a few of the highlights.

BODY

I. **Main idea:** The monuments of Paris came first. *(because)*
    A. We saw a dozen beautiful churches.
        1. Notre Dame was the most famous and the biggest.
        2. Saint Germaine was the oldest.
        3. Sacre Cour had the best view of the city.
        4. Sainte Chapelle was the most beautiful.
    B. We saw many civic monuments.
        1. The Arc de Triomphe was a highlight.
        2. The Eiffel Tower provided the best view of the city.
        3. The Hôtel des Invalides is the world's first military hospital.
        4. The Louvre is more than an art museum.

Transition: We loved the monuments of Paris. But I had always wanted to visit Chartres Cathedral and Versailles Palace.

II. **Main idea:** We traveled to Chartres and Versailles in one day. *(because)*
    A. We spent only three hours at Chartres.
        1. The cathedral is the highest example of medieval Gothic architecture.
        2. Part of the old village is still evident.
    B. We spent four hours at Versailles.
        1. The building is immense.
        2. Ten thousand acres of grounds were designed as a setting for the palace.

CONCLUSION

Summary: Six days won't begin to give you enough time to see France. The museums, the restaurants, the walks, the river were all beautiful, but for me, the monuments of Paris and a day at Chartres and Versailles were the highlights of the trip.

Closing: I fell in love with France. I'll go back some day, and it won't be long.

In this example, the student followed a time sequence in her planning outline. You can develop a planning outline for any organizational strategy you choose. Example 9.9 shows a planning outline that uses space as an organizational pattern, while example 9.10 shows how you might plan to follow a problem-to-solution sequence. Example 9.11 shows a partial

EXAMPLE **9.9**

PLANNING OUTLINE USING SPACE AS AN ORGANIZATIONAL PATTERN
(After an outline developed by Baptist Glenos. Used with permission.)

INTRODUCTION

Opening: Good afternoon. You know me by now.

Name: My name is Baptist Glenos. My family and I moved here just three years ago. Dad retired from the Air Force and bought a farm. When we first came to the farm, I didn't have any idea about farming. I thought all those buildings were just a display of my father's wealth.

Thesis statement: Every building on the property is a working structure.

Transition: I'd like to tell you about three of the most interesting ones to me.

BODY

I. **Main idea:** The barn sits farthest from the house. *(because)*
    A. The barn has two levels.
       1. The loft serves two functions. [Supporting evidence]
       2. The main level has three areas. [Supporting evidence]
    B. The barn is the heart of the farm. [Supporting evidence]

Transition: Having looked at the barn, you might be just as interested in the shop.

II. **Main idea:** The shop lies between the barn and the garage, nearer to the house. *(because)*
    A. Tool repair and maintenance are done in the shop. [Supporting evidence]
    B. Metal and wood parts and equipment are built in the shop. [Supporting evidence]

Transition: The shop is busy all the time at our farm. So is the garage.

III. **Main idea:** The garage is closest to our house. *(because)*
    A. The garage houses cars, trucks, and tractors. [Supporting evidence]
    B. Rolling stock is maintained and repaired in the shop. [Supporting evidence]

Transition: So what have I said so far about our farm?

CONCLUSION

Summary: Of all the working buildings on the farm, the garage, the shop, and the barn seem the most important. Three years ago, I was surprised how important these buildings are to the farm.

Closing: Now I can hardly wait to go home.

EXAMPLE 9.10

PARTIAL PLANNING OUTLINE USING A PROBLEM-TO-SOLUTION ORGANIZATIONAL PATTERN
(After course materials submitted by Tony Divilbis. Used with permission.)

INTRODUCTION

Opening: Hello, again. I'm Tony Divilbis. I'm a junior student majoring in sociology. This morning, I want to talk about the biggest government rip-off in America.

Thesis statement: I think the federal government should drastically change the welfare system.

Definition: By welfare, I mean all federal entitlement programs and give-away programs except Social Security and Medicare.

Importance: The welfare system is costing taxpayers more than it should, and it's doing more harm than good.

Transition: So what are the problems I'm talking about?

BODY

I. **Main idea:** The problems with the current welfare programs seem insurmountable. *(because)*
   A. The economic costs are staggering. [Supporting evidence]
   B. The human costs are unsupportable. [Supporting evidence]
   C. The programs are impossible to administer fairly. [Supporting evidence]

Transition: It's easy to see that the current welfare system presents staggering problems. But what can be done about them?

II. **Main idea:** The solution will require a complete redesign of government's ways of helping people who can't help themselves. *(because)*
   A. The government should abolish all federal entitlement programs and giveaways except Social Security and Medicare.
   B. The government should institute a guaranteed minimum annual cash income for everyone. [Explanation and definitions]
   C. The government should establish the requirement that there are no free lunches by making indigence a crime. [Explanation and definitions]
   D. The government should administer and enforce the new program through the Internal Revenue Service. [Explanation]

CONCLUSION

Summary: In summary, I have argued that the problems with federal welfare programs can no longer be supported. I have urged your support for a plan in which the federal government would abolish those programs and implement a new plan. I have shown you that a guaranteed minimum annual cash income program, carefully designed and carefully administered, would solve the problems and would be a far more effective way to take care of the nation's poor.

Closing: There aren't any free lunches. Someone has to pay for them. If you pay taxes, raise your hand and look around. You folks with your hands up, the federal government wastes your tax dollars by the millions and millions every day.

INTRODUCTION

Opening:

Thesis statement: Our public schools are a mess because of serious underfunding.

Preview:

Transition:

BODY

I. **Main idea:** Our public schools just aren't doing the job. *(because)*
    A. In four critical areas, our city has the highest illiteracy rate in this state.
        1. The students can't read. [Supporting evidence]
        2. The students can't do math. [Supporting evidence]
        3. The students don't know geography. [Supporting evidence]
        4. The students can't run computers. [Supporting evidence]
    B. Our schools produced the lowest SAT and ACT scores in a five-state region. [Supporting evidence]

Transition:

II. **Main idea:** Five factors—all the result of serious underfunding—combine to cause this sorry state of affairs. *(because)*
    A. Poor teaching is a factor. [Supporting evidence]
    B. Overcrowded classes play a part. [Supporting evidence]
    C. Obsolete or nonexistent technology characterizes our schools. [Supporting evidence]
    D. School buildings are antiquated and in disrepair. [Supporting evidence]
    E. The problems are so big that people think nothing can be done. [Supporting evidence]

Transition:

CONCLUSION

Summary:

Closing:

planning outline using an effect-to-cause organizational strategy. All of these organizational strategies are discussed in detail in chapter 8, "Organizing the Body of the Speech."

The planning outline in example 9.12 illustrates the motivated sequence organizational strategy originally developed by Alan H. Monroe in the mid-1930s.[1] Speakers use the motivated sequence to organize many different kinds of persuasive speeches. It works because it conforms to the way people think. Rather than the usual introduction, body, and conclusion, however, this sequence has five steps: (1) attention, (2) need, (3) satisfaction, (4) visualization, and (5) action. Refer to chapter 8, "Organizing the Body of the Speech," for a more complete discussion of the motivated sequence.

PLANNING OUTLINE FOLLOWING THE MOTIVATED SEQUENCE
(Used with permission of Debra Campbell.)

Foreign Language Competence: A Key to Employment in the 1990s

General purpose: To persuade

Specific purpose: I want to persuade my listeners to learn a foreign language as a way to help them get jobs when they graduate.

I. Attention step

Greeting: Wouldn't it be great to walk into a job interview after you graduate, knowing that you have a skill your prospective employer desperately needs—a skill most other applicants don't have?

Preview: Today, I want to tell you about a skill that you can develop here at South that will give you an edge over the competition no matter what your field is. The skill is being able to speak a foreign language.

Thesis statement: Learning a foreign language can mean the difference between landing a job or not.

Transition: Let's look at some of the reasons that speaking a foreign language can help you get into corporate America.

II. Need step
  A. U.S. corporations must look outward, not inward.
      1. Senator Paul Simon stated in 1990 that "Cultural isolation is a luxury the United States can no longer afford."
      2. As businesses continue to expand in Europe, Latin America, China, and Russia, they will have to communicate in their clients' native languages.
      3. Dr. Jerry Murch, chief scientist for Tektronix, explained this need in the March 1989 *Electronic Design.*
      4. Americans can't rely on speaking English slower and louder to make deals.
  B. U.S. companies are looking for employees who can speak foreign languages.
      1. Dr. Carol Fixman, in "The Foreign Language Needs of U.S.-Based Corporations," says they are.
      2. The January 1990 *Management Review* says employers give special weight to people with language skills.
      3. Companies need foreign language capabilities even in the United States.
          a. QMS provides an example of one such company.
          b. Omni International of Mobile provides another example.
          c. Morrison's, Inc. provides a personal example.

Transition: Well, we've seen that corporations need to look beyond the English-speaking world, and they need people who can help them do that. Where does that leave you?

III. Satisfaction step
  A. You can learn a foreign language here at South while you finish your degree.
      1. All Arts and Sciences majors must complete a three-quarter cluster.

EXAMPLE **9.12** CONTINUED

      2. You can take two or more intermediate language classes to fulfill the Humanities requirement.

      3. Just eight hours beyond the intermediate sequence will give you a minor in a language.

  B. The most difficult part is deciding which language to study.

      1. To help you decide, consider which languages are most sought after by employers.

         a. Spanish (44%)

         b. Japanese (33%)

         c. French (8%)

         d. German (5%)

         e. Russian (1%)

      2. All of these languages, plus Greek and Arabic, are offered at South.

      3. All of the sources I consulted advised job seekers to learn the language that most interests them.

IV. Visualization step

  A. Picture yourself as you walk into your first interview.

      1. You are confident because you speak the language this employer needs.

      2. When the interviewer asks, "Do you speak _____ ?" you smile with confidence.

      3. The interviewer makes a note and nods her head.

  B. You know you've got the advantage because you made the effort to meet the company's needs.

V. Action step

Summary: It's all up to you. I've told you about foreign language needs that globalization of business has caused, and I've told you how to prepare yourself to meet those needs. To quote the July 1991 *Forbes Magazine,* "Knowledge of a language usually means money to someone's career."

Closing: Act now. Registration for summer quarter begins in a week. Get yourself into a foreign language class. Your future might depend on it.

MAKE OUTLINE ENTRIES COMPLETE, SIMPLE SENTENCES WITH ACTION VERBS

Planning outlines help you to crystallize your thinking. If you use sentence fragments in your outline, you are presenting only idea fragments. Thus, your outline entries should be complete sentences. In addition, use action verbs whenever possible, since forms of the verb *to be* often seem weak and lifeless. The following outline entries demonstrate these guidelines:

  Wrong: The problems in higher education
  Better: State colleges and universities are in financial trouble.
  Best: State colleges and universities face increasing financial trouble.

PLAN ORGANIZATIONAL LINKS

As discussed in chapter 8, "Organizing the Body of the Speech," organizational links are transitions, signposts, and internal summaries that help listeners to follow and remember your line of thinking. To review, a transition is a unit of speech designed to move listeners from consideration of one idea to consideration of the next. A transition serves as a bridge between ideas. A signpost announces or points to some new or important idea. Signposts can be numbers ("The first issue is . . ."), direct questions ("What is the solution to this problem?"), or highlights of key ideas ("If you forget everything else, remember this . . ."). Like road signs, signposts keep listeners on the right road and help them to find their way through your speech. Internal summaries are short reviews or recapitulations of some part of your message ("To summarize, I've talked about three key areas . . .").

Standard outline practice calls for organizational links to be labeled, without numbers or letters, at the outline's left-hand margin. To illustrate for transitions, suppose your argument includes the following three lines of analysis:

Thesis statement: The budget committee should increase the library budget by 25 percent. *(because)*
I. **Main idea:** Periodical holdings do not support undergraduate major programs in three colleges.
II. **Main idea:** A 25 percent increase in budget would bring the holdings up to the standard needed.
III. **Main idea:** The money is available in existing university budgets.

This complex argument would require a good deal of development. To help listeners follow your analysis, develop a transition between each of the main ideas. Between the first and second main ideas, you could say:

Transition: We have seen, then, that the periodical holdings don't support the undergraduate majors in Arts and Sciences, in Allied Health, or in Business Administration. Will the proposed 25 percent increase in library budget be enough to solve this problem? I think so.

Between the second and third main ideas, you might say:

Transition: We have seen, then, that the periodical holdings don't support undergraduate majors in three colleges and that a 25 percent increase in the library's acquisitions budget would be enough to cover the costs. The next question we have to consider is whether the money is available.

Put it all together and you have the outline in example 9.13. Within outlines, signposts and internal summaries are handled in the same manner as the transitions in the previous example.

INCLUDE SUPPORTING EVIDENCE AND DOCUMENTATION

Your planning outline will not be effective if it includes only assertions and knowledge claims, but no supporting materials. The proofs are your reasons for making the assertions in the first place. Include them in your outline, and document them where appropriate.

EXAMPLE 9.13	OUTLINE OF MAIN IDEAS AND TRANSITIONS

Thesis statement: The budget committee should increase the library budget by 25 percent. *(because)*

I. **Main idea:** Periodical holdings do not support undergraduate major programs in three colleges.

Transition: We have seen, then, that the periodical holdings don't support the undergraduate majors in Arts and Sciences, in Allied Health, or in Business Administration. Will the proposed 25 percent increase in library budget be enough to solve this problem? I think so.

II. **Main idea:** A 25 percent increase in budget would bring the holdings up to the standard needed.

Transition: We have seen, then, that the periodical holdings don't support undergraduate majors in three colleges and that a 25 percent increase in the library's acquisitions budget would be enough to cover the costs. The next question we have to consider is whether the money is available.

III. **Main idea:** The money is available in existing university budgets.

Your speech instructor will probably have a preference about how you document supporting evidence in an outline. Standard practice is to document as you would for a term paper, placing full bibliographical data either at the foot of the relevant page or at the end of the outline. Documentation styles vary, depending on which style manual you are following.[2] Learn a standard style, and use it consistently.

PLANNING OUTLINE CHECKLIST AND EXAMPLE

Table 9.1 presents a planning outline checklist. Use this table to double-check that your planning outline includes all of the necessary information, logically organized, and in an appropriate format.

Example 9.14 on page 212 is a complete, annotated, full-sentence planning outline that was developed in preparation for a six-minute argumentative speech. Although not perfect, the outline exemplifies most of the outlining features described in this chapter.

DEVELOPING A SPEAKING OUTLINE

Once you are satisfied with your planning outline, you can begin to develop a speaking outline. Much briefer than the planning outline, the speaking outline provides you with notes to use while giving your speech. Include only the topics you will discuss. The following pointers will help you to develop your speaking outline:

Table 9.1

PLANNING OUTLINE CHECKLIST

1. Have I labeled the introduction, body, and conclusion as separate parts? Are the labels centered?

2. Have I included the appropriate side-headings in the introduction and conclusion?

3. Have I written out the general and specific purpose and the thesis statement? Do I know clearly what response I want from my listeners?

4. Have I identified and consistently followed an organizational strategy (time, space, problem to solution, motivated sequence, etc.)?

5. Have I followed a standard outline symbol system to indicate superior and subordinate relationships among ideas?

6. Have I used complete, simple sentences and action words?

7. Have I double-checked that the main ideas support the thesis statement and that subpoints support the main ideas? (Have I used the *because* test?)

8. Have I planned and included transitions, signposts, and internal summaries?

9. Have I included supporting and bibliographical material?

FOLLOW THE PLANNING OUTLINE

Use the same standard set of symbols and indentation pattern that you used in your planning outline. If you alter the pattern, you run the risk of confusing yourself during the speech.

BE BRIEF

Because the purpose of a speaking outline is to jog your memory, there is no need for more than a few words. If your outline is too detailed, you may spend too much time studying the outline and not enough time looking at the audience. Keep your speaking outline as brief as possible.

MAKE THE SPEAKING OUTLINE A WORKING TOOL

The speaking outline is a good place to make marginal notes about things you want to re-member. For example, you may have just met a member of the audience and want to mention her name during the speech. Print her name in the margin of the speaking outline at the appropriate place. Similarly, you may wish to remind yourself of any visual aids you plan to use. A marginal note or sketch at the appropriate place in your speaking outline will help you to remember when to use the visual aids.

EXAMPLE 9.14 **PLANNING OUTLINE WITH ANNOTATIONS**
(Used with permission of Cheryl Cope.)

WOMEN IN THE WORK FORCE: ARE THEY BETTER OFF?

General purpose: To change belief.

Specific purpose: To persuade my audience that the Family Medical Leave Act will make the problem (too few women are promoted to upper executive ranks) worse.

INTRODUCTION

Opener: Good morning, class. My name is Cheryl Cope. I'm working on my degree in business. And I'm worried.

Thesis statement: I'm worried because, despite what they tell you on television, things are getting worse for women executives, not better.

Transition: I think I can show you at least three reasons why, whether you're a man or a woman, you should be concerned, too. The number of women employees is growing rapidly, but the number of women executives is not. And now, the Family Medical Leave Act is going to make things worse, not better.

BODY

I. **Main idea:** Very few women gain entry into upper executive ranks.[1] *(because)*

   A. Yet, women make up the majority of new entrants into the work force each year.
      1. The number of women in the work force has grown from 20 million to 50 million in the years from 1960 to 1990.
      2. The percent of women in the work force has grown from 33 percent in 1960 to 45 percent in 1990.
   B. Of the Fortune 500 and Service 500 companies, women make up less than 5 percent of managers at or above the level of vice president.[2]
   C. The number of women promoted to senior management positions increased only 2 percent over a ten-year period.[3]

Transition: You have to conclude from these figures that there aren't many women executives and that, even though the number of women employees is growing rapidly, the number of women executives isn't keeping pace. But why? How can this be true when we hear all the time about how conditions are getting better for women?

It is a good idea to state the purpose of the speech in writing before you begin to outline. This helps you to test the accuracy and completeness of the outline.

Label each part separately. Put the label in the center of the page.

Interest-gathering standard opening that leads up to a startling statement.

Note how this clear thesis statement flows from the specific purpose.

This transition builds the importance and relevance of the topic for the listeners. It also previews the main ideas and alerts listeners to what is coming.

Centered label shows that this is a separate and distinct part of the speech.

The first main idea is stated in a full sentence. It carries only one idea. Also, notice the inclusion of supporting materials and the use of the *because* test. Capital letters indicate subpoints.

Sub-subpoints provide evidence. Notice also, how indentation shows subordination of ideas.

Each subpoint directly supports the main idea.

See how the transition ties the first main idea to the second. It is a good idea to plan and write out transitions. Label them separately from the symbol and indentation system.

EXAMPLE **9.14** CONTINUED

An internal summary helps listeners to remember as well as to follow from one idea to the next.

Internal summary: Sex-role stereotypes may have something to do with the problem. It may be that sex-role stereotyping keeps women out of the executive suite. And things aren't likely to get better.

Full sentences force you to think clearly.

II. **Main idea:** The Family Medical Leave Act that became effective on August 4, 1993, will make it more difficult for women to break through into senior management positions. *(because)*

A. The Family Medical Leave Act makes sweeping changes.[4]

Here the speaker has pulled out of the act only those provisions that support her argument. When asked about other provisions, she was able to answer questions knowledgeably.

1. Any organization that employs fifty or more people within a seventy-five-mile radius must offer workers as much as twelve weeks of unpaid leave for certain qualified medical reasons.

2. Employers must continue health-care coverage during the leave.

3. Employers must guarantee that their employees will return to either the same job or a comparable one.

B. Women are likely to take more leaves than men.

The student expanded this part of the speech with illustrations of three women she knew personally.

1. Women remain the primary caregivers (mothers, wives, etc.).

2. Women have babies.

C. The costs associated with the FMLA will continue to decrease the number of women hired for executive positions.

1. The costs of benefits will inhibit employers from promoting women.
   a. Benefits continue for the person taking leave.
   b. Benefits must be paid for the replacement person.

Speaker could have provided an example or two here to illustrate her ideas by calling personnel officers.

2. The costs of replacing women who take the leave will inhibit employers from promoting and hiring women executives.
   a. Although the women taking leave will not be paid salaries, the employer must still recruit new people to replace them.
   b. Replacement employees will have to be trained at employer expense.

3. The costs of reinstating women employees will also inhibit employers from hiring and promoting women executives.
   a. An employee who has been away for an extended period of time will have to be retrained.
   b. An employee who elects to distribute leave creates a different problem.

This argument would be stronger if the speaker had included testimony. Of course, that would be difficult to secure. No manager could agree without risking litigation.
Speaker developed this illustration using a convincing but hypothetical case.

Example: Employee says to boss, "Beginning next month, I will be gone every Monday and Friday."

EXAMPLE **9.14** CONTINUED

CONCLUSION

This label makes the conclusion a distinct part of the speech.

Restatement of the main ideas helps listeners to remember them. A summary at the end of a speech is always a good idea.

Speaker includes an optimistic note and then doubles back on her introductory idea.

Standard practice is to include footnotes in an outline. Give complete bibliographical information, and be sure to consistently follow your teacher's preferred style manual.

Summary: So, things aren't as good for women in business as you hear. The problem of sex-role stereotyping was keeping women out of the executive suite before the Family Medical Leave Act.

Closing: I don't know what can be done about this situation. Perhaps nothing. As for me, I'm going to do the best I can to make it when I'm finally out there. But I'm going to have to work harder and sacrifice more than men will, and I'm mad about that.

1. "Women in Corporate Management," *Miami Herald,* 27 July 1993.
2. Dow Corporate Communications, "Valuing Diversity: Making the Most of Individual Potential," in *The Point Is: A Summary of Public Issues Important to Dow,* no. 134 (12 September 1990).
3. Dow Corporate Communications, "Valuing Diversity." *ibid.*
4. "Women Slowly Gain Entry into Upper Executive Ranks," *The Mobile Register,* 28 July 1993.

SPEAKING OUTLINE EXAMPLE

Example 9.15 is the annotated speaking outline that corresponds to the planning outline in example 9.14. Compare the two outlines. Notice how the speaking outline follows the same outline format as the planning outline in example 9.14. Yet, the speaker uses only key words and phrases in the speaking outline to remind herself of main ideas, supporting evidence, and examples. She also includes brief notes ("Look." "Breathe." "Pause." and so on) that remind her to slow down and to stay calm.

EXAMPLE 9.15

WOMEN IN THE WORK FORCE: ARE THEY BETTER OFF?
INTRODUCTION

LOOK.   BREATHE.

The speaker used these notes to remind herself to look at the audience and to remain calm.

Opener: Greeting. I'm worried.

Trans: Three reasons to be concerned.

PAUSE.   MOVE.

Notice how the speaker reminds herself to slow down, to pause, to work with listeners.

BODY

I. Few gain entry (*Miami Herald,* 27 July 1993)
   A. Majority of new entrants
      1. 20-M to 50-M, 1960 to 1990
      2. 33% to 45%, 1960 to 1990
   B. Fortune 500 & Service 500—women less that 5% above VP (DOW Newsletter, "Valuing Diversity," Sept. 1990)
   C. Promoted = increased only 2% over 10-yr. period

Note inclusion of source materials. These helped the speaker to build her credibility and to stay calm.

Trans: Not many women executives and number not keeping pace. WHY?

PAUSE.   MOVE.

II. FMLA (Aug. 4) made it more difficult.
   A. Sweeping changes
      1. 50+ people w/in 75 miles = 12 weeks unpaid leave
      2. Employers must cont. health care . . .
      3. and guarantee same or comparable job
   B. Women more likely to take leave
      1. Primary caregivers

Useful reminder.

It was very easy for Cheryl to follow these notes as she spoke.

EX.   MRS.   WILSON

      2. Women have babies.

EX. JEANNIE
EX. DONNA

EXAMPLE **9.15**   CONTINUED

	C. FMLA costs = decrease number of women executives
	1. Benefits = inhibit employers
	2. Recruitment and training = inhibit employers
	3. Guaranteed return to job = inhibit employers
	Example: "Beginning next month . . ."
Useful reminder.	*PAUSE. MOVE IN.*
	CONCLUSION
One word reminds speaker to summarize.	**Summary:**
Speaker includes key ideas of planned closing.	**Closing:** Do best/work harder/sacrifice more. I'm mad.

Summary

Planning outlines and speaking outlines are two tools for simplifying the task of organizing your speech. A planning outline helps you to study the relationships among ideas and to determine the amount and kinds of evidence needed to support your thesis statement. A speaking outline provides you with notes you can refer to while giving your speech.

Within your planning outline, label the introduction, the body, and the conclusion. The introduction usually includes an opening statement or greeting, the thesis statement, a preview of what you are going to discuss, and a transition to your first main idea. The body includes all the main lines of analysis and all of your supporting evidence and arguments. The conclusion often consists of a short summary and a closing statement. Learn to follow a standard outlining format to indicate the various parts of the speech and the relationships among those parts.

A good planning outline depends on a clearly written general purpose, specific purpose, and thesis statement. Once you have a thesis statement, everything else in the outline must support it. Use the *because* test to determine that all of your main ideas support the thesis statement and that all of your subpoints support the main ideas. Outlines should follow an organizational strategy—for example, cause-to-effect or problem-to-solution. The planning outline helps you to consistently follow your organizational plan and indicates whether or not you have supported your ideas adequately. Outline entries should be strong, active, simple sentences, which will help you to resist presenting only idea fragments. Incorporate organizational links, such as transitions, signposts, and internal summaries, into your outline and label them. Also include specific supporting evidence and documentation.

A speaking outline can be developed after you are satisfied with your planning outline. Brevity is the key. Include only enough information to help you remember your key ideas. Make notes to yourself that will make the speaking outline a working tool for your speech presentation.

Key Terms

Because test   Planning outline
Outline   Speaking outline

Application Questions

1. Do you outline before you write? How do your classmates approach the problem? Often, people pattern their ideas in their minds, write the essay, and then make the outline. What are the advantages and disadvantages of this approach?
2. Agree with another member of your class that each of you will write a letter to someone—a local politician, for example, or a favorite teacher. Agree, also, on a thesis statement for the letter. Working alone, select an organizational pattern and develop a planning outline for this letter. Then sit down with your classmate to compare and contrast your work. Notice, especially, the main arguments and supporting materials each of you used to develop the thesis. What did you learn from this exercise? Would you want to send your letter? Why or why not?
3. See if you can develop a full-sentence outline from one of the sample speeches found in appendix A at the end of this book. Bring it to class and be prepared to discuss the following questions:
    *   Do you think the writer developed an outline before writing the editorial? Why or why not?
    *   Did you find any gaps or thin spots in the logic or supporting materials?
4. Select an editorial from *USA Today* or from your local newspaper. See if you can develop a full-sentence outline from it. Then bring the outline to class and be prepared to discuss the following questions:
    *   Do you think the writer developed an outline before writing the editorial? Why or why not?
    *   Did you find any gaps or thin spots in the logic or supporting materials?

Self-Test for Review

Identify items 1–5 as either A (describing a planning outline) or B (describing a speaking outline):

_____1. Full sentences
_____2. Includes supporting material and documentation
_____3. Key words and phrases
_____4. Notes in the margins
_____5. Superior and subordinate relationships tested with the *because* test

_____6. Which of the following best describes the *because* test?
- a. A technique for identifying subordination
- b. A technique for identifying a planning outline
- c. A technique used in speaking outlines for argumentation
- d. None of the above describes the *because* test

_____7. A transition is
- a. a bridge between ideas.
- b. a simple word or phrase that points to an important idea.
- c. a speech unit designed to move listeners from one point to another.
- d. both a and c.

_____8. A signpost is
- a. a statement that serves as a bridge from one idea to another.
- b. a statement that points to an important idea.
- c. a 4-inch-by-4-inch post stuck in the ground.
- d. Both b and c.

Answers: 1.A. 2.A. 3.B. 4.B. 5.A. 6.a. 7.d. 8.d.

Suggested Reading

Brigance, William Norwood. *Speech: Its Techniques and Disciplines in a Free Society.* New York: Appleton-Century-Crofts, 1952. This old chestnut set the standard for outlining for American speech teachers. It is still the best source available.

CHAPTER 10

Beginning and Ending a Speech

OUTLINE

OBJECTIVES

After reading this chapter, you should be able to:

1. *Name* and *describe* the functions of a speech introduction.
2. *List* and *provide* examples of eight different strategies for speech introductions.
3. *Name* and *describe* the functions of a speech conclusion.
4. *List* and *provide* examples of five different strategies for speech conclusions.

© David Young-Wolff/PhotoEdit

*T*his chapter discusses the most effective techniques for beginning and ending your speech. Strong introductions and conclusions ensure that listeners will pay attention to your message and remember your main ideas.

The first part of the chapter explains how a speech introduction should secure attention and interest, establish a positive relationship between the speaker and the audience, prepare listeners for the message, and set the tone for the speech. Quotations, startling statements, illustrations, stories, previews of the main ideas, and simple greetings are effective at the beginning of the speech. Introductions that use humor and rhetorical questions are more difficult for inexperienced speakers but can be used successfully.

The remainder of the chapter examines speech conclusions. A conclusion should review the speaker's main ideas and focus the thoughts and feelings of listeners on what has been said. The conclusion should also lend a sense of completeness or finality to the speech. Summaries, quotations, references to the introduction, calls to action, or a combination of these often work effectively to clarify what you want from listeners.

When the highly rated television program "60 Minutes" first comes on the air, one of the reporters previews the feature stories of that evening's program by saying something like:

> *Tonight, on "60 Minutes," we'll examine the real story behind the Branch Dividian catastrophe in Texas and see how it paralleled the Jamestown disaster. [Cut to videotape for 10 seconds.] We'll go to Los Angeles and visit with Woody Harrelson and see how he's adjusted to life after "Cheers." [Cut to videotape for 12 seconds.] Ed Bradley will show you our investigation of migrant workers in Wisconsin, Ohio, Indiana, and Illinois. [Cut to videotape for 15 seconds.] And Andy Rooney wonders why we ever got into the silly business of handshaking. That, and much more, tonight on "60 Minutes."*

To end the popular program, one of the featured reporters says: "I'm [Ed Bradley]. We'll see you next week on '60 Minutes.'"

Just as a television program must have an effective introduction and conclusion, so must a well-developed speech. A speaker needs to get off to a fast start because the first few moments of a speech can determine whether or not the speech is successful. The end of the speech is just as important. Perhaps you have heard speakers who just do not know how to quit. They come to a logical finishing place but keep right on talking, destroying the impact of their speech and their personal credibility in the process. Problems in either a speech introduction or conclusion can neutralize the effective ideas in the body of your presentation.

THE INTRODUCTION

The **introduction** is the "kickoff" for your speech. While it should not be lengthy, the introduction is vital to the success of your speech and must be prepared carefully.

JOHNNETTA COLE

Johnnetta Cole, President of Spelman College, succinctly captures the challenge of preparing an effective introduction:

Introductions are tricky. Usually, with only a few short minutes at our disposal, we try to communicate the gist, the drift of a person, an idea. Of course, should the introduction drag on too long, you can feel people urging you under their breath to "Please, get to the point!"

Source: Johnnetta Cole, Conversations: Straight Talk with America's Sister President *(New York: Doubleday, 1993), 1. Photo © Bud Smith Photography*

PURPOSES OF THE INTRODUCTION

In general, an introduction should call attention to your subject matter and establish the relationship among you, your listeners, and your speech. In particular, its purposes are to gain attention and interest, establish rapport with the audience, orient audience members to what they are about to hear, and set the tone for the speech.

An audience does not automatically pay attention to what you are saying. You are competing for attention with all the other thoughts that race through listeners' minds. You need to give listeners reasons to listen to you while you prepare them for the ideas you are about to introduce.

Beginning in the introduction, you must convey your credibility to listeners. If they see you as an honest, trustworthy, well-informed, and articulate person, they will be more open to the message you present in the body of your speech.

STRATEGIES FOR INTRODUCTIONS

Effective speakers commonly use eight different introduction strategies to secure listeners' attention (see table 10.1). The sections that follow discuss these in more detail and provide examples.

Quotation

Many introductions incorporate quotations from a recognized, public figure. Example 10.1 shows how one student used quotation in an introduction.

Another student presented a speech that dealt with the elements of leadership and the characteristics that many people in prominent positions should possess. She used a slogan originated by a past U.S. president to suggest the quality of leadership that society needs:

"The buck stops here." This sign, which rested on the desk of President Harry S. Truman, told the world how he felt about responsibility. Mr. Truman made many difficult decisions during his presidency, but he always maintained that, once he made up his mind, he was willing to take the criticism of his choice. He liked to say,

Table 10.1

STRATEGIES FOR INTRODUCTIONS

Strategy	What It Does
1. Quotation	Statement of another (often famous) individual to focus attention
2. Startling statement	Arresting, interesting fact or incident that arouses attention
3. Illustration	Example or case that helps to involve listeners
4. Story	Extended, interesting narrative about the subject to involve listeners
5. Preview of main ideas	Outline of the main points of the speech body to prepare listeners for remainder of speech
6. Simple greeting	Welcoming statement to establish rapport with audience
7. Humor	Amusing story, anecdote, or situation that creates a favorable climate for the speaker
8. Rhetorical question	A question that implies its own answer and leads audience to interest in the topic

---

Example 10.1 — Sample Introduction that Uses a Quotation

Use of quotation to gather attention	The famous American poet Robert Frost wrote in The Death of the Hired Man, "Home is the place where, when you have to go there, they have to take you in." For most of us, that piece of writing is very true. Home is a warm, loving place. It's a place where we keep our fond memories and where we always feel wanted. They "have" to take us in because they love us. But for many people in their teens and twenties, home is a place where they feel rejected. They may have been abused or ignored, shamed by their parents, and severely punished for what you and I would call "no good reason."
Preview of the problem	These people often leave home at a very early age. Sadly, they too often drift into a life of criminal behavior, prostitution, drug and alcohol abuse. These people are America's "throw-away" children, and they can't go home again.
Thesis statement	We must help them. And so, today, I want to argue that the United States government should develop an assistance program for this growing population of young people that will include all the support that you and I draw from our homes.

"If you can't stand the heat, get out of the kitchen" as a way of showing that leadership meant a willingness to stand up for your decisions and not to pass the ball to a subordinate to handle.

You do not always have to quote famous people, but the people you quote should be perceived as credible. One student speaker wanted to support the idea that values should be taught in the home, and not as part of the high school curriculum. In her introduction, she said:

My mother told me three things that have had the greatest influence on my life. She said, "Work hard, love your family, and be honest with everyone." Those words of

Table 10.2

STARTLING STATEMENT EXAMPLES

TOPIC	STARTLING STATEMENT
1. Health	"There's some startling and frightening information out there that you may not know about. Lung cancer is the fastest growing death-causing cancer in the United States. And, get this, cigarette smoking is responsible for 90 percent of lung cancer cases in men and 79 percent among women. Some people call cigarettes the 'cancer stick.' How right they are!"
2. Housing	"So you thought it was expensive to own a home. Well, since 1981, the median price of an existing home in this country has gone from $66,400 to $100,900 in 1992. That's the bad news. The good news is that the cost of owning a home, as a percent of your income, has fallen 16 percent in the same period. So, surprise! It costs more to buy a home, but homes are more affordable because people make more money."
3. Entertainment	"The ABC program 'Nightline'" is a well-established hit opposite 'The Tonight Show.' One night, guest host Cokie Roberts put the show ahead of dinner with the president of the United States. Because she was substituting for Ted Koppel that evening, she had to leave the dinner table at the White House while seated next to President Clinton. Not many of us would walk out on the president, but for this reporter, the news came first." *
4. Taxes	"Most of us think we pay too much of what we earn in taxes. But here's some information that might get your attention. We know that California, New York, and Texas are our most populous states. You'd guess, then, that people who live there probably pay the most taxes. Not true. Residents of the state of Alaska pay at least twice as much per person in taxes as do people living in the largest states. And not far behind is Hawaii. The states that were admitted to the union last also pay the most per person in taxes. Just a coincidence? Let's see."

Adapted from "Fifth Estater," Broadcasting and Cable, 5 April, 1993, 59.

guidance have helped me shape my actions, and they've governed how I react to people and situations in my life. They can be a guide to you in dealing with life and the people you encounter.

Startling Statement

You can introduce your speech with a startling statement of fact or opinion, but be sure that your attempt to startle listeners is appropriate to both the situation and the topic. Your statement should be related to listeners' interests and in keeping with their expectations. Table 10.2 presents examples of startling statements for several topics. In each of the introductions in table 10.2, the objective is to give listeners information that is surprising to them in an effort to arouse interest in the subject.

Illustration

Your introduction can illustrate the issue you plan to discuss. Using an illustration in your introduction works best when you want to involve listeners emotionally in some problem. Make the illustration rich in detail:

> There's a group of tumbledown shacks just outside Rochelle, Illinois, that might astound you. Just half a mile from the city limits, seventeen families of migrant farm workers are living in the pits of poverty. Up to six men, women, and children sleep together in the same hot room. There's a single cold-water pipe that the families share, but there's no bathroom. Instead, they use the old-fashioned outhouse on the property. These families are from Mexico. They were brought here by American businessmen to harvest melons and asparagus. Though their living conditions in that Illinois town are better than they had in Mexico's slums, they are awful.

An introductory illustration such as this stimulates and emotionally involves listeners and also gives them a way of identifying with the situation.

Story

Most people like a good story, especially one that is amusing or provocative. Choose a story that you know well and that applies to the subject you intend to discuss. Try to include many relevant details so that listeners can imagine being personally involved. One student used the following story for an effective introduction:

> Most of you have heard, time and time again, about how important it is to wear a seat belt. Let me tell you about my experience last week.

> My friend Hal and I were returning from a business dinner. He was driving his Miata, and we were talking about some business matters. The street was fairly narrow, with cars parked on the driver's side of the street. We were laughing about some incident of the past week, and I looked off to my right. Hal turned his head toward me, but when he and I looked back at the street, we were about to hit one of the parked cars.

> I braced myself for the impact. We struck the Mazda RX7 at the driver's side headlight. The Miata ran up the hood, onto the roof, and then rolled off onto the pavement. A thousand things went through my mind as we skidded and scraped for what seemed like hours. Suddenly, there was silence.

> I shook my head, reached up to see how much blood there was. Surprise! I wasn't bleeding. I unfastened my seat belt and slid out of the car. Hal was trapped on the crushed driver's side of the car. I helped him get loose and crawl across and come out on the passenger's side. His face was covered with blood, but no sooner was he out of the car than we could hear an ambulance. Someone had called 911.

> They took Hal and me to the hospital. Hal required seventeen stitches to close the cut in his head. I had four small cuts on my hands and a bruised arm. The Miata cost $6,000 to repair. But the important thing to Hal and me is that we're alive. We're

alive because, with the top down in a convertible, we had only our seat belts to keep us from being crushed. Scary experience? Yes, the worst of my life. But believe me, I'll never ride without a seat belt, even on the way to the store.

A story like this sets the mood for the message. It arouses emotions so that the audience will focus attention on the major theme.

In the following story, New York Governor Mario Cuomo illustrates how you can incorporate the theme and some humor in a story for an introduction:

A young Italian immigrant, at the close of the last century, wrote to his family: "Before I came here, they told me the streets were paved with gold. When I came here, I learned three things. First, the streets were not paved with gold. Second, the streets were not paved at all. Third, they expected me to pave them."[1]

Preview of Main Ideas

An easy and effective way to open your speech is to preview the ideas you intend to develop. This approach provides listeners with a clear sense of what you want to do and also shows them how what you are planning to say relates to them. A student speaker used this introduction strategy to preview effectively the values of credit cards:

We've all heard about the problems people have with credit cards. They forget that the charges are "real money," that interest is charged each month when you don't pay the entire balance, and that credit card debt can "eat you alive." Let me give you a different angle. Today, I'd like to show you how a credit card can be used to both pay your expenses and manage your money. Most importantly, it's the best proof you have of payment, and it's accepted almost everywhere. I'll explain to you why each of these reasons should be enough for you to use your credit card instead of your checkbook or cash.

Simple Greeting

Another way to start your speech is with a simple greeting. For example, you might say something like the following:

Good afternoon, members of the Chamber of Commerce. I'm Rosa Ketner, Executive Secretary of the United Way. It's an honor to be with you today. I'd like to discuss with you the issue of . . .

Humor

Humor is a powerful tool for arousing audience interest in both the speaker and the subject. However, *it must be used carefully.* What is amusing to one person may be offensive to another. If you decide to use humor in an introduction, ask yourself: "What will happen if no one in my audience thinks this is funny?" If the opening material is unsuccessful, the rest of the speech is in jeopardy. Clearly, you need an alternate plan if the humor "bombs." In this situation, the best strategy is to return to a straight, factual presentation and to abandon all other plans you had for humorous material. You will gain little by repeating your effort to be amusing.

Jay Leno provided the following general guidelines about the kind of humor to avoid:

AIDS isn't funny. Child molestation isn't funny. Vietnam isn't funny. Jokes that belittle other cultures aren't funny. A subject that's always in the news—a plane crash—isn't funny.[2]

In addition, off-color jokes and racial and ethnic jokes are neither funny nor appropriate. If you want to begin your speech with some light, amusing material, be sure that the humor provides the right flavor for the speech. Ask yourself, also, if your audience will find the humor appropriate.

The use of humor requires a subtle touch. You can use humor in several different ways. Because your needs in public communication may vary, a general knowledge of the categories of humor provides you with useful choices. Table 10.3 lists several categories of humor that could be used in an introduction (or even in the body or conclusion of a speech).

For example, the first category of humor in table 10.3 involves pointing out absurdities. Paul Harvey tells the following story about a physician:

Dr. Roland Cross of Loyola Medical, Chicago, got a bill from the hospital. The **doctor** *got a bill—$309 for anesthesia during Cesarean delivery. Dr. Cross notified hospital auditors that he had not been hospitalized for any reason. And certainly a*

Table 10.3

CATEGORIES OF HUMOR

Category	Definition
1. Absurdity	Using materials that are illogical in thinking or in language
2. Confusion	Misunderstandings or contradictions that are potentially amusing
3. Human problems	Situations in which a person appears foolish or is overcome by events; includes situations where the speaker or the activity of the speaker appears laughable
4. Exaggeration	Overstatement related to persons, places, sizes, the way people feel or act, and personal experiences
5. Playful ridicule	A sympathetic teasing and acceptance of human faults
6. Surprise	Making use of unexpected or unusual feelings, events, or facts

Source: Adapted from Katharine Hull Kappas, "A Study of Humor in Children's Books," MA thesis, University of Chicago, 1965, pp. 53–56.

seventy-year-old male would not be having a C-section. The hospital blamed its computer. But guess what? Now Dr. Cross has been notified by Blue Cross that his hospital bill has been paid. Three hundred nine dollars for anesthesia—during Cesarean delivery—and Blue Cross further offers its congratulations on the birth of TWINS.[3]

Absurd situations like the one in this brief story usually create amusement. People appreciate the absurd—typically, because the situation is so extreme or stupid. Few people are likely to be offended by the discussion of a flawed hospital bill.

Here is another example of the same technique:

At a high school basketball game, Oklahoma City police officer Eldridge Wyatt became dissatisfied that no fouls were being called on No. 21 and walked onto the court to point out the player's elbowing to the referees. When referee Stan Guffey told Wyatt to leave the officiating to him, Wyatt arrested Guffey. Guffey was un-arrested a few minutes later so that the game could continue, but when a reporter asked Wyatt after the game what had happened, Wyatt tried to arrest him, too.[4]

Certainly, the police officer's actions fit under the classification of absurd. Most audiences would find this story amusing.

Another category of humor in table 10.3—confusion—can also sometimes be funny. For example, if you wanted to introduce a situation where misunderstandings over language occurred, this type of humor might be appropriate:

Sometimes, it does all get lost in the translation. "Please leave your values at the front desk," says the sign at a Paris hotel. Hungry? From a Polish menu, select "roasted duck let loose" or perhaps "beef rashers beaten up in the country people's fashion." A Swiss eatery proudly warns, "Our wines leave you nothing to hope for."

A Budapest zoo puts people first: "Please do not feed the animals. If you have any suitable food, give it to the guard on duty." A Rhodes tailor wants early orders for summer suits "because in big rush we will execute customers in strict rotation."[5]

Human problems—the third category of humor in table 10.3—have a unique appeal. We have all felt frustrated or perhaps angry with a problem. The actions that other people take when they are upset can sometimes be quite amusing:

A commuter lost his temper in 90-degree heat at Waterloo station when he asked a British Rail supervisor to explain why his train was delayed and was told that there was no such word as explanation *in the British Rail rule book. . . . Malcolm Stuart's delayed train was still listed on the information board, but after waiting 20 minutes without announcement of a delay, he approached a station supervisor and asked about the train. . . . The supervisor, who was described as "obese" and with heavily tattooed arms, told him: "Look, cloth ears, there's been a points failure. There will be a train when there's a train." . . . Mr. Stuart took out his black (pen) and started writing the word* explanation *on the front of the supervisor's white shirt. Stuart was found guilty of criminal damage and threatening behavior and was fined 250 pounds, 100 pounds court costs, and ordered to pay 50 pounds compensation for the shirt.[6]*

As shown in table 10.3, exaggeration is another category of humor that might be appropriate for your introduction. While the following "Mendoza's Law of Purchasing" may not generate a belly laugh, understanding smiles and nods are likely:

(1) When shopping, never look for something specific, you won't find it. (2) Always shop for nothing, you'll always come back with something. (3) After a heavy day's shopping, the perfect purchase is in either the first or the last place you've looked.[7]

Playful ridicule, the fifth category of humor in table 10.3, is sometimes helpful with a good-natured audience. A visiting missionary used playful ridicule to tease his listeners as he began a fund-raising speech:

A twenty-dollar bill and a one-dollar bill were on their way to final destruction. During the trip, they struck up a conversation. The twenty-dollar bill said, "I've had a good life. I've gone to glamorous places like San Francisco, Montreal, New York, New Orleans, and Las Vegas. It's been a lot of fun, and I've always been excited. How about you?" he asked the one-dollar bill. The dollar bill answered, "Boring, boring. Go to church, go to church, go to church."

The humor category of surprise involves using unexpected or unusual feelings, events, or facts to provide a light touch. The so-called "one-liners" that stand-up comics often use provide examples:

I told my husband I wanted to be surprised for dinner, so he soaked the labels off the cans.

The nice things about dictating letters is that you can use a lot of words you don't know how to spell.

He'd be great in the Olympics. He can hang his chin over a bar for hours.

Behind every successful person stands a devoted spouse—and a surprised mother-in-law.

The types of humor presented in table 10.3 do not cover all possible categories. For example, you can use humor that combines features from several of these types. Rather, the list includes the most commonly used and effective types of humor for inexperienced speakers. Other types of humor are sometimes used by professional comedians and persons skilled in entertainment. Among these are such techniques as slapstick, defiance, and violence, but these are difficult for beginning speakers to present effectively.

It is unlikely that anyone would find any of the previous examples offensive. They set a lighthearted mood and help to relax the audience for the rest of the speech. The best advice for using humor in your introduction is to be as certain as you can that the humor is appropriate for the subject, the audience, and the occasion.

Rhetorical Question

The rhetorical question is sometimes used in a speech introduction as an attention-getting device. The answer to the question is either implied by the question or is part of a strategy designed to get listeners involved in your topic. The question is asked to arouse curiosity, rather than to seek information.

Asking rhetorical questions can be difficult, however, especially for inexperienced speakers. Sometimes, the questions sound trite and detract from the effect of the speech. For example, one student used the following rhetorical question to introduce a speech about the costs of cigarette smoking: "Did you ever think that smoking cigarettes could damage your health?" This question did not work well because listeners had already been barraged with information about the dangers of smoking. The student's second effort was much more successful in getting attention and in preparing listeners for the message:

Most of us know there are many things in life that can cause harm. Sometimes, the damage is immediate; sometimes, it's long-term. How much do you think the cost of smoking cigarettes adds to the national health bill each year?

Another caution regarding the use of a rhetorical question is that, unless you prepare the rhetorical question carefully, you could get the wrong answer. If that happens, you could appear foolish or your introduction could lose its impact. For example, a student asked the following question to introduce a speech to change beliefs: "Don't you agree that drinking ought to be a matter of choice for everyone who has reached the age of eighteen?" The students in the audience lived in a state where the legal drinking age was twenty-one. How do you think listeners reacted? Some listeners were about eighteen, but some were much older. One person was nearly sixty. A few audience members opposed drinking because of their religious beliefs. One woman was a member of MADD (Mothers Against Drunk Driving). Clearly, the speaker's opinion was not shared by many audience members. In this case, the rhetorical question was clearly detrimental to the speaker's goal.

THE CONCLUSION

The **conclusion** of your speech should be the unifying element for the ideas or the tone you develop in the speech body. Listeners need a concise reminder of the ideas or themes that you developed and an indication that you have finished speaking. The conclusion is the final impression you leave with listeners. What do you want listeners to take away from the speech? Decide clearly what the feeling, attitude, action, or information should be. Then, craft your conclusion around that thought, using the techniques outlined here.

PURPOSES OF THE CONCLUSION

A conclusion should (1) focus audience attention on what you have said, (2) signal listeners that you have finished, and (3) give some final thrust to the speech. A carefully planned conclusion provides listeners with a sense of closure and puts them in a mood to do as you have asked or stimulates them to think about your thesis statement.

If you keep the goals of your conclusion in mind, deciding how you want to end your speech is fairly easy. Ask yourself what you have tried to accomplish in discussing this topic. Then develop a conclusion that focuses listeners' thoughts and feelings on the speech's central ideas.

STRATEGIES FOR CONCLUSIONS

As shown in table 10.4, there are five main strategies for "wrapping up" your speech. Consider how each of them relates to your thesis, and then choose the strategy most appropriate for your speech. More detailed discussion and examples of each of these strategies follow.

Summary

Summarizing your main ideas is an effective way to conclude. One student finished her speech against capital punishment laws with the following summary:

> *So, what have I said to you this morning? I've shown you that capital punishment is not an effective deterrent to crime. I've argued that deliberately taking another person's life to punish them is nothing more than legalized murder. And I've shown you an alternative that is more humane than capital punishment. At best, imprisonment without chance of parole, along with intelligent use of the prisoner's lifetime, can do something positive for society.*
>
> *But the law won't be changed unless you act. It's up to you and to other Americans. It's the right thing to do.*

Here is how another student restated the major idea of his speech on additional funds needed for instructional programs:

> *A truly good university consists of an ample library, well stocked with books and periodicals. We must have money for scholarships which will attract the best and*

Table 10.4

STRATEGIES FOR CONCLUSIONS

STRATEGY	WHAT IT DOES
1. Summary	Restates the main ideas of the speech
2. Quotation	Uses a statement by another person to focus audience attention on the theme of the speech
3. Reference to the introduction	May restate the words or reinforce the mood set in the opening remarks
4. Call for action	Asks the listeners to do something described clearly in the body of the speech
5. Combinations	May combine a quotation with a call for action, ask for action and restate the introduction, or any of the other possible combinations

most diverse student body. And our faculty must be the best teachers available because teaching is the primary mission of this school.

A summary, however brief, can be an important part of any conclusion. It helps listeners to remember the main ideas and serves to justify any final appeal you make.

Quotation

Using a quotation in your conclusion helps to focus audience attention. Often, speakers prefer to repeat a quotation that was part of their introduction. Sometimes, a different quote is more effective. The quotation you select, however, whether used previously in the introduction or new, should reinforce the basic theme of your speech.

One student senator used a quotation in his conclusion to urge the student senate to stop postponing an ambitious campus renovation program:

So, in the words of Franklin Delano Roosevelt, "Never before have we had so little time in which to do so much." We must get moving. If we're going to be successful, we must begin today. Time is running out on this project, and our funding will disappear if we don't show considerable movement. Pitch in. Sign up. Become part of the team that will restore the beauty of this truly American campus.

In the conclusion to a speech about how important it is for people to find the fun in their lives and to learn to let go of their troubles from time to time, a student speaker effectively quoted G. K. Chesterton:

I think G. K. Chesterton had a profound message for all of us when he wrote: "Angels can fly because they take themselves lightly." If you want to succeed, you sometimes have to take yourself lightly. Find the fun in your life, or learn how to put fun into your life. Fly.

Reference to the Introduction

A theme that you explored in the introduction can be reused in your conclusion with very powerful effect. After one student related the story of his near-brush with death in a car accident, he developed a speech focused on regular use of safety equipment in cars. Then he closed with a reference to his introduction:

> *I hope that you won't have to be as terrified as I felt when I bumped my head along the pavement. It's not only convertibles that "flip." Remember that most of the fatal accidents happen within five minutes of your residence. Think of that when you jump in the car to drive to the store next week.*

This conclusion was effective because it reminded the audience again of the speaker's frightening personal experience that he related in his introduction. It also reemphasized that any car can turn over in an accident and that most auto wrecks occur near the driver's home.

Call for Action

Your speech will often have a goal of asking listeners to do something. The actions you seek may range from volunteering to work in a food bank to helping with voter registration. When you have goals like these, a straightforward call for action is often best.

A student speaker wanted listeners to volunteer their efforts for the Special Olympics. Her call for action was simple and direct:

> *Most of you know that the Special Olympics is one of the greatest experiences for the mentally and physically disadvantaged kids in this community. You've heard how rewarding this event is to the participants. It's just as rewarding to you when you see the 10- to 20-year-old straining with joy in their opportunity for competition. They don't care so much if they win. They love the chance just to compete. We want your help.*

> *Skip sleeping in next Saturday. Come to the Red Springs track and give us a hand to help your friends. Sign up on the sheet I'm passing around now. I guarantee you'll find it one of the most rewarding experiences you've ever had. Come on—give these kids a hand. You'd want them to help you, wouldn't you?*

What you ask for must be clear and easy to give. If listeners do not understand exactly what you want, or if your request is difficult or confusing, your chances for success are small. As you plan a call for action, ask yourself these questions:

1. Am I asking for something I can hope to get?
2. Will the listeners know what I am asking?
3. Am I making it easy for listeners to act?

EXAMPLE 10.2	EXAMPLE OF A COMBINATION CONCLUSION
	CONCLUSION
Brief summary and restatement of thesis	So what have we seen about the work load of the faculty? Whether we like it or not, work load differs according to the area of expertise and the person's level of talent. Our work load policy should reflect those differences.
How the thesis affects listeners	And we're, finally, the ones who have to change the work load policy. It affects everyone here. Beyond that, we have to remember it touches the quality of teaching, research, and service we provide to our students and the general public.
Reference to introduction, restatement of theme combined with closure that restates speaker position and focuses audience attention	We must act now. Pass this resolution in favor of variable work loads for faculty. What's the alternative? Just like that old truck I mentioned earlier, if we don't take time for maintenance—if we don't insist on time for our own research—we'll surely begin to rust and deteriorate. What will happen to the load we carry if that happens?

Combinations

You probably have already realized that it is possible to combine several conclusion strategies into a single conclusion. A combined approach may provide you with the strongest possible conclusion. Since your closing words may be the ones most clearly remembered by your audience, make them memorable.

In a speech to the faculty senate, Professor Pamela Robbins proposed variable work loads for university faculty. Her conclusion, shown in example 10.2, clearly exemplifies the power of the combined approach.

Summary

How a speech begins and ends is just as important as what comes in the middle. The aims of a speech introduction are to secure the attention and interest of listeners, establish a good relationship between speaker and listeners, and orient listeners to what they are about to hear. An effective introduction sets the tone for the speech.

Eight different introduction strategies can be used to secure listeners' attention. Many introductions incorporate a quotation, a startling statement, an illustration that emotionally involves listeners, a story that makes a point, a preview of the main ideas, or a simple greeting. Humor can be effective in an introduction, but it must be used carefully. Types of humor that inexperienced speakers might want to consider using include absurdity, confusion, human problems, exaggeration, playful ridicule, and surprise. A rhetorical question is also a useful strategy for an introduction but requires thoughtful preparation.

The conclusion of a speech should focus the thoughts and feelings of listeners on the speech's central ideas, signal to listeners that the speaker is finished, and offer some final motivating thrust for the speech. Listeners want closure, with the speech brought to an orderly end that is consistent with the ideas or actions the speaker suggested. Five effective conclusion strategies are: (1) summarizing your main ideas, (2) using a quotation to focus audience attention, (3) referring back to something stated in the introduction, (4) calling for action, and (5) combining several of the previous four conclusion strategies into a single conclusion.

Key Terms

Conclusion
Introduction

Application Questions

1. Working with one or two of your classmates, decide how you might develop an introduction and a conclusion that would relate each of the following topics to your classroom audience. Be prepared to explain your choices.
   a. Automobile repair
   b. Mountain climbing
   c. Money management
   d. Defense spending
   e. Capital punishment
   f. Chocolate mousse

2. Pay attention to the opening moments of your favorite television show. *How* did the show open? What features, if any, could you describe using the ideas in this chapter? Bring your notes to class, and be prepared to discuss your findings.

3. As a small group, select one of the topics in Application Question 1. Working individually, develop the best introduction for your classroom audience that you can imagine, using the suggestions in this chapter. Make notes about the reasoning behind your decisions. Compare and contrast your ideas with those of other group members. What insights can you draw from this experience? How do you account for any differences in approach?

Self-Test for Review

1. Name and describe the functions of a speech introduction.

   _____

   _____

   _____

   _____

2. Match the following introduction strategies to their definitions.

    _____ a. Humor   1. Statement of another individual used to focus attention

    _____ b. Illustration   2. Arresting, interesting fact or incident

    _____ c. Preview of main ideas   3. Example or case that helps to involve listeners

    _____ d. Quotation   4. Extended, interesting narrative about a subject

    _____ e. Rhetorical question   5. Outline of main points of a speech

    _____ f. Simple greeting   6. Welcoming statement to establish rapport with audience

    _____ g. Startling statement   7. Amusing story, anecdote, or situation used to create a favorable climate

    _____ h. Story   8. Question that implies its own answer and leads audience to interest in the topic

3. Name and describe the functions of a speech conclusion.

4. Match the following conclusion strategies to their definitions.

    _____ a. Call for action   1. Restates main ideas

    _____ b. Combination   2. Combines quotation with call for action

    _____ c. Quotation   3. Asks listener to do something described in body of speech

    _____ d. Reference to the introduction   4. Uses statement by another person to focus audience attention

    _____ e. Summary   5. Restates mood or words of opening remarks

Answers: 1. An introduction calls attention to subject matter and establishes relationships among the speaker, the subject of the speech, and the listeners. The goals are to gain attention, establish rapport with the audience, orient listeners to what is coming, and set the tone for the speech. 2. a. 7, b. 3, c. 5, d. 1, e. 8, f. 6, g. 2, h. 4 3. A conclusion should focus audience attention on what has been said, signal that the speech is over, and provide a final thrust to the speech. 4. a. 3, b. 2, c. 4, d. 5, e. 1.

Suggested Reading

Aristotle. *Rhetoric.* Translated by W. Rhys Roberts. New York: Modern Library, 1954. This book is suggested to make the point that speech teachers and rhetoricians have been giving the advice in this chapter for a very long time. *Rhetoric* was written about 340 years B.C.E. See Book III, chapters 13 and 19, especially. The W. Rhys Roberts translation is probably the best.

PART 4

Delivering the Speech

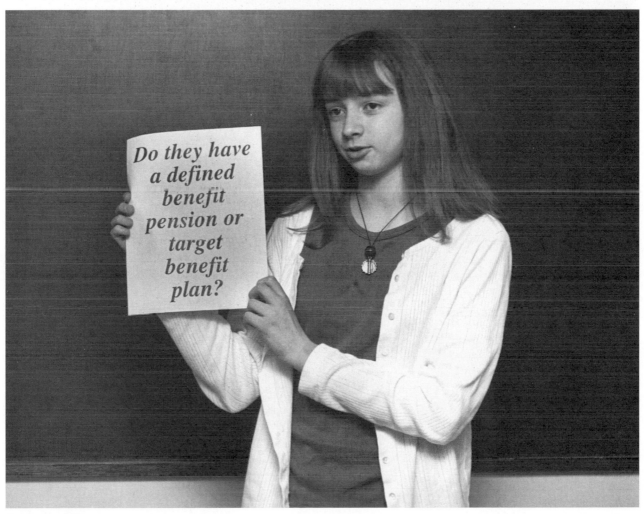

© James L. Shaffer

CHAPTER 11

Language: The Key to Successful Speaking

OUTLINE

OBJECTIVES

After reading this chapter, you should be able to:

1. *Define* the term *language,* and *explain* two reasons why it is important to use language wisely and carefully.
2. *Explain* the relationship between language and cognition.
3. *Illustrate* how language creates emotional affect.
4. *Define, compare and contrast,* and *illustrate* denotative and connotative meaning.
5. *Define* relational meaning and *explain* how it affects the speaker-audience relationship.
6. *Specify* and *explain* the characteristics of appropriate language.
7. *Illustrate* the importance of keeping language simple and clear.
8. *Explain* various ways to make language vivid for listeners.
9. *Explain* how language ambiguity creates problems.

© Daniel J. Olson/Unicorn Stock Photos

*T*his chapter explores the magical human tool of language. Language creates reality. It controls our cognitive behavior and feelings. Language also allows us to share three kinds of meaning: denotative, connotative, and relational. Thus, more than anything else, your success in achieving the effect that you want from a speech depends on how skillfully you select and use language.

This chapter explains how to choose language that is appropriate, simple, clear, vivid, and accurate. Offensive, insensitive, or sexist language always damages a speech, as do trite expressions, big words, and technical jargon. You will learn how to capture listeners' imaginations with vivid imagery, and how to select words and phrases that show listeners that you care about them and your subject.

Good communication gets the effect you want. Communication that does not achieve the desired effect is flawed in some way.

For example, consider the statements in table 11.1, which were taken from actual insurance company accident-report forms. The images and impressions you derive from these statements result from the writers' language choice and usage. Obviously, in these examples, poor language choice and usage obscure the intended message.

If you found humor in the statements, the humor was a result of your surprise at the unexpected and unconventional use of language, not because it was what the writer intended. Any judgments you may have made about the principals involved were, again, based on language usage.

Thus, whether you are writing for an insurance report or preparing a speech, language choices are critical to your success or failure to communicate your message. Develop your language skills, and you will be able to select words and phrases that leave the right impression with listeners.

LANGUAGE: SHARING REALITY AND MEANING

Language can be defined as a system of signs and symbols used by a **speech community** (all of those who use the same language system) to share meaning and experience. The words and phrases you choose create reality, both in your head and in the heads of listeners. They also carry three kinds of meaning: denotative, connotative, and relational. They define the relationship that exists between you and listeners. Thus, how you use language is important to your success in every communication event of your life. It is especially important to your success as a public speaker.

Table 11.1

STATEMENTS TAKEN FROM ACTUAL INSURANCE COMPANY
ACCIDENT-REPORT FORMS

1. I thought my window was down, but found it was up when I put my hand through it.
2. I pulled away from the side of the road, glanced at my mother-in-law, and headed for the embankment.
3. To avoid hitting the bumper of the car in front, I struck the pedestrian.
4. The pedestrian had no idea which direction to run; so I ran over him.
5. I saw a slow-moving, sad-faced old gentleman as he bounced off the hood of my car.
6. I had been driving for forty years, when I fell asleep at the wheel and had an accident.
7. In my attempt to hit a fly, I drove into a telephone pole.
8. That guy was all over the road. I had to swerve a number of times before I hit him.
9. The indirect cause of the accident was a little guy in a small car with a big mouth.
10. I told the police that I was not injured, but on removing my hat, I found that I had a fractured skull.

LANGUAGE CREATES REALITY

Truth and reality are relative to personal experience. What you believe in, trust in, have confidence in, and feel right about constitute your truth, your reality. They may not agree with someone else's notion of truth and reality.

For example, one of your friends may be convinced that President Clinton's domestic policies are right, while another friend disagrees. One of your friends may take a strong position on the issue of abortion, while you may disagree. One of your friends may be a devout churchgoer, absolutely committed to the ideology of the church, while another may be a militant atheist. Where lies the truth? What is real?[1]

If you want others to learn from you, believe you, or be persuaded by you, you use language. If you want others to share understanding or experience with you, you use language. Others use language to perceive and interpret your messages. In this sense, language creates reality.[2] As explained in the next two sections, in the process of creating reality, language works through cognition and affect.

Language and Cognition

Cognition is the act, power, or faculty of apprehending, knowing, or perceiving. According to Dean Hewes and Sally Planalp, cognition requires (1) information or knowledge structures, and (2) cognitive processes.[3] An **information structure** is how information is organized in your cognitive system. More simply, it is what you know—the body of

knowledge you have gathered and assimilated. A **cognitive process** is a mechanism used to handle information in the mind. Cognition is primarily a language activity.

What does all this mean as you consider how to use language in speech making? It means that what listeners comprehend, know, or perceive of your messages and intentions depends entirely upon your skill in choosing language.

Language and Affect

Affect is a combination of physical experience plus the language we use, either consciously or unconsciously, to describe the experience. An affective state is a subjective experience. When people are moved to do things, they always have feelings to accompany their motives. Indeed, sometimes, our emotions provide all the motivation we need—for example, if your excitement and pleasure at seeing your team make a winning touchdown causes you to jump to your feet and cheer.

Human emotional experience requires two factors: (1) We must be aroused or stimulated in some way, and (2) we must make something of that arousal—that is, we have to label our arousal as an emotion. Both are necessary. A word is not emotion without arousal. Arousal is not emotion without a word.

Thus, language is intimately tied to what we think and feel. Without language to process it, the reality outside our skins would seem no more significant to us than the air in the living room seems to your house cat or the water in the pond seems to the fish living there. Without language, our feelings would resemble mere physical experience, devoid of human passion. Clearly, then, if you want to have an impact on the thoughts and feelings of your audience, you need to know how to use language.

Example **11.1**   AN EXERCISE TO STUDY CONNOTATION

Directions: Write a word in the space provided below. For example, you might write the word *Mother.* Then place a check mark ✓ along each continuum according to how you experience the word. Write a word here: _____

Good								Bad
Soft								Hard
Active								Passive
Cruel								Kind
Heavy								Light
Slow								Fast
Honest								Dishonest
Weak								Strong
Hot								Cold

Compare your responses to those of a classmate who chose the same word to see how you two rated the word differently. The differences lie in connotative truth.

LANGUAGE CARRIES MEANING

Language carries three kinds of meaning: denotative, connotative, and relational. Each of these kinds of meaning influences every public speaking event, so you should consider all of them as you think about using language.

Denotative Meaning

Denotation is the literal dictionary definition of a word. It also refers to the associations usually called up by a word among members of a speech community. In other words, denotation refers to the features of a word that native speakers of a language usually accept. For example, when you use the word *chair,* you expect that others who speak English will know what you mean.

All words carry denotative meanings, or we could not exchange messages with each other. But since not everyone always knows the dictionary definitions, you should use simple, clear language when communicating. To illustrate, if a professor started tossing around highly technical terms without first providing definitions of those terms, you probably would feel confused. You might even stop listening. Similarly, if you as a public speaker start using words that your listeners do not commonly use, your listeners may tune you out.

Connotative Meaning

Connotation refers to the affective value or meaning of a word. Connotation is the emotional association an individual brings to or imposes on a word. You can get an idea about connotation by playing with the classic exercise in example 11.1, which is based on

Charles Osgood's idea of semantic space.[4] Osgood's idea was that words stimulate meaning inside people along three "dimensions" that he intuitively described and named: (1) evaluative dimension, (2) potency dimension, and (3) activity dimension.

According to Osgood, the **evaluative dimension** involves overall positive and negative determinations stimulated by a word. Such words as *good-bad, kind-cruel,* and *honest-dishonest* characterize the evaluative dimension. This idea was illustrated by a young mother-to-be, who when asked, "Do you know what you are going to name the baby?" replied:

> *If it's a boy, we'll name him Sam. My husband wants to name the baby Sylvia if it's a girl, but I hate that name. When I was in high school, I knew a Sylvia that I didn't like at all. I surely wouldn't want to saddle my baby with that name.*

Clearly the name "Sylvia" stimulates powerful negative evaluations in the young woman.

Osgood defines the **potency dimension** as a power dimension, involving such judgments as *strong-weak, hard-soft,* and *heavy-light* that people apply to words. The same young mother-to-be also provided a good example of the potency dimension. When asked, "Why the name Sam?" she replied:

> *It's a strong name, an American name. It's got a simple, unassuming power to it. A baby grows up to his name.*

The **activity dimension,** according to Osgood, is a movement dimension and relates to a word's dynamics—to what a word does. *Hot-cold, fast-slow,* and *active-passive* fill this dimension. When you write or speak the name of someone who has influenced your life, you experience an aspect of this dimension. Once again, let the young mother-to-be's struggle to find a name for her baby provide the illustration. When asked, "What girl names are you thinking about?" she replied:

> *I really like the name April. It sounds like springtime and joy and new grass to me. It's got a touch of sunshine in it.*

The point of all this is that people respond to language not only intellectually (the denotative meaning) but also emotionally (the connotative meaning). It is important, then, to choose language that elicits both the cognitive and emotional responses you want.

Relational Meaning

The **relational meaning** in language tells people how speakers define their relationship with listeners. If a person talks down to you, you know it and probably also resent it. If someone builds you up, you know that, too.

Relational meanings are completely subjective. Listeners observe the speaker and then guess (based on what they observe) how the speaker defines the relationship and whether the definition seems appropriate. For example, suppose that you and your friend decide to treat yourselves to a nice dinner in an upscale local restaurant but the waiter treats you with disdain and puts on a haughty "you're not good enough to eat in this restaurant" attitude. You would take offense, and rightly so. The waiter's messages clearly indicate how he defines your relationship, and the definition seems inappropriate.

As another example, if you decide that a speaker is racist, you probably have assigned relational meanings to the speaker's language choices. If a speaker seems sexist, that, too, probably results from the language choices the speaker has made. If a speaker seems prejudiced against old people, or people with disabilities, or gay people, these perceptions and interpretations involve relational meanings.

You can see this phenomenon at work in you classes. Most professors are very careful about how they relate to students, although they may or may not be consciously aware of what they do. They manage the relationship to produce an effect they want from the classes they teach.

Most professors approach their classes with respect. They define the relationship positively and treat students as fully matured adults. Unfortunately, occasional teachers feel superior to their students and make their feelings clear to their classes. Whose classes would you rather take? Which teachers would you rather know? Which teachers are more likely to succeed in the teaching and learning process?

Listeners will monitor your speeches to see how you define your relationship with them and whether or not that definition seems appropriate. When it does seem appropriate, listeners will give you a hearing. When it does not seem appropriate, your audience may give you less than rapt attention.

A good example of a bad speech illustrates the importance that listeners place on relational meanings. The assignment was to prepare and deliver a speech designed to teach class members something they would not be likely to know. Students were required to develop and use visual supporting materials. One male student carried a single sheet of poster paper to the front of the classroom. "You girls don't need this speech," he said, "but you men better listen up." Then he launched into a speech about how to do the laundry: "The first thing you need is a basket. It's to carry your clothes back and forth from the dorm to the laundromat. The second thing you need is a pair of rubber gloves." They were to keep the students from getting dishpan hands, he told them. "Finally, you need a pair of rubber boots." They were to keep students' feet from getting wet when they stupidly put too much soap into the washing machine, and too many clothes, with the result that the machine overflowed.

The speech received an unqualified *"F"* grade. The problem was not that the speaker could not perform. Rather, he defined the relationship between himself and the audience in completely the wrong way. Of the twenty-five students in that class, only about a third were men. The others were women, not girls, who were offended by the student's sexist remark. Moreover, all of the students—men and women—had a right to be respected, but the speaker's talk suggested that he did not care about their rights. It was as though he had said to himself, "I have to give a speech, so I'm going to give one, and to heck with everyone else."

Clearly, the language choices you make carry meanings of different kinds, and at different levels. Language controls the kinds of meaning people will draw from your speeches.

USING LANGUAGE WELL

You have already seen in this chapter that language can create problems. When language is used well, however, it can create many special effects of imagery and mood. What can you do to use language more effectively as you speak?

MARIO CUOMO

As one of the most highly regarded speakers on the American political scene, New York Governor Mario Cuomo has several clear and definite ideas about the speechmaking process, including thoughts on the skillful use of language. Here are a few excerpts from the *Diaries of Mario Cuomo*, with additional commentary by the authors:

Cuomo is one of the few politicians who prepares most of his own speeches. Of one speech, Cuomo attributed success to three factors: "It's an emotional speech; I wrote it myself and, therefore, was familiar with it; and it was typed on cards. There's no question that reading from cards makes the delivery better."

Although Cuomo has used assistance in writing speeches, Cuomo's own diary notes his dissatisfaction with finding a person who could perform the task adequately. What then are the qualities necessary for a Cuomo speechwriter? Someone who "is sensitive, gentle . . . who loves arranging words and singing songs in prose."

Important also in Cuomo's oratorical success is his speaking style. Although he spends many hours writing polished addresses, he has also been known to throw away the speech in favor of simple "talk." At the heart of his approach to speaking is an exchange of ideas with his audience. Referring to his 1983 inaugural address as governor of New York he notes: "I think the principle effectiveness was in the ideas—simple ideas that a lot of people feel good about . . . I think people want to feel good about themselves and the world. We are often a cynical people, but we don't want to be. We'd prefer to believe, to hope, to love . . . if only for a little bit."

Source: Mario M. Cuomo, The Diaries of Mario M. Cuomo: The Campaign for Governor. *Copyright © 1984 by Mario M. Cuomo. Reprinted by permission of Random House, Inc., New York. Photo UPI/Bettmann.*

USE APPROPRIATE LANGUAGE

Appropriate language is language that does not offend and that is not insensitive or sexist. Trite expressions or clichés are also considered inappropriate.

Avoid Offensive Language

If you use language that attacks or insults others, that slurs or slights listeners in any way, that affronts listeners' sensibilities, or that injures them, you are virtually guaranteed that offended listeners will not cooperate with you. Even so, speakers sometimes unintentionally use offensive language. Think about what you are going to say and how you plan to say it well in advance of the actual event.

A good rule of thumb about choosing language is: "If you're in doubt about the appropriateness of a word or expression, don't use it." This injunction extends to impertinence, any kind of inappropriate innuendo, making a joke at another person's expense, and attempting to diminish someone on the basis of religion, race, gender, or disability. Dirty jokes, sexual innuendoes, profanity, and indecency of any kind have no place in public speaking. You never have to do it.

Avoid Insensitive and Sexist Language

Avoiding insensitive and sexist language is as important as avoiding offensive language, and for the same reasons. Three suggestions apply here: (1) Focus on the person, rather than on an irrelevant feature of that person; (2) do not imply anything negative, such as pity, or with disabled people, inability to function; and (3) avoid insulting euphemisms. Tables 11.2 and 11.3 offer some alternatives for insensitive or sexist expressions.

Avoid Trite Expressions

A trite expression, sometimes called a *cliché,* is one that has been overused or simply worn out. Trite expressions leave the impression that your ideas are second-hand. They call attention to themselves to the point that listeners focus on the expression and miss what you are trying to communicate.

Table 11.4 lists two dozen clichés, and you can probably think of several dozen more. Avoid these "like the plague." They may seem "worth their weight in gold," but in the "dog-eat-dog" world of public speaking, a speech full of trite expressions will get your message "signed, sealed, and delivered"—to no one.

USE SIMPLE LANGUAGE

Work to keep your language level as simple as necessary for your audience. Prefer the nickel words to the eighty-five cent words, and avoid twelve-dollar words altogether.

This does not mean that you cannot create vivid images or be powerful in language choice. Match your choice of language to the level you believe your least skillful listener is capable of understanding. As a rule, the larger your audience, the less listeners' collective ability to listen to you, and the simpler your language ought to be.

To illustrate, table 11.5 shows part of a three-page list of suggested language options that the U.S. Department of the Navy circulated in an effort to improve official writing. Keep in mind that the strength of English is in its small, often one-syllable words. Simple language is understood by more people.

USE CLEAR LANGUAGE

Clear language is language that says something. It avoids the modifiers that weaken its impact and spoil its style. The English language is replete with words and phrases that do not say anything. Table 11.6 shows a representative list of say-nothing words, along with a typical sentence for each one. There are hundreds of such words. Try to avoid them.

Eliminate as much meaningless language as you can. Such words lack power and directness. Prove it to yourself by comparing the weaker and more powerful sentences in table 11.6.

Table 11.2

INSENSITIVE EXPRESSIONS AND ALTERNATIVES

Instead of Saying:	Try:
The deaf person	The person
The woman doctor	The doctor
The blind man	The man
The amputee	The person
The mentally retarded child	The child
Ellen is confined to a wheelchair.	Ellen uses a wheelchair.
Ellen is burdened with a grossly disfiguring disease.	Ellen has acne.
Ellen is a victim of cancer.	Ellen has cancer.
Ellen, an exceptional child, . . .	Ellen . . .
Ellen is suffering from . . .	Ellen has . . .

Table 11.3

SEXIST WORDS AND ALTERNATIVES

Sexist	Alternative	Sexist	Alternative
Businessman	Executive, manager, leader, person	Foreman	Supervisor
		Mailman	Mail carrier, letter carrier
Cameraman	Photographer, camera operator	Man and wife	Husband and wife
Chairman	Leader, presiding officer	Manmade	Artificial, manufactured
Cleaning lady	Custodian	Manpower	Workers, work force, labor
Co-ed	Student		
Congressman	Representative	Policeman	Police Officer
Fireman	Fire fighter	Salesman	Salesperson, representative

Table 11.4

EXAMPLE TRITE EXPRESSIONS

Worth its weight in gold	Flat as a pancake
Over the hill	Dumb as an ox
Fresh as a daisy	Red as a rose
Hard as nails	Black as pitch
Make a long story short	Mother Nature
Sick as a dog	Father Time
Sly as a fox	Dog-eat-dog
Rat race	Crack of dawn
Cool as a cucumber	Spring chicken
Crying over spilled milk	Signed, sealed, delivered
Greased lightning	Open-and-shut case
Pretty as a picture	Armed to the teeth

Table 11.5

SIMPLER WORDS AND PHRASES

INSTEAD OF SAYING:	TRY:
Accompany	Go with
Accordingly	So
Advantageous	Helpful
Attached herewith	Here's
At the present time	Now
Close proximity	Near
Cognizant	Aware
Concur	Agree
Constitutes	Is, forms, makes up
Contains	Has
Discontinue	Drop, stop
Enumerate	Count
Fatuous numbskull	Jerk
Feasible	Can be done
Inasmuch as	Since
Inception	Start
Magnitude	Size
Necessitate	Cause
Parameters	Limits
Promulgate	Announce, issue
Pursuant to	By, following, under
Recapitulate	Sum up
Remuneration	Pay
Subsequently	After, later, then
Terminate	End
Transmit	Send

Table 11.6

"SAY-NOTHING" WORDS AND EXAMPLES OF WEAK AND MORE POWERFUL SENTENCES

"Say-Nothing" Words	Example Sentence	More Powerful Sentence
A lot	What we need is a lot of money.	What we need is $300,000.
Kind of	This is kind of a difficult problem.	This is a difficult problem.
Sort of	This idea is sort of problematic.	This idea is problematic.
Perhaps	Perhaps this will solve the problem.	This will solve the problem.
You know	We should act now, you know?	We should act now.
It seems like	It seems like you are hesitating on this.	You're hesitating on this.
I hope	I hope I can get this done by Wednesday.	I'll have this done by Wednesday.
I think that	I think that this will solve your problem.	This will solve the problem.
Very	This engine is very powerful.	This engine is powerful.
Well	Well, the next main idea is . . .	The next main idea is . . .
Definitely	This solution is definitely the best.	This is the best solution.

For a better understanding of the importance of eliminating meaningless modifiers from your speech, examine the student speech sample that follows. The original has been edited to eliminate modifiers that sap the message's vigor and strength.

> *The ~~powerful~~ Federal Aviation Agency has ~~wisely~~ ruled that U.S. ~~commercial~~ airliners must be equipped with ~~a system of a lot of~~ explosive detection devices, ~~and they must have them~~ by ~~sometime around~~ 1994. Currently, ~~what happens is that~~ the airlines ~~sort of~~ screen passengers and ~~all their~~ carry-on bags by using X-ray machines and, ~~you know,~~ metal detectors.*

Sometimes, a speaker gets wrapped up in fancy language. Do not talk like a bureaucrat who has spent a lifetime hiding behind language excess. The more you complicate your sentences, the more you are likely to confuse listeners. For example, read the following notice about an upcoming workshop:

> *The computer tool seminar and workshop, which will be presented on September 15 in the Small Engineering Conference Room, may be of special interest to process engineers, but all interested personnel are invited to attend. Please advise Technical Training of your group's attendance plans before September 8.*

Now read the following edited version of the workshop notice. Which is clearer?

> *If you're a Process Engineer, you will find the computer tool seminar especially interesting. The workshop will be held on September 15 in the Small Engineering Conference Room. If you want to attend, please let us know before September 8.*

Additional suggestions for using clear language include:

- Use a single word instead of three or four words if you can.
- Use common words rather than jargon.

- Avoid stilted (formal, stiff) language.
- Say what you mean (without "beating around the bush").

USE VIVID LANGUAGE

Vivid language is specific. It aims at listeners' emotions. It reverberates with imagery and rhythm. It rings. It moves. Eliminate language that does not promote your message, but add language that does. Four pieces of advice will help you to use language more vigorously and more vividly: (1) Be specific, (2) use action language, (3) use comparison and contrast, and (4) use illustrations.

Be Specific

Listeners must take what you give them. If you want them to form an image, you must provide the specific materials they need to form it. Generalizations do not provide sufficient material.

Dan McDonald, a professor of English, uses what he calls the "Ginger principle" to emphasize the importance of being specific. The "Ginger principle" involves three concrete details—proper nouns, real numbers, and color—that help listeners to form images in their heads. McDonald uses the following sentence to illustrate his idea:

> *His cousin drove me to a nearby wood, where we sat drinking beer and listening to music until very late.*

While this sentence is grammatically correct, it does not provide enough specific information for you as a listener to form the desired image. As a result, the sentence describes a dull and lifeless setting. Notice how the addition of specific details (some "ginger") to the sentence transforms the image:

> *His cousin Ginger drove me to Johnston's Wood in her brand new, cherry red Mustang convertible. We drank a six-pack of Stroh's Light and listened to her collection of old Billy Holiday tapes until 2:30 A.M.*

This second version tells a story. You can imagine the scene because the sentences are specific. Spice your speech with real names, real numbers, and color. People will listen more carefully, and much more effortlessly, to what you have to say.

Use Action Language

One aspect of action language is learning to use the active voice. With active voice, the subject of each sentence does what the verb says. This allows listeners to draw more accurate inferences. In addition, passive voice—the opposite of active voice in that, instead of doing the acting, the subject of the sentence is acted upon—sounds awkward, stilted, and wordy. Consider the following examples:

Active: Congress passed the new bill.
Passive: The new bill was passed by Congress.

Active: Mary likes this poem.
Passive: This poem is liked by Mary.

Active: The critic saw the play.
Passive: The play was seen by the critic.

Active: A rainstorm delayed the ball game.
Passive: The ball game was delayed by a rainstorm.

Action language also includes short sentences, time words, and interrupted rhythms. Compare the passages that follow from a student's speech. The student's "after" version was written following a lecture on short sentences, time words, and interrupted rhythms.

> *Before:* We are now in the midst of a new era—the communications age. But our American schools aren't preparing our students to cope with the new age. Technology is changing so very rapidly that yesterday's advances are already obsolete. But the schools aren't changing, and perhaps they can't. They don't have the technology and they don't have the know-how to change. But clearly, something has to be done, and it must be done now.

> *After:* We are all affected. We can't escape the problems of the communications era. But we're not ready, and the schools are not ready. Technology has changed the educational calendar, but it hasn't changed the educational system. Each day is but a single tick of the giant clock of history. And the hands of the clock move relentlessly toward a new day. They move at a real-world speed that leaves us breathless. It's seventeen minutes before midnight on that clock. We'd better do something, and do it now.

Learning to use action language is not difficult, but it takes practice. Like specific language, action language helps you to *show* your listeners what you mean, rather than merely tell them.

Use Comparison and Contrast

Comparison and contrast add vividness and accuracy to a speech. They help you to clarify your ideas by placing one concept next to another and showing similarities and differences. Different forms of comparison and contrast include analogy and metaphor. **Analogy** explains a particular subject by pointing out its similarities to another subject, usually one that is better known or more easily understood. **Metaphor** is an implied comparison between two unlike things that is used to show some unexpected likeness between the two.

The analogy of the clock in the "After" example in the previous section gives the passage a sense of urgency and force it would not otherwise have had. The power comes from comparing something listeners know to something they do not know. Thus, comparison and contrast help people to comprehend and understand.

Here is how one speaker used comparison and contrast to argue against building an elevated interstate highway spur through downtown Mobile, Alabama. Partly because of powerful speaking like this, that elevated highway spur was never built.

We have lots of evidence that putting an elevated interstate highway through a downtown area creates a slum in the area under the highway. This certainly has been the case in Kansas City, Chicago, Detroit, Denver, Los Angeles, and New York. And it will be true of Mobile, as well.

If you want to see what your support for the elevated highway will bring to Mobile, take a drive to New Orleans on Interstate 10. When you get there, follow along the interstate, but underneath it. You will find empty buildings with broken windows. You will find abandoned cars. You will find winos sleeping in the doorways of abandoned businesses. But be sure to lock your car and close the windows, because you will also find a criminal element on that trip ready and willing to knock you on the head and steal your car and your money.

I can't believe that anyone here wants that to happen in Mobile. But it most certainly will happen to Mobile if this highway is built. It has happened in every metropolitan downtown area where an elevated highway has been built. So the question is not whether we ought to have an interstate highway extension through our city. The question is whether we want to create a slum in our beautiful downtown area.

Comparison and contrast also can be used to build a sense of concreteness. Compare something that exists in the real world to the abstraction you want to make seem real:

Choosing to get married is something like choosing to take a trip on a bicycle built for two. You have to agree where you are going. You both have to work together to get there. To help make the trip pleasant, you probably will take turns at the handlebars. And, of course, preventive maintenance is a must. If you don't oil the bike now and then, and fix an occasional flat tire, you probably won't finish the trip.

Be careful not to overdo comparison and contrast. You might create some unusual associations by accident. Overused and mixed metaphors (using more than one metaphor in a single illustration) are the two most common problems in using figurative language. This argument, produced by the local coordinator of an organization called March Against Crime, illustrates the problem:

The Youthful Offender Act is a sacred cow for trial lawyers and other special interests with clout in Montgomery. . . . The purported purpose of the act is to prevent the "stigma" of the crime from tainting the good name of the criminal. Said unworthy purpose is lost in the dust of the aforesaid cow. That's who's on first.[5]

Additional guidelines for using comparison and contrast are: (1) Follow one line of analysis, (2) drive toward a single purpose, and (3) play fair. Let us look at each of these guidelines in more detail.

Follow One Line of Analysis

You can compare and contrast electric heat and gas heat in numerous ways. For example, you could focus on their comparative efficiency or on their comparative contribution to environmental pollution. In either case, the line of analysis determines what you compare and contrast. Stay with one line of analysis, or you risk confusing your listeners. Let your thesis sentence determine the line of analysis you decide to follow.

Drive Toward a Single Purpose

Comparison and contrast generally has one of the following three purposes in a speech: (1) to clarify something, (2) to show that one thing is superior to another, or (3) to use the comparison as a way of supporting a general knowledge claim. Let one purpose drive your comparison and contrast. Otherwise, you risk confusing listeners.

Play Fair

Argument by analogy can lead you into fallacious reasoning if you are not careful. Play fair with listeners. If you see that your analogy holds in most ways, but breaks down in others, mention this fact to listeners. Listeners will appreciate your candor, and your credibility with them will increase. If you do not, and listeners see the holes in your analogy on their own, your credibility may be in jeopardy.

Use Illustrations

People think about concepts in predictable ways. They begin by trying to visualize a concrete image that makes sense to them. In other words, they seek an illustration. Knowing this, you can help listeners to understand your idea by illustrating it.

Your audience will usually be composed of a broad range of people from different walks of life, with differing abilities to receive and process your message. Abstract ideas that may carry meaning for some members of that audience will have no meaning value for others. Use lots of examples and illustrations to provide audience members with a common ground on which to come to grips with your ideas. You may wish to review chapter 6, "Supporting Ideas with Arguments and Evidence," where illustrations and examples are discussed in detail.

USE ACCURATE AND UNAMBIGUOUS LANGUAGE

Language is nothing if it is not ambiguous. No direct relationship exists between a referent and the word that represents it. When you say *car,* or *rock,* or *tree,* listeners have to process the words and make something of them. That is easy when the word refers to something concrete. For example, when you hear the word *tree,* you get a picture—undoubtedly a composite—in your mind of something you have experienced with regard to this word. Because your experience is unlike anyone else's, you create an image in your mind unlike any other.

Since everyone in your audience does this with language, your success in communicating with them depends on how accurately you use language. To illustrate the problem, consider the italicized words in the sentences in table 11.7. Each of these sentences swings in more than one direction, largely because of the italicized word. Why confuse a listening audience with this kind of talk? Instead, say what you mean and say it simply.

Table 11.7

SENTENCES THAT CAN HAVE MORE THAN ONE MEANING

This is an *acceptable* alternative.
He *admits* that he was home by 10:00 P.M.
He *claims* that he was home by 10:00 P.M.
I *can't* see you this afternoon.
She's a *clever* woman.
She's an *experienced* woman.
She's a *fair* woman.
James Council is an *intellectual*.
James Council is an *impressive* fellow.
James Council has an *obsession*.
James Council's file is *virtually* complete.
James Council is a *freedom fighter. (Terrorist?)*

Summary

More than anything else, your language skills will determine whether you succeed in getting the effect you want from your speeches. Language is the system of signs and symbols used by a speech community (a group of individuals who use the same language system) to share meaning and experience.

Language creates reality because it is intimately tied to what we think and feel. Language also carries three kinds of meaning: (1) denotative (a word's literal definition), (2) connotative (a word's emotional associations), and (3) relational (the speaker's relationship with listeners). Thus, language allows us to share meaning with others and to understand our relationships with them.

To use language well, speakers should concentrate on making their words appropriate, simple, clear, vivid, and accurate. Appropriate language does not offend, is not insensitive or sexist, and does not consist of trite expressions or clichés. Simple language requires the use of nickel words over eighty-five-cent words so that your least skillful listener is capable of understanding. Clear language is language that says something without getting tangled in meaningless modifiers or technical jargon. Vivid language requires providing specific information, using action language, comparing and contrasting, and incorporating numerous illustrations. The accuracy of your language will determine whether you are actually able to communicate your message to listeners.

Learn to use language wisely and well. The quality and success of your speeches depend on it.

Key Terms

Activity dimension of
  language
Affect
Analogy
Cognition
Cognitive process

Connotation
Denotation
Evaluative dimension of
  language
Information structure
Language

Metaphor
Potency dimension of
  language
Relational meaning
Speech community

Application Questions

1. Ask five of your friends who have not studied public speaking or communication: What is language? Notice how their responses compare and contrast. How do you account for the similarities and differences?
2. Pay close attention to a televised commercial. If possible, videotape the commercial and then write out the exact spoken and written language used. Do you notice any relationship between the language choices and the commercial's intended goal? In terms of this chapter, what are those relationships?
3. Make a list of car names (Camry, Mirage, Crown Victoria, Sable, and so on). Do you find any relationship between the kind of car the name represents, the car's name, and the intended market? Make a similar list of truck names (Bronco, Blazer, Trooper), and perform a similar analysis. How might you use your insights to improve your speech making?

Self-Test for Review

1. Which of the following *best* defines the term *language?*
   a. A system of signs and symbols used by a speech community to share meaning and experience
   b. A phonetic sound system used in speech behavior to isolate morphemes
   c. A system of words, plus rules for their use, that allows people to correspond
   d. A complete set of signs and sounds that allows speaking and writing among people in the same community

2. Which of the following is accurate regarding the statement that language creates reality?
   a. This statement is true because language controls what we think.
   b. This statement is true because language controls what we feel.
   c. This statement is true because language both controls what we think and how we feel.
   d. This statement is false. Language does not create reality.

Mark the following items: R = relational, C = connotation, D = denotation.

_____ 3. Refers to associations usually called up by a word in a speech community

_____ 4. Refers to the affective value of a word

_____ 5. Evaluative, potency, and activity dimensions

_____ 6. The dictionary definition of a word

_____ 7. Charles Osgood's semantic space

_____ 8. A speaker's attitude toward listeners

9. What is *relational meaning?*

  a. The relationship between denotation and connotation

  b. The similarities between connotation and denotation

  c. The message that speakers send about how they understand their relationships to listeners

  d. The phenomenon of interpersonal attraction that operates in a public speaking situation

Correct the following statements by striking through meaningless modifiers.

10. Ladies and gentlemen, may I present the charming and beautiful Miss Judy Jackson.

11. Thank you for your kind hospitality so generously extended to me during this visit.

12. Open your wonderful textbook to page 344.

Rewrite these sentences, using the active voice.

13. The new bill was passed by Congress.

14. The play was seen by the critic.

15. The plane was delayed by the weather.

Answers: 1. a. 2. c. 3. D. 4. C. 5. C. 6. D. 7. C. 8. R. 9. c. 10. Ladies and gentlemen, may I present ~~the charming and beautiful Miss~~ Judy Jackson. 11. Thank you for your ~~kind~~ hospitality ~~so generously extended to me during this visit~~. 12. Open your ~~wonderful~~ textbook to page 344. 13. Congress passed the new bill. 14. The critic saw the play. 15. The weather delayed the plane.

Suggested Readings

Eschholz, Paul, Alfred Rosa, and Virginia Clark, eds. *Language Awareness.* 6th ed. New York: St. Martin's Press, 1994. This reader includes some of the most interesting and provocative excerpts about language available in any one source. Contributors include George Orwell, Jeffrey Schrank, Edwin Newman, Hugh Rank, Gordon Allport, S. I. Hayakawa, Neil Postman, and Stephen King.

Fromkin, Victoria, and Robert Rodman. *An Introduction to Language.* 5th ed. New York: Holt, Rinehart and Winston, 1993. This is a comprehensive but easy-to-read introductory text about language. This book should be on the desk of anyone who cares about understanding and using language.

CHAPTER **12**

Supporting Ideas Visually

OBJECTIVES

After reading this chapter, you should be able to:

1. *Specify* when to use visual aids.
2. *Name* what you should support with visual aids and *explain* why.
3. *Describe* the steps in developing a visual aid program.
4. *Explain* how to apply three criteria for choosing the right visual medium for a visual aid program.
5. *Explain* why overhead projectors are popular speaking tools, and *list* several tips for using overhead projectors in your visuals program.
6. *Describe* and *use* the principles of layout and design including (a) the rule of thirds, (b) straight lines and curved lines, (c) the balance of triangles, (d) eye movement and negative space, (e) sketches and illustrations, and (f) language and lettering.
7. *Demonstrate* correctly how to introduce, present, explain, and put away visual aids.

© Bob Daemmrich/Stock Boston

*W*ell-made visual supporting materials enhance most public speeches, but only if they contribute something to the speech. In this chapter, you learn when to use visual aids, what to show on them, how to develop visual materials, and the four-step sequence of visual aid presentation.

Use visual aids to simplify complexity, to help listeners organize your ideas, to control audience attention, and to help listeners understand your ideas and remember them. In addition, a well-designed visual aid program helps you to organize your thoughts and stay on track during a speech. Visuals are especially helpful for showing problems, solutions and benefits, processes, procedures, and steps in a sequence.

Developing a visual aid program involves a number of steps, from identifying the key ideas that need support, to designing thumbnail sketches, to practicing with "rough" visuals, to reviewing and revising the final visuals program. You should also consider the convenience, cost, and communication power of each visual medium. The principles of effective layout and design presented in the chapter will aid you when producing a visual aids program. The chapter concludes with a description of a simple, four-step procedure for using your visual aids: (1) Introduce the visual aid before you present it. (2) Present the visual aid with a minimum of talk so that listeners can concentrate on looking instead of listening. (3) Explain the idea you are trying to illustrate. (4) Then put the visual aid away.

The term *visual* implies looking. The term *aid* implies support. A **visual aid** is any object, photograph, chart, graph, sketch, or lettered poster that supports a speech or the speaker. Visual aids can be three-dimensional, but as a rule, two-dimensional visual materials work better to support a speech. A three-dimensional object small enough to manipulate easily is probably too small to be an effective visual aid, although there are exceptions, of course.

Effective visual aids contribute something to a speech. Either they help listeners to understand or identify with a speech, or they help the speaker. If visual material fails to make a positive contribution, it is not an aid. In fact, some visual materials may even detract from the speaker's goals.

Learning when to use visual aids, what to visualize, and how to develop visual materials will help you to achieve your speaking goals. In addition, a broad range of visual media are available to help ensure that your visual materials will have maximum effect during your speech.

WHEN TO USE VISUAL AIDS

Full and frequent use of visual materials will help you to succeed in almost every kind of speech. Probable exceptions would be speeches in which you introduce another speaker or acceptance speeches for receiving an award or nomination. For these types of speeches, visual aids probably would not be necessary. But in most other speeches, visual aids can contribute to your speech goals. Table 12.1 lists six important uses of visual supporting materials.

Table 12.1

SIX USES OF VISUAL SUPPORTING MATERIALS

1. To simplify complexity
2. To help listeners organize your ideas
3. To control audience attention
4. To help listeners understand abstract ideas
5. To help listeners remember
6. To help you remain organized while speaking

TO SIMPLIFY COMPLEXITY

You should always try to present ideas as simply as possible. However, sometimes, you must discuss complex material that listeners may have trouble following. For example, engineers and financial people often need to present very technical information to managers or other decision makers who do not have technical training. In these situations, listeners often need the help of visual materials to understand the speaker's ideas.

To help listeners understand such technical information as statistics, projected costs, or complex policies and procedures, simplify your presentation with a visual program. Charts, graphs, tables, models, and flowcharts will make complex information easier for listeners to understand (see figure 12.1).

TO HELP LISTENERS ORGANIZE YOUR IDEAS

Suppose you want to discuss two or three main ideas, each of which you want to break down into two or three subpoints. Or perhaps you want to describe both a problem and a solution to the problem, each part of which has two or three main ideas. Visual supporting materials will help listeners to follow your organization. Figure 12.2 shows three visual aids a college debater might use to help listeners follow a complex ten-minute speech.

TO CONTROL AUDIENCE ATTENTION

Listeners must pay attention before they can learn or be persuaded by what you say. As a speaker, you face the important task of controlling listener attention, and visual aids can help in that regard.

Take a lesson from television. Advertisers know how to use visual material to hold viewer attention. To see how they do it, watch your television set for any two-minute period. Turn the sound off, and count the number of times the picture changes. Examine the movement on the screen. Those changes, that movement, hold viewer attention so well that a few people cannot focus on anything else.

Figure **12.1**

Visual aids can take many forms, but often they serve a common goal—to simplify complexity.

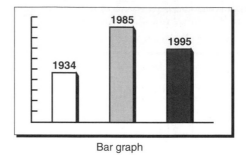

Bar graph

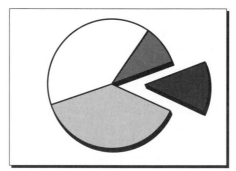

Pie chart

	1985	1995
1.	673.50	1,283.40
2.	2,196.30	443.50
3.	95.90	95.90
4.	3,433.75	6,423.40
5.	87.30	92.55
	$6,486.75	$8,338.75

Two-column statistical table

As a speaker, you can use visual materials with much the same effect. If you present an idea, refer to a visual aid, then put the visual away, you move the audience's attention from yourself to the visual and then back to yourself again. Careful timing of visual presentations will help you to get listeners' attention and to keep it.

TO HELP LISTENERS UNDERSTAND ABSTRACT IDEAS

Occasionally, you may need to present abstract ideas, ideas that are difficult for listeners to conceptualize. Abstract concepts presented without visual materials can overwhelm your audience. One student had to deal with abstract ideas when he tried to describe the

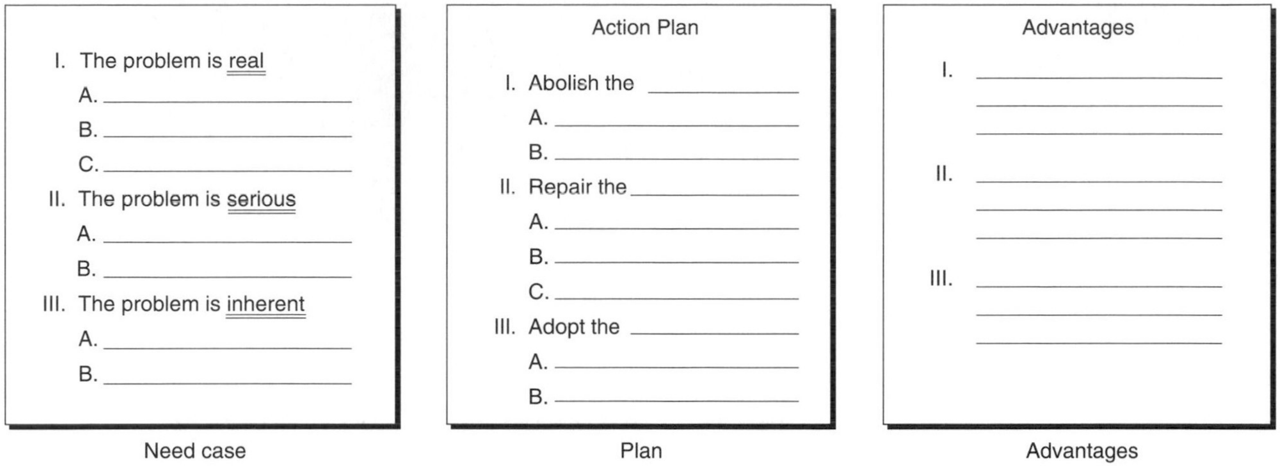

I. The problem is <u>real</u>	Action Plan	Advantages
A. _____	I. Abolish the _____	I. _____
B. _____	A. _____	_____
C. _____	B. _____	_____
II. The problem is <u>serious</u>	II. Repair the _____	II. _____
A. _____	A. _____	_____
B. _____	B. _____	_____
III. The problem is <u>inherent</u>	C. _____	III. _____
A. _____	III. Adopt the _____	_____
B. _____	A. _____	_____
	B. _____	
Need case	**Plan**	**Advantages**

engineering involved in building the world's longest underwater tunnel between France and England. Although the speech needed focus, the student's visual materials made his complex ideas easy to follow, as the following speech excerpts and illustrations show:

A private company built a tunnel between Dover, England, and Calais, France. It is the longest underwater tunnel in the world, and it makes car travel from England to France almost as fast as airplane travel.

At this point the student presented his first visual aid—a simplified map of the English Channel (see figure 12.3). It showed the location of the tunnel and related statistics.

The speaker presented a second visual to show how such a tunnel could be drilled (see figure 12.4):

A soft but waterproof layer called marl chalk *lies just below the surface of the channel bed. It runs most of the way from England to France. Because it's both soft and waterproof, and close to the channel floor, it was easy to drill a tunnel through that layer. Two giant boring machines, one working from England, and one from France, met near the center of the tunnel.*

Here the speaker presented his third visual aid, showing one of the boring machines (see figure 12.5). He used the visual aid to describe how the drilling machine works and to point out several of its interesting features.

Actually, they drilled three tunnels—two for the trains, and a third, in the center, for service vehicles.

Here the speaker displayed a fourth visual aid (see figure 12.6) and explained that two tunnels were needed because the trains had to run both directions and that a third, smaller tunnel is used to service the other two. Without his four visual aids, the student would have had a difficult time helping his audience to understand and be interested in such technical information.

Figure **12.2**

When strict organization is critically important in a speech, a visual aid showing the organization can be useful.

Figure **12.3**

The first of four visual aids for a speech about the Eurotunnel: A simplified map of the English Channel.

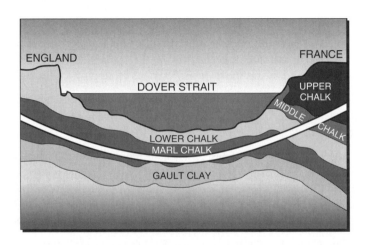

FACT LIST
- 32.2 MILES LONG
- $12-BILLION COST
- LONDON-PARIS IN 4 HOURS

England

DOVER

CALAIS

France

Figure **12.4**

Visual aid diagram showing layer of marl chalk.

ENGLAND

FRANCE

DOVER STRAIT

UPPER CHALK

MIDDLE CHALK

LOWER CHALK

MARL CHALK

GAULT CLAY

Figure **12.5**

Visual aid diagram of the boring machine.

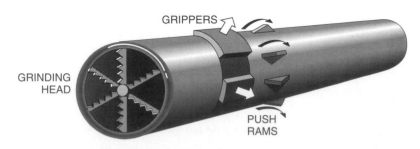

THE MOLE

GRIPPERS

GRINDING HEAD

PUSH RAMS

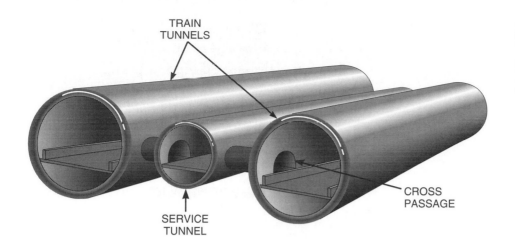

Figure **12.6**

Visual aid diagram of the three tunnels of the Eurotunnel.

TRAIN
TUNNELS

CROSS
PASSAGE

SERVICE
TUNNEL

TO HELP LISTENERS REMEMBER

Good visual aids not only teach—they help audience members to remember. Both functions are critical.

To illustrate, a student lawyer told her audience of student court members that they needed to understand and remember the answers to three questions if they were going to reach a fair decision about her client. The student on trial was accused of damaging university property through malicious mischief. Apparently, he had broken up with his steady girlfriend, drunk too much beer, and then smashed a lamp by throwing it across his dormitory room. The student court had the authority to expel the defendant if court members thought he was guilty and if the situation warranted such a response.

"You must remember these three questions," said the defendant's representative, while displaying a poster like that in figure 12.7. "Did Tom Johnston do malicious mischief?" She pointed to the first question on the poster. "Were there any extenuating circumstances?" She pointed to the second question. "Was what he did really serious enough to warrant expulsion from this university?" She pointed to the third question on the poster and then explained her position:

> Tom surely did break the lamp. He surely did throw it across the room. He did smash university property, and he has since bought a new one. Those are the facts, and the facts are not in question.

> But did Tom do malicious mischief? He didn't just tear up the lamp in his room for the fun of it. He didn't do an act of common vandalism. He didn't set out in advance to trash his dorm room. What he did was thoughtless, unpremeditated. It wasn't malicious mischief, and that is what he is being tried for. The answer to the first question is "no."

> And clearly, there were extenuating circumstances. Tom's behavior can't be condoned, but it can be understood. Wouldn't you also feel like throwing something if you had just broken up with someone special to you?

Figure **12.7**

The members of the student court were more likely to remember Tom Johnstons's defense summary because his student lawyer provided a visual aid showing the main points of her speech.

But let's suppose he had set out, in advance, to trash his room. And suppose, also, that Tom had not just broken up with his steady. We deny these things, but suppose them anyway. You still have to consider the third question. Was what he did serious enough to merit throwing him out of college?

Certainly not. A broken-up lamp is not worth a broken-up education. A smashed light fixture is not worth smashing a man's college program.

So, as you consider what you will do about Tom Johnston, please keep these three questions in mind. They make the difference in this case.

After concluding her speech, the student walked to her chair, leaving the poster and its three questions on the easel in front of the student court. It was a dramatic use of visual material to help listeners remember the purpose of her speech.

TO HELP YOU REMAIN ORGANIZED WHILE SPEAKING

Your visual aid program can also be the "notes" you use during your speech to keep yourself on track. This use of visual materials works so well that the market for "presentation software" has grown into a multi-million-dollar industry in the United States. Figure 12.8 shows how one such program, Microsoft PowerPoint for Windows, helps use visual materials for notes. The outline in figure 12.8 becomes a series of transparencies. Figure 12.9 displays one of these transparencies; the software allows the presenter to provide the visual aids with or without a border.

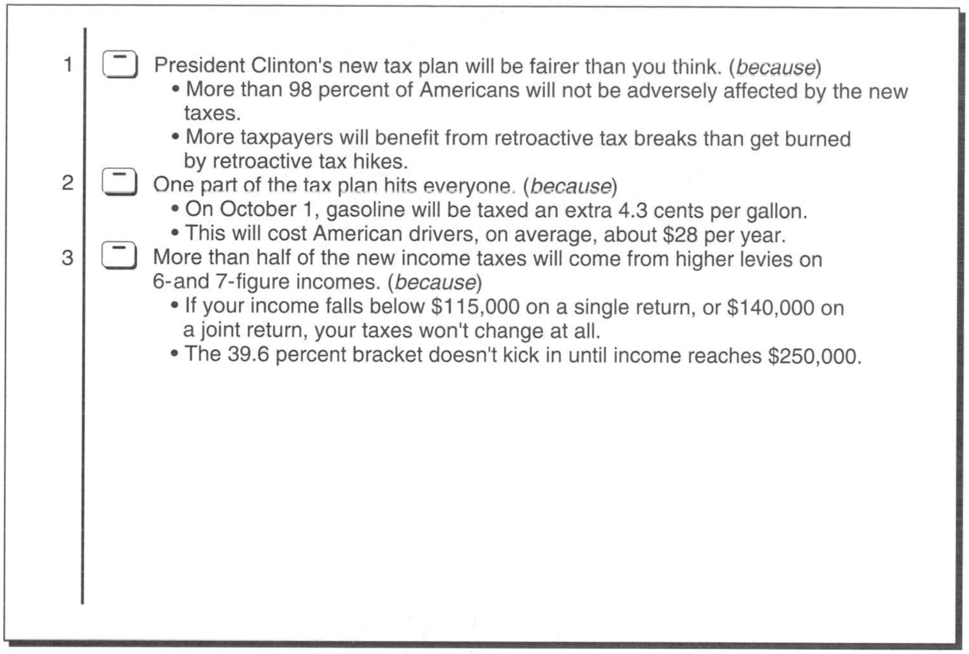

Figure **12.8**

Part of a speaker's planning outline generated by Microsoft PowerPoint for Windows.

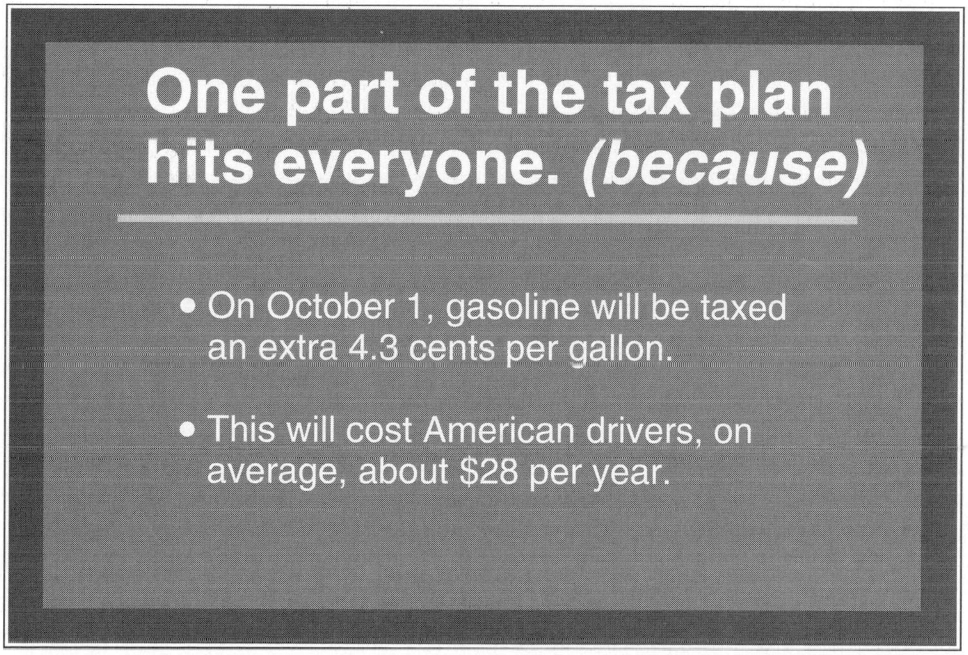

Figure **12.9**

A transparency generated from speaker's planning outline in figure 12.8.

What audience members may not realize is that these transparencies serve the speaker as much as they serve audience members. The same visuals that help listeners to follow your ideas also help you to follow your speech plan.

WHAT TO SUPPORT WITH VISUAL MATERIALS

A student speaker complained: "I just don't think I need any visual aids in this speech." By now you probably know that the student was emphasizing the wrong thing: *You* may not need any visual aids, but listeners almost certainly will need them. Keep your focus on the audience as you consider what to support with visual materials. Visual materials are especially helpful for showing problems, solutions and benefits, processes, procedures, and steps in a sequence.

SHOW PROBLEMS

As a speaker, you will often need to ask listeners to understand or care about a problem. For example, an engineer working in the paper industry wanted her management group to budget more money for preventive maintenance. She also wanted authorization to shut down any machine briefly when she felt preventive maintenance was necessary. But shutdowns are costly. Each minute that a paper machine is not operating can cost thousands of dollars.

A major problem in the papermaking process is corrosion. Corrosion plays havoc with paper machines, but it occurs slowly, almost imperceptibly. At the same time, people do not make decisions to solve problems they cannot see or identify. The engineer knew that before members of her management group would agree to a shutdown, or to increase the maintenance budget, they would have to be shown that the problem really existed. Beyond that, the problem would also need to be seen as important, compelling, and high priority.

This is where visual supporting materials played an effective role. Because the engineer could not bring management group members to the problem (corrosion is slow and difficult to observe), she decided to bring the problem to them. A new motor housing that had been installed in her section provided the opportunity she needed. Every three days over a four-week period, she took close-up photographs of the new motor housing. Before taking each picture, she placed a small sign on the housing that showed the date and time. Thus, she had a photographic record of the effects of corrosion on the new housing over a four-week period.

In addition, she photographed many examples of corrosion in other parts of the plant and calculated the costs of that corrosion in terms of machine failure, accidental shutdown, and machine-part replacement. She put all of this information into visual form, along with cost estimates of preventive maintenance and planned shutdown.

When she presented her findings to management group members, they authorized her proposal. Her visuals helped them to understand the problem clearly and to feel compelled to act. The engineer's presentation probably would not have been successful without the visual materials. People will not try to solve problems they cannot understand or see. Sometimes, you have to show them.

SHOW SOLUTIONS AND BENEFITS

Imagine that you have to propose a particular solution to a well-known problem. Your speech must show that your idea will solve or resolve the problem better than other alternatives. Your chances for success rise dramatically when you display visual materials that show listeners the likely solutions and benefits you propose.

To illustrate, a group of city officials determined that the city should build a large convention center on the downtown waterfront to attract major conventions. The hope was that a new center would bring people and money to town and revitalize the decaying downtown area. The proposal's short-term advantages were new jobs and enhanced cash flow in the local economy. But the project was going to be expensive. How do you persuade the citizens of a fairly conservative community to spend more than $30 million?

To persuade the press corps, and through them the local community, city officials had an architectural firm develop a series of impressive illustrations of the proposed center. They also hired a consulting firm to project, as realistically as possible, revenues and a rate of return. The data were presented in a series of easily read and visually appealing graphs and pie charts that illustrated the convention center's potential financial benefits. When all was ready, the mayor and other local dignitaries called a press conference to announce the new initiative. They used the visuals to show how the proposed convention center was a solution to the problem of a dragging local economy and to illustrate the benefits that this center would accrue for the community. Although a few audience members were skeptical, the project received favorable press from that meeting onward.

By illustrating solutions and benefits with visuals, you enhance the persuasive power of your speech. The visuals also help to involve listeners emotionally and to show them how a fairly complex plan of action holds together. People have to *see* what you mean.

SHOW PROCESSES, PROCEDURES, AND STEPS IN A SEQUENCE

In addition to showing problems, solutions, and benefits, visual aids help people to understand processes and to follow procedures and sequential steps. For example, the personnel office of a large midwestern corporation decided to change its health-care benefit program from one insurance company to another. In making the transition, management determined that employees within five years of retirement should have the right to choose whether to remain with the old program or to enroll in the new. If they chose the new program, they would have to specify the coverage they preferred. This meant that each employee making the change would have to fill out a complicated form. The personnel director decided to meet with those employees and teach them how to fill out the form. So she developed a series of overhead projector transparencies to illustrate each step in the procedure. The meeting lasted one hour, and sixty-two of sixty-five people filled out the form correctly.

Whenever your speech topic calls for explaining a process, describing a procedure, or presenting the steps in a sequence, visual supporting materials will make your job easier. Not only will listeners understand your presentation better—they will also tend to remember it longer.

STEPS IN DEVELOPING A VISUAL AID PROGRAM

So far, you have studied what to support with visual materials, and when, but developing the actual visual materials is another matter. The remainder of the chapter focuses on steps in developing a visual aid program, choosing the right medium for visual supporting materials, designing and making your own visual materials when your circumstances require it, and using those materials to maximum effect.

Assuming that you have a fairly clear notion of what you want to say in your speech, the steps involved in developing a visual aid program should fall neatly into place.

THINK ABOUT KEY IDEAS

The first step is to think about your ideas. Which of your ideas seem complex? Which ones stand on their own? Which ones require visual support? Review the discussion of how to use note cards to help you plan the main ideas of your speech (see chapter 7, "Gathering Supporting Materials and Using the Library"). Those note cards can help you with this part of speech preparation, too. Lay them out again, or look closely at your planning outline (chapter 9, "Outlining the Speech").

DEVELOP A ROUGH PLAN FOR THE VISUAL PROGRAM

From the listener's point of view, what kinds of visual materials would be most useful to understanding your ideas? Which of your key ideas seem most difficult, most important, most memorable? Decide what kinds of visual materials you intend to use and what ideas these materials will illustrate or support.

DESIGN THUMBNAIL SKETCHES OF EACH VISUAL AID

Lay out a series of thumbnail sketches of planned visual aids. Do you need to add any? Delete any? Figure 12.10 shows a series of thumbnail sketches for a visual program for a speech on the communication model. The layout includes six separate visuals for a six-minute speech. What do you think? Are there too few? Too many? Only practicing your speech with your visual aids will tell you if your visual aids program is too ambitious, or incomplete.

Leadership behavior is communication behavior.

Objectives for Session #1

- Separate personal from interpersonal communication.
- Explain three key principles.
- Name five interaction guidelines.
- Define communication.

**Key Principle #1.
Maintain or
enhance self-esteem.**

**Key Principle #2.
Listen and respond
with empathy.**

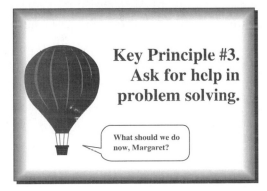

**Key Principle #3.
Ask for help in
problem solving.**

What should we do now, Margaret?

Five Interaction Guidelines

- Say *what* you want to discuss, and *why*.
- Gather and review details.
- Explore alternatives.
- Agree on actions.
- Agree on follow-up.

PRODUCE ROUGH VISUAL AIDS FOR PRACTICE

Use colored markers to produce rough mock-ups of your visuals on 8½-by-11-inch sheets. The artwork does not have to be fancy. As you practice your speech with these mock-ups, you should get an idea of whether or not the visuals you have chosen are needed or require any design changes.

Figure **12.10**

Thumbnail sketches for a speech about the communication model.

PRODUCE THE FINISHED VISUAL AIDS
FOR THE PROGRAM

If you have access to a computer with a good word processor or presentation manager, producing the finished visual aids for your speech is easy. But even without these tools, you do not have to spend a lot of money to produce good visual aids. Also, using a computer probably will not teach you any more about visual aids than if you choose paper as your medium. Regardless of the medium you use, think about your visual aids from the listener's point of view.

Consider using flip-chart paper and felt-tip markers for your visual aids, since these are versatile and also the least expensive of all the media. If you elect to use this approach, draw each visual out in pencil before you apply ink or paint. Print—do not write words out in longhand. Print big, and limit the amount of language. Keep any drawings simple. And if you plan to use felt-tip markers, put a sheet between the one you are working on and the one behind it to catch any bleed-through ink.

REVIEW AND REVISE THE FINAL PROGRAM

Practice your speech using the final visual aid program. If your visual aids are on a flip-chart easel, practice with the easel. If you are using overhead transparencies, turn on the projector and use the visuals as you practice your speech. You may still discover ways of enhancing the visual aids or of making them more useful to listeners.

CHOOSING THE RIGHT VISUAL MEDIUM

Choosing the right visual medium for your visual aids program requires thoughtful analysis. Three criteria should guide your thinking: (1) convenience of use, (2) costs versus benefits, and (3) communication power.

CONVENIENCE OF USE

Convenience of use should be one of your first considerations in choosing a visual medium. You want visual aids to assist you, not hinder you.

For example, for a long time, many corporate speakers chose 35-millimeter slides as visual aids for presentations. A slide-supported presentation has several advantages, but developing it is time consuming and costly. More importantly, however, a speaker who depends on photographic slides for visual support must manage the equipment, the lights in the room, and a screen. Is the medium convenient to use?

For a classroom speech, the time you take to make an elaborate visual aid, such as 35-millimeter slides, would almost certainly be better spent in practicing and improving your speech. Add the troubles of securing a projector and screen and determining who will run the equipment, and you must decide whether the visual aid's potential value is worth its inconvenience.

COSTS VERSUS BENEFITS

Cost is another important consideration in choosing your visual medium. Table 12.2 compares a number of different communications media by cost, by the size audience they accommodate, and by lead times needed. In fact, some of the more costly alternatives in table 12.2 are realistically open only to business and professional speakers. In choosing visual media, ask yourself: Is the payoff worth the price?

COMMUNICATION POWER

The term **communication power** refers to the degree of potency and memorability of visual or other symbolic material. Communication power has to do with the impact a particular communication strategy has on listeners. An enormous industry has emerged to service demands for more and more communication power in presentational speaking. To illustrate, the *Directory of Video, Computer & Audio-Visual Products,* published each year by the International Communications Industries Association, lists and illustrates more than fifteen hundred different products, including both hardware and software technology in computer, video, audiovisual, presentation, and multimedia.[1] For each entry, it describes computer compatibility; gives technical specifications; provides size, power, and weight information; and lists optional accessories. In addition, it includes a directory of service providers and a useful glossary of terms.

Given the enormous range of choices suggested by the *Directory,* ask yourself how much communication power you really need. Table 12.2 may help you with this question.

OVERHEAD PROJECTORS: THE ULTIMATE SPEAKING TOOL?

Overhead projectors (OHPs) were invented during World War II but did not catch on until about 1970. Recently, they have enjoyed a dramatic increase in popularity. You will find these powerful tools in classrooms, training centers, and conference rooms all over the country.[2] Coupled with computer software and liquid crystal displays,[3] OHPs may be the ultimate speaking tools available. Newer OHPs are bright, lightweight, inexpensive, and easy to use. Table 12.3 presents tips for using overhead projectors wisely.

HOW TO MAKE A TWO-DIMENSIONAL VISUAL AID

Because they apply to every visual aid you will ever make, two evaluative criteria should guide your thinking about two-dimensional design: simplicity and accessibility. With regard to visual aids, **simplicity** means plain, immediately obvious, easy to see from a distance, unmistakable even to a person who is not familiar with the subject, while **accessibility**

Table 12.2

A GUIDE TO MAKING AUDIOVISUAL EQUIPMENT DECISIONS

EQUIPMENT[1]	REASONS FOR USING EQUIPMENT	EQUIPMENT COSTS (WEIGHT)[2]	PRESENTATION MATERIALS COSTS[3]
Flip chart	Short lead time; little investment warranted	$63 (15 lb)	Per word cost: $25–40 for 1–5 words per page: $75–90 for charts, cartoon, etc.
Chalkboard	Informal in-house communications in boardrooms and offices	$13–134	None
Velcro boards, felt boards, etc.	Informal but professional presentation to valued audience	$70–100 (21–33 lb for portables)	$4.50 per letter
Overhead projector (3M)	Complex materials requiring extensive discussion	$230–490 (15–21 lb for portables)[4]	$4–7 made in-house; $25–85 professional.*
Slides (one-projector presentation) (Kodak)	Important audience and message; professional tone wanted	$140–770 (10–15 lb)	Type only: $5–50; Art: $15–75+.**
Filmstrip with sound, pulse advance (Singer)	Mechanically somewhat easier than slide and sound	$125–160 (20 lb+)	Same as slides
16-mm sound movies (Kodak)	Highly important audience; greatest impact; long life; simple, universal display	$735–1,775 (35–40 lb)	$1,500–6,000 per minute of finished film
Videotape 1. Seen on monitor from prerecorded videocassette (Sony) 2. Seen projected on screen (Sony)	1 and 2: Important audience; credibility; cheaper, quicker production than film; quality not as critical as film	$299–600 for ½ @ $1,250 for ¾ plus tape $4–15 (½) $60 (¾)	1 and 2: Anyone with a steady hand can make a videotape; studio quality can run to half the cost of film

[1]*Other specialty systems that may be of interest are: 3M's sound-on slide: multimedia using multiple slide projectors on slides with movies; Super 8 sound movies; sound tape presentations or sound with auxiliary materials; and opaque projectors, which are best for small conference situations.*
[2]*Figures are based on information available in 1993.*
[3]*Overtime for professional assistance or studio or lab time can add 50 to 100 percent to production costs.*
[4]*Software programs designed to generate overhead transparencies and that cost about $50 are now available. The computer equipment required can be under $1,000, including the price of a printer.*
Source: Copyright May, 1979. Reprinted by permission of *Public Relations Journal,* Published by the Public Relations Society of America, New York, New York.

AUDIENCE SIZE	IMAGE AREA SIZE	PREPARING SCRIPTS	LEAD TIMES NEEDED	
			PRODUCING MATERIALS	EQUIPMENT REHEARSAL AND FIRST SETUP TIME
10 or under	27" to 34" maximum	From hours to days	Up to 18 pages per day per worker	Minimal but needed
Approximately 16	18" × 24" to 48" × 96"	None	None	None
Up to 24	48" × 36" to 72" × 48"	From several days to weeks	Usually several days	3–4 hours or more
48 maximum	60" × 60"		Up to several days	Allow a few hours
Usually limited only by room size	6' or more	Plan on 2 or more weeks	Ideally, several weeks from storyboard to finished art	Several hours or longer for script-presented lines; less with programmed tape
Same as slides	Same as slides	Same as slides	Same as slides (Note: Frame ratio is different from slides)	Same as slides
Usually limited only by room size	6' or more	Several weeks	1–5 minutes of usable footage per day's shooting	One hour or so
1.1 person per 1¢¢ of monitor size; e.g., 25 for 25¢¢ monitor size 2. About 36	1. up to 25¢¢ for regular monitor 2. Any size for large-screen projection	1 and 2: days to weeks	1 and 2: Instant	Instant

If you have a computer with a good word processor, and access to either a laser printer or any other printer and a good photocopy machine, you can make serviceable overhead transparencies for the cost of your time plus about thirty cents.

**A computer program for making transparencies and color slides can cost as little as $150 from mail-order houses. These usually include an adequate library of "clip art."*

Table 12.3

TIPS FOR USING AN OVERHEAD PROJECTOR

1. Keep your transparencies simple. Resist using all the fancy fonts, borders, colors, and illustrations that you may have available on a computer program.
- Prefer horizontal to vertical layout. This makes better use of the usual OHP image and screen size.
- Use large type. People must read your visual aids easily from the back of the room. Generally, do not go much smaller than 24-point bold-faced type unless you know that your farthest audience member will be close enough to read the smaller type easily.
- Use heads and subheads. These help listeners to focus on content and to understand your ideas.
- Use less, not more. Limit yourself to two or three key ideas, each expressed in no more than three or four words. If your visual has to be more complex than this for listeners to understand your explanation, consider giving listeners a handout.
- Do not let background "wallpaper" and other patterns overpower your visual aids. Just because your machine can generate them does not mean you have to use them. Use color instead.
2. Plan the room layout if you can. Work to ensure maximum visibility, both for yourself and your visual program (see figure 12.11).
- Choose a screen large enough to guarantee that people in the back seats will be able to see easily. Raise the screen high enough so that people in the back can see the bottom of the screen. Get an OHP whose lenses will throw the images to the screen without too much distortion.
- Think about sight lines, and do not put seats in the corners near the front.
- Ask for a projector stand on wheels so that you can move the OHP out of the way when you want to. If the stand has a recessed area for the projector, and a space where you can put your transparencies, so much the better. If possible, set the stand where the projector's lenshead will not be in anyone's sight line.
- Try to dim the lights immediately above the screen. You can use an OHP in full light, but listeners will see the image better if the lights immediately above the screen are dimmed. One experienced speaker removes the fluorescent tubes from the panel immediately over the screen.

means that the audience must be able to understand the visual material. Mere numbers or lists of statistics, for example, may confound audience members, even if they know how to work with figures.

Good visual materials result when you consider listeners and their possible reactions to your message and then tie this consideration into your layout and design. You do not have to be an artist to make intelligent choices, but neither should you leave the selection and design of visual materials to chance or take them for granted.

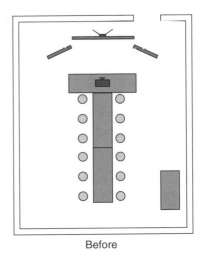
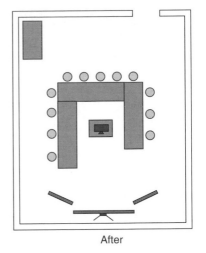

Before　　　　　　　　　　　　　　After

Figure **12.11**

Plan the room layout if you can. This illustration shows seating accommodations before and after rearrangement by the speaker. The "after" arrangement facilitates attention and interaction for the speaker and the audience, and makes it possible for listeners to view the visual aid program easily.

A complete course in two-dimensional layout and design cannot be presented in a public speaking textbook. However, a few basic principles will make it easier for you to develop your own visual supporting materials and to judge the quality of visual aids that others may develop for you.

THE RULE OF THIRDS

Two-dimensional visual aids are more pleasing when design elements conform to what people expect. The **rule of thirds** is based on the idea that the center of interest in your visual aids should fall on (or close to) imaginary intersections that divide the plane into thirds, both horizontally and vertically.

Figure 12.12 shows how those imaginary lines have guided the composition of one speaker's visual aid. Her subject was the vocal mechanism, and she wanted her audience to be able to name and locate the primary resonating chambers for speech. Notice that the key elements in the visual fit the rule of thirds.

STRAIGHT LINES AND CURVED LINES

Straight lines suggest strength and purpose, while curved lines suggest calm and delicacy (figure 12.13). If you want to suggest vitality, energy, and action, incorporate angles and straight lines in your visual aid. If you want to suggest tranquility or peace, use curved lines.

Lines can also suggest movement. If you draw the eye from right to left along a line, you pull viewers into the image, perhaps because this direction contradicts our training to read from left to right. When eye movement is from right to left, viewers feel compelled to follow the line of movement. An image that draws the eye from left to right suggests movement toward the viewer (see figure 12.14).

Figure **12.12**

Attention to the rule of thirds will improve the visual appeal and effectiveness of your visual aids.

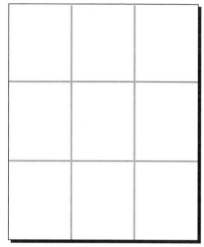

The Rule of Thirds

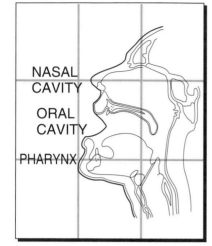

Visual aid showing the rule of thirds

Figure **12.13**

Straight lines and angles imply action and purpose, while curved lines suggest calm and delicacy.

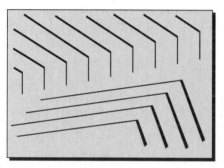

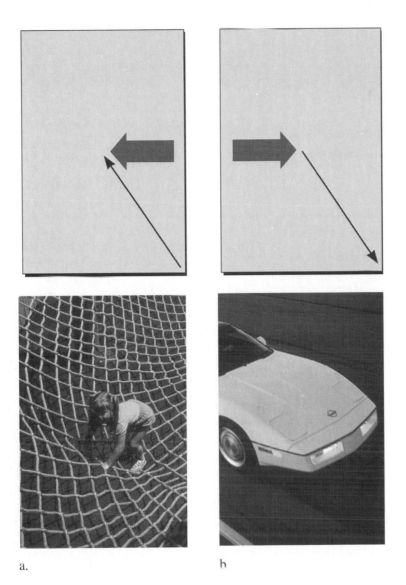

Figure **12.14**

(*a*): Eye movement from right to left draws viewer into frame. (*b*): Eye movement from left to right suggests movement toward viewer.

© *Eric Meola/The Image Bank*

a.   b

THE BALANCE OF TRIANGLES

Triangular compositions typify most Western painting and drawing. In a simple triangulated layout, the dominant element in the design is located at the apex of the triangle. You can experiment with triangles of different shapes to discover the most pleasing composition. Usually, the left-hand side of a two-dimensional plane is perceived as lighter than the right-hand side. Therefore, it can carry more material than the right-hand side without upsetting the design's psychological balance (see figure 12.15).

Figure **12.15**

Three examples of triangulation. The viewer's eye is able to travel from left to right and up and down the page relatively easily when you incorporate a triangular composition in a visual aid.

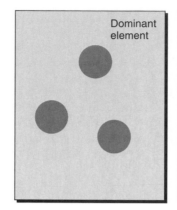
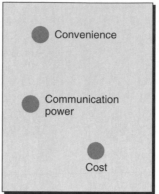
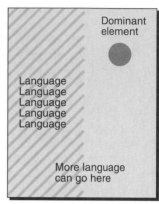

Figure **12.16**

As with triangular composition, negative space facilitates and directs the movement of the viewer's eye.

Too full: no negative space.

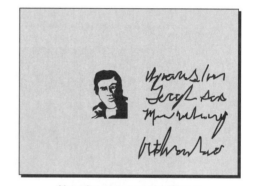

Negative space moves the eye.

EYE MOVEMENT AND NEGATIVE SPACE

In two-dimensional design, blank space can be as, or more important than, the filled area. Graphic designers call blank space negative space, and they use it to control eye movement. If you put too much material onto a two-dimensional plane, you eliminate the negative space and lose opportunities to control the eye movement and attention that negative space offers.

Figure 12.16 illustrates the power of negative space in controlling eye movement. Notice that one of the illustrations is so full of material that negative space is virtually nonexistent. Consequently, the eye does not know where to focus. However, in the other illustration, the eye immediately comes to rest on the important feature of the visual aid.

SKETCHES AND ILLUSTRATIONS

Carefully rendered drawings, paintings, or other art illustrations are usually more trouble than they are worth for visual supporting material. Still, developing a simplified sketch is sometimes necessary to illustrate your idea. A detailed, copiously labeled technical illustration, however, will not be helpful. Keep your sketch or illustration as simple as possible. A freehand cartoon often works better than a meticulously rendered drawing.

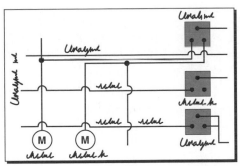

Wiring diagram

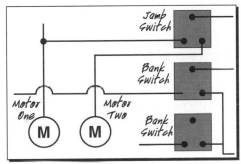

Simplified wiring diagram

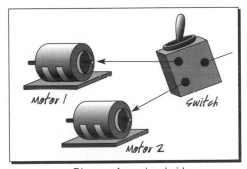

Diagram for a visual aid

Figure **12.17**

Most of us do not understand wiring diagrams—or any complicated system—at first glance, so we are attracted to a visual aid that shows only the essentials.

Compare the three drawings in figure 12.17. Each drawing illustrates the same technical idea. Which one do you think carries the idea more forcefully? Notice that lack of labeling in the visual aid diagram does not inhibit the visual aid's ability to communicate the speaker's goal.

Student speakers occasionally try to reproduce the kind of illustrative materials they find in their textbooks. A speaking situation, however, presents different kinds of receiving problems for listeners than reading situations present for readers. Readers have time to study illustrations in a textbook. Indeed, students often study the illustrative materials without reading the text. Consequently, authors tend to present more information in textbook

Figure **12.18**

An example of what not to do with a visual aid. The drawing is unclear, and the overall effect is very confusing. Two drawings would have been better.

illustrations than listeners could possibly comprehend in a public speaking situation. Listeners do not have time to study a visual aid. They must assimilate information at the speaker's speed.

Figure 12.18 reproduces a visual aid used to support a student's speech on rock climbing. The student had just returned from a two-week camping experience in the mountains. She wanted to show how climbers can hang from the surface of sheer rock and to describe the devices that make this feat possible.

The label "Mountaineering" does not contribute anything special to this visual aid. Without it, however, the visual aid would be incomprehensible. If you look carefully, you can make out the silhouette of an individual hanging from the face of the rock. The two objects to the right represent the anchoring devices the student planned to describe. These items are not immediately obvious or recognizable. Since the student's purpose was to show how rock climbers anchor themselves to the surface of sheer rock, she should have developed a separate drawing for each of the anchoring devices (see figure 12.19).

LANGUAGE AND LETTERING

Do not clutter a visual aid with extraneous language. Rather, include only enough information to guarantee that the visual aid will be immediately understandable. Compare the two drawings in figure 12.20. One drawing is cluttered with labels. In the other, all extraneous language has been removed, with the result that the visual aid seems cleaner, simpler, and easier to grasp.

Piton   Nut

Figure **12.19**

These sketches of a piton (*a*) and a nut (*b*) will give a listener a clearer idea of how a climber hangs from a sheer rock face than could the student's visual aid in figure 12.18.

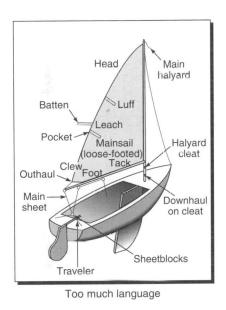

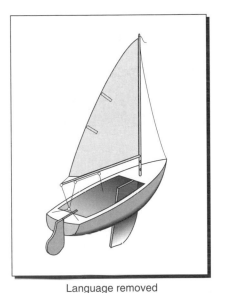

Too much language   Language removed

Figure **12.20**

Keeping labels to a minimum is an important aspect of creating simple, easily understood visual aids.

Most speech visual aids consist entirely of language—for example, outlines and other word-only visual aids that help listeners to follow your ideas. These can powerfully support your speech. They also have the potential for confusing listeners, however, if they are overcomplicated. Let simplicity guide your design choices.

Lettering does not have to be a problem. If you are using an overhead projector, an inexpensive computer program that includes suggestions for format and layout and that provides a variety of type styles and sizes can make the lettering of overhead transparencies simple. More elaborate programs that import pictures and drawings, put borders around the transparencies, and so on also are available.

But you do not need elaborate computer programs to make serviceable OHP transparencies. You can make an effective transparency by laying a piece of clear plastic over tablet paper and using the lines to guide you as you letter the plastic with a felt-tip pen. Or, you can mount a visual aid on 8½-by-11-inch paper and then use a copy machine to convert it into an OHP transparency.

Flip charts, chalkboards, and marker boards are commonly found in classrooms and conference rooms, and some speakers elect to use these to generate visual aids "on the fly"—that is, they write down key ideas or terms on these media while delivering their speeches. You also may occasionally use these media, but beware. Your lettering skills may not be sufficient to the task when you are under pressure and working in front of an audience. You also risk turning your back on your audience for long periods.

When the nature of the speech requires quality lettering and you do not feel adept enough to tackle it, find someone to help you do it right. In most situations, however, your own lettering will suffice if you remember the following pointers:

1. Print, don't write.
2. Print big.
3. Use block letters.
4. Use the simplest words you can.
5. Eliminate every word you can.

HOW TO USE VISUAL MATERIALS: MATTERS OF DELIVERY

The skills involved in handling and using visual aids come easily if you think about what your audience needs. Unfortunately, many speakers fail in this regard. Your visuals do not deliver your speech—you do. If you do not have a reason for a visual aid, don't use one. Focusing audience attention on yourself is far better than presenting a visual that is not motivated by the need to explain or reinforce your key points. Table 12.4 presents additional pointers regarding visual aid use.

Effective public speakers generally follow a predictable four-step sequence when presenting a visual aid: (1) Introduce the visual, (2) present it, (3) explain it, and then (4) put it away.

INTRODUCE THE VISUAL

When you are about to present a visual aid, you should prepare audience members for a shift in attention with a simple introductory statement, such as: "To illustrate this idea, I would like to show you a sketch that identifies the most important part of this problem . . ." Such a statement tells listeners that they are going to have to depend more on their eyes than on their ears. Do not take this shift in receiving for granted. Listeners need your help to prepare for this shift.

PRESENT THE VISUAL

Present the visual aid without much talk. After introducing it, put the visual on the easel or display it on the screen and then step out of the way for a moment. Give audience members time to adjust to the shift from listening to looking. Remember, too, that they need time to satisfy their curiosity about the visual you have presented.

Table 12.4

HOW TO USE VISUAL AIDS

DO	DON'T
Simplify visual materials as much as possible.	Stand between your visual aid and the audience.
Stay with two-dimensional visual aids. Print big, block letters.	Leave a visual aid on display when it is not in use.
Use simple words and as few as possible.	Develop elaborate visual aids.
Err on the side of too many visuals rather than too few.	Write longhand on a visual aid.
Think about the convenience of using a visual aid.	Assume that all necessary equipment will be available.
Design visual aids following the rule of thirds.	Assume that everyone in the back row will be able to see a visual aid clearly.
Triangulate the design of visual aids. Use lots of negative space.	Use the chalkboard if you can avoid it. Pass items around for your audience to study while you talk.
Follow this sequence when using a visual aid: introduce it, display it, discuss it, and then put it away.	

EXPLAIN THE VISUAL

After a moment of silence, audience members will be ready for you to point to and discuss the visual aid. Do not assume that they have made all the connections you want them to make. Take the time to explain the visual aid and to highlight its important points.

If you are using a flip chart or poster board, move back to the visual, stand beside it, and face your audience. You can more easily gesture to a portion of the visual aid from this position, without turning your back on the audience.

If you are using an overhead projector, lay a sharpened pencil on the transparency so that the pencil's shadow is projected onto the screen and becomes a pointer. Do not point to items on the transparency with your finger. Do not "fence" with the transparency by moving the pencil pointer with your hand as you speak. The pencil pointer that is moved only a couple of inches on the transparency creates a shadow that may move a foot or more on the screen. Such exaggerated movement draws attention away from the visual and the point you are trying to illustrate.

One young man walked over to the projector and pointed to an item on the transparency with his middle finger. Moving slowly up and down on the wall behind him was a finger gesture about 5 feet high. No audience member could resist the humor of the situation, and very few got the point of the visual aid.

When your visual is displayed on an overhead projector, stand to the right of the projector—to listeners' left. Stay in this position when pointing out details on the screen. Gesture with your left hand. Since the normal reading pattern moves from left to right, this position helps you to gain control of audience attention.

PUT THE VISUAL AWAY

After you have used the visual material, get rid of it. Too often, speakers introduce and discuss an attractive and effective visual aid and then leave it displayed as they move to their next point. Visual aids are designed to get and hold attention. Audience members who can still see and think about your last visual aid may not be thinking about what you are presently telling them. Why risk losing audience control? Put the visual away.

Summary

Visual supporting materials can enhance most public speeches, but only if they actually contribute something to the speech. A visual aid is any object, photograph, chart, graph, sketch, or lettered poster that supports a speech or the speaker. Visual aids simplify complexity, control audience attention, and help you to remain organized while delivering your speech. They also help listeners to organize your ideas, understand abstract concepts, and remember your main points. Visual materials are especially helpful for showing problems, solutions and benefits, processes, procedures, and steps in a sequence.

Before developing a visual aid program, you should think about your key ideas and decide what kinds of visual materials you intend to use and what ideas these materials will illustrate or support. You can then design thumbnail sketches of each visual aid and make rough visual aids for practice. When you feel satisfied with your visual aids program, produce the finished visual aids and then review and revise your presentation, if necessary.

Convenience of use, costs versus benefits, and communication power are the three Cs that help you to select the right visual medium for your particular situation. Overhead projectors, coupled with computers and software, may be the ultimate speaking tool. When using OHPs, however, resist the temptation to make your transparencies fancy—simple visual aids work best. Also, work to ensure maximum visibility, both for yourself and your OHP visual program.

The best visual materials are simple and accessible and conform to certain principles of two-dimensional design, such as applying the rule of thirds, using straight and curved lines to create moods, experimenting with triangulation to produce a pleasing composition, controlling eye movement with negative space, and developing effective sketches, illustrations, and lettering.

When using a visual aid, introduce it, present or display the visual smoothly and quietly, explain it, and then remove the visual from view so that listeners can concentrate on your next point.

Key Terms

Accessibility
Communication power

Overhead projector (OHP)
Rule of thirds

Simplicity
Visual aid

Application Questions

1. Agree with a group of your classmates to spend some time watching television with the sound off. Count the number of times the picture changes during a two-minute period. Include every camera change, each time the camera angle changes by panning or zooming, and each time language is superimposed on the picture. Notice how these changes are used to focus viewer attention. Now turn the sound on and pay attention to the sounds. How do the sounds and the sights work together? Return to your group and compare notes. Can any of this information be applied to public speaking?
2. This chapter is filled with illustrative materials. Even so, it is not as visually rich as a magazine. Bring a magazine to class. With a group of classmates, go through the magazine looking for examples of curved and straight lines, triangulation, and the use of blank space to control eye movement. Are the examples easy to find? What can you learn from this exercise about developing visual supporting materials for a speech?

Self-Test for Review

Mark the following statements: A = Good advice about using visual aids, or B = Bad advice about using visual aids.

_____ 1. "Try to present ideas as simply as possible."
_____ 2. "Visual aids can help to simplify complex information."
_____ 3. "A visual aid should not be just words. You ought to use some kind of graphic on every one."
_____ 4. "Remember, visual materials help you control audience attention, so use them often."
_____ 5. "The first and most important criterion for selecting a visual medium is *consistency.*"

6. List what you should support with visual aids.

   a. _____

   b. _____

   c. _____

   d. _____

   e. _____

7. Which of the following are **not** recommended steps in developing a visual aid program?

   a. Think about key ideas.
   b. Think about the available communications media.
   c. Develop a rough plan for the visual program.
   d. Develop an outline of visual materials you will produce.
   e. Design thumbnail sketches of each visual aid.
   f. Make "dummy" visual aids full-size, on newsprint sheets.
   g. Produce the finished visual aids in the media you selected.

8. Which of the following is the *best* definition of the rule of thirds?

   a. Divide topics into three main ideas.
   b. Divide a plane into thirds, both horizontally and vertically.
   c. Use one third of your preparation time for audience analysis, one third for speech preparation, and one third for practice.
   d. People think in threes—therefore, they will best remember what is divided into thirds.

9. What are the two characteristic features of all well-designed visual supporting materials?

   a. Simplicity and accessibility
   b. Convenience and communication power
   c. Creativity and clarity
   d. Low cost and convenience of use

Mark the following true or false.

   _____ 10. The amount of language on a visual should be limited as much as possible.

   _____ 11. Eye movement can be best controlled by filling blank space with design elements.

   _____ 12. Straight lines and angles suggest calm.

   _____ 13. The virtual standard of Western visual design is a plane divided into fourths.

   _____ 14. A distributor cap—a small plastic part about the size of half a grapefruit— would be a good visual aid for a speech about the electrical system of a car.

   _____ 15. Leave a complex visual aid before audience members throughout the speech so they will have plenty of opportunity to understand it.

   _____ 16. A visual aid is any object, photo, chart, or lettered poster that supports a speech.

Suggested Readings

The following two periodicals constitute the best resources for information on visual aids anywhere. Dozens of other similar periodicals may be found at your local newsstand.

AVC Presentation for the Visual Communicator (Melville, N.Y.: PTN Publishing).

Publish: The Art and Technology of Graphic Design (San Francisco, Calif.: Integrated Media).

CHAPTER 13

Delivery

OUTLINE

OBJECTIVES

After reading this chapter, you should be able to:

1. *Compare and contrast* four different methods of delivery (manuscript delivery, memorized delivery, extemporaneous delivery, and impromptu delivery), and *explain* what is meant by "invisible" delivery.
2. *Differentiate* between written and oral styles of speaking.
3. *List* characteristics of your speaking voice that you can control or change.
4. *Explain* how nonverbal elements, such as gestures, eye contact, and personal appearance, contribute to effective public speaking.
5. *Specify* four procedures for making your speech practice more effective.

UPI/Bettmann

*D*elivery is the vehicle speakers use to transmit ideas to listeners. This chapter focuses on both the verbal and nonverbal aspects of effective delivery. The setting or the audience often suggest different methods of delivery, such as reading directly from a manuscript, memorizing your speech, preparing an extemporaneous presentation, and delivering impromptu remarks. In addition to the four different delivery methods are two speech styles: written and oral. Written style is more formal and stilted, while oral style sounds more like conversation.

Your speaking voice—in particular, the rate, pitch, and volume of your voice—and your nonverbal messages, such as your gestures, eye contact, and personal appearance and behavior, affect how listeners perceive you and your message. In this chapter, you learn how to use your speaking voice and gestures to compliment your speech, rather than contradict it.

Practicing your speech will help you to polish your methods and style of delivery, your speaking voice, and your nonverbal messages so that all of these elements work together to deliver your message in the most effective way possible.

Delivery is the verbal and nonverbal expression of ideas, feelings, and impressions, and involves using the voice and the body to convey a message to listeners. Effective delivery concentrates the audience's attention on the message instead of the speaker. The following comments from audience members suggest elements of poor and good delivery.

> *Poor delivery:* "That speaker had a wonderful voice. It was loud and nicely pitched."
> "I liked the speaker's gestures. They seemed so spontaneous and smooth."
> *Good delivery:* "That was a dynamite speech. The speaker had a clear idea and seemed interested in the subject."
> "I hadn't thought about foreign languages in the way that speaker talked about. That topic isn't as simple as I thought it would be."

As these comments indicate, when listeners comment on the speaker's voice or gestures, instead of on the speaker's message, then the delivery must have been ineffective. Audience members who later talk about the ideas they heard in the speech listened to a clear message, effectively delivered.

Good delivery helps you to realize your specific purpose. Any aspect of your delivery that interferes with reaching that goal is a distraction and should be eliminated. When listeners comment on your voice or behavior, they are attending to the delivery and not to the content. Delivery is effective when verbal and nonverbal elements of your delivery merge with your content.

CHOOSING A METHOD OF DELIVERY

An important and difficult choice every speaker makes is the method of delivery for the speech. Should you recite from a manuscript, deliver your speech from memory, speak extemporaneously, or try an impromptu style? Your decision will directly affect your likelihood for success.

Table 13.1

HAZARDS OF MANUSCRIPT DELIVERY

PROBLEM	REASON
Your eye contact is restricted to your manuscript.	You concentrate on the manuscript and not on the audience because you want to be certain that you say everything that is written.
The speech sounds stilted.	There are substantial differences between written and spoken language (see the section "Differences between Written and Oral Styles" later in the chapter).
You appear "wooden."	You are "tied" to the manuscript and cannot deviate from the written material.

Good delivery is *invisible*—that is, it does not call attention to itself. Listeners should not notice the delivery choices you have made. Instead, your choices should help them to understand and think about your ideas.

The setting or the audience may suggest the most appropriate method of delivery. Consider what is expected of you in this particular speaking situation and also consider what the audience expects. Choose a delivery method that is consistent with the occasion, your listeners, and your message. As you read about the methods of delivery—manuscript, memorized, extemporaneous, and impromptu—decide which concerns about setting and audiences apply to you and the speech you plan to deliver.

MANUSCRIPT DELIVERY

You may feel tempted to write out your speech and then read it from the manuscript. **Manuscript delivery,** however, has a number of disadvantages (see table 13.1). Even so, delivering a speech from a manuscript may be appropriate when:

- You must weigh your language carefully.
- You must present your material in a specific sequence.
- You need to use technical assistants for cueing (television, lighting, and so on).

Important business and government speeches are frequently read from a manuscript. In class situations, however, teachers often discourage manuscript delivery.

If you decide on a manuscript delivery, read the manuscript aloud many times before the actual speech. Be familiar with every word, and be certain of the correct pronunciation. Have at least one dress rehearsal during which you flip every switch, show every visual, and turn each page. Try to make the speech sound spontaneous—as though it has just occurred to you for the first time. If you have a problem, go through the speech again as many times as necessary.

Delivery from a manuscript requires great skill. This speaker has lost contact with the audience.

© *James L. Shaffer*

MEMORIZED DELIVERY

The advantages of **memorized delivery** lie in the advance planning that this method allows. Yet, the disadvantages of memorization outweigh the advantages (see table 13.2). Unless your speaking situation requires a memorized address, you should probably avoid this style of delivery.

Memorized speeches create considerable fear because speakers worry about memory lapses. Few situations are more agonizing for a speaker and more uncomfortable for an audience than the silence where a forgotten line should have been. Nearly as worrisome is the half-remembered argument, which leaves listeners with an incomplete jigsaw puzzle of an idea.

Another problem of a memorized speech is that it *sounds* memorized. Speakers who are preoccupied with remembering every word tend to speak in either a monotone or singsong pattern that advertises memorization. When speakers must work at remembering each word in sequence, they lose the vocal emphasis and variety needed to sound interesting or enthusiastic. A memorized speech leaves the impression that you are more involved in remembering your speech than you are in communicating with your audience.

Finally, the memorized speech does not give you the opportunity for any audience feedback. When you have decided in advance exactly what you are going to say, there is no incentive to look at the audience, since feedback will not change your speech. You tend to be less sensitive to audience reaction. Your speech lacks flexibility, which makes it difficult for you to adapt.

Table 13.2

ADVANTAGES AND DISADVANTAGES
OF MEMORIZED DELIVERY

ADVANTAGES OF MEMORIZATION	DISADVANTAGES OF MEMORIZATION
You can choose the exact wording.	You can easily forget a sentence or phrase, which can lead to an embarrassing silence.
The timing will be exact.	Your speech may sound memorized because of a lack of vocal variety, emphasis, and changes in rate.
You know exactly what you want to say.	It discourages audience response.
The sequence of ideas will be precise.	It may increase listeners' apprehension about the speech.
The subtle implications can be prepared and worded carefully.	You cannot be flexible in idea development or change.

EXTEMPORANEOUS DELIVERY

Extemporaneous delivery is planned carefully, but the speaker has minimal notes. It is different from impromptu delivery, which is a no-notes, "off-the-cuff" type of presentation.

Your concern in an extemporaneous speech is presenting ideas and supporting proofs in a logical sequence. Your goal is not a word-for-word progression of ideas. Because you have prepared carefully using an outline, all you typically need are a few notes to remind you of your key ideas in the order in which you plan to present them (see chapter 9, "Outlining the Speech").

Figure 13.1 shows an example note card that helps you to remember your main ideas and the order in which you want to present them. Meta-notes are notes about your notes. Use them to remind yourself of such things as preplanned movement or where and when to use visual materials (see figure 13.2).

Practicing with your notes increases confidence and gives you a better command of your ideas. Each time you go over the speech, you develop and refine your language.

Extemporaneous speaking has most of the advantages of memorized speaking and manuscript speaking, but few of the disadvantages. It is more direct and spontaneous than either memorization or manuscript reading. You are free to interact with audience members, and listeners are more likely to view you and your speech as an interpersonal event that involves them as individuals.

Extemporaneous speaking does require extra preparation so that you can be spontaneous and appear more confident during the presentation of ideas. Poise during delivery and a clear grasp of all the material are hallmarks of the extemporaneous style.

Figure **13.1**

An example note card. A few handheld notes will help you to remember your main ideas and their sequence while not bogging you down and taking your attention away from the audience.

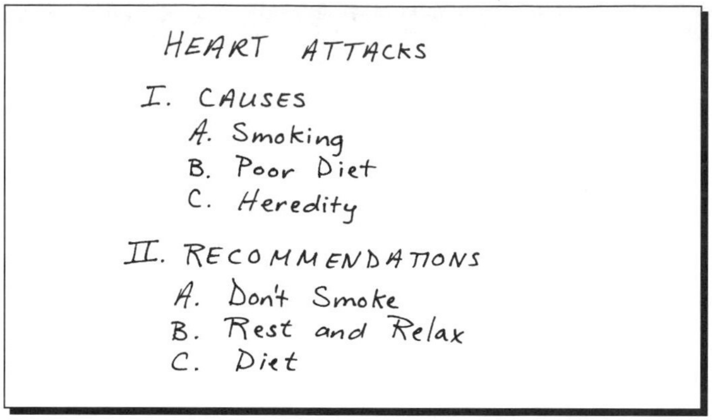

HEART ATTACKS

I. CAUSES
   A. Smoking
   B. Poor Diet
   C. Heredity

II. RECOMMENDATIONS
   A. Don't Smoke
   B. Rest and Relax
   C. Diet

Figure **13.2**

Meta-notes serve as reminders to attend to other aspects of the speech, such as when to display visual aids or read quotes.

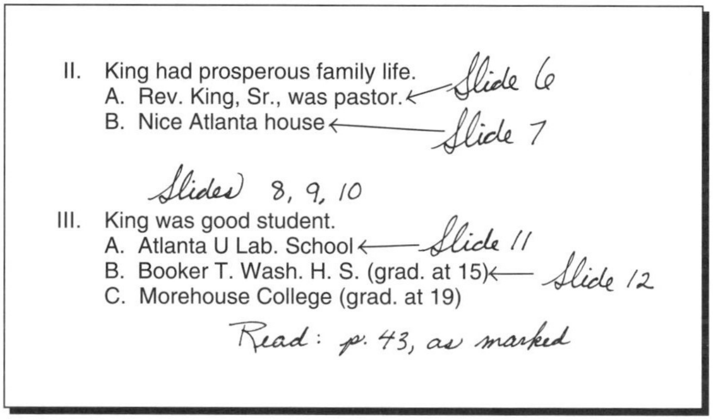

II. King had prosperous family life. *Slide 6*
   A. Rev. King, Sr., was pastor.
   B. Nice Atlanta house *Slide 7*

Slides 8, 9, 10

III. King was good student.
   A. Atlanta U Lab. School *Slide 11*
   B. Booker T. Wash. H. S. (grad. at 15) *Slide 12*
   C. Morehouse College (grad. at 19)

Read: p. 43, as marked

Students are sometimes concerned that the extemporaneous method does not afford them any help in remembering what they are going to say next. They worry that they will forget where they are going and where they have been. With notes and practice, however, you have all the basic tools to be successful. Table 13.3 lists characteristics of extemporaneous delivery and potential advantages of these characteristics.

IMPROMPTU DELIVERY

Impromptu delivery is speaking without preparation or advance planning. It is "spur-of-the-moment" speaking with no notes. Speech teachers generally do not assign impromptu speeches. If, however, you are sufficiently knowledgeable about a subject and have been asked to share your ideas without notice, the following techniques for impromptu speaking may be helpful:

- Take a moment to organize your thoughts. Ask for this time. No one will be offended by the momentary delay, and your speech and your credibility will benefit.

Table 13.3

CHARACTERISTICS OF EXTEMPORANEOUS DELIVERY
AND THEIR ADVANTAGES

CHARACTERISTIC	ADVANTAGES OF CHARACTERISTIC
1. Speaker engages in extra preparation and practice.	Increases speaker's confidence and spontaneity
2. Speaker uses minimal notes.	Allows speaker to have more audience contact and feedback
3. Speaker talks directly to listeners.	Greater "conversational tone" in the speaker's voice
4. Speaker uses visuals as notes (see chapter 12, "Supporting Ideas Visually").	Visuals beneficial for both audience and speaker

- Make a few notes. Just a word or two can stimulate a complete idea. Begin by identifying the point you want to make or the position you want to take. Then quickly sketch out the subpoints.
- Organize around a simple, repetitive pattern. Many speakers who find themselves in this kind of situation rely on a familiar approach. They "tell them what they're going to tell them, tell them, and then tell them what they've told them." That technique also makes it easy for both the speaker and the audience to remember the main ideas.

DIFFERENCES BETWEEN WRITTEN AND ORAL STYLES

When we write, we use language that may be fairly complex, rather abstract, and formal in expression. These are desirable characteristics for written material. But if this material is read aloud to a group of listeners, those same characteristics tend to make the information confusing and harder to understand.

In the same way, speakers who use a **written style** of speaking sound like they are reading from books or prepared papers. They seem to lack spontaneity or real enthusiasm. The following passage from a student speech is a good example of the written style:

It is imperative that we discontinue foreign aid to nations that show so little regard for human rights and personal dignity. For centuries, many countries have run roughshod over the concerns of the poor, minorities, certain religious groups, and women. The majority has disregarded the fundamental precepts of these people and not only denied them their basic rights but persecuted them.

Table 13.4

COMPARISON OF ORAL AND WRITTEN STYLES

ORAL STYLE	WRITTEN STYLE
Short words	Polysyllabic words
Short sentences	Long sentences
Much repetition	Little repetition
Contractions	Few contractions
Concrete terms	Abstract language

This is not the way we talk in normal conversation. It is much more stilted and formal, uses long words, and does not have the repetition that listeners need. The following is another version of the same message—presented in **oral style:**

> *Foreign aid is abused by countries like Iraq. We shouldn't continue to help them deny the rights of minorities. They deny equal rights to women. They don't give the Sunni Moslems their rights. They persecute and kill the Kurds in Iraq. Many citizens are shot for trying to get their rights. We shouldn't send taxpayer money to countries that abuse their own people.*

This passage sounds more like the way we talk. In general, the oral style sounds as if someone is talking to you, while the written style sounds as if it is being read from a page.

Memorized delivery and manuscript reading are the two kinds of delivery that encourage written style. When speakers talk as if they are reading from books or prepared papers, however, audience members often do not feel compelled to listen. Extemporaneous delivery, on the other hand, relies on oral style, which tends to free you from your notes and allow you to act more spontaneously. This in itself tends to attract listeners' attention.

Table 13.4 compares and contrasts the oral and written styles. It is obvious why the oral style is more appealing to listeners. Simple, informal language and lots of repetition make listening easy.

THE SPEAKING VOICE

Would you recognize your own voice if you heard it played back on a tape recorder? Some people do not recognize their own voices because the sound inside their heads is different from the sounds others hear when they speak. Many elements contribute to the unique sound of each of our voices, including the different size of our vocal chords, the size and shape of our heads, our sinus cavities, and the size and shape of our mouths. These are not characteristics that you can change.

Actor James Earl Jones is best known for his deep, resonant voice. In his autobiography, Jones recalls being advised by his teachers to focus on his message, not his voice:

I was sufficiently warned by all my teachers in college and since then not to become obsessed with my voice. Once you start listening to your own voice, you risk becoming trapped into affectation. The speaker's last concern should be how he sounds. The listeners, not the speaker, should be aware of how the voice sounds. The speaker should be concerned with what he seeks to communicate by the sound of his voice.

Source: James Earl Jones and Penelope Niven, Voices and Silences *(New York: Charles Scribner's Sons, 1993), 373. Photo UPI/Bettmann*

You do have some control over several characteristics of your speaking voice, however, and you can alter these to your speaking advantage. These characteristics are rate, pitch, and volume. To understand and to manage these characteristics is to have control of the transmission system for your speech.

RATE

The term **rate** describes the speed at which a person speaks. A typical rate of speech is approximately 140 to 160 words per minute. People speak at a variety of rates. For example, President John F. Kennedy spoke at about 180 words per minute, with bursts up to 200 words per minute. President Franklin Delano Roosevelt spoke much more slowly, in a smooth, melodious voice, at about 120 words a minute.

Many famous speakers change their rate of speaking within their speech. Table 13.5 shows how rate changes affect the message.

You send many message to your audience by the rate of your speech.

1. You tell listeners if you are uneasy. The faster you speak, the more likely that listeners will sense your anxiety. Listen to yourself and attempt to speak slowly. Monitor your rate by tape-recording a practice run-through of your speech.
2. You tell listeners if ideas are important. Speakers do not rush through material that they think is important for others to understand.
3. You tell listeners how important they are to you. When you are concerned with people, you take your time talking to them. A frantic rate of delivery suggests that you only want to be finished with the speech, that you are not vitally interested in your listeners and in getting the ideas across to them.

Also, remember that the larger the audience, the slower you have to speak. Most of us get into a rhythm that is appropriate for talking to a small group and forget that floor noise, distance, poor lighting, and other distractions require a much slower delivery. Unlike

Table 13.5	
HOW RATE CHANGES AFFECT THE MESSAGE	
FAST RATE	SLOW RATE
Conveys a sense of urgency	Stresses the idea
Can show anger and surprise	Can show sadness or concern
Is less persuasive	Is more persuasive

Source: George B. Ray, "Vocally Cued Personality Prototypes: An Implicit Personality Theory Approach," in *Communication Monographs, 53,* 1986: 266–76.

the conversational setting, your listeners cannot see you easily in public address, hear each nuance of your voice and its inflection, pick up on micro-momentary changes in muscle tone, or read your lips. You can help to compensate for these disadvantages by taking your time and slowing down.

PITCH

Pitch is the level of the vocal sound at which your voice mechanism works with maximum efficiency and ease. Your natural pitch is the level at which you usually carry on conversation. Generally, women have higher pitched voices than men. Singing voices are also classified by pitch into groups of sopranos, altos, tenors, and baritones.

A higher than normal pitch shows emotion or excitement. Listen to the excited voices at an athletic contest or the vocal pitch of your close friend who tells you about an "A" on a final exam. A lower than normal pitch suggests that a person is intense or quite serious. When an event requires us to express ourselves carefully and seriously (such as when giving testimony in court or giving an order to another worker), we attempt to lower our pitch to demonstrate intensity and feeling.

Changes in pitch reflect our feelings. Sometimes, we are not even conscious of our pitch changes, but listeners hear the difference. People in public speaking situations often speak at a higher than normal pitch. Their voices reflect the tension and excitement of appearing in front of a group. Usually, speakers' vocal pitch and rate return to normal after they become convinced that they can succeed.

A short-term change up or down in pitch within a sentence or short passage is called **inflection.** For example, rising inflection (pitch) at the end of a sentence suggests a question, while a downward inflection is associated with the completeness of a thought and gives emphasis to an idea. In the middle of sentences, the rising and falling of our voices emphasize certain points and minimize others. In the following sample sentences, give rising inflection to the word or words that are underlined:

Fred *did* understand the assignment for tomorrow.

Did *Marie* buy that new Mercedes?

A vacation in New Hampshire is a *special event.*

Without a *ticket* to the concert, you have *no chance* of getting in.

I refuse to spend another cent on *food* from that lousy restaurant.

Now experiment with changing the meaning of these sentences by moving the inflection to other words. The message can change drastically.

Thus, rising or falling inflections within sentences emphasize different words and ideas. Voices without inflections are called "flat." Individuals with "flat" voices do not introduce any vocal variety into what they say, and for that reason, their voices are uninteresting. Their lack of inflection also suggests that all of their words are equally important.

Your knowledge of pitch and inflection gives you important tools to improve the effectiveness of your delivery. Vary your pitch and use changes in inflection to emphasize ideas or words within statements. Pitch and pitch changes within sentences can alter much of what you say.

VOLUME

The **volume** or loudness of your voice determines whether or not people can hear you. You have adequate voice volume if the persons seated farthest from you do not have to strain to hear your words. Listening should be easy for them.

Outside the classroom, the setting for a speech may be noisy or large. You may need to use a microphone to enhance your volume so that everyone can hear you. Do not hesitate to ask audience members if they can hear you. Then make whatever adjustments are necessary to assure that they can.

Embrace the attitude that your message is worthwhile, that you will speak out and speak up. People are lazy listeners. Make it easy for them to listen to you by speaking at a volume level that keeps their attention.

NONVERBAL MESSAGES

You have often heard the statement, "What you do speaks more loudly than what you say." Or someone may comment to you: "I don't think you like this idea. In fact, I know you don't because of the way you're acting." Nonverbal cues are important in communication, and the field of nonverbal communication is complex. A complete exploration of this field can be found in some of the "Suggested Readings" at the end of this chapter. Here, however, discussion focuses on those nonverbal elements that play a significant role in effective public speaking: (1) gestures, (2) eye contact, and (3) personal appearance and behavior.

GESTURES

When you move your hands or body to help communicate an idea or feeling, you are using gestures to complement your words, to help you emphasize what you say. Gestures are vital to the flow of a speech. Without them, speakers would have to pause more, and

listeners would have more difficulty remembering parts of the message.[1] Yet, movements and gestures must appear natural, be emphatic enough to be noticed, and be consistent with your words. Include gestures in your speech only if you think they will help to convey your message.

After you have given a speech, ask your speech teacher if your gestures and movements were noticeable. If the gestures contributed to your speech, they were probably invisible. Invisibility means that the gestures were effective because the audience was listening to your words instead of watching your movements. Invisible gestures are your goal in public communication.

In public speaking, three categories of gestures can work with the speaker's words to effectively communicate a message: (1) gestures that relate to the speaker's words—descriptive or abstract, (2) gestures that operate like visual punctuation, and (3) gestures that suggest a speaker's feelings.[2]

Gestures Related to the Speaker's Words

Gestures that relate to the speaker's words could also be called "illustrators" because they are tied so closely to what the speaker says. If the words are concrete, the speaker can use very descriptive gestures. If the message is abstract, the gestures may be less specific, such as when a speaker raises both hands when talking about "Heaven." Table 13.6 presents several examples of the kinds of physical movements that help speakers to convey their message nonverbally. These examples represent only a few gestures tied to words. When you listen to any speaker, you will see others that fit in these categories.

Table 13.6

DESCRIPTIVE AND ABSTRACT GESTURES

DESCRIPTIVE GESTURES	ABSTRACT GESTURES
Pointing (to indicate person or object)	Sketching the air with a hand (to show movement of an idea)
Drawing (to show a shape or movement)	Expansion and contraction gesture (to show the scope of the subject)
Waving (to indicate hello or goodbye)	Circular hand movements (to show you mean more than the words)

Source: Mark L. Knapp and Judith A. Hall, *Nonverbal Communication in Human Interaction*, 3d ed. (Orlando, Fla.: Harcourt Brace Jovanovich, 1992), 199–203.

Gestures for Visual Punctuation

President Harry S. Truman was famous for his frequent use of a hand-chopping gesture to emphasize important ideas. The next time you see film or videotape of President John F. Kennedy, watch how he used a stabbing index finger motion to indicate strong feelings about ideas. Visual punctuation gestures can also be used to show divisions. When you discuss one point, you show one division by holding your hands a foot or so apart. Then, when you discuss a second idea, you move your hands slightly, keeping the same space between them, to show that there is another, equally important part to your discussion. Or visual punctuation gestures can be used to show that a subject has divisions and subparts, or that a detail is only a minor part of the topic (holding the index finger and thumb of one hand slightly apart).

Speakers use visual punctuation to stress important ideas. Help listeners to understand the significance of your oral message by using these types of nonverbal supplements.

Gestures That Suggest a Speaker's Feelings

Speakers who convey feelings about their topic often show these feelings in gestures that do not fit into either of the gesture categories already discussed. Physical action is so important to speaking—especially speaking with feeling—that if people consciously refrained from using gestures while talking, it would damage their train of thought. They would pay less attention to what they were saying and focus more on what they were doing. Thus, gestures that suggest a speaker's feeling, while not neatly categorized or identified, nevertheless are critical to receiving the speaker's entire message.

EYE CONTACT

Because our eyes indicate the object of our attention, a speaker's eye contact with listeners is an important way for the speaker to demonstrate concern and interest in an audience. Since audience members are central to the communication process, regular eye contact is crucial.

Speakers who are interested in their listeners look at them. While that sounds simple, it is hard to do. Standing in front of a group of people often makes speakers feel vulnerable. One way to feel less threatened is to engage in common avoidance behaviors, such as looking at the floor, gazing at note cards for the entire presentation, staring out the window, focusing on a spot slightly above listeners' heads, and concentrating your eyes on the lectern or desk. These avoidance behaviors are typical ways of dealing with the tension and concern you may feel when people are focusing their attention on you. By looking at the floor or out the window, you can "pretend" that there is no one else in the room. This strategy, of course, creates problems for you as a public speaker.

Listeners want you to make eye contact with them. It is one way for them to decide if you are sincere and if they should believe what you are saying. The eye contact does not have to be long. Most visual attention, even in conversation, lasts only about 3 to 4 seconds. Then we generally look somewhere else before once again looking at the person.

The same approach works in a public setting. Try looking at each person for a few seconds before moving on to another member of your audience. You will find that they are looking at you and appear pleased that you care enough about them to make eye contact.

One caution here is that you should avoid staring at one person or one part of your audience. Just as you may feel threatened under the constant scrutiny of audience members, so, too, do listeners who are confronted with a speaker who stares at them.

Regular eye contact does not just happen—it takes work and practice. During your early speeches, you may find it difficult to look beyond the people in the front of the room. In your practice, concentrate on "sweeping" the room with your eyes. However, avoid giving the impression that this is a verbal tennis match, where you look first to your right and then to your left and then back to your right again.

In addition to making audience members feel "connected" to you, eye contact provides you with audience feedback. You see listeners' reactions and notice their interest, or lack of it, and are able to make any necessary adjustments.

PERSONAL APPEARANCE AND BEHAVIOR

Your personal appearance and behavior are other nonverbal elements that help you to present your message. How you look and what you do speak just as loudly as what you say. If you are confident and well poised, listeners will view you and your message as more believable and interesting. Table 13.7 compares positive and negative speaking behaviors.

Consider yourself a salesperson of ideas. Your role is to "close the sale" of your ideas—to fulfill your thesis statement (specific purpose). Sales are closed by people who are confident, well groomed, poised, and interested in their subject and their listeners. Be confident and believe in yourself. This type of contagious behavior will be reflected in your appearance.

SPEAKING BEHAVIOR DO'S AND DON'TS

WHAT TO DO	WHAT TO AVOID
Stand quietly or have a reason for your movement.	Don't fidget or play with your hair or clothes.
Smile and appear interested in listeners.	Don't stand on one leg or wrap your legs around each other.
Approach the front of the room with apparent confidence and interest.	Don't shuffle to the front of the room and keep your head down.
Return to your seat with apparent confidence, acting satisfied with your presentation.	Don't shake your head and act disgusted with your presentation.

PRACTICING YOUR SPEECH

Your success in speaking is a direct function of the amount and quality of your practice. Do not wait until the night before your presentation to begin working with your ideas. You must determine your purpose, analyze the audience, select and narrow the subject, gather materials, and make an outline before you can even begin to practice.

Your speech practice will be more effective if you follow certain procedures:

1. **Keep your practice sessions brief and flexible.** In your early practice, go over the speech two or three times each session. Do not worry about the exact language or about forgetting some parts. *Avoid memorizing any part of the speech.* Experiment with your notes and with the way you have organized your ideas. If you want to make changes, this is the ideal time.

2. **Practice in different settings.** You do not have to wait until you are alone or in a vacant classroom to practice your speech. You can run through it while driving to work or walking your dog. Try to present your speech to at least one of your close friends. That will give you another practice opportunity and the chance to receive some honest suggestions from someone you trust.

3. **Practice with your visual aids and mechanical equipment.** If you plan to use visual materials, prepare them before you speak. Then you can practice using them. Flip charts do not flip themselves, and overhead projectors must be aimed and focused carefully. Experience in using pointers, placing transparencies in the proper direction, and leaving slides projected long enough for the audience to understand them is important. You avoid mistakes by practice.

4. **Practice until you are comfortable.** As you first practice your speech, you make changes until the ideas and general language seem right. When you are comfortable with your ideas and language, stop practicing. With good planning, you should reach this stage a day or two before you speak. Then you can relax and just add any "finishing touches" you think are appropriate.

Summary

Delivery is the verbal and nonverbal expression of ideas, feelings, and impressions, and involves using the voice and the body to convey a message to listeners. Good delivery is invisible; that is, delivery is effective when listeners do not "see" or pay attention to any aspects of the delivery but instead concentrate on your message.

The setting and the audience may suggest the most appropriate method of delivery. Manuscript delivery and memorized delivery are usually avoided because they discourage audience responses, sound stilted, and do not allow speakers to be flexible. Impromptu delivery also tends to be avoided because it involves speaking without preparation or advance planning. Extemporaneous delivery, on the other hand, increases speakers' confidence and spontaneity, allows for more audience contact and feedback, and helps to make the speech an interpersonal event.

The language you use in presenting your ideas is part of the impression you convey to your audience. Oral style is characterized by short words and sentences, much repetition, concrete terms, and contractions, while with written style, statements are longer, langauge is more complicated, and there is less repetition.

During a speech, you communicate with your voice and through nonverbal messages. The effective speaker talks at a rate all people can understand, varies pitch and inflection to emphasize ideas or words, and speaks loud enough that all listeners can hear. Nonverbal elements that play a significant role in effective public speaking are gestures, eye contact, and personal appearance and behavior. These should all visually compliment your message, appear spontaneous, and not call attention to themselves.

Practice your speech in a series of brief sessions and in different settings, and become accustomed to your visual aids and equipment in advance. Your success in speaking is directly related to the amount and quality of your practice.

Key Terms

Delivery	Manuscript delivery	Rate
Extemporaneous delivery	Memorized delivery	Volume
Impromptu delivery	Oral style	Written style
Inflection	Pitch	

Application Questions

1. Think of a speech you heard recently. What speaker behaviors do you remember most clearly? Did they add to or detract from the message? Were these behaviors verbal or nonverbal? Which type seemed most important in the speech?
2. Of the prominent speakers you have heard, who is the most effective? What method of delivery does this person use? Why do you think that the speaker has chosen that method? Identify the individual's speaking strengths and weaknesses.
3. What are the most common nonverbal behaviors you see exhibited in classroom presentations? How do they contribute to or detract from speaker effectiveness?

Self-Test for Review

Mark each of the following as either true (T) or false (F).

1. It is possible to determine a person's feelings by the sound of his or her voice.
   (T)   F
2. When you are speaking to a large audience, you should increase your rate slightly.
   T   (F)
3. When you present an impromptu speech, you talk from a few notes on a topic you prepared in advance.   T   (F)
4. Eye contact with the audience is an important component of nonverbal delivery.
   (T)   F
5. Oral style makes use of slightly longer and more complex sentences than written style.   T   (F)
6. Extemporaneous delivery refers to a style of presentation that is carefully prepared but that has a conversational, direct approach.   (T)   F
7. Audiences tend to discount a speaker's physical appearance.   T   (F)
8. An important principle of speech practice is to know the material word for word so you won't forget anything.   T   (F)
9. Using effective delivery to make the correct impression at the beginning of a speech can have a major effect on the rest of the speech.   T   F

Answers: 1. T, 2. F, 3. F, 4. T, 5. F, 6. T, 7. F, 8. F, 9. T.

Suggested Readings

Brigance, William Norwood. *Speech Composition.* New York: Appleton-Century Crofts, 1937, 1953. This is one of the classic works on preparing and delivering a speech. Its principles have been adopted in various forms by virtually all public speaking teachers. For an interesting and comprehensive study of public communication and the constancy of its presentation, this book is the prime source.

Hickson, Mark L., III, and Don W. Stacks. *NVC—Nonverbal Communication: Studies and Applications.* 3d ed. Dubuque, Iowa: Brown & Benchmark, 1993. This work is a veritable annotated bibliography of the research literature on nonverbal communication, but it also includes lucid explanations of scholars' theoretical and practical approaches to nonverbal communication.

Knapp, Mark L., and Judith A. Hall. *Nonverbal Communication in Human Interaction.* 3d ed. New York: Harcourt Brace Jovanovich, 1992. This latest revision of a standard work offers a wealth of illustrative and scholarly information on the communicative effect of physical and vocal cues. The references and the array of investigations into this area of communication make this a valuable reference source for anyone interested in nonverbal messages.

PART 5

Common Types of Speeches

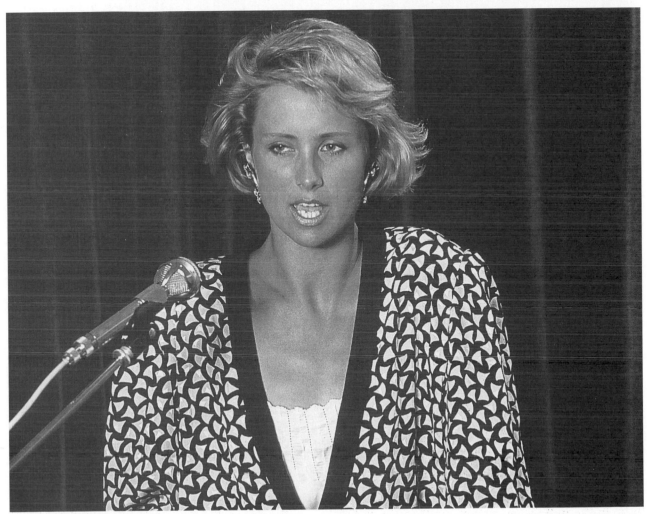

CHAPTER **14**

Informative Speaking

OBJECTIVES

After reading this chapter, you should be able to:

1. *Explain* why listeners must know that your speaking goal is to inform.
2. *Name, define,* and *explain* three ways of characterizing informative speaking.
3. *Name, define,* and *choose* appropriately among the four kinds of informative speeches.
4. *Describe* how to develop each of the four kinds of informative speeches.
5. *Name* and *explain* four guidelines for informative speaking.
6. *List* seven techniques for generating attention and interest.
7. *Explain* how to keep an informative speech simple.
8. *List* ways of making an informative speech credible.
9. *Describe* techniques for making informative speeches memorable.

© Santi Visalli/The Image Bank

*I*n informative speaking, ideas are passed from a speaker to an audience. The message can be as simple as explaining how a pump pulls water from a well or as complex as a discussion of how intelligence is tested.

This chapter explains how a speech to inform can be differentiated from a speech to persuade on the basis of the speaker's intention, the function of the information in the speech, and how listeners perceive the speech.

The chapter also describes how informative speeches generally can be categorized according to whether you want to define, demonstrate, describe, or explain. Whichever of these is your goal, you need to generate attention and interest, keep your language and organizational structure simple, build your credibility, and make your message memorable—easy for listeners to understand, retain, and recall.

The essence of informative speaking is transmitting an idea from one person's mind to another person's mind—sharing ideas. Ideas are shared frequently in a college atmosphere, most often between instructors and students. An instructor's primary function is to convey information, so in all your formal education, you have been exposed to various forms and styles of informative speaking. Speakers who seek to inform want to add to the general storehouse of knowledge that other people have.

Table 14.1 describes the steps that effective public speakers follow when preparing to inform. This checklist will be helpful as you plan for and prepare your informative speaking assignments.

WAYS OF CHARACTERIZING INFORMATIVE SPEECHES

Speeches to inform differ from speeches to persuade on the basis of three characteristics. The first is the speaker's intention—how does the speaker categorize the speech? Second, what is the function of the information in the speech—does it teach or explain, or does it support some argument? Third, how do listeners perceive the speech? The comparison of these three characteristics that follows will give a better understanding of both informative and persuasive speaking and also will help you to know what you must do to get the desired response from listeners.

Your credibility rests on audience members being sure of your intentions. If they develop a skepticism about what you are trying to do, they may begin to criticize your ideas or doubt your honesty. Make sure that listeners understand what you are trying to accomplish with your speech.

Table 14.1

STEPS IN PREPARING AN INFORMATIVE SPEECH

Step	What to Do	Pointers
1	Select your topic and do research.	See chapter 4, "Selecting and Narrowing Your Topic." Go with what you find interesting. Stay with what you know.
2	Analyze your audience.	See chapter 5, "Audience Analysis." Be as realistic as you can. Do not imagine that listeners know more than they do. Look for ways to tie your subject matter to their interests and to their worlds.
3	Decide on a single, observable goal.	See chapter 4, "Selecting and Narrowing Your Topic." What do you want listeners to do, or to be able to do, after they have heard your speech?
4	Identify the main ideas.	What do you have to do to bring listeners to the goal you have in mind for them? Consider writing out each main idea as a single sentence.
5	Organize the main ideas.	See chapter 8, "Organizing the Body of the Speech." Given what you want from listeners, which idea should come first? Next?
6	Develop the supporting materials.	What evidence do you need? What explanations, stories, examples, illustrations, and so on, do you need? See chapter 6, "Supporting Ideas with Argument and Evidence," and chapter 7, "Gathering Supporting Materials and Using the Library."
7	Plan the introduction and the conclusion.	See chapter 10, "Beginning and Ending a Speech." Remember that an introduction is supposed to get attention and prepare listeners for what is coming. Try to develop their curiosity. Build their desire for your information. State your thesis clearly. Remember the purposes of a conclusion: to summarize the key ideas and to focus listeners' thinking and feelings on your key point.
8	Develop your visual aids program.	See chapter 12, "Supporting Ideas Visually." Thumbnail sketches will help. For each main idea, and for each supporting idea, try to imagine how you might use visual materials to strengthen the speech. Keep your specific purpose in mind. After you have a good idea of the overall visuals program, develop a "dummy" of each visual aid.
9	Practice the speech.	Use the "dummy" visual aid program as you go through the speech. Keeping your specific purpose in mind, do you think anything needs to be changed? Would it be better to rearrange the ideas? Strengthen the support? Eliminate irrelevant materials? Drop one or more of the visual aids? Do you need to add any visual aids?
10	Complete the final visual aids program.	Develop and number each visual aid in the overall program.
11	Practice the speech again—and again.	See chapter 13, "Delivery." Think about your impact on listeners. You will know you are ready to give the speech when you feel confident that your ideas make sense, that you know what you are talking about, and that your message "fits" the audience and the occasion. *Do not memorize the speech.*

The primary goal of an informative speech is to transmit information.

THE SPEAKER'S INTENTION

The speaker's intention boils down to a simple question: What does the speaker want from listeners? In other words, what does the speaker want listeners to do or be able to do after hearing the speech? Chapter 4, "Selecting and Narrowing Your Topic," revolves around this central question.

In an informative speech, the speaker wants listeners to know something, to understand something. For example, a speaker who says, "I want you to know three things before you leave here today," leaves no doubt about an intention to inform. The same would be true of a speaker who began a speech with, "Scientists are studying ocean currents by tracking a spilled cargo of Nike sneakers. I'd like to tell you how this works."

By contrast, in a persuasive speech, the speaker wants belief or action and is likely to say something like: "We've just got to take a stand, right now, to protect our environment from industrial pollution." Listeners know immediately from that sentence that the speaker intends to persuade. A call to action in the next sentence ("Won't you please help? Won't you please sign this petition . . . ?") confirms the speaker's persuasive intention.

Thus, the speaker's intent helps to differentiate informative speaking and persuasive speaking. Is your primary objective to transmit information, or is your speech intended, primarily, to change feelings or beliefs? When you can answer that question, you have decided whether your goal is informative or persuasive.

ARTHUR ASHE

In his memoirs written shortly before his death from AIDS, former tennis great Arthur Ashe spoke of what had become one of the most important functions in his life: educating audiences about AIDS. In the following excerpt, he emphasizes two important characteristics of informative speaking: the need to know your audience and the sharing of ideas:

I also found satisfying, although sometimes in a different way, my speeches to a wide range of professional groups, from a luncheon gathering of the National Press Club in Washington, D.C. in May to a morning speech to five hundred public-school teachers at the Sheraton Hotel in Manhattan in October. I have spoken to groups of pharmacists and employees of drug companies, to journalists on the issue of privacy and press freedom, and to businessmen wanting to know firsthand about the magnitude of the AIDS problem. Every group seems to have a different perspective on the problem, so that I constantly find myself being educated even as I try to teach. One of my most satisfying speeches of the year started with a simple letter to me from a student at Greenwich High School in Connecticut who was disturbed by the apparently cavalier attitude toward the disease exhibited by many of her classmates. On short notice, squeezing my visit between two flights out of town to more formal speaking engagements, I drove up from Manhattan to address an assembly of students there. I hope my talk made a difference, at least to some of them.

Source: Arthur Ashe and Arnold Rampersand, Days of Grace: A Memoir *(New York: Alfred A. Knopf, 1993), 256–57. Photo UPI/Bettmann*

FUNCTION OF THE INFORMATION

A speech to inform presents information, while a speech to persuade usually includes elements of both information and persuasion. A persuasive speech needs both elements because, if you want to persuade listeners to change their belief or to act, you have to include information on which to base that change. Determining whether a speech informs or persuades depends to some extent on what the information in the speech is intended to do.

For example, suppose you are listening to a lecture about technological advances in the housing industry. The speaker says that the new technology saves energy, protects the environment, and even helps people with disabilities to live more comfortably and more conveniently than was possible before. Would you classify this as a speech to inform or to persuade?

The answer lies partly in how the information *functions.* Ask yourself: "What does the information do?" When information explains or clarifies an idea, it informs. In contrast, when information supports or proves an argument, it persuades. If the speaker's goal in this example is to inform, you might expect to hear, "This is how the new technology improves housing." But you would know the speaker has a persuasive goal if you hear, "We must incorporate these desirable advances into the city building code." Thus, the function of the information—what it does—indicates whether the speech is informative or persuasive.

LISTENERS' PERCEPTION

Listeners also *perceive* whether a speech is informative or persuasive, and their perception strongly influences how they respond to the speech. For example, some students might think that a classroom lecture on the Roman Catholic idea of the Holy Trinity is informative, while others might believe that the lecture has a persuasive goal. Any differences in perception flow from what listeners *think* the speaker is up to ("What's this guy doing? Is he trying to convert me?"). It is a speech to inform if the listener thinks that the speaker is trying to teach (or is giving authoritative information regardless of motive). It is a speech to persuade if the listener thinks that the speaker is trying to persuade or has an ulterior motive.

Listeners' perceptions can affect your credibility as a speaker and thereby influence the effectiveness of the speech. For example, suppose you decide to give a speech that compares and contrasts several brands of minivans. You begin the speech by talking about Chrysler, Volkswagen, and Ford/Nissan minivans. You compare and contrast these machines in terms of acceleration, braking power, maneuverability, and price. "Overall, the Dodge Caravan appears to be the better value," you say. So far, so good. Assuming that you have dealt with each of these comparisons equally and fairly, listeners will perceive the speech as informative. But suppose, as the speech progresses, that you point out (in an effort to show listeners that you are a knowledgeable source) that you have worked at a Dodge dealership for some time. Suddenly, listeners have to wonder if you are trying to persuade. Could you have an ulterior motive for making such comparisons? Clearly, audience perception can make an important difference to your credibility, and therefore, to the overall impact of your speech.

TYPES OF INFORMATIVE SPEECHES

Although there is some overlap, most informative speeches fall primarily into one of four categories: definition, demonstration, description, and explanation. These categories serve distinctly separate informative functions.

DEFINITION

Definition refers to the formal statement of the meaning or significance of a word or phrase. You use definition as the focal point in an informative speech when you want to teach listeners what something means. Table 14.2 lists several titles of successful **definition speeches.**

Table 14.2

POSSIBLE TITLES FOR A DEFINITION SPEECH

What is euthanasia?	What does it mean to pull yourself up by your bootstraps?
What is a bit, and what is a byte?	
What is the national debt?	What is behaviorism?
What is baroque art?	What is a fact?
What does pro-choice mean to me?	What is artificial intelligence?
What are the limits of personal freedom?	What does post-metaphysical thinking mean?
What does the grade "C" mean?	What is presentational painting?
What does foreign policy mean?	What means success?
What is laser light?	Discipline or child abuse?
What does it mean to argue?	Some call it terrorism.
What is friendship?	

Thus, you define and explain a topic in ways your audience can understand and appreciate. Most speakers use one or more of the following techniques when they give definitional speeches:

Comparison and contrast work as definition when you show how something is similar to or different from something listeners already know. For example, one student speaker compared his first experience with "virtual reality" to "being inside a living video game."

Synonyms are words that have the same, or nearly the same, meanings as other words. For example, a thesaurus might list the following six synonyms for the abstract word *loyalty:* devotion, allegiance, homage, faithfulness, fidelity, fealty. **Antonyms** are words that have the opposite meanings from other words. For example, *short* is the antonym of *tall.* Both synonyms and antonyms work well to define some concept or term.

Etymology means study of the history of change in the meaning of a word. Using etymology to define a term, then, involves talking about the word's origins and history. For example, the English word *democracy* comes from the Greek *demos,* meaning "people," and *karetin,* meaning "rule." So *democracy* means "rule by the people." The *Etymological Dictionary of Modern English* and the *Oxford English Dictionary* are two interesting and useful resources.

Differentiation involves defining by separating or distinguishing something from other members of its class. One student speaker wanted his listeners to be able to identify how a swallow is different from other birds. He used a number of drawings to differentiate the swallow from other types. A transcript of part of his speech follows:

Swallows have slender bodies and long wings. You can tell a swallow mainly by its tail, however. The tail is deeply forked, and the male's outer tail feathers form long streamers. You can also tell a swallow by watching it fly. The swallow can go as high as ten thousand feet or more. It beats its wings evenly and gracefully, and it makes sudden changes in direction, up or down, side to side, without apparently changing this rhythm, and without any apparent loss of speed.

Table 14.3

POSSIBLE TITLES FOR A DEMONSTRATION SPEECH

How an internal combustion engine works	How a cello is made
How to remove water marks from furniture finishes	How to use your nine-iron
	How a sailboat moves upwind
How to make chicken curry	How a laser printer works
How to make a mortise and tenon joint the old-fashioned way	How to clean out a pea trap
	How to hook your television to your stereo system
How to draw the human form	
How to change an electrical switch	How to change a car tire
How to encourage wildlife into your garden	

Swallows love company. When they migrate, the flocks can have hundreds, even thousands of individuals. When they nest, they usually prefer rural areas and farms. They build their nests in rafters, on beams in sheds, or in open chimneys. Sometimes, you can find swallow nests in the understructures of bridges. The nests are built of mud mixed with saliva. They are open at the top and are lined with grass and feathers.

Operational definition means defining something by describing what it does. A student speaker used this approach when she talked about what she, as a physical therapist, does:

I help people get well. For example, one of my patients had a bad automobile accident and was laid up in a cast that held his arms in place for eleven weeks. In that time, the muscles had atrophied. I mean, they had gotten weak from not being used. So my job was to help the patient learn to use those muscles again. I started by actually holding his arms and moving them, making the muscles move. Then we added some weight training, and my job was to develop the weight training program. As the patient got stronger and stronger, I increased the weights until he was able to recover most of the strength he originally had.

DEMONSTRATION

If you wanted to show your audience how to judge the difference between a good-quality touring bicycle and a poor-quality bicycle, you would probably have to give a demonstration speech. To *demonstrate* means to describe, explain, or illustrate by examples, specimens, experiments, and the like. When you demonstrate, you exhibit something. Thus, in a **demonstration speech,** more than in any other kind, you try to show how something works, how it is made, how it is done, or how it happens. Most demonstration speeches rely heavily on visual aids, so you may wish to review chapter 12, "Supporting Ideas Visually." Table 14.3 lists possible titles for a demonstration speech.

Table 14.4

GUIDELINES FOR DEMONSTRATION SPEECHES

1. Do I know enough about this subject to demonstrate it clearly? To focus it and narrow it down?
2. Can this subject be demonstrated in the time limit?
3. Will the location of the speech support or allow the speech?
4. Can I relate this subject to the interests and needs of my listeners? Do they have a reason to care about this subject? Is this subject appropriate for this audience?
5. Will the necessary visual aids be visible? Easy to manage? Convenient? Readily available?

One glance at the list of possible titles in table 14.3 shows that the perceived value of a demonstration speech rests entirely with the listeners. If you already know how to change a car tire, you might perceive a speech on this task to be irrelevant, trite, boring, useless, and redundant. If you do not know how to change a tire and plan to accompany your aged grandmother on a long car trip, that same speech may seem highly relevant and useful.

This means that, as you plan a demonstration speech, you must understand and adapt to listeners' needs and interests. If listeners have no interest in the differences between good-quality and poor-quality bicycles, a speech on that subject will likely bore them. You must find a way for listeners to identify with your ideas. Then, you must focus and narrow the speech, paring it down to manageable limits. It takes a long time to demonstrate something.

One student decided to teach listeners how to build a router table. Given the time limits of the assignment (6 minutes) and the diversity of the listening audience (twenty-four men and women, ranging in age from nineteen to forty-seven), the student did not have a chance of completing the speech adequately. To demonstrate the particulars, the speaker would have had to show listeners:

How to select the appropriate building materials

How to calculate the angles of the various cuts

How to measure and mark the materials for cutting

How to set up and use a saw to make the cuts

How to select and use wood fasteners

Each of these items would take a good deal of time to learn. In addition, the student would have needed a variety of equipment—saws, measuring tapes, and the like. The guidelines in table 14.4 will help you to succeed when you have to demonstrate something.

Table 14.5

POSSIBLE TITLES FOR A DESCRIPTIVE SPEECH

Terrorism in America: What's next?	The rape crisis center volunteer
What to look for in a news magazine	Karate is for everyone
Choosing the right watch	Indo-European origins of English
How the brain controls emotions	Cajun country: The Atchafalaya Basin
Do you need a spread sheet?	Coming out: The problems of a
What computer should you buy?	homosexual in the U.S. military
	AIDS in the nineties

DESCRIPTION

Description means using language to picture some object, phenomenon, or event. **Descriptive speeches** to inform require precise, concrete, and colorful language. As shown in table 14.5, which lists some possible titles for descriptive speeches, many of the lectures you hear take the form of descriptions.

Descriptive speeches succeed when student speakers take the time to polish their language skills. You may wish to review chapter 11, "Language: The Key to Successful Speaking," which examines how to use language wisely.

The following is part of a transcript from a student's descriptive speech about what it means to be a stepparent. The student had married a man with two small children. Notice how vividly she uses language:

> *I've had to learn a lot about kids. I've also had to learn a lot I didn't anticipate, and didn't want to know, about myself. For me, stepparenting offered the challenge to create a close-knit, happy family in which everyone is happy and contented. This meant I had to love both my stepchildren equally and instantly, and to receive love from them instantly.*

> *But they didn't want me. One was quiet about it; the other was openly hostile. This came out the first time at one of our evening meals. After their mother died, my husband and his kids lived on his cooking. That meant macaroni and cheese dinners. I decided the way to those kids' hearts was through their stomachs, so I spent the better part of that day planning and cooking a gourmet meal. I had veal picatta, with all the trimmings, and a lovely dessert. I set a beautiful table, including cut flowers. I had candles. I served wine for us, milk in stemware for the children. I put classical music on the CD. When everything was ready, I called my new family to dinner.*

> *It was a disaster. The kids hated every minute of it. Ken was trying to make the children appreciate my efforts. "Mind your manners," he'd say. "Sit up straight, and be careful not to break the stemware." I was trying to act as though the meal was no big deal. The kids wanted macaroni and cheese, wouldn't eat the "funny stuff," spit out the veal, and turned up their noses at the bread pudding I'd spent two hours making.*

Table 14.6

A CHECKLIST OF QUESTIONS TO HELP YOU DESCRIBE

1. What *size* is the thing you are describing? How does that size compare to something the listeners are likely to know?
2. What is the thing's *weight*? You can say that something is "heavy," or you can say that something weighs 2,000 pounds. Either way (subjective or objective), you clarify a description of weight by comparing it to something with which listeners are already familiar. For example, you might say something like: "That cat weighed 17 pounds—about twice the weight of a normal tabby."
3. *Shape* can produce difficult description problems. What shape is the thing you want to describe? Square? Round? Triangular? Spherical? Cylindrical? Some objects in nature are irregularly shaped, so you will have to approximate to a geometric form. An example of a shape description is: "The dome house is a hemisphere. It looks something like half of a huge basketball with doors and windows cut in."
4. What *color* describes the thing? The human eye is capable of perceiving more than a million different values and hues, so merely to say that a thing is red does not describe it very well. Try comparing the colors to things listeners are likely to know. Say: "blood red," or "dark green, like grass under an oak tree on a sunny afternoon in June."
5. What *material* is the thing you want to describe made of? If you tell listeners what something is made of, they can see it better. Listeners can see a "snowball," but they have to guess what a "ball" looks like. Is it leather? Aluminum? Rubber?
6. How old is the thing? *Age* changes things. They get used, dog-eared, weather-beaten, worn out.
7. In what *condition* is the thing you want to describe? Age, alone, may not tell the story. For example, a 1957 Chevy can be a pile of junk or a collector's item in pristine condition.

Finally I couldn't stand it. I think I must have proved to those kids that I was the wicked stepmother they thought I was.

The checklist of questions in table 14.6 may help you describe things more vividly.

EXPLANATION

Explanation means making clear by describing or interpreting how something works, how to evaluate it, or why it occurred. Every social, political, or economic issue, every historical event, every process, principle, theory, or hypothesis, every piece of music, artistic movement, novel, movie, or drama bears explanation. Table 14.7 lists titles for possible **explanation speeches.**

Is this visual aid visible?
Easy to manage?

© *James L. Shaffer*

Table 14.7

POSSIBLE TITLES FOR AN EXPLANATION SPEECH

The national debt	*Gone With the Wind*
Truman's 1948 whistle-stop tour	The defeat of the Spanish Armada
Pro-choice is pro-life	Africanized killer bees
The theory of generative grammar	Evolution
Cubism	How to make home brew
Compost heap	How snow fences work
Madame Butterfly	Backyard boat building

When you explain something, you expose its essence to listeners. Thus, your analysis of the topic must reveal the essence. Develop your focus by asking the following helpful questions:

What is really important here?

How does it work?

Why does it work?

What difference does it make to me?

What difference does it make to my listeners?

Can I show my listeners how this subject makes a difference to them?

In developing a successful informative presentation, you need to be concerned with effective and accurate transmission of your ideas to listeners. Four important guidelines help you to accomplish your objective: (1) Generate attention and interest, (2) keep it simple, (3) make it credible, and (4) make it memorable.

GENERATE ATTENTION AND INTEREST

Two skills generate listener attention and interest.[1] First, to get and hold interest, you have to keep your ideas moving, and listeners have to feel that the ideas are going somewhere. Second, your ideas must seem relevant to listeners so that they have a motive to keep on listening. They must believe that your ideas bear directly on them—their hopes, wants, customs, needs, and lives.

About the worst thing a beginning speaker can do to listeners is leave them wondering, "So what?" Every speaker needs to anticipate the "So what?" question. If you do, listeners will lean forward in their chairs with interest. If you do not, listeners will decide that there is no reason to keep on listening. Boredom dooms a speech faster than any other audience response.

Seven techniques for generating attention and interest—for keeping your ideas moving and making your ideas relevant to listeners—are: (1) Provide specific details (concretion), (2) build suspense, (3) show action, (4) introduce conflict, (5) hook ideas to the familiar, (6) associate derived interest, and (7) tie ideas to listeners' self-interests.

Provide Specific Details (Concretion)

The term **concretion** refers to the act or process of making something real, tangible, or particular. You make something concrete when you ground it in specific facts, actual circumstances, and conditions. Do not say "a lot" when you mean "eighty-three." Do not say "recently" when you mean "last Wednesday afternoon." Do not say, "The weather was lousy," when you mean, "It rained 4 inches in two hours, and the wind blew drenching gusts up to 70 miles per hour." Chapter 11, "Language: The Key to Successful Speaking," also discusses how specific details enhance your speech.

Build Suspense

Suspense means mental uncertainty and excitement. When listeners cannot anticipate how something will turn out, they pay attention. Knowing this, the great storytellers of all time have held listeners' and readers' attention with suspense.

Suspense works in two ways. In the first, you do not know how something will turn out, and the suspense comes from the questions *who, what,* and *how*. In the second, you know how something will turn out, but you do not know *when* or *by what means*.

Apply the principle of suspense to your informative speech. For example, do not say, "This will solve the problem." Ask, "What will solve the problem?" The question creates tension and suspense and also involves listeners in the search for a solution.

Show Action

Action commands attention. The street performers in New Orleans' Jackson Square understand the action principle. One Saturday afternoon in February, a juggler spread out a carpet, opened his case, and took out a number of colored balls. Without saying a word, he began to juggle first two brightly colored balls, then three. Passersby paused. He spoke to them but kept on juggling. Soon, he had four balls in the air. The crowd grew larger. "Who wants to help?" the juggler cried. Then he moved toward where a little boy stood watching the four colored balls suspended as if by magic. "Hold my coattail," he said. The boy grasped his coat, and the juggler moved into the center of a ring of people. The boy giggled shyly. The pleased crowd laughed. The juggler built the suspense. "I have a fifth ball in my pocket," he said, "but I can't get it because I'll drop these other balls if I do. Can you get it?" Now the juggler led the boy around, pretending to have to move in order to keep the balls in the air, all the while the little boy tried to remove a ball from the juggler's coat pocket. The crowd continued to grow because people want to know what other people find interesting ("Something must be going on there, or all those people would not have stopped to watch.") Finally, the boy got the ball out of the juggler's pocket, and after another ten minutes or so, was able to toss the ball into the mix. Now five balls, then six balls. For a finale, the juggler pretended to pick up the boy and juggle him, too. Of course, all the colored balls came crashing to the ground, and the show was over. It had lasted about 45 action-filled minutes. The applause was satisfyingly loud, and the dollar bills filled up the cigar box the street performer had placed on his little carpet.

You can apply the juggler's action principle to your informative speech because activity happens in the mind, too. You can make it happen if you choose action words. Do not say, "It rained hard," when you mean, "Water slammed to the earth in such density that you couldn't see to the other side of the street." Do not say, "He ran a marathon." Your listeners cannot see that. Try, instead, to show the action:

> For the first few miles, he was part of the pack, running easily at a pace that covered a mile every seven minutes. By the eighth mile, the pack had thinned to sprinkles— four runners here, two more there, a group of three up ahead. Gradually, the distance between runners and between groupings increased, but not the pace. A mile every seven minutes. Mile after mile, through the heat, through the pain in the thighs, through the shortness of breath, through the stitch in the side, the runner thinks only of the pace. Go up the hill. Round the turn. Pound out the pace—seven minutes per mile, a mile every seven minutes.

Introduce Conflict

Conflict—whether between people on a collision course or between ideas—holds attention and stimulates interest. *Conflict* in this sense means antagonism or opposition between interests or principles; or to be at variance. The suspense felt during a compelling speech may well flow from the conflict of issues. You can build interest by placing conflicting ideas in juxtaposition (side by side).

Hook Ideas to the Familiar

People pay attention to the familiar—what they know and have seen before, what they are conversant about. Hook your ideas to listeners' experiences—whether those experiences were direct or vicarious—and you hold their interest.

Two examples may illustrate this principle for you. Suppose you buy a two-year-old Toyota Camry. Before you bought the car, you never paid much attention to the Toyota Camrys on the road. Now, you always notice how many Camrys you pass because Camrys are now a part of your experience—they are familiar to you. Or suppose you are reading a Civil War novel in which the story line takes you to the area around Moline and Rock Island, Illinois, and Davenport, Iowa. Because you lived in that area for a few years and it is familiar to you, you pay particular attention to the narrative.

The principle is a simple one, and so is the conclusion to be drawn: If you want listeners to pay attention, talk in terms of their experience.

Associate Derived Interest

Derived interest means interest that flows from associating a new subject with something listeners already care about. For example, a young mathematics teacher was having trouble interesting a group of military academy students in plane geometry. But then he noticed several of his students hanging out near the pool tables in the student center. The teacher played eight-ball well and so determined to use this ability to derive interest. He walked up to the best student player, slapped down a twenty-dollar bill, and said, "Game of eight-ball?" The student saw an easy mark and agreed. The teacher gave the student the first shot, waited patiently until the student missed, and then ran the table, calling out each shot in advance. Of course, the story of the game spread rapidly among the students. The next day in class, the teacher said, "I won twenty dollars last night because I understand geometry." The teacher's plane geometry class was lively after that.

To associate something new with ideas listeners already find interesting, you must know what listeners find interesting. You cannot afford to guess or to leave this matter to chance. You have to do your homework. Ask yourself: Can I arouse interest in the familiar—a story, a book, a recent news event, an on-campus event, a basketball game, and so on—and then tie it to my subject matter?

Tie Ideas to Listeners' Self-Interests

If you can show that your subject, your ideas, or your point of view will help listeners to get what they want, they will pay attention. The principle, then, is to tie your ideas to listeners' self-interests. Table 14.8 lists fourteen things that listeners really want, without including the obvious, like money, goods, and services. You can undoubtedly add to the list.

As mentioned earlier in the chapter, your speech should not leave listeners wondering, "So what?" Show them how what you have to say can help them to fulfill their self-interests.

All of the techniques discussed in this section (concretion, suspense, action, conflict, the familiar, derived interest, and self-interests) generate attention and interest and give audience members a reason to listen to you. The next sections present additional guidelines for making your informative speech successful: keep it simple, make it credible, and make it memorable.

Table 14.8

FOURTEEN THINGS LISTENERS WANT

1. Power
2. To feel good about who they are
3. To be recognized in a positive way—as having good sense, good judgment, etc.
4. To find or keep a job, and to be promoted
5. To meet personal goals without sacrificing their moral principles
6. To believe that what they are doing really matters
7. To be listened to—and heard
8. To be liked, respected, valued, included
9. To be treated with respect
10. Excitement, travel, adventure, good food, fun
11. The truth
12. To avoid getting trapped, boxed in, caught
13. To avoid trouble, risk, put-downs, hassles, insecurity that comes from surprises and changes
14. To avoid betrayal—by you or anyone else

KEEP IT SIMPLE

A speech to inform must be simple. *Simple* means basic, uncomplicated, not complex, readily understood, without superfluous materials, fundamental, and easy to follow. The essence of simplicity in an informative speech is a structure that contains the following:

1. A clear thesis statement
2. A few main ideas, clearly expressed
3. Materials that support and explain the main ideas

From what you have read in previous chapters, you probably recognize these as the ingredients of a well-organized speech. Informative speaking is intended to present ideas in a way that is easy for listeners to follow. Simple ideas are easy for people to understand during a speech and easy to recall after the speech. Simple language means that your thoughts are expressed in words that are basic, clear, and understandable to all your listeners. As you sift through your ideas, work hard to keep your organizational structure and language simple.

You do not have to sell out an idea to keep it simple. Indeed, the simple speech is often the strongest speech.

MAKE IT CREDIBLE

Credible means believable. Audience members invest credibility in you as a speaker, and they do not take this investment lightly. You have to earn it. The suggestions that follow can help to increase your credibility with listeners.

Be Prepared

When you know your speech and your audience, when you have planned and practiced carefully, your credibility will soar. Listeners can sense when you have your act together. You speak with greater confidence, you seem knowledgeable, and your fluency and command compel audience members to listen.

Be Audience-Centered

Make sure listeners hear and understand that your emphasis is on them. Talk in terms they understand. Show them how they will benefit from your ideas and why they should listen to you. Show how your ideas bear upon their interests and needs. When listeners sense a speaker's focus on them, they pay attention, get interested, and believe in the speaker's credibility.

Be Enthusiastic

You have to care if you want your audience to care. Let your enthusiasm shine through, and your audience will believe in you. Enthusiasm starts with having a positive attitude about your topic and then showing that you really want listeners to get the information. Lack of enthusiasm is evident in poorly made or sloppy visual aids, as well as in lackluster body language and subdued or boring voice dynamics. Take the time to plan and prepare carefully. Look like you care. Listeners need and deserve your enthusiasm, and you need the credibility that listeners can bestow.

Be on Time

Listeners observe your behavior and then draw inferences about you on the basis of what they have observed. What inferences do audience members draw about a speaker who arrives late and delays a program? Your punctuality can reflect on your credibility. It says, "I care enough about these listeners not to waste their time." Get there in time. Start on time. Your credibility may depend on it.

MAKE IT MEMORABLE

Memorable means worthy of being remembered—easily retained and recalled. If you want your informative speech to have an impact on listeners, you must make it memorable. This means, of course, that you must first have an idea that is worth hearing. After that, you need to help listeners understand, retain, and recall your idea. How do you do that? Table 14.9 lists techniques you can use to make your informative speeches memorable.

Appendix A, "Sample Speeches," includes a good example of an informative speech. Read the speech by Siok Tan and evaluate whether it follows the guidelines for informative speaking presented in this chapter.

Table 14.9

TECHNIQUES FOR MAKING INFORMATIVE SPEECHES MEMORABLE

WHAT TO DO	WHY	EXAMPLE
Repeat the key ideas.	Repetition places emphasis on an idea. Thus, repetition makes it more likely that listeners will remember the idea you repeat.	"One fourth of all Americans will have cancer by the time they reach fifty. Think of it—one out of every four men and women."
Tell how the ideas relate to listeners.	People pay attention to things that bear on their own lives.	"What does this mean to you? Well, let's try something. Look at the person to your left. Now look at the person to your right. Now touch the person in front of you. If one of those people doesn't get cancer by age fifty, you will."
Suggest memory aids.	People need help. Just as you determine ways to remember important information for yourself, you can point out ways to help listeners remember.	"When you find yourself trying to compensate for an alcoholic's behavior in your life, remember the three Cs. You didn't *cause* it, you can't *cure* it, and you can't *control* it."
Polish transitions.	Listeners need your help in following you from one idea to another. Allow transitions to make this movement clear.	"So you see the problem. Secondhand smoke is as dangerous as smoking directly. Now we come to the hard part. What are we going to do about it? Ladies and gentlemen, I want to argue that smoking must be banned from all public places in our city."
Use appropriate humor.	Listeners usually remember the point of a story that takes the light approach, and they are likely to associate their pleasure in the humor with the idea you want them to remember. (Stay with what you know, and with what is relevant to the audience and the occasion.)	(In a speech about the problems facing the Mobile County Schools) "I'm not kidding—some of the schools in Mobile County are so old-fashioned, the kids have to raise their hands and get permission before they punch the kid at the next desk."
Use visual aids.	Listeners are more likely to remember what they *see* as well as *hear*.	See chapter 12, "Supporting Ideas Visually."

Summary

Because speeches to inform and speeches to persuade overlap, listeners often become confused about what speakers are trying to accomplish. If listeners misconstrue your intention—for example, if they think you are trying to persuade when you are trying to teach—they might never give you what you want. Such confusion damages both your credibility and the impact of your speech.

Informative speeches differ from persuasive speeches on the basis of three characteristics: (1) the speaker's intention—what does the speaker want listeners to do or be able to do after hearing the speech? (2) how the information in the speech functions—does it teach or explain, or does it support some argument? and (3) how listeners perceive the speech—what do listeners think the speaker is trying to do?

Most informative speeches aim at definition, demonstration, description, or explanation. Definition speeches teach listeners what something means through comparison and contrast, synonyms, antonyms, etymology, differentiation, and operational definition. Demonstration speeches show how something works, how it is made, how it is done, or how it happens. Description speeches use precise, concrete, and colorful language to picture some object, phenomenon, or event. Explanation speeches describe or interpret how something works, how to evaluate it, or why it occurred.

Whichever type of informative speech is your goal, you can generate attention and interest by providing specific details, building suspense, filling the speech with action, introducing conflict, hooking ideas to the familiar, associating derived interest, and tying ideas to listeners' self-interests. Keep your language and organization of ideas simple, direct, and straightforward. You can increase your credibility with listeners by being prepared, audience-centered, enthusiastic, and on time. And your informative speech will be memorable if you repeat the key ideas, tell how the ideas relate to listeners, suggest memory aids, polish transitions, use appropriate humor, and present visual aids.

Key Terms

Antonyms	Demonstration speech	Etymology
Comparison and contrast	Derived interest	Explanation speech
Concretion	Descriptive speech	Operational definition
Definition speech	Differentiation	Synonyms

Application Questions

1. In your experience as a listener, what kinds of topics have made the most interesting informative speeches? Why do you think so?
2. Select the professor who, in your experience, gives the best (most interesting, most informative) lectures. Attend one of the lectures, and pay particular attention to the professor's speaking strategies. Try to consider all of the techniques that apply—for

example, generating attention and interest, keeping it simple, and making it credible and memorable. Make careful notes to share with your classmates in public speaking class. Does the professor's style of speaking agree with suggestions in this chapter? If not, in what ways? What can you learn from this that will help you to give better informative speeches?

3. Effective teachers try to build new ideas on information you already have. Attend an informative speech (classrooms are full of such speaking) with this idea in mind. Do you think the speaker was successful in introducing and building new ideas on the foundations of information you already had? If so, how was that accomplished? If not, what suggestions could you make to help the speaker do it better?

Self-Test for Review

1. For an informative speech to be successful, audience members must believe that the speaking goal is *to inform* because

   a. listeners can respond to a speech even if they do not understand the goal.
   b. audiences always project themselves into the speech situation.
   c. a confused listener always stops listening.
   d. listeners who think the speaker may be trying to persuade may resist the persuasion they think they are being subjected to.

2. The three characteristics of informative speaking are

   a. definition, description, and explanation.
   b. intention, function, and perception.
   c. inclusion, control, direction.
   d. illustration, example, and anecdote.

3. Match each of the following speech characteristics with the type of informative speech in the right-hand column to which it applies.

   _____ a. Formal statement of the meaning or significance of a word
   _____ b. To explain or illustrate by examples, specimens, experiments
   _____ c. Using language to picture a phenomenon or event
   _____ d. Interpreting how something works or how to evaluate it
   _____ e. The defeat of the Spanish Armada (speech title)
   _____ f. How to use your nine-iron (speech title)
   _____ g. What is "baroque" art? (speech title)
   _____ h. The rape crisis center volunteer (speech title)

   1. Explanation
   2. Description
   3. Definition
   4. Demonstration

Evaluate each of the following statements for you personally by checking one of the three alternatives.

4. I understand and can name six ways to develop   ____Yes ____ Needs work ____ No
   a speech of definition.
5. I know how to develop a demonstration speech. ____Yes ____ Needs work ____ No
6. I can use differentiation as a technique for   ____Yes ____ Needs work ____ No
   defining a term.
7. I know how—and why—to use specific   ____Yes ____ Needs work ____ No
   details in a descriptive speech.
8. I know how to bring an explanation into focus   ____Yes ____ Needs work ____ No
   for an audience.
9. I can specify two general speaking skills that   ____Yes ____ Needs work ____ No
   generate listener attention and interest.
10. I can describe two techniques for building   ____Yes ____ Needs work ____ No
    suspense.
11. I can name seven techniques for gaining   ____Yes ____ Needs work ____ No
    listener attention.
12. I know how to use derived and self-interest to   ____Yes ____ Needs work ____ No
    establish an idea as relevant to my listeners.
13. I can name and explain four techniques for   ____Yes ____ Needs work ____ No
    building credibility.

Answers: 1. d. 2. b. 3. a. 3. b. 4. c. 2. d. 1. e. 1. f. 4. g. 3. h. 2. Only the reader can judge the accuracy of items 4 through 13.

Suggested Readings

Freeley, Austin J. *Argumentation and Debate: Critical Thinking for Reasoned Decision Making.* 8th ed. Belmont, Calif.: Wadsworth, 1993. This old chestnut (first edition appeared in 1961) is still one of the best resources available to public speakers. For example, Chapter 4, "Analyzing the Controversy," includes a lucid and thorough explanation of how to define terms.

Goss, Blaine. *The Psychology of Human Communication.* Prospect Heights, Ill.: Waveland Press, 1989. This little text (142 pages, plus end matter) may be the clearest presentation of how people process information to be found anywhere between two covers. The prose is lively and clear, and the materials are directly relevant to the task of adapting informative speeches to listeners.

OUTLINE

OBJECTIVES

After reading this chapter, you should be able to:

1. *Cite* several ethical guidelines for persuasive speakers.
2. *Present* a brief history of the study of persuasion, discussing Aristotle's artistic proofs, the intensification/downplay and evoked recall models of persuasion, and Rokeach's hierarchy of beliefs.
3. *Describe* how values can be differentiated from beliefs and why speakers should appeal to both values and beliefs of listeners.
4. *Describe* the three elements of the effective persuasive speech.
5. *List* and *explain* four credibility components of the persuasive speaker.
6. *Explain* the concept of logical completeness and how it relates to message credibility and propositions of fact, value, and policy.
7. *Describe* and *give examples* of four kinds of persuasive message strategies: (1) one-sided versus two-sided arguments, (2) explicit versus implicit conclusions, (3) evoked recall appeals, and (4) organizing in a motivated sequence.
8. *Cite* the eight primary needs that underlie the use of evoked recall appeals as a persuasive message strategy.
9. *Discuss* two research-supported principles with regard to the use of fear appeals as a persuasive message strategy.
10. *Explain* why the five steps of the motivated sequence—attention, need, satisfaction, visualization, and action—comprise an effective organizational strategy for persuasive speeches.

UPI/Bettmann

*P*ersuasive speaking aims at influencing the attitudes, beliefs, and behaviors of listeners. For that reason, persuasive speakers must be responsible and accountable for what they say. This chapter examines four theories and models of persuasion that have developed over time and then explores the characteristics of effective persuasive speeches. For a persuasive speech to be effective, the speaker must have high credibility with listeners, the persuasive message itself must be credible, and the speaker must use message strategies that ethically appeal to listeners' rational and emotional needs.

Persuasive speaking is common in our everyday lives. We often attempt to influence the thoughts, beliefs, or actions of others. For example, we might say:

> "Hey, I've had enough studying for one night. Let's go get a pizza."

> "You know the concert tickets go on sale today, and the good seats will go first. Do you want me to pick up a ticket for you when I get mine tonight?"

> "You certainly look nice, but I've got to tell you that I like the first shirt better with those slacks. Maybe you should . . ."

Statements like these are common in our daily lives, but most of the time, we do not perceive them as persuasion. They seem, instead, to be merely part of the conversational climate that ties together the events of our existence. However, these statements are more sophisticated, rhetorically, than they first appear because they use a variety of persuasive appeals.

Kathleen Reardon defined **persuasion** as "the activity of attempting to change the behavior of at least one person through symbolic interaction."[1] Thus, in persuading, we choose and implement a strategy that we hope will produce some *observable* change in others. If it is done right, the change occurs, but sometimes, our persuasive efforts are not effective. This chapter describes rhetorical strategies that will increase the likelihood that your persuasive efforts will have the effect you want.

ETHICAL CONSIDERATIONS

An understanding of how to persuade implies certain ethical considerations, as discussed in chapter 1, "Introduction." The following ethical guidelines summarize the chapter 1 discussion:

1. Strive to benefit your listeners as well as yourself.
2. Respect your listeners by valuing their diversity.
3. Be candid as you reveal your thoughts and feelings. Your honesty is your most valuable personal asset.
4. Do not make arguments you cannot support, and do not support arguments with misleading evidence.
5. Do not oversimplify complex matters.
6. Do not use emotional appeals you cannot support with evidence and reasoning.

7. Do not pretend to be sure of something when you are not.
8. Do not coerce or mislead listeners. Let them make up their own minds.
9. Sometimes, preserving harmony and peace may be more important than speaking your mind. When this is the case, keep your mouth shut.
10. Take care never to misuse the enormous power of language to create reality inside other people.

THEORIES OF PERSUASION

People have tried to understand how persuasion works since well before Aristotle wrote his *Rhetoric* about 350 B.C.E. That effort has produced a large number of theories. Four theories are especially helpful to beginning persuasive speaking students: (1) Aristotle's artistic proofs, (2) the intensification/downplay model, (3) the evoked recall model, and (4) beliefs and values.

ARISTOTLE AND ARTISTIC PROOFS

Aristotle was one of the first writers and theorists in persuasion. His work was so influential that much of modern persuasion builds upon his principles. Aristotle described the kinds of appeals that a persuader could create, control, and use. He called these **artistic proofs.** The artistic proofs included **ethos** (the kind of person you are, including your education, honesty, reputation, and skill in delivering a speech), **logos** (appeals to the rational intellect), and **pathos** (appeals to the passions or to the will—the so-called emotional proofs). You may wish to reread the section in chapter 6, "Supporting Ideas with Argument and Evidence," that explains and illustrates the use and importance of these artistic proofs.

INTENSIFICATION/DOWNPLAY MODEL OF PERSUASION

In the 1970s, Hugh Rank developed the **intensification/downplay model of persuasion.**[2] He discovered that people use two persuasive tactics: They either (1) play up their own strong points and their competitors' weak points, or (2) they play down their weak points and their competitors' strong points.[3] Ford Motor Company used the first strategy when it showed pictures of a Ford Tempo beside a Honda Civic, along with a narrative similar to the following:

> *A Honda Civic with radio, automatic transmission, and air conditioning costs $1,500 more than a comparably equipped Ford? What are you spending your money for? See your local Ford dealer.*

Persuaders also play down their own weaknesses and their competitors' strengths. For example, the American Plastics Council showed a picture of a picnic table with the caption, "How to Save the Planet and the Picnic at the Same Time." Plastic wrap covered the hot dogs, salad, and watermelon. The message claimed that plastic saves energy but neglected to mention that plastic comes from petroleum, a nonrenewable fossil fuel. The council also neglected to mention its competitors' strengths, which, in many cases, would be reusability or renewability.

EVOKED RECALL MODEL OF PERSUASION

The **evoked recall model of persuasion** came on the scene in the mid-1970s.[4] It argues that pulling a persuasive message out of a receiver is easier than putting one in. Evoked recall works by relying on a set of memories, experiences, attitudes, and opinions that people already hold. For example, Proctor and Gamble advertised using a full-page photograph of a smiling young woman hugging a package of its Charmin toilet tissue. The only part of the package that shows between the arms of the young woman is imprinted with the picture of a beautiful baby and the name, Charmin. The legend is, "So much squeezable softness, you gotta hug it." Clearly, the advertiser is attempting to evoke a recall—that is, the advertiser wants viewers to make a connection between the images on the screen and something inside themselves. This process, called **identification,** is the most important part of persuasion in the evoked recall model. All of us carry images from the past that can influence our perceptions in the present.

BELIEFS AND VALUES

In addition to carrying images from the past, we all have developed a set of beliefs and values that have grown out of the training and experience of a lifetime. Persuaders can work with these.

Beliefs and values control what people accept as true and important. To illustrate, consider your position on the pro-life/pro-choice controversy—whether or not the government should permit and support abortions. Your position on this issue depends on your values and beliefs. You accept or reject what people tell you about this controversy according to what seems consistent or inconsistent with your values and beliefs.

Suppose you believe that life begins at conception—that the moment the two cells combine, they constitute a living human being. Suppose, further, that you feel that only self-defense or national defense justifies taking the life of another human being. Given these beliefs and values, you probably would oppose a proposal that the government make abortion available to women on demand. Issues of this sort are rarely that simple, however. You also may hold other related opinions. For example, you may feel that a baby should have some chance of happiness, including parents who want the baby and can support it. Or you may feel that a conception resulting from rape or incest would be repugnant.

You can hold all of these opinions at the same time. They are not necessarily inconsistent, and they do not seem inconsistent to the people who hold them. However, they obviously confound the question of whether to support or oppose using federal funds to pay for abortions.

Your position on abortion is not the question here. Rather, this example shows that a position on any issue depends on your values and beliefs. As a persuasive speaker, you need to understand how beliefs and values work so that you can present information to strengthen your arguments and to develop your personal credibility.

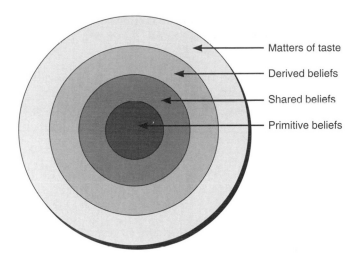

Figure **15.1**
Rokeach's structural
hierarchy of beliefs.

Matters of taste

Derived beliefs

Shared beliefs

Primitive beliefs

Beliefs

A **belief** is a statement that something *is*. A scholar named Milton Rokeach felt that some
beliefs are more significant than others and that this explains why people can hold conflicting beliefs at the same time without discomfort. Rokeach developed a structure of beliefs and placed them in a hierarchy (see figure 15.1).

Primitive Beliefs

According to Rokeach, **primitive beliefs** are beliefs that we have about ourselves, about
existence, and about our personal identities. These primitive beliefs are more central to
our lives than other beliefs. Typical belief statements in this category might be:

1. "I'm an honest person."
2. "I always have bad luck."
3. "Life is never fair to me."
4. "Darkness frightens me."
5. "I think I'm a good-looking person."
6. "I can't do anything athletic."
7. "I'm very affectionate."
8. "I can do anything if I set my mind to it."

We rarely express primitive beliefs aloud, but they substantially influence our communication behavior.

Shared Beliefs

According to Rokeach, **shared beliefs** result from experiences we are willing to discuss
with others. They are the basis for our talk with other people and are less central to the hierarchy than are primitive beliefs (see figure 15.1). We express a belief, others confirm or

deny it, and we accept or reject their confirmation or denial. Because we share this level of belief with other people, shared beliefs become a common ground of understanding. Examples of shared beliefs include:

> "It seems to me that people should be willing to tell where they stand on an issue. We can agree to disagree!"

> "Hopefully, you will agree with me that we can't afford to cut our defense budget any more."

Derived Beliefs

Derived beliefs usually emerge from a combination of other beliefs and, as shown in figure 15.1 of Rokeach's belief hierarchy, are less central than either shared or primitive beliefs. To illustrate, suppose you discover that someone changed your schedule for the winter term and enrolled you in Philosophy 101. You say to your friends: "I don't know why they changed my schedule and put me in a course that'll be boring." Amy says, "Last year I took the same course and felt just like you. But it was great. I learned more about myself in that course than anything else I took for the entire year." Henri agrees: "You're going to thank the Registrar for changing your schedule. I'll bet you a pizza that you'll tell us at the end of the term that was the best course you ever had. The teachers in that department are great, too." After this conversation with your friends, you decide to give the course a chance, especially because the people who share your ideas also enjoyed it. Based on the information gleaned from conversations with others, you have derived a belief about the new course.

Matters of Taste

Matters of taste lie at the outer rim of the Rokeach model (see figure 15.1). They are arbitrary and rather insignificant beliefs about the world, such as:

> "I like country music better than soft rock."

> "The flowers at Bellingrath Gardens seemed more beautiful than usual today."

> "I love the view in the Napa Valley."

> "If you ask me, Helen Hayes was one of the finest performers in this century."

Changing Beliefs

The closer a belief is to the outside of the ring in figure 15.1, the easier it is to change. In other words, matters of taste are easier to modify than shared beliefs or derived beliefs. If you make a statement that appears inconsistent with someone's core primitive beliefs, the listener may think that your position is not credible, even if you support your statement with compelling evidence and argument.

People hold beliefs regardless of whether or not their beliefs can be verified. As a speaker, of course, when you make a claim, you should support it with evidence. Your credibility depends on you doing so. Supporting evidence does not compel listeners to accept a claim, however, especially if the claim goes against their deeply held belief structure.

Similarly, some beliefs seem so obvious that speakers do not think to support them. However, just because a claim seems self-evident to you does not guarantee that your listeners will accept it. For example, each of the following claims seemed self-evident to the people who made them, but the truth of these statements may not be obvious to listeners:

"The violence in Northern Ireland is primarily a religious conflict."

"If given a chance, American farmers could feed the world."

"Racism is the fundamental source of social problems in America's large cities."

"Nationalism is the principal cause of conflict in Eastern Europe and the Middle East."

"Controlling hospital costs will reduce most of the health care crisis."

Marshall information, evidence, and argument to support your ideas and to give listeners an opportunity to modify their beliefs. To illustrate the importance of using adequate supporting material, suppose that you have decided to give a speech about cleaning up the waterways in your area. To be effective, you have to present information and design appeals that seem consistent with listeners' beliefs. Belief statements you might use as the main ideas in the speech include:

The stream is polluted.

The chemical plant upstream polluted the water.

The managers of that chemical plant bear responsibility for the pollution.

For an audience to accept these statements, you need to provide proof. A listener might ask:

How do you know that the stream is polluted? How do you know that the chemical plant is the source of the pollution? How do you know that the managers of the chemical plant are responsible? Are they directly responsible or indirectly responsible? How do you know that?

To persuade listeners to accept your statements, you must present evidence and arguments with enough persuasive strength to prove your claim. Some listeners may be skeptical because their belief systems differ from yours. What seems important to them may be quite different from what is important to you. For example, they may think: "Well maybe there is some pollution, but because we need the jobs that the chemical plant brings, we should tolerate some pollution to keep the plant operating." If your arguments are to seem credible, they have to overcome the effects of listeners' belief systems.

Values

A **value** is a statement containing the words *should* or *ought,* or such subjective terms as *good, beautiful, correct,* or *important.* Consider the following value statements:

"Driving seventy-five miles per hour was a dumb thing to do. You ought to drive that car a lot slower. So much speed isn't safe. And besides, you ought to obey the law."

"That is a very interesting and informative course. And the information is so important. In fact, the course probably ought to be required. Maybe we should require it some time during the sophomore year."

Notice that each of these statements implies the existence of a set of rules or standards—a value system—that justifies the claims *should* and *ought.* When you use such terms as *dumb, interesting,* or *important,* you are also applying a value system.

Values are internal—they are inside you. For example, while the law states that you cannot drive over sixty-five miles per hour on interstate highways, laws are external and not necessarily part of your value system. You may or may not agree with the law. Your internal value system may allow you to choose to drive faster than the law allows.

People often base their thinking on their value systems—on what *ought* to be. As a persuasive speaker, you have to think of ways to adapt to or overcome resistance from listeners' value systems.

Look again at the driving example to see how you might construct persuasive arguments based on value systems. Suppose that you have decided to make the following arguments:

1. Most people are responsible.
2. Therefore, most people will act responsibly, given the choice.
3. In any case, people should be given the freedom to choose the responsible option.
4. The speed limit law in the United States does not permit individual drivers freedom to choose a responsible option.
5. A deliberate choice to exceed the speed limit might be the most sensible choice. For example, you might break the speed limit to move freight more quickly or because your car operates safely at high speeds.
6. Thus, the law that limits speed should be replaced with a general law that gives people a choice about what speed is safe and reasonable.

These are controversial claims. If you want to persuade listeners to accept them, you will have to choose evidence and arguments that are consistent with *listeners'* ideas about what they should and ought to do.

Appealing to Beliefs and Values

Beliefs and values work together in listeners' minds. In fact, people often cannot distinguish between them. Therefore, as a persuasive speaker, your choice of evidence and argument must appeal to *both* their beliefs and values. If a listener says, "How do you know?" "Oh, yeah? Show me," or "So what?", you need to provide a satisfactory answer that seems consistent with what the listener already believes or values. Otherwise, the listener probably will reject your statements. You must have solid arguments to support your position, and specific examples and clear-cut evidence to develop those arguments.

CHARACTERISTICS OF THE EFFECTIVE PERSUASIVE SPEECH

An effective persuasive speech, one that achieves the desired audience response, is generally characterized by three elements. First, the speaker must have established a high level of credibility with listeners. Second, the message must be credible. Third, the speaker's

Table 15.1

COMPONENTS OF SPEAKER CREDIBILITY

ELEMENT	DEMONSTRATED BY A PERSON WHO:
Trust	Is honest, fair, and open-minded and has personal integrity and a good reputation
Knowledge	Is experienced, well-informed, trained, intelligent, qualified and cites evidence
Appearance	Dresses appropriately, demonstrates good grooming, has inner bearing or poise
Audience identification	Is able to establish a bond and to identify with listeners

chosen message strategies should appeal to both the rational and emotional needs of listeners. Including these three elements in a single speech requires hard work and concentrated effort. The discussion that follows explores how you can develop and include these characteristics in your persuasive speeches.

SPEAKER CREDIBILITY

Speaker credibility is the degree to which listeners believe in you as a source. It is not just the message and your presentation of ideas that makes a persuasive speech effective. The audience also judges your believability and intellectual and physical attractiveness in deciding whether or not to accept your arguments. If a speaker seems incredible (that is, not credible) to the audience, then no matter how well drawn, the message will not be persuasive. Four components of speaker credibility warrant your attention: (1) trust, (2) knowledge, (3) appearance, and (4) audience identification (see table 15.1).

Trust

If listeners do not trust a speaker, the speaker has no chance of successful persuasion. No one likes deception, and we rarely follow people we believe will deceive us. Persuasion researchers who have studied the perception of trustworthiness have found that trustworthy speakers present facts honestly, are fair to both sides of an issue, have a high level of personal integrity, are open-minded, and enjoy good reputations. Each of these characteristics is a matter of personal choice. If you wish to be a successful persuader, you must choose to be trustworthy.

Knowledge

Speakers who appear experienced, well-informed, trained, intelligent, and qualified are likely to enjoy more credibility with listeners than speakers who do not project these qualities. In other words, if you wish to succeed in persuasion, you must seem

Table 15.2

CHARACTERISTICS OF KNOWLEDGEABLE SPEAKERS

CHARACTERISTIC	HOW TO DEVELOP AND PROJECT CHARACTERISTIC
Well-informed	Know what you are talking about. Show that you know by presenting facts, figures, names, dates, and so on.
Qualified	You must have the necessary academic and experiential background, and listeners must know of your background. Either mention it yourself, or have someone else mention it, either in writing or orally.
Experienced	To perceive you as experienced, listeners must believe that you have a history of involvement and concern with the topic. They learn of your experience when you or someone else tells them of it. Never try to manufacture experience you do not have.
Intelligent	In a speaking situation, intelligence includes both what you know and how clearly you articulate it. Thus, the marks of an intelligent speaker include organization of ideas and language usage.
Trained	Training involves both experience and credentials. While a scout master with a bachelor's degree might be fully capable of setting a broken bone, a licensed physician has more credibility by reason of training. You or someone else must tell listeners that you have appropriate credentials and experience.

knowledgeable to listeners. Bear in mind that this means that you must also always speak to audience members' level of understanding and provide listeners with proof that you are a knowledgeable source. Table 15.2 describes what is involved in developing and projecting knowledge.

Appearance

The appearance dimension of speaker credibility concerns the way you present yourself, not your physical features. Thus, with this aspect of speaker credibility, as with every other, your personal choices make the difference. In public speaking, appearance boils down to three features: (1) how you dress, (2) how careful you are about grooming, and (3) your presence, bearing, or poise.

You can always choose to dress in a way that increases your credibility. For example, if you are going to speak about the importance of investing your money wisely, you need to present yourself as a person who has achieved success in this activity. That is why bankers and brokers wear business suits and dresses instead of polo shirts and shorts. Dress appropriately for the occasion and the audience.

The rules of good grooming seem equally obvious. Clean and press your clothes, shine your shoes, take a bath, and comb your hair.

The manner in which you conduct yourself reflects your inner bearing and poise. Stand up straight. Hold your head up. Speak and move confidently, even if you do not feel confident.

Audience Identification

We are attracted to people who confirm us, who remind us of ourselves, and we find such people more credible. As a public speaker, you should try to establish a bond between yourself and listeners. Look for the common ground you share—whether it is a place, a problem, or an attitude—and then tell listeners how you share this common ground.

Listeners do not place high credibility in people whose values and judgments are distinctly different from their own. For example, they may tolerate a message that is contrary to their basic beliefs about educational values, but they are unlikely to change their attitudes because of the message. They may decide instead that the speaker is not well informed and has a peculiar sense of value.

This does not mean that you should only tell audience members just what they want to hear. Analyze your listeners, and develop a strategy that will help them to identify with you. That way, you can hope for change, rather than rejection of your entire argument.

MESSAGE CREDIBILITY

As we saw in the previous section, one of the three characteristics of effective speeches—speaker credibility—includes trust, knowledge, appearance, and identification with listeners. A second kind of credibility—message credibility—is equally important to your success as a persuader. A message will seem credible if it is logically complete.

The **logical completeness** of a message exists to the extent that listeners think that a statement is warranted by the evidence and arguments presented. For example, if you were caught out in a pasture, standing under the shelter of an oak tree during a sudden summer shower, you would undoubtedly accept the logical completeness of these knowledge claims:

1. That shower came up in a hurry.
2. It's raining hard.
3. The shower won't last long.

Each of these statements is a knowledge claim about what is. Such statements are called propositions. A **proposition** is an assertion of a speaker's general position on some subject. Its logical completeness depends on the weight of evidence and analysis that renders an audience willing to accept the knowledge claim as true.

There are three kinds of propositions: (1) fact, (2) value, and (3) policy. Table 15.3 defines and separates these three types.

Every persuasive speech includes such propositions. They constitute the basic arguments that the speaker tries to get listeners to accept. To be logically complete, every proposition requires enough evidence to answer listeners' unspoken "How do you know?" and "Show me."

Table 15.3

THE THREE TYPES OF PROPOSITIONS

TYPE	FEATURES	EXAMPLES
Fact	Something *is*	That is an oak tree. Most forest fires are caused by human carelessness. Asphalt highways don't last as long as concrete highways. Lake Superior is the deepest of the Great Lakes.
Value	Judgment terms, such as *good, right,* and *beautiful*	Swimming is the most effective form of total body exercise. People were wrong in boycotting McDonald's for selling animal meat. AIDS is the most frightening disease of our time.
Policy	Something *should* or *ought*	We should lower tuition costs at this institution. The government should require all citizens to vote in national elections. Businesses ought to give a discount for cash purchases.

Placing a proposition into one of the three categories—fact, value, and policy—helps you to more clearly define and organize your ideas and also determines what persuasive appeals you should use to enhance message credibility. Thus, knowing the three types of propositions and their characteristics helps you to assure the logical completeness of your ideas. Let us look more closely at each of these three kinds of propositions.

Propositions of Fact

A **proposition of fact** is a statement that something is true. Your persuasive task is to introduce enough information to convince listeners that your claim is factually accurate. Table 15.4 presents examples of propositions of fact. Notice how the use of argument and evidence in these examples helps to prove the position taken. When the argument is complete enough, listeners will usually accept it.

For example, if you wanted to concentrate on the proposition in table 15.4 that asphalt roads do not last as long as concrete highways, you would compare the durability of concrete and asphalt as paving materials. You could support your case with examples of

Table 15.4

EXAMPLE PROPOSITIONS OF FACT

PROPOSITION OF FACT	ARGUMENT	EVIDENCE
Most forest fires are caused by human carelessness or arson.	Natural causes account for only 10 percent of forest fires.	Statistics and cases from the National Park Service and the Department of Agriculture
Asphalt highways don't last as long as concrete highways.	Asphalt has a half-life of only five years, compared to twelve for concrete.	Highway repair information from the U.S. Department of Transportation
Lake Superior is the deepest of the Great Lakes.	Water temperature is an accurate indicator of depth.	Report studies from the U.S. Geological Survey

highways paved with asphalt and highways paved with concrete. You would want to show that, under similar traffic and weather conditions, concrete pavement lasts longer than asphalt.

Propositions of Value

A **proposition of value** attempts to establish that something is good, bad, valuable, worthless, right, or wrong. Your job, as a speaker, is to introduce the information, the appeals, the criteria, and the evidence so that your audience arrives at the same conclusion you have.

Propositions of value may also have a component that you can discuss factually. For example, the proposition of value "People were wrong in boycotting McDonald's for selling animal meat" also has the following factual component: "Does eating red meat cause substantial physical harm to all people?" This component of the proposition is either true or false. However, whether boycotting McDonald's for selling animal meat was a "right" or "wrong" action is another aspect of the question. If you want to explore the *value* dimension, you examine whether or not the vegetarians who picketed selected McDonald's were wrong. Persuasion happens when you present evidence and arguments that establish your position in listeners' minds as the most accurate or correct one.

A proposition of value should agree with what listeners *already* believe or feel. Otherwise, your audience probably will reject your position. Success here requires both rational and emotional appeals. Be prepared with facts, but listeners will also judge you according to their personal feelings and values.

Propositions of Policy

A **proposition of policy** argues that some action should be taken. These propositions always involve both fact and value and, like the values discussed earlier in the chapter, typically contain the words *should* and *ought*.

Many situations require "should" and "ought" decisions: "Should I cut this class?" "Which outfit should I buy?" "Should I spend the rest of my money on a pizza or on a movie?" We spend much of our time thinking about possible courses of action, which is one reason why propositions of policy are so important in persuasion. Any time you use the words *ought* or *should,* you are asking audience members to make a decision. If you want to persuade them that your position is the correct one, you need to provide them with evidence, while also considering their beliefs and attitudes. This task requires an appeal to both reason and emotion.

MESSAGE STRATEGIES

Speaker credibility and message credibility should work together to evoke some kind of identification in listeners. Listeners process information using both sides of the brain.[5] The left side of the brain processes rational argument and evidence (what Aristotle called logos), while the right side of the brain deals more with feelings and emotions (pathos and ethos). When a persuasive message appeals and adapts to both sides of listeners' brains—to both the rational and emotional sides of audience members—persuasion is likely. But it will not happen unless you, as a speaker, choose wise message strategies.

The discussion that follows examines four kinds of message strategies for persuasion: (1) one-sided versus two-sided arguments, (2) explicit versus implicit conclusions, (3) appeals to evoked recall, and (4) organization in a motivated sequence.

One-Sided versus Two-Sided Arguments

Presenting only one side of an issue enables you to make a strong case for your position. One-sided arguments have a negative aspect, also, however, in that you leave listeners unprepared for arguments from the other side. When these arguments arise, the effects of your message may unravel.

For example, a candidate for the U.S. Senate used the "one term" and "citizen on leave" argument in the campaign. The candidate asserted that there were too many career politicians and that he would serve only for six years and then return to life as a private citizen. A year after election, the senator took a different position. It was important, he said, for senators to have seniority to advance the interests of the nation and their constituents. The senator then acknowledged ignoring the other side of the issue during the campaign: "I was wrong. There is an advantage to the state and the nation that arises from experienced legislative representation." Naturally, this upset the senator's supporters. They had never contemplated this argument in favor of reelection. Support for the senator waned in his home state, and the public criticized his position that citizens would benefit from the six years of experience in Congress. Many supporters of the senator became angry, and the senator seemed genuinely surprised that people would question his change of heart. The problem was that the senator had failed to sketch for voters the other side of the issue—the arguments in favor of longevity. Not surprisingly, at the next election, the senator had the fight of a lifetime.

Malcolm X, one of the most militant and visible leaders of the Black Power movement of the 1960s, recognized the persuasive impact of the two-sided argument. In this excerpt from his autobiography, Malcolm X describes that strategy and the exhilaration he felt in swaying an audience:

But I will tell you that, right there, in the prison, debating, speaking to a crowd, was as exhilarating to me as the discovery of knowledge through reading had been. Standing up there, the faces looking up at me, the things in my head coming out of my mouth, while my brain searched for the next best thing to follow what I was saying, and if I could sway them to my side by handling it right, then I had won the debate—once my feet got wet, I was gone on debating. Whichever side of the selected subject was assigned to me, I'd track down and study everything I could find on it. I'd put myself in my opponent's place and decide how I'd try to win if I had the other side; and then I'd figure a way to knock down those points.

Source: Malcolm X with Alex Haley, The Autobiography of Malcolm X *(New York: Ballantine Books, 1964), 184. Photo UPI/Bettmann*

Two-sided arguments increase the speaker's believability.[6] Most people realize that nearly every issue has more than one side, and they like speakers to be honest in presenting a case. In fact, speakers gain an advantage if they present not only the arguments in favor of their position but deal also with the opposing point of view. Even in cases where listeners are not aware of the other side, the two-sided approach is more desirable.[7] Essentially, you prepare audience members for later situations when they may face the other side head-on. Listeners feel more confident of their position if they hear the opposition arguments presented and countered.

Finally, depriving listeners of information that will help them to reach an informed decision is difficult to justify ethically. In addition, the preponderance of research shows that two-sided presentations persuade more listeners. The long-term results of two-sided presentations are also encouraging. When people encounter the other side at a later time, they understand the arguments.

Explicit versus Implicit Conclusions

Should a speaker tell listeners what to do in the speech conclusion? Most research indicates that drawing **explicit conclusions** for listeners—that is, telling them precisely what you want them to do or believe—is more effective than implying or hinting at the goal you have in mind.

Some people have argued that intelligent, well-educated, or well-informed listeners might resent a suggestion about their actions, but research does not support that argument. In fact, research clearly indicates that effective persuasive speakers specifically tell listeners what information or conclusion the listeners should get from the speech and also describe any actions that are necessary. This makes the actions easy to perform.[8]

Drawing an explicit conclusion for listeners also has considerable ethical merit. If you are "open" with your audience about the fundamental goals of your message, listeners do not have to wonder what they are being asked to believe. If you only implied or hinted at your conclusion, different audience members could reach varying conclusions, based on information they already have and their interpretation of your message. An explicitly drawn conclusion leaves no room for varying interpretations.

Evoked Recall Appeals

Motivation research has provided information about eight compelling needs that drive humans to believe or act.[9] Some have called these needs "hidden persuaders." In this text, they are called **evoked recall appeals** because they cause people to change their attitudes and beliefs and to act on their feelings.

Need for Emotional Security

As the world shrinks, events come closer to us each day via the news media. We read about and see wars, famine, disease, and civil discord. In our own lives, we constantly expose ourselves to actual and potential harm. Whether at school or work, with friends, family, or strangers, events happen that hurt our feelings or make us fearful. Life requires that we expose our feelings and emotions to a certain amount of insecurity, and thus it is natural to look for some kind of security that will protect us from emotional distress. This need for security may take the form of finding a close group of friends, wanting to buy a large home, or having financial protection.

To illustrate, a recent issue of *Kiplinger's Personal Finance Magazine* ran a full-page ad, showing a pensive, professionally attired woman. The caption read, "You've insured your house, your health, your car. Even your grandmother's antique pearl necklace. But what about your valuable nest egg?" Numerous advertisers appeal to people's emotional security:

"Beef—Real food for real people."

"AT&T—Technologies for the real world."

"Get Met—It pays."

"GMC Truck—The strength of experience."

As a speaker, you can use this need for emotional security to persuade. For example, you could use a vividly drawn word picture to help listeners to visualize what would result from adopting of your proposal. Illustrations and metaphors will also help you to create a positive, emotionally secure picture in listeners' minds.

A good deal of research has studied the effects of this need for emotional security. One especially interesting set of questions centered on the use of fear appeals. **Fear appeals** involve using evidence or argument designed to induce fear in listeners as a means of motivating them to some decision or action.

Research in the use of fear appeals is inconclusive but suggests at least two principles. First, messages that create a substantial level of fear or anxiety in listeners will have greater effects than messages that fail to arouse much fear.[10] However, you should not conclude that the more fear you can create, the greater your chances for success. It is

Table 15.5

EXAMPLES OF MODERATE FEAR APPEALS

TYPE OF PROOF	APPEAL	RATIONALE
Pathos: "It's hard to maintain self-dignity lying helpless in a hospital bed while AIDS steals your body."	"Practice 'safe sex.' Don't end up like me."	"AIDS can be transmitted only through bodily fluids or blood."
Ethos: "I'm Yul Brenner and I'm dying of cancer."	"I've had my larynx removed. I have to fight this cancer. So, I quit smoking. Don't wait as long as I did. Quit today."	"The Surgeon General of the United States says that smoking causes cancer."

Source: Adapted from Deidre D. Johnson, *The Art and Science of Persuasion,* (Dubuque, Iowa: Brown & Benchmark, 1994), 130.

difficult to manage the level of fear you may arouse in listeners.[11] Additionally, if you succeed in arousing a high level of fear, audience members may choose not to listen to your arguments simply because the material disturbs them. For example, in a stop-smoking campaign, smokers were shown photographs of the lungs of smokers versus those of nonsmokers (blackened, crusty tissue compared to pink, flexible flesh). This strategy was self-defeating because the photographs created such a level of disturbance that the smokers did not listen to subsequent information. A moderate level of fear may yield maximum attitude or belief change from your message. See table 15.5.

The second principle suggested by research with regard to the use of fear appeals is that the message should offer reasonable solutions to the level of fear. Campaigns against AIDS or cigarette smoking often ask listeners to engage in behaviors that, for them, are virtually impossible. Cigarette smokers crave nicotine, while sexually active young adults regard abstinence as incomprehensible. The solutions a speaker offers in these situations should be aimed at hitting a resonant chord. A reasonable solution moderates the fear. For example, a reasonable solution for smokers might be to use the "nicotine patch," while for persons potentially exposed to AIDS, it might be always using appropriate protection from sexually transmitted diseases.

As a persuasive speaker, you should ask yourself the following questions about using fear as an appeal:

- Does your use of fear appeals overstate or exaggerate the danger to listeners?
- Is your appeal based on the latest available evidence from reliable expert sources?
- Have you allowed your personal biases to cloud the accuracy and completeness of the appeal?
- Is there likely to be a negative consequence to listeners if you use these fear appeals?

The human need for emotional security, then, is a powerful message strategy. Use it wisely, and take care that you do not let its awesome power to persuade overcome your basic ethical responsibilities.

Need for Reassurance of Worth

As the population has become increasingly mobile, it also has become more competitive, hurried, and impersonal. In many cases, we have given up long-term associations with family and friends. The result often is that people begin to feel less secure and personally unimportant. Our technologically advanced society has produced a rapidly changing world where people can feel isolated, powerless, and not valued. They need continual reassurance of worth.

Corporations have been quick to appeal to the need for reassurance of worth, as evidenced by these contemporary advertisements:

"When you're traveling abroad, it's nice to hear a familiar voice. AT&T."

"When you know your worth—Omega, the sign of excellence."

"With one of America's largest managed care networks, we understand the importance of taking care of one another. But, more importantly, we offer a program that recognizes one truth for employer and employee alike—the greatest wealth of all has little to do with money. The Travelers."

As a public speaker, you can also reassure your listeners of their worth. For example, a student used this appeal effectively in a speech asking for financial gifts to the United Way campaign. "You know that your help is needed," the speaker said. "And you know that you'll have done the right thing. Can you think of a more worthy thing to do?"

Need for Ego Gratification

Everyone needs attention that goes beyond the recognition of worth. We like to think, "I'm not only worthy, I'm very special." We want reassurance from those who matter to us. Advertisers know how to appeal to this need for ego gratification:

"New Cadillac Deville. New Owner Privileges. New Cadillac Smart Lease. $499 a month."

"Washington's second best address. Stouffer Mayflower Hotel."

"Not many people need a personal computer with 16 megabytes of RAM and a 250-megabyte hard drive. But, it's a special feeling knowing that the power is there just in case."

People buy, rent, or lease these things because it makes them feel special. It reinforces their egos.

Public speakers also can make use of the human need for ego gratification, and one did so directly in a speech to an audience of two hundred bankers: "If you are special, please stand up," directed the speaker. Most, but not all, of the listeners stood. "Everyone is special," said the speaker. After waiting a moment, the speaker then said, "If someone near you is not standing, please encourage them to stand up. Tell them that they are special." The speaker waited as the crowd warmed to the activity. Then the speaker said,

"Ladies and gentlemen, there are some other special people in this city, and they need your help." Then the speaker asked for support for local youngsters who were hoping to attend the Special Olympics.

As a persuasive speaker, you should analyze listeners carefully to consider how you can make them feel special, a cut above the crowd. Then you can integrate appeals reflecting that need into the structure of your message.

Need for Creative Outlets

Humans have always shown a desire to build and create things. From cave paintings to the graffiti on city walls, people have sought ways to express their individuality and self-worth through creative expression. People satisfy that need today in a wide variety of ways—by writing poetry, cooking with a secret recipe, designing their own clothing, collecting political memorabilia, creating a new offensive set for a football team, or building their own salad at a restaurant, to name just a few.

One of the most successful commercial approaches to this need for creative outlets is that taken by the company Jim Walter Homes. The company prepares a building site and constructs a "shell" home. Buyers then can choose a variety of room arrangements and exterior features. They can enlarge a room, add a garage, or eliminate a wall. The company also offers purchasers the option to have the home "roughed in" (80 percent completed with unfinished walls and partial wiring and plumbing) or 90 percent completed (needing only finish painting and carpet installed). The needs and creative eyes of buyers help them to decide about the design and the degree of completion they can afford and want. The homes are less expensive than many, and they also reflect the creative characteristics of their owners. They are not all "look-alikes."

We all have the inner desire to help create something special. In persuasive speaking, your task is to help listeners to *visualize* the creation you are suggesting (whether it be a better school, a cleaner city, or improved legislation) and to see themselves playing a significant role in its completion.

Need for Love Objects

Everyone needs outlets for their loving feelings. For example, in homes where children have grown and gone, parents often acquire pets to help them deal with the empty-nest syndrome. Inanimate objects also sometimes function as a substitute. For example, some people love their cars, lavishing attention and care on them as they might on a child. Still others talk to their plants or their gardens.

This need for love objects is not limited to parents whose children have left home. People of all ages and from every walk of life need outlets for their affections. Advertisers know this, too, and they appeal to this need constantly.

That is why Lee blue-jeans advertised its line of Lee Riders for Kids in *Redbook* magazine in a two-page spread showing only four cute youngsters and the caption: "Jeans Tough Enough for the Wrecking Crew." The need for love objects explains why Michelin Tire Company shows a baby sitting in one of its tires when it advertises that "There's a lot riding on my tires." It is why Ralston Purina Company advertises its animal food by showing a photograph of a dog licking an obviously happy older man. The caption reads,

"Help lick loneliness with every Purina purchase." And what is Oscar Mayer really selling when it shows a daddy playing with the eighteen-month-old cherub on his shoulders and the caption "Food that's great for people of all ages"?

You can use the need for love objects as a persuasive tool in public speaking. One of the best ways is to develop a vivid story that helps audience members to imagine a real person with a genuine need for their caring.

Need for a Sense of Power

U.S. society teaches children from the moment of birth to need power. This may be more true of U.S. society than of any other on earth. Our attraction to power and symbols of power has not been lost on advertisers, as the following examples demonstrate:

- Ford advertises its Bronco by showing it climbing steep hills and over boulders and rocks.
- Nike and Reebok feature athletes wearing Nike and Reebok shoes slam-dunking basketball shots.
- Nordic Flex stresses its role in "The Evolution of Strength Training."

Power can also be expressed in nonphysical ways. Psychological and moral power are ingredients of a sensitive and well-rounded person. The power to refuse drugs, the power to refuse a dare to shoplift, or the power to stand up for what you believe is right are contemporary examples of moral and psychological power.

Public speakers often use this need for power to persuade. A student made the following statements in a speech about the importance of becoming a Rape Crisis volunteer:

You have it in your power to make a difference. You can make all the difference between a victim who recovers and a victim who doesn't. You have it in your power to help families who really need you. They often don't understand, so they blame the rape victim. You have it in your power to lend a helping hand to husbands and boyfriends over a crisis for them as well as for the victims they love.

As this excerpt illustrates, power can be integrated with other needs, resulting in a strong combination of power needs and love needs.

Need for Roots

As mentioned earlier, U.S. society has become increasingly mobile. Americans move, on average, twelve times in the first ten years after graduating from college. Most of these moves are from one neighborhood to another, but some are from city to city in the same state. At least one of the moves, on average, is cross-country. It is not unusual today for parents and siblings to live in at least three or four states in different sections of the country. People who continue to live in the location where they grew up are the exception today, rather than the rule. As a society, we have developed a need for roots that will increase as society continues to displace workers and families.

The need for roots explains the following kinds of appeals:

- "Remember Grandpa's tomatoes? Think back. You may have been just a child. . . ."
- "Getaway to yesterday. Visit the Inn in the Berkshires with. . . ."
- "Family-style meals. All you can eat."
- "Escape from the bustle of the city. Come home to Fairfield Acres, the classic community just 15 minutes from. . . ."

Public speakers frequently appeal to the need for roots. One student speaker used this appeal when talking about the importance of giving aging parents a home and a hand:

> *Do you remember how nice it was when you came in from playing in the cold? Mother stood, in the kitchen, surrounded by the unforgettable smell of that fried chicken dinner. Remember the sizzle as the snow melted from your mittens and dropped onto the hot stove in the corner? And, can you remember the times when she came to you in the night to comfort you when you'd had a bad dream? How many times did she kiss a hurt well?*

At this point, the student mentioned that 35 percent of Americans over age sixty-five live alone or are in nursing homes. The speaker's argument was that most of these elderly should be living with their families, that it was time for the children to take care of the parents, just as the parents had taken care of the children.

Need for Immortality

One of the most difficult topics for most of us to discuss is our own mortality. Both individually and as a society, death may be our most deep-seated taboo. We do not like to think or talk much about it. When we do speak of death, we often use euphemisms, such as *gone to their reward, passed on, expired,* or *met their Maker.*

We all feel a need for immortality. This need may have become even more profound today because people increasingly are being replaced by machines or computers. People feel like they have lost control of their lives.

The advertising community takes advantage of our need for immortality. We are urged to buy "a piece of the rock" instead of just life insurance, and we are told that "the difference between a shattered windshield and a shattered life" is a new layer in a windshield by DuPont. Our need for immortality may explain our fascination with fitness centers, facial creams, hair dyes, and cosmetic surgery. It is even one of the reasons people choose to have children.

Most of us want to satisfy our need for immortality by passing something on to future generations. It may be in the form of children, a philanthropic contribution, writing a great novel, or becoming involved in politics, service, charity work, or fund-raising. As a persuasive speaker, you can appeal to this need for immortality. Encourage listeners to become part of a movement or to take action individually through an appeal to listeners' need to leave a legacy for future generations.

Table 15.6

THE MOTIVATED SEQUENCE REVISITED

STEP IN THE MOTIVATED SEQUENCE	PURPOSE	DESIRED AUDIENCE RESPONSE
1. Attention step	Get attention	"This is interesting. I will listen to this."
2. Need step	Show the need; show the problem	"Something needs to be (felt) (decided) (changed)."
3. Satisfaction step	Satisfy the need; show a solution to the problem	"Yes, this is what we ought to (feel) (decide) (change)."
4. Visualization step	Visualize the results of accepting the solution	"I can see myself in the future, enjoying the benefits of (feeling) (deciding) (changing) this."
5. Action step	Ask for action or approval	"I will (feel) (decide) (change) this."

Organizing in a Motivated Sequence

In chapter 8, "Organizing the Body of the Speech," you read about the **motivated sequence,** a pattern for organizing persuasive speeches. The motivated sequence reflects a predictable pattern of thinking when many people analyze a new idea. Table 15.6 reviews and describes the five steps and provides a brief example of the desired audience response at each step. Refer to chapter 8 for a more detailed discussion of the motivated sequence.

Summary

All persuasion, including persuasive speaking, seeks to change people's behavior through the use of symbols. Persuasive speakers are ethically responsible and accountable to listeners to communicate honestly, without misleading, oversimplifying, coercing, or presenting unsupportable arguments and emotional appeals.

So common are attempts at persuasion that thinkers have tried to understand how the process works for as long as recorded history. Aristotle discussed three artistic proofs: ethos, logos, and pathos. Hugh Rank developed an intensification/downplay model of persuasion that states that people use two persuasive tactics: They either (1) play up their own strong points and their competitors' weak points, or (2) they play down their weak points and their competitors' strong points. The evoked recall model of persuasion makes it clear that persuasion is not something people do to others: It is something we do to ourselves. The persuader presents images in an effort to cause us to identify and respond. Milton Rokeach described a hierarchy of beliefs and values, and showed how they influence the kinds of choices people make.

Persuasive speeches that succeed in achieving their goals are characterized by three elements: (1) The speaker must have a high level of credibility with listeners, (2) the message must be credible, and (3) the speaker's chosen message strategies should appeal to both the rational and emotional needs of listeners.

Speaker credibility depends upon the extent to which the speaker's choices demonstrate trustworthiness and knowledge of the subject, reflect a concern for personal appearance, and establish a bond or identification with listeners. A message will seem credible if it is logically complete. That is, propositions must seem warranted by the speaker's evidence and arguments. Propositions of fact state that something *is,* propositions of value use judgment terms, and propositions of policy argue that some action *should* or *ought* to be taken.

For speaker credibility and message credibility to work together to evoke some kind of listener identification, the speaker must select message strategies that have both rational and emotional appeal to listeners. Persuasive message strategies include presenting two-sided arguments; drawing explicit conclusions; using evoked recall appeals that center on humans' needs for emotional security, reassurance of worth, ego gratification, creative outlets, love objects, a sense of power, roots, and immortality; and organizing the message in a motivated sequence.

Key Terms

Artistic proofs
Belief
Derived beliefs
Ethos
Evoked recall appeals
Evoked recall model of
  persuasion
Explicit conclusions
Fear appeals

Identification
Intensification/downplay
  model of persuasion
Logical completeness
Logos
Matters of taste
Motivated sequence
Pathos
Persuasion

Primitive beliefs
Proposition
Proposition of fact
Proposition of policy
Proposition of value
Shared beliefs
Value

Application Questions

1. When you listen to a public speech, how do you determine the credibility of the speaker? How important is speaker credibility in most of the speeches you have heard?
2. Which message strategies do most prominent speakers use? What is your usual reaction to fear appeals and one-sided persuasion? Why?
3. How important a role do you feel ethics plays in the communication strategy of most public speakers? Is it more important for prominent speakers to observe ethical procedures than for the average person? Why?
4. Have most of the persuasive speeches you have heard included propositions of fact, value, or policy? Which type of proposition seems to be appropriate for most of your discussions? Why?

Self-Test for Review

Mark each of the following as either true (T) or false (F).

1. Aristotle's artistic proofs are ethos, pathos, and probos.   T   F
2. "Income taxes are too high for the average American" is a proposition of policy. T   F
3. Persuasion is the activity of attempting to change the behavior of at least one person through manipulation.   T   F
4. Explicit conclusion drawing is an effective strategy because it avoids confusion in the minds of listeners.   T   F
5. Fear appeals always increase the effectiveness of a persuasive speaker.   T   F
6. In the intensification/downplay model of persuasion, people emphasize their own strong points and their competitors' weak points.   T   F
7. The term *logos* refers to the use of emotional appeals in an argument.   T   F
8. If your audience is aware of contrary arguments, it is best to use two-sided persuasion.   T   F
9. According to Rokeach, primitive beliefs are harder to change than derived beliefs   T   F
10. The persuasive speaker develops credibility primarily through the message.   T   F

Answers: 1. F, 2. F, 3. F, 4. T, 5. F, 6. T, 7. F, 8. T, 9. T, 10. F.

Suggested Readings

Engel, S. Morris. *With Good Reason: An Introduction to Informal Fallacies.* 3rd ed. New York: St. Martin's Press, 1986. This lively book in the field of reasoning is filled with contemporary illustrations, making it ideal for anyone interested in reasoning and, especially, fallacies in contemporary argument. The book is extremely interesting and informative.

Johnston, Deidre D. *The Art and Science of Persuasion.* Dubuque, Iowa: Brown & Benchmark, 1994. This recent offering views persuasion from the process perspective, with allied emphasis on the components of persuasion and its societal impact. It is an excellent contemporary source for research and application of theory and ethics in the persuasion process.

Larson, Charles U. *Persuasion: Reception and Responsibility.* 7th ed. Belmont, Calif.: Wadsworth, 1995. This latest edition of the roots and techniques of persuasion is especially strong in its analysis of the persuasive campaign and movements. For student speakers who are looking for a strong, contemporary understanding of applied persuasion theory, this book should be required reading.

O'Keefe, Daniel J. *Persuasion: Theory and Research.* Newbury Park, Calif.: Sage, 1990. This offering is a highly effective collection of the research findings and implications of contemporary investigations into persuasion. One of its interesting strengths is its thorough and heavily documented discussion of the factors that influence persuasive effects.

Reardon, Kathleen Kelley. *Persuasion in Practice.* Newbury Park, Calif.: Sage, 1991. This work is especially valuable for researchers pursuing persuasion theory and practice. It is aimed, to a substantial degree, at the application of persuasion to the contemporary business and industrial environment and is a fine source of summary research findings in interpersonal, mass media, organizational, and political settings.

CHAPTER 16

Speeches for Special Occasions

OBJECTIVES

After reading this chapter, you should be able to:

1. *Explain* how special occasion speeches differ from other types of speeches.
2. *Name* and *separate* into three subgroups nine different kinds of special occasion speeches.
3. *Explain* the purpose of each of the nine special occasion speeches discussed in the chapter.
4. *Cite* criteria for evaluating the nine special occasion speeches presented in the chapter.
5. *Explain* how to secure information for an introductory speech.
6. *Define* and *explain* five techniques of humor: satire, irony, exaggeration, parody, and reversal of values.

© Bob Daemmrich/Stock Boston

*T*he special occasions of life often call for speech making designed to praise or pay tribute, to inspire, or just to have fun. This chapter describes how to develop nine different kinds of special occasion speeches: (1) introductory speeches, (2) presentation speeches, (3) acceptance speeches, (4) eulogies, (5) commencement speeches, (6) keynote speeches, (7) welcoming speeches, (8) after-dinner speeches, and (9) roasts. These speeches can be grouped into three categories: speeches of praise and tribute, inspirational speeches, and speeches given for the sake of humor.

Most of your public speaking will be informative or persuasive, but on occasion, you may find yourself preparing to speak in a ceremonial setting. For example, you might be asked to introduce Tim Arthur, whom you have known since high school, or you might be asked to present an award to Betty Simpson, who has worked with you for the last four years. In both cases, the ideas suggested in previous chapters for informative and persuasive speaking may seem somewhat inappropriate. Special occasion speeches call for a different approach.

The number of different kinds of ceremonial occasions defies description, and this chapter cannot tell you how to prepare a speech for each of them. However, much of the chapter information also applies to speeches for numerous other special occasions. What you need to remember for all special occasion speeches is that the purpose of the special occasion always determines what you must do as the speaker. Adhere consistently to that purpose. Find out what function your speech has to contribute. Since you cannot say everything about anything, focus on the audience and occasion. That focus marks all of the better special occasion speeches. The quality of special occasion speeches also depends on brevity, appropriateness, timing, and pacing.

Finally, most people enjoy giving special occasion speeches because such occasions are usually rich in human warmth and caring. The best special occasion speeches reflect the speaker's warmth and caring as well.

SPEECHES OF PRAISE AND TRIBUTE

Praise is an expression of your approval or admiration, while *tributes* are acknowledgments of your gratitude, esteem, or regard. Let these definitions guide your thinking when presenting any of the following speeches of praise and tribute: (1) introductory speeches, (2) presentation speeches, (3) acceptance speeches, and (4) eulogies.

INTRODUCTORY SPEECHES

One day, someone probably will ask you to introduce another speaker—to present an **introductory speech**—to an audience. The speaker might be an old friend, a political figure, or a company or community dignitary. The frequency of such requests is why introductory speeches are discussed first in this chapter.

Occasions for speeches of tribute are frequent.

© *Art Gurmankin/Unicorn Stock Photos*

Introductory speeches have two purposes. First, you want to focus listener attention on the person you are introducing. Second, you want to set up or prepare listeners for the speech that will follow. For example, you might wish to help establish speakers' credibility by talking about their qualifications. Or you might want to change the mood or to "pump up" a group that has been together through a long session already.

Limit yourself to a few minutes when introducing a speaker. Your function as introducer is important, but secondary. Arouse anticipation, focus attention on the speaker, then get out of the way.

Table 16.1 lists questions you may want to ask yourself as you prepare to introduce a speaker. The biographical and audience-centered information implied by these questions will provide you with the raw materials for your speech.

If you do not personally know the speaker, arrange for an in-person or over-the-phone interview to get vital information. Get as complete a picture of the total person as you can. If an interview is not possible, then ask the speaker's friends or relatives for information. Again, the questions in table 16.1 are helpful for these interviews.

Try to find out if the speaking situation contains any special conditions or expectations that might influence the speech. For example, in an introductory speech, audiences usually expect the introducer to not mention the name of the person being introduced

Table 16.1

INTERVIEWING CHECKLIST FOR INTRODUCTORY SPEECH

1. What are the speaker's qualifications?
2. What credentials does the speaker have in the field of his speech?
3. What do the speaker and the audience have in common?
4. How well do you know this person?
5. How long and in what way have you been acquainted?
6. What do you think is this person's most outstanding characteristic?
7. Why do you think this person has been so successful?
8. How is this person different from the average person?
9. What four words do you think best describe this person?
10. How do this person's contemporaries regard her?
11. Do you know any anecdotes that show the person's ability or character?

Table 16.2

CRITERIA FOR AN INTRODUCTORY SPEECH

An introductory speech should:

1. Be brief.
2. Discuss the speaker's general qualifications.
3. Explain the speaker's credentials in the topic field.
4. Give audience members reasons to listen.
5. Demonstrate a thorough knowledge of the speaker.

until the last moment. This technique creates suspense and allows the person making the introduction to emphasize the name of the speaker as the last information given. If that is what your audience expects, you should conform.

The great orator from Illinois, Senator Everett Dirksen, ignored this rule at the 1964 Republican convention. His job was to introduce presidential candidate Barry Goldwater. Early in the speech, he mentioned Goldwater's name. This error resulted in a demonstration by delegates that lasted more than ten minutes. Meanwhile, Senator Dirksen could only stand and wait for the tumult to subside. Although he resumed his speech after the demonstration, Dirksen never again captured listeners' attention. His early mention of Goldwater violated the basic expectation of his audience that the candidate's name would be mentioned only at the close of the speech. Table 16.2 shows general criteria for an introductory speech.

Example 16.1 presents a sample introductory speech that was given at a Rotary Club meeting. Notice how the introduction is brief, outlines the speaker's qualifications and credentials, and stresses the similarity of aspiration and accomplishment between the speaker and Rotary Club members. Thus, the speech meets all the criteria for successful introductory speaking mentioned in table 16.2.

It's an honor for me to introduce the mayor of Centertown to you. At a time when everyone else seems to be calling for reductions in every kind of federal program, this man's enormous knowledge of the problems of rural people in our state has made him an outspoken advocate for increased government aid to the farmer. In fact, last year he led a delegation to Washington. He personally presented the petition many of you signed for more liberal farm loan conditions to the secretary of agriculture.

As a farmer himself, the mayor understands the needs of rural people. If ever there was a dynamic representative of farmers and their concerns, he's it. Join me in welcoming a successful farmer and a hard and dedicated worker whose primary concern is the future of the American way of life. It's my pleasure to introduce a man some have called "Mr. Rural America." He's here tonight to talk to us about promises of the future for agriculture in America and what that means to us here in Jefferson County.

Please give a warm welcome to Ben Edelblute.

Table 16.3

CHRONOLOGICAL STEPS IN MAKING A
PRESENTATION SPEECH

---

1. Name the reason for giving the gift or award.
2. Name and describe the criteria used in making the decision to present the gift or award.
3. Show how the person receiving the gift or award met the criteria.
4. If the award was made competitively, praise the other participants who were not selected.
5. Call the person forward to receive the award or gift.
6. If the award or gift carries an inscription, read it aloud to the audience.

PRESENTATION SPEECHES

A **presentation speech** is the talk given almost every time a person receives an award or a gift in public. Table 16.3 lists the chronological steps that nearly all presentation speeches follow.

Every year, the Student Government Association (SGA) at most colleges and universities holds an awards banquet. An SGA president gave the presentation speech in example 16.2 at one such banquet. Notice how the speech generally follows the steps suggested in table 16.3.

EXAMPLE 16.2	SAMPLE PRESENTATION SPEECH

Ladies and gentlemen, every year the members of the Student Government Association honor the senior student who has done the most to foster good government and to advance the school.

So many people have done so much to advance student government, and to make this university a great one, that this year we had a lot of trouble deciding upon the recipient. We looked at the service records of the nominees. We considered the overall grade point averages of the nominees. We collected letters of recommendation and support from faculty and staff, and from students within and outside the Student Government Association. Then we talked and talked before we finally made our selection.

This year's recipient has been a member of the Student Senate for four years. She has served as president of SGA. She was vice president of SGA. She served as president of Jaguar Productions—the group that screens and coordinates all on-campus concert and theatrical productions brought in from outside.

She has been president of Delta Zeta sorority, as well as rush chairperson. She was a member of the Pan Hellenic Council for three years. She serves as a rape-crisis volunteer, giving one twenty-four-hour period each month to be on call to rush to the Medical Center when she is needed.

And this year's recipient is a fine student. She carries an overall grade point average of 3.85. She has been on the Dean's List or the President's List every quarter that she has been a student at South.

I'd like to add that she has accomplished all of these things while working twenty hours each week to help pay her way through college.

Martha Williamson, will you please come forward to let us recognize you?

[Pause until the honored person is standing next to the presenter.]

Ladies and gentlemen, this award includes a plaque and a $350 honorarium. Her name will be inscribed on a permanent tablet that hangs in the University Center. I'd like to read the inscription on the plaque.

The Student Government Association Outstanding Service Award for 1993 is given to Martha Williamson in recognition of her unstinting service to the university and the community.

Congratulations, Martha.

A speaker has just presented an award—a common public speaking situation.

© Bob Daemmrich/Stock Boston

Table 16.4

CHRONOLOGICAL STEPS IN GIVING AN ACCEPTANCE SPEECH

1. Thank the people who gave you the gift or award.
2. Thank the people who helped you to achieve the goals that resulted in the award or gift.
3. If appropriate, express your intention to live up to the honor.

EXAMPLE 16.3   SAMPLE ACCEPTANCE SPEECH

How can I possibly tell you how grateful I feel right now? I am honored to receive this award. And I am completely surprised. What I did I did out of love. I love this university. I have loved every minute of my four years here. And I am so very grateful to the Student Government Association for giving me the opportunities to learn about government, and to grow as a person. So I thank you all for this award. It really belongs to all of you.

But I would like to name some of the people here who have been especially helpful to me. Abby Ratcliff, you should share in this award. You have been there when I've needed you these past four years. Ladies and gentlemen, I met Abby during freshman orientation four years ago, and we've been friends ever since.

How could I have done anything without Michael Kim Wong? I think he lives in the SGA office. I'd like to tell you that Mike knows more about how this university works than anyone I know. Thank you, Mike, for your advice.

And thank you all, again, for this high honor.

ACCEPTANCE SPEECHES

A presentation usually calls for the recipient to make an **acceptance speech** to thank the presenter and the organization that gave the gift or award. Table 16.4 lists the chronological steps in giving an acceptance speech.

The acceptance speech should be short and simple and should allow the recipient's warmth and gratitude to show. Example 16.3 shows how Martha Williamson accepted the Student Government Association Outstanding Service Award mentioned in example 16.2.

EULOGIES

The word **eulogy** means to praise or speak well of a person. Eulogies most commonly occur at a ceremony following a death—but not always. Sometimes, we eulogize the living. To illustrate, the adult children of one family threw a surprise eighty-fifth birthday party for their father. One of his sons gave the eulogy in example 16.4.

Eulogies are always informative speeches. Listeners expect and want you to teach them something about the person being honored. But more than inform, eulogies seek to inspire others through careful use of language. As you plan a speech of this kind, try to move beyond mere history. Portray a sense of the core values listeners share with your subject. Paint an image with words. You want to arouse or heighten listeners' appreciation and admiration for your subject. Table 16.5 shows the chronological steps to follow when giving a eulogy.

Do not give a eulogy for a person you do not know, or if you are not familiar with the person's accomplishments or character. Without that information, your speech will sound like an awkward series of empty generalizations.

Table 16.5

CHRONOLOGICAL STEPS IN GIVING A EULOGY

1. Identify your knowledge of the person.
2. Recognize the person's humanity.
3. Describe ways the person's life touched others, and give specific examples.
4. Restate the person's most basic characteristic.

EXAMPLE **16.4** SAMPLE EULOGY
(Reprinted with permission of Joseph C. Feldman.)

Ladies and gentlemen, this happy occasion honors my father, Solomon Feldman. I have loved him, admired him, respected him, and feared him for slightly more than fifty years.

My father is something of an institution around here. He owned the first automobile dealership in this city. He was elected mayor when he was thirty-five, and again when he was approaching sixty. He has served on nearly every civic board it is possible for a person to serve on in our town. He was president of the Kiwanis Club three times. He was once Chairman of the Board of Education. And he was once even incarcerated in our local jail. His offense was that he didn't grow a beard during the Daniel Boone Days Celebration.

I could list everything I know about my father's accomplishments, and then you, his dear friends, could undoubtedly add to them. So I would like to pay tribute to the Sol Feldman who's not a local legend—Sol Feldman, ordinary man, Sol Feldman, extraordinary father.

I remember taking my father for granted. He was always there for us—steadfast and supportive. Now, looking back from my adult perspective, I am amazed when I recall how much time my father found to give his children. I will never forget my father's careful guidance in basic things that children must know. He taught us moral values by his example, by his engaging conversations. And, occasionally, he taught moral values by placing his hand firmly on one of our backsides. He taught us the value of work. He taught us the value of worship. He taught us the value of play, too. But he did all this teaching, it seems to me now, in a very low key, and with enormous patience. Mostly, he taught by example.

One day, I recall, the phone rang. It was Dr. Virtle's office. Could Daddy come right away to the hospital? And since we were alone in the house—I don't remember where Mama was—he said "Come on. Now. There's been an accident. Someone needs blood." I asked him who it was, and he said "I don't know, son. But God gave us each a special kind of blood. When they need our kind, we're the only place they can get it." That's the way my father has lived his life for eighty-five years—untiring, unstinting, selfless.

So, ladies and gentlemen, my father taught us what it means to love. It seems to me that one word, *love*, characterizes him more than any other. My father has always been, and still is, a great lover. He loves his family. He loves his community. He loves this place.

I know that you have all gathered here to honor Solomon Feldman on his eighty-fifth birthday, and I know you will all have a way to tell him that tonight. I'd like to speak for my family.

Daddy, we don't tell you enough that we love you back.

Table 16.6

Table 16.6

CRITERIA FOR A COMMENCEMENT SPEECH

1. Comment on the nature of the occasion.
2. Acknowledge the contributions and sacrifices of the graduates and the audience.
3. Provide challenge, or define the role of graduates, and suggest methods for success.
4. Avoid clichés.
5. Express sincere, simple feelings.
6. Be brief.

Listeners expect a tribute to focus on a person's human side. Point to your subject's significant, human characteristics. Discuss what made the person unusual or outstanding. And do not worry that the person may not have been a world leader or that you may not be a great orator. Plain, simple people and their basic goodness form the basis of our society. Plain, simple people usually give the best eulogies, too.

INSPIRATIONAL SPEECHES

Inspirational speeches are meant to arouse, to animate, to quicken. Commencement speeches, keynote addresses, and welcoming speeches all fall into this category.

COMMENCEMENT SPEECHES

A **commencement speech** is an address given during graduation ceremonies. Perhaps the most common failing of commencement presentations is that they are long-winded. Audience members want to hear brief, glowing statements about their children, relatives, or friends. Their primary concern is with the ritual: They want to see the presentation of diplomas. Whatever precedes that presentation of diplomas should be brief, complimentary, and perhaps slightly challenging. Table 16.6 lists the main criteria for a commencement speech.

University President Tim Laird delivered the commencement speech shown in part in example 16.5. Applying the criteria in table 16.6 to this speech shows that Dr. Laird systematically met each standard. He acknowledged personal sacrifices and paid tribute to parents and students. He recognized the movement of the students into the work force. He suggested guidelines for career success. Best of all, he spoke for only ten minutes. Remember that, on ceremonial occasions like this, audiences want brevity, simplicity, and clarity.

EXAMPLE **16.5**   SAMPLE COMMENCEMENT SPEECH

I want to be the first to applaud these graduates for their efforts and the sacrifices they made to be here today. I know the hours they've spent cracking the books when the sounds of spring called them outside to toss a Frisbee or join their friends at the movies. I know how tempting it is to put off the reading or writing assignment that is due until that last minute because the personal calendar is full of events that are much more attractive—events like a stop at Taco Bell or a cruise down fraternity or sorority row.

I want to recognize the efforts so many of you have made in your personal quest for the degree. I applaud you, the part-time student. It's not easy to hold down a full-time job and succeed in classes. I applaud you veterans who have returned from military service to "be the best that you can be." I applaud you full-time students whose major efforts are directed toward the beginning of a new career. For some of you, your education has been an enormous drain on your energies and meager financial resources. For many others of you, though, it was your folks who placed your needs for education ahead of their own desires. They had to dig deeply to pay the tuition bills, and skip the dinners out they thought they would be able to afford once you had gotten beyond high school. They suffered along with you about your goals for your life and your job opportunities after graduation. They have wanted for you the chances they never had. They're the model parents. Yes, they may have a fault or two, but they want for you a life just a bit better than they have had. And isn't that what you will want for your children? So this is an occasion for recognizing both the accomplishments of the graduates as well as the sacrifices of the parents.

Today, I want to challenge each of you graduates to be a success. And becoming a success is not easy. But I think I may be able to give you three suggestions about how you can be a success, regardless of what kind of job you choose to take.

Keep up-to-date in your field. The level of your job doesn't matter. You could be a customer service representative or a store manager. In any case, you must stay aware of developments in your field. You must know your job and the information needed to do your work effectively. Because your formal education may have ended does not mean you should stop being intellectually curious. Look, question, and read. New ideas are the best source for improving yourself and your work. You must know what others are doing or suggesting should be done.

Give it your best. There's no substitute for applying your efforts to your job. No one wants to hire or keep a lazy employee. All jobs become boring in one way or another, but you'll need to work your way through those times with the same energy and effort you show in the interesting and exciting moments. [Dr. Laird briefly discussed work and working. He then outlined how hard work and knowledge of the job are the keys to success.]

Finally, you need to believe in yourself and your talent. I call it self-confidence. You must believe you can perform. You must approach each task with a positive mental attitude. Your actions, attitudes, and accomplishments are significant if you trust yourself. You can succeed at your chores if you believe in yourself.

The road to success is difficult at best. Many people have made sacrifices to provide you graduates with the opportunity to succeed. But your degrees today are no guarantees of success. Society expects much from you. You are the intelligentsia of the modern generation. You are the experts in your field.

Your employers expect you to know your subject, remain abreast of new developments, and work hard with all the information available. They'll provide you with the place to work, the opportunities for success, but you must make your own contribution. And don't forget that you must believe in yourself, whether things are going your way or against you. Persevere.

I challenge you to be all that you and those who know you realize is possible. Can you meet that challenge? [Dr. Laird concluded with a restatement of his earlier formula for success.]

Even veteran speakers, such as Jim Lehrer the co-anchor of the Public Broadcasting Station's "The MacNeil-Lehrer News-Hour," occasionally feel apprehensive about presenting a speech. With absolute fear and petrification, he accepted Vassar College's invitation to speak at his child Jamie's commencement. Lehrer recalls the anxiety he felt:

The last thing I wanted to do was write and deliver a speech of any kind, much less one as important and perilous as a commencement address to a class to which one of my very own belonged. There is simply no way for any child of any commencement speaker to do anything but sit in frozen fear while a parent makes a commencement speech. What if nobody laughs at the jokes? What if everybody does laugh—but at the wrong places? From the parent/speaker's point of view, the potential for grief and destruction is enormous. Nothing could be worse than being a cause of embarrassment to your child on graduation day—one of the most important days of your child's life.

Lehrer at one point even considered using his recent heart attack to duck out of the commitment. He continues:

I made the speech. And I am glad I did it. It was a gorgeous day in Poughkeepsie that May 20. The students and their parents and other family and friends received what I had to say about as well as could be expected for any commencement address. I have always believed that the most irrelevant speaker at any graduation is, in fact, the speaker.

Source: Jim Lehrer, A Bus of My Own *(New York: Plume, 1992), 195–96. Photo courtesy of MacNeil-Lehrer Productions.*

KEYNOTE SPEECHES

A **keynote speech** is given at the beginning of nearly every social or business function. An official, a celebrity, or perhaps a local dignitary addresses the audience to set the tone or mood for the meeting and the people attending. The speech can be inspirational, challenging, or problem oriented, as long as it sets the tone and gets things moving.

Most keynote speeches have the same objective: to generate enthusiasm and audience arousal. Like speeches of introduction, they should be brief and clearly stated. Unlike an introductory speech, however, a keynote speech is a major focus of the meeting. The keynote speaker does not play second fiddle to the rest of the program or to the next speaker. Indeed, the keynote speech may receive more attention than any other part of the meeting.

Table 16.7

CRITERIA FOR A KEYNOTE SPEECH

1. Determine the purpose or theme of the meeting.
2. Use the theme as the central part of your speech.
3. Show the importance and relevance of the theme to listeners.
4. Gear the speech to the common concerns of the audience.
5. Show your personal concern for the central theme of the meeting.

Studies of conferences, conventions, business meetings, and the like show that getting off to a good start is essential. The keynote speech can establish the mood for the entire session. Thus, as a keynote speaker, you should state the theme or goals, and try to generate excitement and enthusiasm. Table 16.7 suggests criteria for a keynote speech.

Example 16.6 shows a portion of a keynote speech given at the annual sales meeting of a paper company. A study of this speech shows that the speaker integrated several of the table 16.7 criteria into his message.

WELCOMING SPEECHES

Welcoming speeches occur most commonly when groups visit organizations and local businesses. Someone welcomes them to the company and may also conduct a tour of the facility. Similarly, groups of high school students and their parents often visit college campuses for "get acquainted days" that typically involve a number of welcoming speeches.

Welcoming speeches acknowledge the visitors and extend the hospitality of the organization. Thus, such speeches are usually brief and pointed. Table 16.8 suggests the chronological steps to follow in making a welcoming speech. Example 16.7 shows how one speaker welcomed a group of students and their parents to a "get acquainted day" recently.

SPEECHES FOR THE SAKE OF HUMOR

So far, we have looked at what you must do to succeed when giving a speech of praise or tribute, or when you are trying to inspire others. Many special occasions, however, call for speeches that have humor as their primary goal. The word *humor* refers to a comic quality that causes amusement. Speeches in this category seek to be funny and comical, to show a sense of fun, and to produce laughter. They include after-dinner speeches and roasts.

EXAMPLE 16.6   SAMPLE KEYNOTE SPEECH

Fred Allen once defined the term *conference* to mean "a gathering of important people who singly can do nothing, but together can decide that nothing can be done." He could not have been thinking of this group.

As I look around this room this morning, I see dozens of success stories seated around me. I see people who have learned how important Shelter Paper and its products are to daily living. But their learning didn't stop there. You decided it was important that all those paper users needed to understand that we stand for quality and service more than any other company in our business.

That's not an easy job, but who ever said that Shelter Paper looked for the easy market and the easy sales? We've been leaders because we've taken on the opposition head-to-head for years and always come out the winner. Your attitude, your work, and your success are the reasons we continue to be the leader in paper product sales for the thirty-fifth consecutive year.

We're not here as a mutual admiration society. You and I are at this annual sales meeting to find out why we've been successful, why we lost some of those sales we really should have made, and to be updated on the latest products and techniques in our business.

But this is important. We need to remember that we are winners. What company in this business can claim to have larger sales, better paid salespeople and managers, or a more efficient home office staff? Your answer to that question is the same as mine: None. And no one will even come close if we continue to think and act like the winners we at Shelter have become over the years. Yes, it's the power of positive thinking. We're the best, and no one is going to take that position from us.

We work harder and have a better product. But most of all, we have the best people in the industry working for us. When you have the best people and the best product, you're going to be a winner.

That's what we have here today. Winners sitting next to winners. Our margin of victory is greater today than ever before and that is because each of you has thought, acted, and sold positively.

AFTER-DINNER SPEECHES

After-dinner speaking is one of the most common forms of public address. Nowadays, **after-dinner speeches** follow almost every kind of social meal. They are usually brief— no more than about ten minutes—and they often are designed to be entertaining.

Almost any subject can serve as the topic for an after-dinner speech if it lends itself to the light touch. Let your own good taste guide you. But you obviously would not want to talk about cancer or herpes, child abuse, or the abortion issue.

Not everyone understands this common-sense suggestion. In one situation, a group of about 150 law enforcement officers and administrators had to sit through a tasteless presentation about automobile accidents immediately after they had eaten lunch. The speaker even showed full-color 35-millimeter slides. Many of the listeners simply got up and left the room.

The first thought most people have when someone invites them to give an after-dinner speech is that it must be funny. Humor, of course, plays an important part, but you do not have to be a stand-up comedian to succeed. Still, timing and a sense of the comical do not come readily to everyone. So after dinner speaking can provide a special problem for people who do not easily poke fun. If you are one of these, and if you find yourself faced with having to give an after-dinner speech, either decline the invitation or focus

EXAMPLE **16.7**   SAMPLE WELCOMING SPEECH

Good morning, ladies and gentlemen, and welcome to this get acquainted day. And especially to you students who are visiting us, welcome. My name is Tyrone Pate. I am a junior majoring in political science, and I am one of the two junior class senators in the Student Government Association.

On behalf of everyone connected with the university, I'd like to say how happy I am that you have joined us today. You honor us by coming out today. I know you could be visiting a different college right now.

It's going to be a full day if you do everything we've planned. But of course, you don't have to do it all. You're welcome to come and go anywhere, of course, or just to hang around in the library or the University Center if you want.

If you'll look at the schedule that we placed in your chair, you'll see that our activities begin in about fifteen minutes with tours of the campus. That will take about an hour, maybe an hour and a half. Then you will meet some of our faculty. You have already indicated which departments you would like to visit. All the meetings are going to happen in two buildings, and the tour guides will show you where to go. After you meet the faculty, the tour guides will bring you to lunch. We've got a special music program for you at noon.

In just one more moment, Jack Reed will get you together with your student tour guide. They're all standing in the back, wearing red, white, and blue uniforms. Before we break up, let me say again, how glad I am to see you. We're proud of this school, and we'd like to share it with you. If there is anything I or any one of the tour guides can do to make your stay more pleasant, please speak right up. I'll see you at lunch.

Table 16.8

CHRONOLOGICAL STEPS IN GIVING A WELCOMING SPEECH

1. Greet the group, tell them who you are, and how you connect to the organization.
2. Express pleasure that the group has arrived for its visit.
3. Explain what will happen next, and offer to be of any service you can.

---

your attention on *interesting* the audience. Before you take this option, however, double-check that taking an "interesting" (as opposed to "funny") approach will seem appropriate to listeners in that particular context. Discuss this matter with the person who invited you to give the speech.

Strip after-dinner speeches of technical detail and contentiousness. This is not the time to champion your point of view or to grind an ax. Rather, take a light-hearted, imaginative, stimulating approach. Make a point, but do it with consideration for the feelings and expectations of listeners.

Most after-dinner speakers prefer delivering either one-point speeches or pleasantry speeches. In the **one-point after-dinner speech,** the speaker states a central thought and then wraps stories, anecdotes, quotations, and the like around that central thought. In the **pleasantry speech,** the after-dinner speaker gently pokes fun. Almost anything can be a "target" for pleasantry: the audience, some institution, some person who represents a group or institution, some idea.

Pleasantry is not satire. **Satire** is the use of ridicule to expose, denounce, or deride. Thus, satire is negative and hurtful, and has a cutting edge. In contrast, pleasantry is usually expressed as (1) irony, (2) exaggeration, (3) parody, or (4) reversal of values.

Irony is saying one thing but meaning the opposite—on the condition that the result is a humorous insight. Be careful. When irony takes on a cutting edge, it is satire or sarcasm. For example, several people spoke at a retirement banquet honoring a local judge. They were generally full of praise for the judge's skill and insight over the course of her career. You can imagine the laughter, then, when the district attorney said, "She once handed down a judgment that was so subtle and cognitively complex nobody knew what she meant."

Exaggeration means blowing things up beyond the limits of truth, to increase or enlarge abnormally. For example, a school swimming coach made the following remark about his best woman freestyle swimmer—an Olympics contender—after a sports banquet: "She started her competitive career in swimming as a lifeguard at a car wash."

Parody is imitation for the sake of humor. This is a common form of humor on late-night television. An example of parody would be someone, for the sake of humor, imitating the president of the United States, but changing the content of what the president might say. Television's "Saturday Night Live" has used parody for years as a mainstay of its humor.

Reversal of values is a technique in which the speaker makes something significant out of the trivial, or something trivial out of the important. The fun is in the surprise turn. When a professor of geography was selected to give the Dean's Lecture—an honor that falls on some member of the faculty at the University of South Alabama once each year—the dean said:

> *He is not only a fine geographer with an enviable publication record, ladies and gentlemen, he's also a fine cartographer. His work in mapping the silt deposits flowing out of Mobile Bay and the Mississippi River have made him quite a reputation. He's published more than twenty separate maps over the past six years. Now if only he could show us how to refold them.*

A story is told of Supreme Court Justice Felix Frankfurter that also illustrates reversal of values. A friend asked Justice Frankfurter to officiate at her wedding ceremony. Justice Frankfurter explained that he did not have the authority to perform the ceremony. "What?" his friend exclaimed. "A Supreme Court Justice doesn't have the authority to marry people. Why not?" Frankfurter replied, "I guess it's because marriage is not considered a federal offense."

Table 16.9 suggests steps in preparing an after-dinner speech.

ROASTS

One special occasion violates nearly all the rules about after-dinner speaking. A **roast** involves numerous speakers who aim exaggerated insults at the subject of the roast. In a roast, speakers use extreme satire as their primary means of having fun. Both the subject of the roast and listeners know that the satire is not intended to be hurtful. When a group selects someone to roast, they do that person great honor. Both the subject and listeners understand this honor and are also expected to understand the satire.

Table 16.9

STEPS IN PREPARING AN AFTER-DINNER SPEECH

1. Determine the interests that audience members share in common.
2. Determine the approach you will take.
   A. If you decide to take the one-point approach:
      Select a central theme.
      Look for the fun in the theme.
      Select stories, anecdotes, quotations, and so on that bear on that theme.
      Organize your ideas so that they build to a high point.
   B. If you decide on pleasantry as your approach:
      Select a "target" subject.
      Look for irony, exaggeration, parody, and reversal of values.
      Tie the speech to a central theme that holds the various pieces together.

EXAMPLE 16.8 — SAMPLE GAG LINES FROM A ROAST

"Jack may be good at his job, but after a few drinks, he loses complete control."

"He works in the office as controller, but at home he has no power over his kids. He can't even control his own TV set."

"He's usually out of the office so much that he has to run things by remote control."

"Jack is so ugly that, when he looks at the account ledger, the ink fades."

"He can keep the company expenses within limits, but you ought to see his credit card statements."

"He's not much of a detective. Last time he got on the right track, he went in the wrong direction."

"Jack really likes his job—it allows him to get plenty of sleep."

"Actually, he's so good at reporting errors that he ought to be a baseball announcer."

"Jack's so dumb that last Wednesday he sharpened his new ballpoint pen."

"He once said he could even improve the Ten Commandments. He'd just cut them down to six or seven."

If you are invited to roast someone, hook your remarks to things that listeners are likely to know about the subject. And remember, if you know someone well enough to roast, you know enough not to be hurtful. Take care, even in a roast, never to offend someone else.

To illustrate what goes on during a roast, example 16.8 shows some gag lines used when friends roasted Jack, the corporate comptroller of a local business. Table 16.10 offers suggestions for how to stage a roast.

You do not have to be a joke writer to develop humorous materials for a roast. At the library you will find many books under the listing "Wit and Humor." Help yourself to what is there. Authors and publishers of such books expect you to take their materials without giving credit.

Table 16.10

STAGING A ROAST

1. Select speakers who know the target of the roast well, and who speak easily and confidently.
2. Assign each speaker a place in the speaking order program and a specific time limit. Be sure that all the speakers understand that they must adhere to the time limit. The total speaking time should not last more than thirty to forty minutes.
3. Before the roast, ask the speakers to rough out their remarks and to then attend a meeting in which the speakers compare notes. This eliminates unwanted duplication, serves as a rehearsal, and allows you to check on the overall program time.
4. Invite the target of the roast to prepare a rebuttal. Suggest a time limit of about seven to ten minutes. The target's rebuttal is the last part (and, hopefully, the highlight) of the program.

Summary

Our lives include many special occasions that call for speech making. Speeches for special occasions require different approaches from the other types of public speaking situations discussed in this book. However, they share the need for effective and thorough preparation, knowledge of the audience, and speaker understanding of the person or occasion. All are audience centered, and your success in these settings is largely determined by the carefulness of your preparation.

Speeches of praise and tribute include introductory speeches, presentation speeches, acceptance speeches, and eulogies. The introductory speech has two purposes: to focus listener attention on the person being introduced and to prepare listeners for the speech to follow. It is characterized by brevity and the presentation of basic biographical information about the speaker, such as qualifications and credentials. Gather facts and background information to create a picture of the total person. Remember that your purpose is only to introduce the main speaker. The audience is there primarily to listen to the other person, not you.

A presentation speech is the special occasion speech given when a gift or award is presented. The speaker names and describes the reason for giving the gift or award and the criteria used in deciding who should receive it. The speaker may then describe the recipient's personal qualifications for receiving the award. After the recipient has been called forward, the speaker reads any inscription on the award.

A presentation usually calls for the recipient of the gift or award to make an acceptance speech. The recipient thanks the people who gave the gift or award and the people who helped the recipient to achieve the goals that resulted in the presentation.

Eulogies are usually presented at ceremonies following a death, although the living are also sometimes eulogized. Eulogies require speakers to inform listeners about the person being honored—especially the person's significant human characteristics and specific ways in which the person's life touched others.

Inspirational speeches are meant to arouse and inspire. Commencement speeches, keynote speeches, and welcoming speeches fall into this category. Commencement speeches should acknowledge the personal sacrifices of parents and students, and should define the role of graduates and suggest methods for achieving success. Such ceremonial occasions require speaker brevity, simplicity, and clarity.

A keynote speech is a special occasion speech that sets the tone or mood for the meeting and the people attending. It is the major focus of the meeting and is designed to create audience enthusiasm. To accomplish this emotional arousal, the speaker must determine the theme of the meeting, show how the theme is important to the speech and to listeners, gear the speech to the common concerns of listeners, and show a genuine interest in the topic and the audience.

Welcoming speeches are commonly presented when groups visit schools or organizations. The speaker briefly greets the group, expresses pleasure that the group has come, explains what will happen next, and offers to be of service.

Many special occasions call for speeches that have humor as their primary goal. Speeches for the sake of humor include after-dinner speeches and roasts. After-dinner speakers usually take a humorous approach, although some prefer to focus on interesting audience members rather than entertaining them. One-point after-dinner speeches and pleasantry speeches are commonly used formats. Successful after-dinner speakers often employ the techniques of irony, exaggeration, parody, and reversal of values.

A roast is a special occasion involving numerous speakers who aim exaggerated insults at the subject of the roast. Everyone involved understands that the insults are meant to be funny, not hurtful or offensive.

Key Terms

Acceptance speech	Irony	Presentation speech
After-dinner speech	Keynote speech	Reversal of values
Commencement speech	One-point after-dinner	Roast (speech)
Eulogy	speech	Satire
Exaggeration	Parody	Welcoming speech
Introductory speech	Pleasantry speech	

Application Questions

1. What special occasion speech have you heard most recently? In what category would you place it? Using the criteria provided in the chapter, how well did the speech meet those standards?

2. Prepare a list of special occasion speeches that you have heard. What were the predominant strengths and weaknesses of each one? Given your reading of this chapter, could you suggest ways to improve the speeches? What changes would you recommend, and why?

3. Assume for the sake of this exercise that any meal is a special occasion. After a meal with friends or family members, make a little speech in which you praise the people at the table with you. Follow the suggestions in this chapter. Then report your experience to the class. What effect did your speech have on the people you praised? Would you judge the speech a success? Looking back, would you have changed the speech in any way?

Self-Test for Review

1. Match the kinds of special occasion speeches in the left-hand column with the categories of special occasion speeches in the right-hand column.

    _____ a. Welcoming speech   1. Speech of praise or tribute
    _____ b. Roast   2. Inspirational speech
    _____ c. Eulogy   3. Speech given for sake of humor
    _____ d. After-dinner speech
    _____ e. Commencement speech
    _____ f. Keynote speech
    _____ g. Acceptance speech
    _____ h. Introductory speech
    _____ i. Presentation speech

2. Match the kinds of special occasion speeches in the left-hand column with the statements in the right-hand column that best describe them.

    _____ a. Welcoming speech   1. To focus listeners' attention on the speech they are about to hear
    _____ b. Roast   2. To give a gift or award in public
    _____ c. Eulogy   3. To thank a presenter or an organization for a gift or award
    _____ d. After-dinner speech   4. To praise or speak well of someone
    _____ e. Commencement   5. To acknowledge contributions and sacrifices, and to provide a challenge
              speech
    _____ f. Keynote speech   6. To set the tone or mood of a meeting
    _____ g. Acceptance speech   7. To greet a group and extend the hospitality of the organization
    _____ h. Introductory speech   8. To provide a light or humorous finish following a meal
    _____ i. Presentation speech   9. To honor an individual with extreme satire and friendly insult

3. Mark the following statements: 1 = Good advice about speaking for special occasions; 2 = Bad advice about speaking for special occasions.

_____ a. It is usually not a good idea to ask people about themselves before introducing them. Instead, ask someone who knows them.

_____ b. Try to understand if the speaking situation assumes expectations that can influence the speech.

_____ c. Always name and describe the criteria used in deciding who should receive an award.

_____ d. In an acceptance speech, it is a good idea to thank the people who helped you achieve the award.

_____ e. Do not eulogize a living person.

_____ f. Eulogies are always persuasive speeches, but the persuasion has to be subtle and in line with the achievements of the person you are eulogizing.

_____ g. Keep a commencement address short and sweet.

_____ h. Let the theme of a meeting guide your keynote speech.

4. Match the definitions in the left-hand column with the correct terms in the right-hand column.

_____ a. Use of ridicule to expose, denounce, or deride	1. Irony
_____ b. Pretending the trivial is significant or the significant is trivial	2. Exaggeration
	3. Parody
_____ c. Imitation for the sake of humor	4. Reversal of values
_____ d. Blowing something up beyond the limits of truth	5. Satire
_____ e. Saying one thing and meaning another for humorous insight	

Answers: 1. a. 2, b. 3, c. 1, d. 3, e. 2, f. 2, g. 2, h. 1, i. 1, j. 1, 2. a. 7, b. 9, c. 4, d. 8, e. 5, f. 6, g. 3, h. 1, i. 2, 3. a. 2, b. 1, c. 1, d. 1, e. 1, f. 2, g. 1, h. 1, 4. a. 5, b. 4, c. 3, d. 2, e. 1.

Suggested Readings

Johannesen, Richard L., R. R. Allen, and Wil A. Linkugel. *Contemporary American Speeches.* 7th ed. Dubuque, Iowa: Kendall-Hunt, 1992. This book is a good source for model special occasion speeches. The authors explain each speech type, give the criteria, and outline the major features of the speeches they include.

Vital Speeches of the Day. Southhold, N.Y.: City New Publishing. This is the premiere source of contemporary speeches in American society. Published twice each month and found in nearly every college library, *Vital Speeches* contains speeches of all kinds about current national and international concerns.

Appendix A

Sample Speeches

The sample speeches presented here represent various levels of polish and speaking experience. Of course, manuscripts are not speeches. A speech does not exist until it is being spoken. As you read these speeches, try to imagine the voice, how the speaker sounded. Or read the speeches out loud, pausing where you think the speakers might have, stressing the ideas you think the speaker might have stressed. In this way, you will get a sense of the oral nature of the speeches.

In those sample speeches where marginal notes appear, read the speech through the first time without looking at the marginal notations. Try to get a sense of the speech before you analyze it. The marginal notes are designed to stimulate your thinking and your criticism. Use them, then, as a guide only. Let your own speech criticism flow from what you know and how you feel. If you do, reading these speeches will contribute to your overall growth as a speech maker.

These sample speeches have been organized in order according to the relative experience of the speech makers, with least experienced speakers first. You will surely notice differences, then, in the levels of polish and sophistication. Be assured that none of these speeches is perfect. No speech ever is. No speech ever needs to be. Your own speech making will show improvement with experience, just as these speeches reflect the value of experience.

The first speech, by international student Siok Tan, is a clear example of informative speaking. You can almost hear his voice as you read the manuscript.

Stephanie Kaplan, University of Wisconsin–Madison, gave her speech about "organoids" in a speech competition among college students. You will enjoy studying how she builds her speech using facts and testimony.

Amy Olson, of Bradley University, uses information to persuade her listeners that a very real problem exists in the movement to recycle paper. As you read this speech, bear in mind that what you are reading is a transcript of a spoken message. Her listeners cannot have missed her argument that there is a problem.

Jerry Stalick, of Eastern New Mexico University, goes further. His use of evidence and argument forms a compelling case for each of us learning to make the cross-cultural sojourn. When you finish reading this fine example of student work, you may find yourself enrolling in a foreign language course!

Elizabeth Glaser's address to the Democratic National Convention will move you. It is a special occasion speech, and at the same time, an emotionally involving oration. You will enjoy reading it most if you concentrate on hearing her voice. Imagine a large hall full of people enjoying a partisan political convention. Glaser gathers their attention, pulls them into her subject and her speech, and leaves them breathless.

Robert Cizik and J. Peter Grace are both businessmen. Their speeches show a level of polish that ordinary people can achieve with practice. Cizik's speech is an empassioned plea that listeners do something to improve the business climate in California. Pay attention to how well he builds the tension with short, simple sentences. Imagine yourself sitting in his audience in Los Angeles. Would you be able to resist his conclusion?

J. Peter Grace balances humor, facts, and testimony to hold listener attention. Notice, especially, how he humanizes facts and figures. For example, pay particular attention to his use of Cicero to make his point about the size of the national debt.

Bernard Shaw is a professional communicator. You would expect his speech making to be excellent, and you would be right. His argument that democracy is not a smooth sauce is superbly crafted.

Mario Cuomo is a gifted public speaker. His speech for the governorship of New York is classic campaign oratory at its best. Read this speech out loud if you want to hear how important voice can be to the compelling force of a speech.

Vernon E. Jordan, Jr.'s commencement address provides a good model for epideictic speaking, a speech that reinforces a certain set of values. You will certainly notice that this speech takes on a political edge, however. Politicians do that. If you are ever invited to give a commencement address, you probably would be wise not to follow Jordan's example.

UNTITLED

SIOK TAN, *INTERNATIONAL STUDENT FROM SINGAPORE*

Introduction

This introduction follows the pattern recommended in chapters 2 and 10: Greeting, name, topic and importance.

Good morning, classmates. My name is Siok Tan. I am an international student from Temasek. You don't know my country by that name, however. You know it by the name *Singapore.* My purpose this morning is to tell you interesting details about my country because I want to help break an American student stereotype that everyone from Asia is like the Japanese. Don't misunderstand my idea. I like the Japanese, and this idea of mine does not attack the Japanese people. But Singapore is different.

Effort to develop curiosity in the classroom audience.

My country is a small island country in Southeast Asia. It is about as big as the city of Chicago. It is only one-fifth as big as your smallest state, Rhode Island. And in fact, when you come to my country, you think you are coming to a large United States city.

Reveals structure of the speech as transition.

I will tell you where we are located, some brief facts about our history, and interesting ideas about our economy.

Body

Siok's first main idea demanded use of a map.

When you look on your map, you will find Singapore just at the southern tip of the Malay Peninsula. (points to map) Right here. We are separated from this big island of Sumatra by the straight of Malacca. You can see that we're close to Borneo, Viet Nam, Thailand, and not far from Sri Lanka and India. This tells you about our population and our culture. We are about three million people, including Chinese, Indian, Malay, and others. We have four official languages—Chinese, English, Malay, and Tamil. And we get along great.

Interesting information, but only marginally related to the first main idea.

Appendix A

Singapore has an ancient history, but we are a new nation. In fact, we didn't become an independent country until 1965. Before that, we were part of Malaysia for two years. From 1824 until then, we were controlled by Great Britain. Now we are proud to be an independent republic.

Second main idea.

Specific details suggest that Siok is an expert. They build his credibility.

In ancient times, Singapore was known as *Temasek*. It is a Japanese word that means "sea." We live on a tiny island surrounded by the sea. In fact, Singapore was destroyed at the end of the fourth century by the sea. As the saying goes, Temasek was not discovered again until the eleventh century A.D. Prince Nila Utama landed on the island, and he saw a strange looking animal. Later, he learned that the animal was a lion, so he named the island Singapura, which is from two words. Singa means lion, and Pura means city.

Supporting materials for the main idea.

Transition needed. We suggested that Siok include an internal summary leading up to his description of Singapore's economy.

Third main idea.

To tell you about our economy, Singapore is one of the twenty richest countries in the world today. This is because of many factors. For example, Singapore has a literacy rate of about 90 percent. And we have always been a financial center in the region, since we have had a stable political environment. Our government has worked hard to make Singapore a place to attract big banks from around the world. Our seaport is the world's busiest seaport. Did you know that? And also, we have only small unemployment— 1.7 percent. So you can see that we have a very strong economy. In fact, we're so busy that Singapore has three hotels that were voted to be among the top ten business hotels in the world. This was a study by a British publication called *Business Traveller*.

Conclusion

Summary

Here Siok tried to use a "kicker" that introduced a new purpose into his speech. It was charming but irrelevant.

So, in conclusion, I have explained to you our history and our economic background and where Singapore is located. I am proud of my country and my people.

So in conclusion, I invite you to come to Singapore for a visit.

Thank you.

UNTITLED

STEPHANIE KAPLAN, *UNIVERSITY OF WISCONSIN–MADISON*

When manufacturers began using Gortex, a brand-name plastic polymer, to produce indestructible sleeping bags, tents, and rainwear, outdoor enthusiasts oohed and aahed, and everyone else said, who cares? But now a team of Maryland researchers has discovered a use for Gortex which will make the whole world sit up and take notice. Gortex is used as the foundation for groups of human cells which act like real human organs, producing substances that the body needs, such as hormones, and breaking down harmful products in the body. Scientists predict that within the next few years, these neo-organs, or organoids, will enable them to successfully treat AIDS, diabetes, hemophilia, and Alzheimer's disease. Within our lifetime, they will actually replace dysfunctioning organs, dramatically reducing our need for organ transplants. As Ward Kassos of the National Heart, Lung and Blood Institute explains, "In this era of designer genes, all of these things are now possible." In a world where great medical advances are made almost daily, organoids are unique because of their tremendous versatility. In order to understand why scientists, doctors, and their patients are so excited about this new technology, we will examine what organoids are and the applications which they allow, and the drawback which may limit their use.

With little more than Gortex fibers, gelatin, and natural growth factors, scientists have created what John Thompson of the University of Alabama–Birmingham calls a "cauldron filled with all the right stuff " to create a new organ. While scientists are still slightly unsure exactly why organoids form, they're quick to recognize that they will revolutionize the way we treat diseases. Organoids will be able to help out overworked or dysfunctioning organs by duplicating some of their functions. They demonstrate two of the essential characteristics of real human organs: the ability to secrete proteins and grow new blood vessels.

The process of creating an organoid involves a number of steps, according to the *Washington Post Weekly* of September 4, 1989. First, very thin Gortex fibers are coated with gelatin and then matted to form a spongelike shape. This sponge is then coated with natural growth factors, which encourage cells to grow and develop. The sponge is then surgically implanted in a site appropriate for its intended use—for example, in the abdominal cavity near the pancreas or the liver. So far, implants have been performed on rats, mice, rabbits, and monkeys, and scientists predict that the first human implants will take place in the next year or so. Next comes the mysterious part. According to *Science* of September 8, 1988, for unknown reasons, immature cells from unknown organs migrate to the fibers and colonize them. The growth factors encourage these cells to multiply and mature. After about a month, the sponge is surgically removed, the cells are scraped off and cultivated in a petri dish. It is at this part of the process that the tremendous potential of organoids becomes apparent. Using a new technology known as gene therapy, scientists are able to insert new genes into these cells, changing their DNA from that of the original host. The genetically altered cells are then placed on a new Gortex sponge and reimplanted in the same general area, where they will grow into an organoid, where they will act just like a real human organ, producing substances which the body needs and secreting them into the bloodstream and growing new blood vessels. And, because organoids are grown from the cells taken from the patient's own body, there's no chance of rejection as sometimes happens with transplant organs.

Organoids will allow scientists to do what they have previously only dreamed about. W. French Anderson, Chief of Molecular Hematology for the National Heart, Lung and Blood Institute, explains that what's amazing about these new structures is that they can secrete proteins directly into the bloodstream. "Consequently," Anderson concludes, "what you end up with is, basically, a new organ." By combining these new organs with gene therapy, which allows researchers to insert new genes into cells, they have created a technology with a wide variety of applications. As Thomas Messick, Chief of Molecular Biology at the American Red Cross' Jerome Hollins Laboratory, explains, this will have a major clinical impact on a wide variety of diseases.

By combining gene therapy with organoid technology, scientists have created what W. French Anderson calls "the ability to treat any genetic disease which can be corrected by the secretion of a product." This includes diabetes, hemophilia, and the immune disease known as ADA deficiency. For example, as the *Washington Post* of September 3, 1989, explains, diabetes could be treated by insulin produced by an organoid. First, genes for insulin production would be inserted into cells taken from the patient. These cells would then be placed on a Gortex sponge and implanted near the pancreas which—when working properly—produces the body's supply of insulin. There, they would grow into an organoid which, according to the *Post,* would act like a little insulin factory. This would replace the current treatment of diabetes, which requires the self-monitoring of insulin levels and the self-administration of animal or artificial insulin. The organoid would monitor blood sugar levels and release insulin into the bloodstream as needed, all by itself.

But organoids won't be limited to just treating genetic disease. As *Science* of September 10, 1989, explains, first on the agenda is a cure for AIDS. Scientists now know that the AIDS virus penetrates cells and begins to replicate itself by binding to what are known as CD-4 protein receptors. Various researchers have speculated that if CD-4 protein could be introduced directly into the bloodstream, the virus might bind to these decoy proteins rather than the patient's cells. The decoy CD-4 would then be secreted from the body, taking the AIDS virus with it. In fact, the Food and Drug Administration has recently approved the first human tests for CD-4. So far, however, researchers had remained stumped by how to keep a constant supply of CD-4 in the bloodstream without permanently hooking the patient up to an IV. Organoids will solve this problem. As Rachael King, of Genetic Therapy, Incorporated of Rockville, Maryland, explained during a February 2, 1990, phone interview, cells could be placed on a Gortex sponge which when implanted would grow into an organoid that would produce CD-4 and release it constantly. Organoids may also allow us to treat neurological disorders, such as Alzheimer's disease. John Thompson, of the University of Alabama–Birmingham, explains that in addition to growing new blood vessels, organoids produce what look like nerve fibers. What he says this means is that we may be able to grow new nerves for Alzheimer's victims.

The ability of scientists to bolster the secretions of dysfunctioning organs has led some to speculate about someday simply replacing these organs with organoids. The *Washington Post Weekly* of September 4, 1989, speculates that within our lifetime, doctors will be able to routinely replace damaged or aging organs, such as the spleen, liver, pancreas—and even the heart—with fresh organs grown inside our own bodies. This would dramatically reduce the need for transplant organs, practically eliminate transplant rejection, and perhaps extend the average life span.

While doctors are very excited about the potential organoids offer, they do list one major drawback. Because the growth factors used to stimulate cell development are so strong, some researchers question whether an organoid could grow out of control and into a tumor. Ward Kassos of the National Heart, Lung and Blood Institute explains that these factors are so potent, it's conceivable they could cause problems. So far, the answer to this question remains unknown. But W. French Anderson, also of the Institute, points to six months of experiments with rats which show no evidence of tumors. Anderson goes on to explain the assumption that if something went wrong with an organoid, you could simply go in and snip it out. And, because they develop so quickly, it would be relatively easy to replace problematic organoids.

Today, we've examined an amazing new technology by looking at what organoids are and the applications they'll allow, and the drawback which may limit their use. It seems almost impossible to believe that a fiber once known for its water resistance has become the basis of a technology which will allow us to treat AIDS, diabetes, hemophilia, and Alzheimer's disease. The ability to remove cells from patients' bodies, genetically alter these cells, and then cultivate them on Gortex sponges, has given scientists a new technology with a wide variety of applications. Not only will it allow us to treat a variety of genetic and acquired diseases, it may someday replace our pressing need for transplant organs. Indeed, it is easy to agree with Robert Gallup, co-founder, uh, co-discoverer of the AIDS virus, who is now working with organoids, who explains, "The whole thing is incredible."

Reprinted with permission of the American Forensic Association.

UNTITLED

AMY OLSON, *BRADLEY UNIVERSITY*

After reading the news, eyeing the ads, and catching up on the latest misadventures of Calvin and Hobbes, what do you folks do with your Sunday newspapers? In our ever more ecologically aware community, it becomes fairly standard to save newspapers for recycling. However, according to an August 17th, 1989, article in the *Washington Post,* in Arlington, Virginia, in the first week of June, all of the newspaper recycling organizations were wiped out. A sign in front of the local Boy Scout collection post read: "Due to the current oversupply in the market, there's no outlet for our collective newspapers. Thanks for your loyalty to the Scouts." So why is it that even the Boy Scouts can't do their good deeds?

As we enter the 1990s, the recycling of paper and other goods has become standard in many communities . . . with 34 states having recycling legislation, according to the February 25, 1990, *Chicago Tribune.* However, while consumers are asked to save goods for recycling, we lack the facilities to complete that recycling process. So what happens when the individuals do their parts but the capacity does not exist to recycle their goods?

In order to better approach this major concern, we must first take a look at what has caused this glut of paper in the recycling market. Next, we'll see how this glut has had not only an environmental effect but a detrimental economic effect on the community as well. And finally, we'll see how, as a community, we can solve this all too real problem of too many recyclable goods.

The year is 1990. The year of video telephones, robots, and the paperless office. So much for Jeanne Dixon's forecast. We have more paper now than we have ever used before. Each year, Americans use over 67 million tons of paper, . . . That's over 600 pounds per person, according to the book *Waste Paper, the Future of a Resource.* Now with each ton of waste paper taking up three cubic yards of ever-decreasing landfill space, waste disposal is no longer the easy solution. Waste paper can be burned like wood to create electricity, but environmentalists have proven that the gases produced are dangerous, according to a November 14, 1989, article in the *Christian Science Monitor.*

Now in response to these concerns, ten states and many cities have begun mandating recycling. In theory, all this paper that we used to either throw away or burn can be recycled.

And, in theory, this is a good thing. Reality holds one not-so-insignificant problem. These hundreds of thousands of tons of waste paper that we are so diligently collecting, for the very noble purpose of recycling, have no place to go. According to the September 10, 1989, edition of the *New York Times,* there are only eight mills in this country capable of de-inking paper for recycling. Other than those eight mills, there are hundreds of others that can't, and it would cost them over $50 million each in de-inking equipment in order to make recycling profitable. None of them have plans to make such an investment. Well, these mandatory recycling laws are creating hundreds of thousands of tons of waste paper that can no longer go in the landfills but should be recycled. But they cannot be recycled because there aren't enough plants. So why aren't the plants responding to this obvious need? Because the market for recycled paper products just doesn't exist. According to a December, 1989, article in *Sierra* magazine, although AT&T runs a highly profitable in-house recycling program of selling their neatly bailed waste products to use within the corporation itself. . . . According to a January 19, 1990, article in the *Wall Street Journal,* Ameritex yellow pages are now being recycled for use in tissues, paper towels, and toilet paper. But nobody wants to buy. Well, there seems to be some stigma attached to using recycled toilet paper, which is, in effect, killing the recycling market. Now you might do your part by buying the occasional recycled birthday card, but how many of you in this room actually use recycled paper in your typewriters? As your computer paper? As your ballot? And as James L. Baker, president of the Garden State Paper Company says, "If you can't sell it, there's no sense in making it."

Now, the effect of this glut of paper upon the recycling market has been two-fold: environmental and economic. Environmentally, with landfills already operating over capacity, the ever-increasing amount of waste paper that's not recycled will only speed the impending crisis of landfill space. As mayor of Chicago, Richard M. Daley, recently pointed out, "There just aren't enough dump sites in this nation to dump all this material." A bit more disheartening is the fact that groups, like the Boy Scouts out in Arlington, Virginia, and organizations just like them all across the country can't fulfill their original purpose. They can collect the newspapers, but then where does it go? Now, economically, this glut is not only going to hurt nonprofit organizations. According to that December '89 article in *Sierra,* most recycling laws address only the separation of recyclables from garbage. They don't require anybody to buy or reuse the collected materials. Well, consequently, some of our country's brave new recycling programs are stuck with piles of newspapers that administrators have to pay to get rid of, just like garbage. In a January 8, 1990, telephone interview with Ann Greggs of the Chicago Recycling Coalition, she noted that less than 12 weeks ago in Chicago, a recycling plant was paying over $100 a ton for recyclable waste paper. Now not only is there no money given for the waste paper, but money must be raised to transport the goods to the plant. Well, community organizations, town and city governments alike are having to pay to get rid of their waste paper, to transport it to plants, possibly farther away, that can still take their goods. But how much longer will they have that option?

Now obviously, the solution is not to stop recycling paper. But with ten states and many cities mandating the collection of paper for recycling, the market's not going to let up in the near future. In the long term, there is only one option, more plants must become equipped to recycle, and industry must use those newly created recycled products. The government could offer economic incentives in order to promote the building of more recycling plants. On January 22, 1990, President Bush submitted to Congress a national levy on certain raw materials in order to promote industrial recycling. Individual states have begun to take similar measures. According to that November 14th article in the *Christian Science Monitor,* Florida had begun to levy a 10-cent tax on virgin paper rolls. Other states, including California and Connecticut, have passed minimum content, roughly 20 percent, of recycled fibers. Now these minimum content laws are important. Because not only do they encourage recycling, but more importantly, they lighten up that glut of paper already existing in the market.

As a community, we can encourage the recycling market by purchasing recycled paper products on a large scale for our schools and our offices. According to a February 8, 1990, telephone interview with Bob McDowell of the Environmental Protection Agency, he supports procurement programs, whereby offices are required, by law, that a certain percentage of the paper products purchased for the office are made from recycled fibers. Well, for instance, according to an April 4, 1990, article in the *Chicago Tribune,* in one year, a single typical Chicago law firm goes through over 1.8 million sheets of paper. Stack that up, that's over 67 stories high. Just recently, over 250 million census forms were sent out. That's over 5 trillion sheets of paper. Imagine the effect on the recycling industry if even half of those sheets of paper, printed by our government, had been printed on recycled paper.

Well, for the rest of us, we too can encourage the recycling market by purchasing recycled paper products on a regular basis for ourselves. Earthcare Paper Company boasts a computer paper that's not only more durable and flexible than regular computer paper, but it costs 24 percent less. Hallmark card stores carry several lines of cards printed only on recycled paper. And stores all across the country, even here in Tuscaloosa, are opening to carry exclusively recycled goods. Well, the point is, if we're not going to buy it, the proverbial they are not going to invest millions of dollars to make it. And then no matter how noble our recycling efforts, we're right back where we started from, with hundreds of thousands of tons of newspapers that nobody wants.

Now, according to Herschal Cutler of the Institute for Scrap Recycling, much of what the municipalities have us so zealously collecting for recycling is going to end up in the landfills after all. Well, there's not enough space in the landfills for all the paper that we generate. And at the moment, there aren't enough plants to recycle it. There's not going to be any more landfill space, so there must be more plants equipped to recycle. It's up to us to encourage the recycling industry by purchasing those recycled paper products, not only for our schools and our offices, but for ourselves.

By taking a look at what caused this glut of paper in the recycling market, its economic and environmental effects, and finally how we as a community can solve the problem of too many recyclable goods, we can salvage the recycled paper product market. And hey, if only for those Boy Scouts out in Arlington, Virginia, isn't it about time that we returned the good deed?

Reprinted with permission of the American Forensic Association.

THE *MOKUSATSU* MISTAKE
Communication across Cultural Barriers

JERRY STALICK, *EASTERN NEW MEXICO UNIVERSITY, NEW MEXICO*
COACHED BY ANTHONY SCHROEDER

Mokusatsu. In Japanese, it can mean either "to withhold comment," or it can mean, "to ignore." If you were a translator given a statement by the Japanese prime minister to translate into English, which meaning would you choose? Oh, a word of caution. If you choose the wrong meaning, you will cause the deaths of over 150,000 people in the next two weeks. Seem farfetched? On July 28, 1945, it happened. And as a result, less than two weeks later, on August 6, the first atomic bomb dropped on Hiroshima. The destruction of Nagasaki soon followed.

But how is a translator supposed to know which meaning Prime Minister Suzuki had in mind when he issued his fateful statement containing the word *mokusatsu?* Our communication is so subtle and intricate between native English speakers, is it any wonder that international communication is difficult and often misunderstood?

The *mokusatsu* example clearly demonstrates the need for improved understanding between the nations and the cultures. Intercultural communication is critical, but so far, it has not received nearly the research or application associated with other more well-known areas of communication. UNDERSTANDING INTERCULTURAL COMMUNICATION IS OF THE UTMOST IMPORTANCE IF WE ARE TO FUNCTION IN THE NEW GLOBAL SOCIETY.

In order to demonstrate the need for increased understanding of other cultures, we will first analyze the inevitable coming of the global society. Next, we will see some of the problems associated with learning about other cultures. And finally, we will cross over the barrier from simply learning about another culture to actually understanding the people of that culture.

Like the British of 200 years ago, the new global society is coming. In recognition of this fact, there are some attempts currently being made at expanding intercultural knowledge, and while these efforts must be acknowledged, we must also realize that it is far too little, far too late. We must be prepared to actively learn about, and not just passively survey, other cultures. The sense of urgency is apparent when we realize that cultures and subcultures are no longer able to hide behind isolationist walls. People from different cultures are blending and mixing now more than ever, and this trend is leading to a breakdown of the barriers between the cultures. Dean C. Barnlund, an expert on intercultural communication, insists the preparation comes now because, he says, "within a decade or two, many of us will spend at least a portion of our lives immersed in another culture." And Dr. Linda Moore reports, "One million immigrants a year make their homes in the United States . . . it's a far smaller world; we must know more about other cultures and understand our similarities as well as our differences."

Differences can arise in any situation, and many of the customs that Americans take for granted, such as punctuality, are very different in other cultures. For instance, in the United States, if you plan a party to start at 7, people will begin arriving at 7. This societal standard, however, is by no means universal. In Arabic countries, for example, being thirty minutes late is expected. In Italy, it may be two hours or more before guests begin arriving for social occasions, and in Java, the guest may never arrive. The invitations were accepted only to prevent the host from losing face.

Technology is a key tool helping to tear down the cultural barriers. Marshall McLuhan, a media expert and critic, said in *Modern Maturity,* June/July, 1991, that "television has turned the world into a global village." CNN and the networks are bringing the people from the corners of the globe together and exposing us to more cultural interaction. In ten minutes we may use (insert current news topics). Each one of these things is foreign to us, but behind the headlines are real people living real lives. It is imperative that we begin to understand these very real people half-a-world away. Soon they will be half-a-block away.

Competitive speakers use current event topics often taken from the morning paper.

Now that we understand the need for more understanding between cultures, let's look at some of the problems associated with learning about other cultures.

Learning about a culture may sound fairly easy, but like juggling, it often takes more than desire to learn. There are several critical problems that face those trying to learn more about other cultures. One of the key problems is the fact that the entire concept of intercultural communication is relatively new. The newness of intercultural communication means that there are fewer resources available to draw knowledge from. In many cases, these limited resources are inaccurate or misleading. With more study and experience, communication between the cultures will be easier and more productive, but for now, the level of success is disappointingly low.

Another problem in learning about other cultures comes from the types of people needing to learn about intercultural communication. Varied needs produce varied results, and often, the results are not interchangeable from group to group. Michael Argyle, another intercultural expert, defines five different types of people that need to learn about other cultures. They are tourists; short-term business, government, and university visitors; businessmen planning on a long overseas stay and overseas service people, such as Peace Corps volunteers; immigrants; and people who stay at home but during the course of their lives come into contact with visitors from other cultures. Which category do you fit in? In the rapidly approaching global society, we will all find ourselves in at least one of these groups.

The different training required by each group presents a considerable obstacle. Tourists may just need enough of the language and major societal customs to function for a short period. Long-term businessmen and Peace Corps volunteers will require not only training in the language and customs, but in history, theology, habits and values.

Some might suggest that merely learning the language would be an adequate base for beginning to function in another culture. They would argue that there is sufficient cultural and value system ideology present in the language and its structure to serve the visitor. However, in the 1950s, the United States government spent millions of dollars developing a system to translate Russian. The final result, according to Edward T. Hall, was "computers [that] could spew out yards of printout, but they meant very little. The words and some of the grammar were all there, but the sense was distorted."

The problem with knowing the language only was illustrated at the beginning of my presentation when we looked at the situation in Japan in 1945. The word *mokusatsu* was there—the meaning was not.

Now that we clearly understand some of the difficulties faced when we try to learn about another culture, let us examine some of the methods used to overcome the cultural barrier.

Many organizations are very interested in intercultural communication. As corporations become multi-national conglomerates, their employees must become mainstreamed into their new society. The United States military is also taking an active interest in intercultural communication. Now, because it is more interested in cooperation than in confrontation, the Navy has been developing a system to teach servicemen and women how to integrate into other cultures. The Navy system comes as a result of studying how the State Department, businesses, and the Peace Corps have trained their personnel in cultural differences. Some of the different techniques that these groups use include learning the language, reading about potential difficult situations within the society, role-playing, and possibly most important, interaction with current or former members of the culture. The technique the Navy uses combines these techniques into an integrated training system. Michael Argyle, quoted earlier, reports that Naval personnel stationed in Japan claimed higher levels of satisfaction and comfort within their new culture after going through the integrated system.

On a more personal level, we need to realize the role we can play in helping cultures to blend without the friction of the past. Attempts at improving intercultural communication are being made, but the effort must expand to actively include each one of us, and this effort cannot begin next month or this summer. It must start immediately. We already live in a global society. In order to get this blending started, we need to know what we can do as individuals to learn more about other cultures. First, each of us can use the methods currently being used by the government and various internationally oriented groups. Furthermore, many colleges and universities offer intercultural communication classes, and many libraries have dozens of books with information on cultures from around the world. Learning the language, while insufficient by itself, serves as a good supplement to the student of intercultural communication. Traveling is also a good way to overcome the cultural barrier. Even travel within the United States can be beneficial for the intercultural student. Places like San Francisco's Chinatown and New York's Little Italy are virtual microcosms of the larger overseas cultures.

Felipe Korzenny suggests another way to overcome the cultural barrier. He suggests understanding and overcoming the natural ethnocentrism common to most people. There is, according to Korzenny, "an innate tendency . . . to attribute increased importance to those who are closer to the self." Ethnocentrism is natural, but we must not allow it to strengthen the wall we are trying to pull down. Overcoming ethnocentrism may well be the first step toward attaining and understanding the inevitable global village.

By examining the coming global society, looking at some of the problems in learning about other cultures, and some of the methods that we can use to cross the cultural barrier, we have uncovered the need and a possible solution for improving intercultural communication.

On July 26, 1945, the United States, Great Britain and China issued the Potsdam ultimatum. It outlined the terms of surrender for Japan. The Japan high command was determined to accept the surrender at all costs but was not yet prepared to tell the battered Japanese public that surrender was eminent. In a press conference on July 28, Prime Minister Suzuki said the cabinet was holding to a policy of *mokusatsu*. A translator at the

Domei News Agency in Tokyo translated it as "ignoring" the ultimatum. What the prime minister and the cabinet meant, however, was that they were withholding comment for the time being. When the Allies got the translation, they interpreted his remark as implying the Japanese had no intent to surrender. The punishment for the mistaken translation was swift and severe.

Intercultural communication is critical. People are mixing and blending now more than ever. We must take the effort and time to learn about the people around us, or we run the terrible risk of repeating again and again the *mokusatsu* mistake.

Interstate Oratorical Association Winning Orations, 1992. Reprinted by permission.

ADDRESS TO THE DEMOCRATIC NATIONAL CONVENTION, JULY 1992

ELIZABETH GLASER

Elizabeth Glaser, a young mother who contracted AIDS through a blood transfusion in 1981, gave a ringing political speech at the 1992 Democratic National Convention. Her thesis was "We need a leader." Her argument was that under the Republican administration, America was not responsive to the plight of people with AIDS and that Democratic administration would be more responsive. The speech lasted only about eight minutes, not counting interruptions for applause.

Name and startling statements of fact and opinion draw attention, establish the speaker as qualified, and set the tone for what's coming.

I'm Elizabeth Glaser. Eleven years ago, while giving birth to my first child, I hemorrhaged and was transfused with seven pints of blood. Four years later, I found out that I had been infected with the AIDS virus, and I had unknowingly passed it to my daughter Ariel through my breast milk, and my son, Jake, in utero.

Twenty years ago, I wanted to be at the Democratic Convention because it was a way to participate in my country. Today, I am here because it's a matter of life and death. (APPLAUSE)

I am in a race with the clock. This is not about being a Republican or an Independent or a Democrat. It's about the future of each and every one of us.

This claim foreshadows the thesis statement. You can almost hear it coming.

I started out just a mom, fighting for the life of her child. But, along the way, I learned how unfair America can be today, not just for people who have HIV, but for many, many people—poor people, gay people, people of color, children. A strange spokesperson for such a group, a well-to-do white woman. But I have learned my lesson the hard way, and I know that America has lost her path and is at risk of losing her soul. America, wake up. We are all in a struggle between life and death. (APPLAUSE)

Notice how skillfully Ms. Glaser develops her need case.

I understand—I understand the sense of frustration and despair in our country because I know firsthand about shouting for help and getting no answer. I went to Washington to tell presidents Reagan and Bush that much, much more had to be done for AIDS research and care and that children couldn't be forgotten. The first time when nothing happened, I thought they just didn't hear me. The second time when nothing happened, I thought maybe I didn't shout loud enough. But now I realize they don't hear because they don't want to listen. (APPLAUSE)

When you cry for help and no one listens, you start to lose your hope. I began to lose faith in America. I felt my country was letting me down, and it was. This is not the America I was raised to be proud of. I was raised to believe that others' problems were my problems as well. But when I tell most people about HIV in hopes that they will help and care, I see the look in their eyes. It's not my problem, they're thinking. Well, it's everyone's problem. And we need a leader who will tell us that. (APPLAUSE)

We need a visionary to guide us, to say it wasn't right for Ryan White to be banned from school because he had AIDS. (APPLAUSE)

To say it wasn't all right for a man or a woman to be denied a job because they're infected with this virus. We need a leader who is truly committed to educating us.

I believe in America, but not with a leadership of selfishness and greed, where the wealthy get health care and insurance and the poor don't. Do you know . . . (APPLAUSE)

Do you know how much my AIDS care costs? Over $40,000 a year. Someone without insurance can't afford this. Even the drugs that I hope will keep me alive are out of reach for others. Is their life any less valuable? Of course not. This is not the America I was raised to be proud of, where rich people get care and drugs that poor people can't. We need health care for all. (APPLAUSE)

We need a leader who will say this and do something about it.

I believe in America, but not a leadership that talks about problems, but is incapable of solving them. Two HIV commission reports, with recommendations about what to do to solve this crisis, sitting on shelves, gathering dust.

We need a leader who will not only listen to these recommendations, but implement them.

I believe in America, but not with a leadership that doesn't hold government accountable. I go to Washington, to the National Institutes of Health, and say show me what you're doing on HIV. They hate it when I come because I try to tell them how to do it better. But that's why I love being a taxpayer, because it's my money, and they must feel accountable. (APPLAUSE)

I believe in an America where our leaders talk straight. When anyone tells President Bush that the battle against AIDS is seriously underfunded, he juggles the numbers to mislead the public into thinking we're spending twice as much as we really are. While they play games with numbers, people are dying.

I believe in America, but an America where there is a light in every hope. A thousand points of lights just wasn't enough. My house has been dark for too long. (APPLAUSE)

Once every generation, history brings us to an important crossroads. Sometimes in life, there is that moment when it's possible to make a change for the better. This is one of those moments. For me, this is not politics. This is a crisis of caring.

In this hall is the future. Women, men, of all colors saying, take America back. (APPLAUSE)

Thesis statement repeated three times. The theme, "We need a leader," of course, was the central message of the entire Democratic National Convention.

Notice, too, this dramatic parallel structure, ringing through the speech.

Transition and buildup to the solution.

Here Ms. Glaser makes clear
what she wants from the
audience. They knew it, of
course, before she started.

We are just real people wanting a more hopeful life. But words and ideas are not enough. Good thoughts won't save my family. What's the point of caring if we don't do something about it?

A president and a Congress that can work together so that we can get out of this gridlock and move ahead, because I don't win my war if the president cares and the Congress doesn't, or if the Congress cares and the president doesn't support the ideas.

This emotional appeal was
designed to stimulate the
listeners, but it really doesn't
fit the remainder of the speech
very well. It does, however,
provide a transition to the
dramatic challenge in the last
line.

The people in this hall, this week, the Democratic party, all of us can begin to deliver that partnership. And in November, we can all bring it home. (APPLAUSE)

My daughter lived seven years, and in her last year, when she couldn't walk or talk, her wisdom shone through. She taught me to love, when all I wanted to do was hate.

She taught me to help others, when all I wanted to do was help myself.

She taught me to be brave, when all I felt was fear.

This was the country that offered hope. This was the place where dreams could come true—not just economic dreams, but dreams of freedom, justice, and equality.

We all need to hope that our dreams can come true.

I challenge you to make it happen. Because all our lives, not just mine, depend on it. Thank you. (APPLAUSE)

From Elizabeth Glaser, Address to the Democratic National Convention, July 1992.

WILL CALIFORNIA BE INVITED TO THE NEXT INDUSTRIAL REVOLUTION?
BUDGET DEFICIT REDUCTION AND ECONOMIC GROWTH

ROBERT CIZIK, *CHAIRMAN AND CEO, COOPER INDUSTRIES, INC., AND CHAIRMAN NATIONAL ASSOCIATION OF MANUFACTURERS*

Delivered to Town Hall of California, Los Angeles, California, June 30, 1993

LONG AGO, a poet wrote a hymn of praise to the sturdy pioneers who settled in California. The poem and its author are long forgotten, but one line remains for all to see—etched in granite over the entrance to the California State Archives building in Sacramento. The line reads: "Bring Me Men to Match My Mountains."

If that poem were written today, that line would surely read, "Bring Me Men *and Women* to Match My Mountains," for it took both to tame a wild frontier. The point is still valid: A land needs determined, self-reliant people, with the ruggedness of mountains, to achieve greatness.

Sometimes, when our problems appear to be overwhelming, we describe them as "mountainous."

Today, in California, and across the nation, we have just such a problem. It's the need to create millions of new jobs while becoming more productive and more competitive in global markets. To meet the jobs challenge, we're going to need plenty of resourceful men and women.

And I'm proud to say we have those people in manufacturing.

As Chairman of the National Association of Manufacturers, I welcome every opportunity like this one, to talk about the importance of manufacturing to our economy. There are more than three trillion dollars worth of manufacturing transactions in this country every year.

Even some of the *words* we use are manufactured.

I was reminded of this a few years ago when Cooper Industries acquired McGraw-Edison, a corporation that descended from Thomas Edison's original company.

Thomas Edison received one thousand and ninety-three U.S. patents. We're all familiar with the light bulb, the phonograph, and motion pictures—to name just a few. But every day we use one of his inventions, for which he never received a patent, or a dime in royalties.

The story is that Edison had made a lot of significant improvements to Alexander Graham Bell's telephone and telephone switching system. The problem was that people were uncomfortable with it.

They didn't like the idea of picking up a telephone and talking to a total stranger. Also, there was no standard greeting to hail someone on the other end of the line. Bell suggested to his customers that they use the nautical term "Ahoy."

But Edison would have nothing to do with "Ahoy." So he put pen to paper and coined a brand new word all his own.

That word was "Hello."

It first appeared in American literature in 1880, when Mark Twain described the first telephone operators as "hello girls." Before long, everyone was saying "hello" to one another. In 1883, the only word Edison ever invented was published in the Oxford English Dictionary.

And so, I say to all of you—AHOY!—and thank you for inviting me here today.

About the time Edison and Bell were arguing over what to say on the telephone, Horace Greeley, the publisher and editor of the *New York Tribune,* was advising young men to go west and seek their fortunes on the new frontier. And west they went.

To California. The promised land. A land where dreams come true. By the 1920s, companies were flocking here—attracted by a pro-business political climate and a state economy larger than that of most nations.

It seemed there would be no end to it. Until now.

Recent news stories, about California's economic crisis, sound like bad movie reviews:

According to *Fortune* magazine, the state's current economic upheaval has spawned a "widespread fear that California's future might, indeed, be worse than its present."

Or as the *Los Angeles Times* succinctly put it: "The go-go days may be gone-gone forever."

I think, however, that the *Wall Street Journal* went a bit too far by suggesting that "The nation's economic landscape would look much better if California were floated out to sea."

Everyone in this room is painfully aware of the problems:

- The U.S. recession ended in March of 1991, but the California economy has continued in recession.
- The rest of the nation went from recession to a "jobless recovery," but California continued to lose ground as 900,000 jobs left the state.

- The Bank of America predicts that another 400,000 jobs will have left California by 1995.
- Last year, Los Angeles County lost 63,000 jobs—most of those from the manufacturing sector.

So, how *do* you stop the bleeding?

To answer that, we need to answer three questions:

First, we need to understand *why* we're not creating enough jobs in California, or the rest of the nation.

Second, we need to understand *why* President Clinton's job-creation efforts won't work.

And *third,* we need to consider *what* it will take to put more people in California, and more people in America, back to work.

Nationwide, we are experiencing a jobless recovery because of structural problems that are deterring normal job growth.

These problems were caused by excesses of the 80s, and by a whole new set of challenges.

The excesses included:

- Too much debt—both private and commercial.
- Too many empty office buildings.
- Excess industrial capacity, and
- A huge federal deficit that has kept interest rates high.

Couple these with:

- Scaled-back defense spending;
- A huge increase in non-production costs for companies, and
- The drive to increase productivity.

The result is *low growth* and *low profit margins*.

In the '60s, manufacturing profits averaged 9 percent.

In the '80s, they dropped to 7 percent.

Today, they average 5 percent.

Each tick downward precipitates more restructuring to bring costs into line.

There was a time when corporations could maintain profit margins in the face of cost increases by passing the increases on to customers as higher prices. This is rarely possible in today's world—where companies are basically price-takers, not price-setters.

Today, cost increases are seldom passed on to customers because doing so risks erosion of market share.

Instead, cost increases are shifted *backward*—in the form of reduced employment, lowered profits, and deferred capital spending.

This profit margin/job squeeze is being accelerated by enormous growth in nonproduction costs. By that I mean such things as health care costs, regulatory costs, legal costs, and increased payroll taxes.

Federal regulatory costs, for example, exceed $100 billion dollars a year.

That's *more* than the annual after-tax profits of *all* U.S. manufacturers combined!

This profit and job squeeze is a double whammy for California because of the high cost of doing business in this state.

California is losing one manufacturing-related job every minute of every working day.

They are being driven out by the runaway cost of worker's compensation, excessively high sales and use taxes, and the highest corporate tax rate of any of your six neighboring states.

Here in Los Angeles, before a new business can open its doors, it must gather at least a dozen permits from a maze of seventy-two city, county, regional, state, and federal regulatory agencies.

If you want to plant a tree in Los Angeles, you need eight permits.

If you're a manufacturer and you want to turn that tree into furniture, you need forty-seven permits.

Peter Ueberroth, who chairs the Council on California Competitiveness, suppressed his frustration recently by saying, "California is the most highly tuned, finely honed, *job-killing machine* that this country has ever seen."

And so it is—that the economy of our largest manufacturing state—the world's seventh largest trading partner—is in danger of running aground.

Obviously, it's time to change directions and to *do something to improve the business climate of California.*

It has never been more important to do so, ladies and gentlemen, because America has it within its power to turn this jobless recovery into much more than cyclical economic bounce.

We have the power to create a *new industrial revolution* in which new technologies and new processes enable dramatic increases in production and usher in a new age of opportunity.

Will California be invited? That's up to you, your elected representatives and the governor.

In a few minutes, I'll discuss what it will take to bring about a new industrial revolution. But first, let's examine why President Clinton's plan—*his* cure for American's economic problems—won't do it.

During his campaign—and in the Little Rock economic conference and his message to Congress—Mr. Clinton talked about his plan to reduce the deficit, generate more jobs, and renew the American Dream for our children.

Who could disagree with *these* objectives?

However, analysis leads us to conclude that the president's plan, as it is now structured, just won't work.

N-A-M's econometric model indicates that, by 1998, gross domestic product will be sixty billion dollars *lower* under the president's plan than it is today.

And, there will be 600,000 *fewer* jobs in the economy than if we did absolutely nothing at all!

The reason is, when you add up all the proposed tax increases in the president's plan and compare them to the proposed incentives through 1998, the tax *increases* far outweigh the tax *incentives.*

The difference—one hundred and twenty billion dollars in new taxes on business—creates *no* jobs, buys *no* capital equipment, and trains not a *single* worker. The president's emphasis on deficit reduction and job creation is right, but, his plan fails to reflect that purpose.

It's a plan that's internally inconsistent.

It ignores the fact that the deficit is out of control because spending is out of control. And spending is out control because neither Congress nor the administration is willing to control it.

Manufacturers want deficit reduction, as do all Americans. But we want it less as an end in itself than as a means to the *far more important goal* of long-term growth.

Manufacturing now generates 21 percent of gross domestic product with 16 percent of the work force. It supports half of all economic activity. It produces 80 percent of our merchandise exports, which was the one bright spot in our economy through the recession.

Exports and productivity are in our corner. But if the United States is to remain an economic superpower in the twenty-first century, we must *increase* exports and *raise* productivity far beyond current levels.

To do *that,* we must invest *more* in what I call the three T's—Tools, Training, and Technology.

The *tools*—new plants, equipment and machinery—require large-scale capital investment.

It takes cash to make business investments in new jobs, plants, and equipment. If we don't have the capital, we can't make the capital investments.

When I tell this to officials at the White House, they nod and say, "Yes, the president's plan will reduce cash flow, but that will be offset by a reduction in long-term interest rates."

Statements like that remind me of the veterinarian who decided to expand his business by cross-training as a taxidermist. Then, he put a sign in the window that said, "Either way, you get your *dog* back."

The Clinton Economic Plan originally included investment tax credits intended to encourage investment in new plants and equipment. But Clinton's I-T-C's with their offsets and limitations, fell far short of what was needed to stimulate capital formation.

Investment tax credits are usually good for the economy. But after some soul searching, N-A-M recommended that these weak proposals be abandoned in favor of lower corporate tax increases.

What's really needed is a permanent, nonincremental, 10 percent investment tax credit, targeted for productivity-enhancing equipment. That would raise real gross domestic product by $120 billion. It would create more than one-and-a-half million manufacturing jobs over the next five years.

As Ross Perot is fond of saying, "It's that simple."

What's not so simple is the current tax bill, now in the House-Senate Conference Committee. N-A-M was instrumental in removing the BTU tax from the Senate tax bill. But we can't say with any certainty that the BTU tax is dead—because it's still in the House version of the bill. There's always the possibility that it could be resurrected.

In fact, if the president has his way, it *will* be resurrected.

At this moment, it appears that the final version of the tax package will, nevertheless, fulfill Mr. Clinton's campaign promise to "soak-the-rich." And in the process of soaking wealthy individuals—his higher tax rate will also "soak" small businesses and small manufacturing companies.

"But, wait a minute!"—you're thinking—"Individual tax rates wouldn't affect small companies."

Wrong! Or as today's youngsters would say, "Not!"

The individual tax rates in the president's plan will affect almost every small business owner in this room. That's because many of you don't pay federal income taxes at the *corporate,* or Schedule C rate.

You file as "Subchapter S" corporations and are subject to the same tax rates as partnerships and sole proprietors. Your profits are declared as personal income and taxed at the *individual* rate.

The Clinton plan increases the tax rate for Schedule C corporations from 34 to 35 percent. That's a one percentage point change, for a tax increase of about 3 percent.

For individuals, however, the top rate will go from 31 to 42.5 percent. That's a tax *increase* of 37 percent!

In addition to partnerships and sole proprietors, these higher federal tax rates will affect one-and-a-half million Subchapter S companies. That includes almost *half* of all manufacturing companies.

These are the very same small businesses and small manufacturers that account for 90 percent of the new jobs in this country.

So let me ask the small business owners here today: Can *you* raise the prices of your products enough to offset a 37 percent tax increase, and still sell them? If not, that tax is going to come out of *your* pocket. *You* are going to make up for it by postponing the purchase of the *tools* you will need to participate in the new industrial revolution.

The second of my three Ts is for training.

The president is also emphasizing the importance of expanding and improving worker training.

Administration efforts are underway to consolidate training programs, provide better school-to-work transition, and improve on-the-job training.

Again, we agree with the president's call for a better-trained work force.

But if we want a world-class work force in the twenty-first century, then we in business and industry had better start growing our own, *with* or *without* government assistance.

Increasingly, in manufacturing we need people who are literate and numerate, people who can use a computer, read instructions, and solve problems. Some companies are teaching these skills to employees. But the most desirable way of instilling them is to make sure students don't leave school without them.

That's why companies are getting involved in business and school partnerships to improve the quality of public education.

The federal government can best spend our *tax* dollars by identifying training programs that work and encouraging their adoption on a nationwide basis.

I'm happy to say that N-A-M is already working with the Department of Labor—and has been for two years—to identify successful training strategies.

If we do nothing, a poorly educated work force will make us *all* poor.

Now, about my third T—technology.

Robert Solow won the Nobel Prize for showing that the rate of technological progress is more important to an industrialized country's growth—than the size of its labor force—or its investments in plant and equipment.

In other words: Technology drives economic growth.

The Clinton administration correctly embraces that concept. The president has proposed an increase in federal R&D to boost manufacturing competitiveness.

This is desperately needed in *process* innovation—in the *way* products are made—where manufacturing progress has been most impressive, and the challenge most daunting.

Ninety percent of large manufacturers in the United States use some form of advanced technology. Three out of four use computer-aided production equipment. Two out of three are skilled in computer-aided design. But less than half use manufacturing cells. Fewer, still, are adept at computer-aided and computer-integrated manufacturing or just-in-time manufacturing.

Many people don't realize that *half* the manufacturing in this country is performed by companies that employ less than fifty people each. Among these companies, the technology gap is wider and deeper than the Grand Canyon. The technology they need is on the shelf. The biggest obstacle to their adopting it, other than a lack of capital, is the inability of their workers to understand and use it.

This brings us full circle to the need for investment in tools and training.

My three Ts don't include trade, but they all feed into it. With 5 percent of the world's population, the United States produces 25 percent of the world's output.

We are *the* economic *superpower*.

As such, we cannot turn our back on the global economy. And we must take the *long-term* view of international trade.

Last month, I testified before the Senate Finance Committee in favor of the president's request for new fast-track authority for the Uruguay Round of the General Agreement on Tariffs and Trade.

In other forums, I'm often asked about NAFTA—the North American Free Trade Agreement. I always tell people that N-A-M is for it—my company is for it—and I'm for it, even though it may cause some *short-term* growing pains.

Since 1986, U.S. exports to Mexico have more than tripled. This growth has already increased U.S. employment. Fears of permanent and massive job losses, as a result of NAFTA, are simply unjustified. Jobs that are under pressure to move outside the U.S. will go, with or *without* NAFTA.

We need to remember that NAFTA will create the world's largest and richest free trade area.

Exports create jobs.

A rule of thumb is that every billion dollars in new export sales creates 24,000 American jobs.

U.S. exports to Mexico now provide jobs for more than 600,000 Americans. Under NAFTA, that could easily increase to *one million* American jobs—and California would benefit the most.

I've covered a lot of ground today, so let me sweep everything into one pile.

Here's what the nation, and therefore California, really need from the Clinton administration:

First, budget deficit reduction.

Some new tax revenue may be unavoidable, but cuts in government spending should be the driving force.

Second, we need incentives for real economic growth.

The best incentive would be an investment tax credit to enhance productivity.

The prescription for California is not so different.

In the movie *Cool Hand Luke,* Paul Newman is having a hard time adjusting to prison life in the deep South. The warden says to him, "What we have here is a *failure to communicate.*"

That's how I feel about the deep divide between manufacturing and our elected representatives. Many people in state capitols, in our nation's capitol, and in the White House, have never set foot in a factory—much less worked in one.

So what we've had here is a "failure to communicate."

The National Association of Manufacturers is trying to resolve this problem with a nationwide effort—to communicate the value of a strong manufacturing base to full economic recovery. We're trying to show elected officials, at all levels of government, the economic impact of manufacturing in the districts and the states they represent.

If you believe, as I do, that California's economy, and our national economy, need a strong manufacturing base to generate jobs and opportunity, you can help us communicate this message to your legislature, the Congress, and the administration.

Tell them it's time to *invest* in tools, training, and technology.

It's time to *revive* the American Dream.

It's *time* for a new industrial revolution.

From Robert Cizik, "Will California Be Invited to the Next Industrial Revolution?" in Vital Speeches, 669–672, August 15, 1993. Copyright © 1993 City News Publishing Co., Mount Pleasant, SC. Reprinted by permission from Robert Cizik, Chairman & CEO Cooper Industries, Inc.; Chairman, National Association of Manufacturers.

BURNING MONEY
The Waste of Your Tax Dollars

J. PETER GRACE, *CHAIRMAN, W. R. GRACE & CO. AND CO-CHAIRMAN,*
CITIZENS AGAINST GOVERNMENT WASTE

Delivered before the Commonwealth Club of California, San Francisco, California,
March 19, 1993

THANK YOU very much, Mary. I understand the Commonwealth Club celebrated its ninetieth anniversary last night, so I would like to congratulate the club and its 17,000 members and radio affiliates on their long record of public service to the citizens of the United States.

Now there's a lot of talk coming out of Washington these days about reducing the deficit and, at the same time, increasing govermnent spending. Well, let me tell you, that's like trying to lose weight on a diet of french fries and Big Macs.

The federal debt will reach $4.4 trillion at the end of the current fiscal year. That's $17,600 for every man, woman, and child in America. The average family of four owes $70,400 or more than double its annual income of $34,000.

What's more, despite all the hoopla about the Clinton tax increases and spending cuts, the debt will increase at an average rate of $200–$400 billion per year, which means that—at the end of the next four years—it will be somewhere between $5.2 and $6 trillion.

So what are we talking about here? Even if the Clinton program succeeds, which is unlikely, the debt will be a staggering $5.2 trillion in four years. All this talk about deficit reduction is just chicken feed. The debt is still rising year after year after year and, unless we do something, we're all doomed.

I'd like to read a statement.

"The budget should be balanced, the Treasury should be refilled, public debt should be reduced, the arrogance of officialdom should be tempered and controlled, and the assistance to foreign lands should be curtailed lest we become bankrupt."

Does that sound like a Johnny-come-lately statement to you, ladies and gentlemen?

Well, let me tell you, I am a plagiarist, but I am giving my source right now so that there will be no misunderstanding. I am disclosing my source immediately before you get me on this. These are the exact words of Cicero in 63 B.C., 2,056 years ago.

If that doesn't sound like a long time ago to you, you have a point because it is only 6½ percent of a trillion seconds. It takes 31,700 years, or 317 centuries, to count to a trillion seconds, and we are only in the twentieth century, so there's the same 6½ percent coming right back at you.

As a father and grandfather, I am greatly concerned about the future of our children and grandchildren. What right do we have to saddle them with a $5 trillion debt? This is intergenerational rape. It's stealing from piggy banks. As Thomas Jefferson said a long time ago, and I quote:

"The question of whether one generation has the right to bind another by the deficit it imposes is a question of such consequence as to place it among the fundamental principles of government. We should consider ourselves unauthorized *to saddle posterity with our debts, and normally bound to pay them ourselves."*

If present trends continue, there are only two possible outcomes—the Argentina model or the New York City model, and I know a little about both of them. We could go the way of Argentina and have massive inflation. When I first went to Argentina in 1946, the peso was trading at four to the dollar. Today, it's two trillion to the dollar—two trillion! Over the last five years alone, the inflation rate in Argentina has averaged 500 percent. You just keep printing money to pay off your debts, and eventually, the currency becomes worthless. Is that what we want for our children and grandchildren?

Or we could go the way of New York City in 1975. We could go bankrupt. People will stop buying our debt. We'll have no credit. Then what happens? We'll be a banana republic.

So we're not talking about the real issue when we talk about reducing the deficit from $332 billion this year to $293 billion next year, or by $339 billion over four years as claimed by the Clinton administration. That's not going to solve our problems.

The real solution is to eliminate the deficit entirely and then get rid of the federal debt. If we were really serious, we'd try to eliminate the debt in twenty years, or at the rate of $200 billion in a year.

That would take real sacrifice. That would mean a swing of $500 billion from our present pattern—$300 billion to eliminate the deficit and $200 billion to pay down the debt. That would be a real achievement.

The only way we can do this is by reducing wasteful spending and encouraging economic growth.

Let's talk about wasteful spending first, and let me give you an example of the kind of waste I'm talking about. This is a letter we received from one of our supporters in Citizens Against Government Waste, and it's addressed to the Secretary of Agriculture in Washington. It goes like this:

"Dear Sir:

"My friend, Ed Peterson, over at Wells, Iowa, received a check for $1,000 from the government for not raising hogs. So I want to go into the 'not raising hogs' business next year.

"As I see it, the hardest part of this program will be in keeping an accurate inventory of how many hogs I haven't raised.

"My friend, Peterson, is very joyful about the future of the business. He has been raising hogs for thirty years or so, and the best he ever made on them was $422 in 1968, until this year, when he got your check for $1,000 for not raising hogs.

"If I get $1,000 for not raising fifty hogs, will I get $2,000 for not raising one hundred hogs? I plan to operate on a small scale at first, holding myself down to about four thousand hogs not raised, which will mean about $80,000 the first year.

"Now another thing, these hogs I will not raise will not eat 100,000 bushels of corn. I understand that you also pay farmers for not raising corn or wheat. Will I qualify for payments for not raising wheat and corn not to feed the four thousand hogs I am not going to raise?

"Also, I am considering the 'not milking cows' business, so please send me any information on that too.

"In view of these circumstances, you understand that I will be totally unemployed and therefore plan to file for unemployment and food stamps.

"Be assured you will have my vote in the next election.

Patriotically yours,
/s/ John Partridge"

We found that in 1935, when there were 6.3 million farmers, the Agriculture Department employed twenty thousand people. Today, with only 2.1 million farmers, 50 percent of whom farm part-time, the number of federal farm-related employees has tripled to sixty thousand. At this rate, there will be one Agriculture Department employee for each farm in the year 2040.

Ten years ago, we argued that charging uniform deposit insurance premiums, regardless of the risk profile of the insured institution, was crazy. We strongly recommended risk-related premiums so that, say, the Morgan Guaranty Bank wouldn't pay the same deposit insurance premium as some fly-by-night S&L. But no action was taken. The deposit insurance mess has grown since then from a $20 billion problem in 1983, to what is now known as the $500 billion S&L bailout. And they still haven't taken our advice—uniform premiums are still charged, although belated charges are proposed for the future—$480 billion too late. That one recommendation of the Grace Commission would have saved taxpayers $480 billion.

We have 1,132 different and distinct domestic social programs being run at the federal level that will spend more than $1 trillion by 1997, or 61 percent of the budget. If the Russians have figured out that socialism doesn't work, how long before we catch on?

Why don't we give the president the line-item veto so he can knock out the federal study of cow belches or leafy spurge biocontrol? That's what the governors of forty-three states have—why not the president? The line-item veto would save taxpayers $10 billion in just the first year.

It's a sad fact that in the Congress of the United States there are only three CPAs—certified public accountants. Most of the rest are lawyers and, in my experience, lawyers use numbers like a drunk uses a lamppost—for support rather than illumination.

Here's my prescription for eliminating wasteful government spending:

First, give the president the line-item veto—one-year savings: $10 billion.

Second, cut government overhead by 10 percent across the board. When businesses get into trouble, they slash overhead and reduce spending. That's exactly what the federal government should do—one-year savings: $27 billion.

Third, implement the remaining recommendations of the Grace Commission—one-year savings: $20.5 billion.

Fourth, eliminate all unnecessary and redundant Defense Department procurement regulations—one-year savings: $7 billion.

Fifth, eliminate all agricultural subsidies—one-year savings: $5.9 billion.

Sixth, require federal, state, and local agencies to issue a W-2 form to Welfare recipients—one-year savings: $5 billion.

Seventh, close all unnecessary military bases—one-year savings: $2 billion.

And the list goes on and on and on.

All told, the Council for Citizens Against Government Waste—that's CCAGW—estimates that at least $125 billion in one-year savings is available and ready to be implemented right now. They have 537 well-documented examples of government waste, 3½ times the number Clinton is talking about. So what are we waiting for?

The other key to eliminating the deficit and reducing the debt is strong economic growth. By increasing the tax base, we can generate additional revenues and, at the same time, create new jobs for all Americans.

Unfortunately, during the last four years, we have managed to turn the clock back to the failed policies of the 1970s. We have turned away from the *politics of growth* and allowed a return to the *politics of envy.* We are now divided against one another, and the great engine of American economic growth has been stopped dead in its tracks.

In the meantime, after forty-five years of sacrifice and perseverance, we have won the Cold War. We have witnessed the total failure of communism on the European continent and in the former Soviet Union. Yet in the last four years, we have, at the same time, allowed our own system to gravitate back to the failed socialistic concepts of income redistribution and broadening federal intrusion in the marketplace. At the height of the West's triumph over communism, we have embraced the very ideas which are at the root of its collapse.

There is a well-known Russian joke about two neighbors—one who had a cow and one who didn't. The neighbor without the cow was consumed by jealousy night and day that he didn't have a cow and his neighbor did, until one day he found a bottle by the side of the road. In the bottle was a genie who was so grateful for being released that he granted the cow-less Russian one wish—anything he desired. The Russian needed only a second to answer and shouted: "I wish that you would kill my neighbor's cow."

Now that's what I call the politics of envy. Everyone is reduced to the lowest common denominator. The 1993 version goes something like this: if you work hard and are successful, you should be penalized for your hard work. In other words, the only people who should pay more in taxes are the very people who save and invest and make the economy go in the first place. These are mainly two-income families who work hard and save to provide a decent living for themselves and their children.

That is the same kind of thinking that brought us the so-called "luxury tax" that was imposed on expensive cars, yachts, jewelry, and private aircraft. Policymakers looked at "X" number of cars and yachts sold before the tax was imposed and easily calculated the potential tax revenue with a pocket calculator. But a funny thing happened on the way to the treasury: People stopped buying expensive yachts and cars. Instead of the rich suffering from this tax, 17,000 middle-class workers in the boat-building industry were thrown out of work. The net effect on the treasury was a loss of hundreds of millions of dollars in payroll and income taxes. The luxury tax was a classic example of the politics of envy at work.

As Margaret Thatcher has said:

"When you take into the public ownership a profitable industry, the profits soon disappear. The goose that laid the golden egg goes broody. State geese are not good layers."

What the politicians don't tell you is that 90 percent of all the personal taxable income in America is reached at the $45,000 level.

Seventy-five percent of all the personal taxable income is reached at the $25,000 level.

So when the politicians say they're going to tax "the rich," hold on to your wallet. They mean, as we all know by now, anyone making more than $30,000 a year.

Of the top 20 percent of U.S. taxpayers, 83 percent are two-income families. So if you and your spouse both work hard and make $30,000 a year each—look out, you're both rich.

Since 1947—over the last forty-six years—every time Congress raised taxes by $1, they increased spending by $1.59. Is it any wonder then that, in all but two of those years, we have run staggering deficits? Or that the last time the federal budget was balanced was in 1969? History tells us that the one sure way *not* to reduce the deficit is to raise taxes.

Okay, then what about economic growth? Bad news again. Here's how the new administration plans to stimulate job creation:

(1) increase corporate and personal income taxes;

(2) increase the cost of doing business with a new tax on energy consumption;

(3) tighten all environmental regulations so U.S. companies spend more on compliance—much more—than their foreign competitors;

(4) threaten regulations and price controls, causing corporations to postpone decisions;

(5) threaten private corporations with quota lawsuits, since most jobs are created in small companies which don't have the staff to fight them.

So this is just foolishness and another example of the politics of envy that is polarizing our great country.

According to the National Association of Manufacturers, the Clinton administration's proposals add up to $56.5 billion in business tax cuts and $170.1 billion in business tax increases between now and 1998. The net reduction of $113.6 billion in corporate cash flows will inevitably reduce investment over the next five years.

Similarly, the N-A-M economists calculate that the entire Clinton program will generate only 150,000 new jobs by next year, not the 400,000 claimed by the administration. And, more importantly, it will actually *reduce* new job creation by 1.2 million over the next five years.

We're slowly killing the goose that laid the golden egg.

Let's get our priorities straight.

Let's not penalize hard work and success; let's encourage it.

Let's not make the economic pie smaller. Let's make it bigger.

Let's not raise one dime in new taxes until we've *first* cut wasteful government spending to the bone.

Here's what the new Secretary of Transportation said last week in an interview with *USA Today:*

> *"There's a lot of waste in the federal government. We have more people than we need . . . I'm constantly amazed at what my department has. I was intrigued to learn we have three hundred planes. I have two planes at National Airport I don't use. I fly coach commercial. But one of the planes cost $24 million. We have forty-something cars. We don't need all those things. What astounds me is we were all told we had a very austere, conservative government in place for the last twelve years that was very much committed to cutting government, and I see all these perks, lavish perks all over the department, and I ask the question, 'Why?' "*

Thank you, Mr. Secretary. The taxpayers of America join you in asking the same question—"Why?"

So let's not start any new spending programs until we first get rid of the waste that is everywhere in the government.

Get behind Citizens Against Government Waste and join the 535,000 Americans who care about the future of their country and are willing to stand up and be counted. Call 1–800–BE–ANGRY and find out how you can get involved.

Remember, Congressmen have only two objectives: the first is to get elected, and the second is to get re-elected.

Harry Truman once said that limiting Congressional terms would "help cure senility and seniority, both terrible legislative diseases." If we can put a stop to the imperial Congress, to the power of incumbency; if we can make our elected representatives run scared and be held accountable for their actions, then we are on our way to a better America and a better future for us all.

But if we sit back and do nothing, if we simply let events run their course, when our children and grandchildren grow up and realize what we've done to them, ask yourselves—will they ever forgive us?

Thank you very much.

From J. Peter Grace, "Burning Money: The Waste of Your Tax Dollars" in *Vital Speeches,* July 1, 1993. Copyright © 1993 City News Publishing Co., Mount Pleasant, SC.

OUR ATTITUDE ABOUT WOMEN
DEMOCRACY IS NOT A SMOOTH SAUCE

BERNARD SHAW, *CNN PRINCIPAL WASHINGTON ANCHOR, LECTURER*

Delivered at the Alfred M. Landon Lectures on Public Issues Series, Kansas State University, Manhattan, Kansas, November 20, 1992

The ancient Greek sophists taught their speech students to introduce a harsh or unpleasant comment or passage with gentle and positive remarks. Bernard Shaw must have been mindful of this advice. The first six minutes of the speech compliment and build up listeners, only hinting at the harsh message he plans as the focus for the remainder of his speech.

LADIES AND GENTLEMEN: I come to you at the invitation of one of the finest universities to grace this land. I come to you as a fellow-midwesterner—just two states away—an Illinoisan who is fond of simplicity and directness, two of many characteristics Kansans appreciate.

The introduction seeks to establish speaker credibility. "I am one of the good guys. Our Democratic system is also good, but it may not always seem so overseas."

I come to you as a fellow American . . . proud that our nation—once again—has changed presidential leadership without one mortar shot fired in the process . . . and *relieved* that a numbingly too-long campaign is over!

There were two surprises in this election: Bob Dole was re-elected . . . and Kansas voted Republican!

In capitals around the world, leaders and their advisers are squirming. Most were pulling for our incumbent president. Had you polled them after the euphoric Desert Storm victory in the Gulf War, when George Bush was riding an 80 percent-plus popularity wave, those leaders would have said Bush was a re-election certainty.

But as our electoral marathon for the White House unfolded and as candidates dwindled—so did the certitude in world capitals about who would be raising his hand to take the oath of office on January 20th, 1993.

Overseas, observers seem to forget that Americans are utterly serious about choosing a president—that they are capable of surprising holders of the smart money—that Americans are capable of electing a general, a peanut farmer, an actor, a haberdasher, a governor from Arkansas.

Generally, as a people, we have been blessed to have solid performances from most of the forty-one presidents in our nation's history.

Democracy is not a smooth sauce. Democracy is a chili of different currents, changes, and contradictions. Democracy is the lone dish in constant need of seasoning, stirring, tasting. Democracy is never . . . never done.

Here begins a long transition. Notice how cleverly Mr. Shaw turns the focus from pride to shame. He seems to be saying: "Our diversity is our source of strength. We are the beneficiaries of that diversity, and we're good. We've been generous to a fault. We have provided international leadership, and we have adapted to shifting pressures with many important changes." All of this leads up to the thesis statement.

The United States of America were not always united. We were not and will never be a nation of one race . . . one religion . . . one tongue.

Some think, indeed some say—if only we had the homogeneity of the Japanese, the Chinese, the British—we wouldn't be bothered by problems which slow us down.

That cannot be because this is not our history. Our richness is directly because of what we are—*many* forming *one*. Our nation's greatness is its potential to become greater.

Each of us is an instrument for change. Most of us want to awaken one morning—in *this* lifetime—to say our long racial nightmare is over, our fire in the night has been put out.

But as we begin streaming by the millions into cinemas to see the movie *Malcolm X* . . . as we wonder when and where will the next Los Angeles explode in deadly fury . . . as we struggle to dissolve with reason and understanding racial and ethnic stereotypes, we know the next generation will receive from us the state of the nation as we leave it for them.

If you, an American, fear for your country . . . if you, an American, agonize over our faults and fissures, remember this: no other nation—no other nation on the face of this earth—is struggling to do what we as a people profess to believe in and have undertaken to make reality.

"You ought to believe something in life . . . believe that thing so fervently that you will stand up with it till the end of your days."

Dr. Martin Luther King Jr. said those words.

Alfred M. Landon believed and acted out those words.

Landon. King. Two Americans who made their lives instruments for change.

What they felt, the many causes they fought, held this nation's and this world's interest and attention.

We are the beneficiaries of their legacy. It is regrettable that we sometimes take for granted what two of our finest sons did *unselfishly* to make life better for all.

Globally, we Americans have been selfless to a fault.

Japan's and Europe's ashes of war became our challenge to help rebuild with billions of dollars in massive aid and assistance. Some argue we did the job too well.

Today the playing field is not level.

Europe is acquiring economic and trading muscle that cannot be ignored, and Japan's proficiency in the international marketplace is legendary.

For decades we helped the world community while paint was peeling off our walls back home.

We have sent life-saving care and medicines abroad, knowing full well that our own people in urban and rural communities were and are in need.

World events whipsawed our leaders in Washington.

First things first: Our collective defense of ourselves and our allies had priority.

Communism's demise has been the most expensive death in the political history of mankind. Our federal treasury bears the bruises of this long, worthwhile fight. Our national debt—our federal budget deficits are the shrapnel of battle.

Those world leaders and their advisers worry because, regardless of the language they speak, they understand clearly what the American people said when they voted on November 3rd: Instead of fixing the world's problems, fix our problems now!

Those same American voters know their nation's role is too pivotal to tolerate withdrawal symptoms, too crucial to relax vigilance.

They know that United States leadership is costly, but they are demanding and expecting action at home on several fronts.

Ironic, isn't it? Ironic that the relatively peaceful and prosperous corridors we helped carve out are now the gauntlets along which we must compete for jobs and marketshare.

We as a people know what is happening. The alarms have long since sounded. We are mobilizing.

Our schools must be and are becoming better. Our production lines are leaner and more efficient. Everyone hearing my voice knows that competition is global.

But ladies and gentlemen, we are not putting on the field *all* our players. Nor are *all* those players being rewarded fairly.

Thesis statement, repeated in three different forms.

That is what I really have come to speak to you about this morning.

We cannot win this fight if we do not change our attitude about women. Sexism is a poison we have been drinking for too long.

Twenty-two months ago, the United States led twenty-seven other nations in the Gulf War. Erase the hot exchange of words, put aside Saddam Hussein, and you see *why* that war was fought.

The Gulf War was about a resource precious and essential to the industrialized world—black gold—oil.

In the fullness of time, everyone in this auditorium will be dead. To learn about us, people will either read or watch hours of video images. "They fought a war to protect a valuable resource," some will conclude.

But *some* looking more closely at *how* our society functioned—looking more *critically*—some will say, "But *why* weren't those Americans as fierce and as passionate about their greatest resource, their people?"

Exemplary use of rhetorical questions, followed by evidence and arguments designed to prove that America abuses women in principle and in fact.

Especially—*why* . . . *why* . . . did they abuse women—in principle and in fact? Why?

In a letter to her husband John, Abigail Adams wrote . . .

"If particular care and attention are not paid to the ladies, we are determined to foment a rebellion, and will not hold ourselves bound by any laws in which we have no voice or representation."

She wrote that more than one hundred years ago.

In Washington, before election night, Mrs. Quentin Burdick of North Dakota, Barbara Mikulski of Maryland, and Nancy Kassebaum of Kansas were surrounded in one of the most exclusive male-oriented clubs in this country.

Now they have company—from Illinois . . . from Washington state . . . from California.

Regardless of your opinion of how the all-male members of the Senate Judiciary Committee comported themselves in the confirmation hearings of Supreme Court Justice

Clarence Thomas last fall—the *manner* in which law Professor Anita Hill was questioned and treated—had a profoundly catalytic and yes . . . explosive impact on American politics and American women. This nation will never be the same.

More than one Senate candidate said she was outraged by the tough and rude handling of Professor Hill and what she was insisting happened.

Resonating throughout this election campaign was one undeniable truth: Most American men possess in their psyches a winking double standard for the charge, the complaint of sexual harassment.

Reminder: In the 1988 presidential election—by nearly *6* million—women outvoted men, or by almost 20 percent.

Ladies and gentlemen, women now constitute nearly *50* percent of the United States work force. Yet, where they work full time, they barely earn an average of 75 cents of the dollar taken home by their male co-workers.

Why?

And then there's the stench of discrimination in promotions along executive row—described by one of the most odorous euphemisms ever thought up—"The Glass Ceiling."

Promotion—pay. What do you think of these words from Dr. Fran Conley? She's a neurologist at Stanford University. Quote:

> *"I've been told over the years I don't need to be paid as much because I'm a woman—because I'm married. They're married!"*

Women are fighting this poison in our workplace on all fronts, enduring the frustration of proving job discrimination, of proving sexual harassment and abuse, of resisting the dumping ground for female managers.

Talk about barriers to the top!

The Center for Creative Leadership says on average nine out of ten female managers are pushed into staff jobs, such as human resources and public relations, positions that do not lead to the top.

If people are not given work experiences to broaden themselves, how can they ever get the opportunity to be more responsible?

Presently fewer than 6 percent of all the top executives in the United States are female.

This problem is exacerbated by a natural human tendency to surround yourself with people like you. Labor Secretary Lynn Martin says if the person at the top is male and white, quote:

> *"Invariably . . . he picks people around him just like him."*

As this happens each day in our cities and each day in our states, *each day* we as a nation of people *suffer*.

Thesis statement. Notice the shift, now, to a more emotional tone. Shaw is angry, and is using his anger with powerful effect.

And when this great nation suffers, we *lose* another step in competition, because we are failing to use fully our most precious talent and resource, our own people.

Federal, state, and local laws are there. But laws are given life and force by people and companies willfully looking after their best interests, and fortunately that *is* happening, but too slowly.

Some companies and some executives are acting with conscience to "change" the way the marketplace and society treat women.

Some!

Folks, we are talking about our very existence, our survival as a competing nation, a nation whose greatness is its ability to become greater!

But the hour is late.

I have discussed, very briefly, matters of money, position, wealth. But what of the essence of life . . . health?

Internal summary used as a transition.

Did you know that heart disease is the number-one killer of American women? Sixty-one percent of the people dying from strokes are women. According to studies, heart disease many times goes undetected in women until it is virtually too late. The director of the National Institutes of Health, Dr. Bernadine Healy, says, as a result, 49 percent of women suffering heart attacks die within one year, compared with 31 percent of men.

One reason for this gap is that over the years billions more research dollars have gone into studying heart disease among men, than women, especially women over sixty-five.

That is a damned outrage! Women outlive men, and they have heart attacks *later* than men.

My point in all this is simple: We must change. We must change—*now!* Our attitudes must change, and change in some most basic of ways.

Restatement of central idea again. The speaker never lets his audience forget what he's talking about. Notice, also, how Shaw balances a general statement with specifics. Principle—specific instance, principle—specific instance.

Example: My boss is Ted Turner. When we are together, I don't greet him by saying, "Hi, Ted, honey, or darling, or sweetie."

If I don't do that with him, or with other males with whom I work, what makes me think I should be able to do it with the women!

We must stop subjecting women to subtle and blatant abuses we men would never tolerate!

And I will recognize the instant that time arrives, especially in the business I know—television news.

Example: There are men, over age fifty, on television reporting news. They are wrinkled, they are gray, they are *experienced!*

It is time for television and our nation in general to stop this deluding fixation with youth and respect the right of women, especially in television news, to wrinkle . . . and to gray . . . on the job.

Ladies and gentlemen, we must change so that those who study what we did, correctly conclude that our society matured and affirmed that a woman does not have to out-man a man to be respected—and respectable.

From Bernard Shaw, "Our Attitude About Women" in *Vital Speeches,* 245–249, February 1, 1993. Copyright © 1993 City News Publishing Co., Mount Pleasant, SC.

SPEECH TO THE POLICE CONFERENCE OF THE STATE OF NEW YORK

MARIO M. CUOMO

Presented during the campaign for the governorship of New York, Albany, March 24, 1982

I'm pleased to be here. Peter [Reilly, president] made it sound as though I were doing you a big favor by coming, and I'm not. You do me the favor by having me.

I'm pleased to have this opportunity to talk to you today for a few minutes. The reason I need to start early and get out on time is that the governor has a meeting at ten o'clock with just the legislative leaders. We have trouble again on the budget—it has not been put together. We're trying desperately hard to avoid the kind of debacle we had last year, when we were forty-two days late—at which time, when asked about a budget not coming in on time for three years in a row and how I felt about that, I said frankly, "I feel very bad, because it's another symptom of a society that's gone lawless."

We all talk about violent crime and the increase of violent crime; we all know about that. But if you look around, it's happening everywhere. In every part of our society there's a loss of discipline, a lack of respect for authority, for the rule, for the necessity to defer to the rule. And here is a legislature and a whole government assembled in Albany whose principal function legally is to get the budget done on time. And three years in a row, we didn't live up to the law, while at the same time we were trying to tell the people of this state that they must. So the budget debacles are a serious problem that goes way beyond the $30 million it cost us last year to be late. And that's what we're talking about at ten o'clock this morning.

I wish that I could talk to you about libraries and education and economic development and the things I would do with money in this state if I were the governor—if I were the king. All the wonderful things we've not done that we'd want to do.

We have a whole generation of people in wheelchairs who will never live a reasonable existence because we can't figure out how to transport them. We have senior citizens in Clinton County and Essex County literally stealing from free lunches so that they have something to eat at night. We have 14 percent of the population unemployed in Buffalo. We have problems of every kind that we ought to be directing our attention to, and we're distracted by another problem that we have to talk about whether we want to or not.

I don't like saying it, because it's a disgrace that we have to say it, but the biggest problem in this society today, the one that comes before all the others, is the problem of keeping law and order.

Some time ago a fellow—Teddy White—wrote a book, *In Search of History.* He was talking about Chungking in 1939 and the Communists and why it was that communism was so appealing to the Chinese at that time. White said, "It's because the first obligation of government is to keep people safe from one another and from the hordes, from the attackers, and they did that."

We're not doing it in this state. It's never been worse. We talked about it at the last convention. I've talked about it ever since. I've talked about it for seven years, and it gets worse every year.

I've talked about being born and raised in the 103rd Precinct in South Jamaica. You know that was supposed to be a tough community in those days. Everybody fought. You had gang wars, and someone might even stick you with a knife occasionally. But it was nothing like what it is now. The violence is sick, it's deep, it's penetrating, it's irrational, and it's everywhere.

What do we do about it as a society? Well, I'll tell you. I said in my announcement—and again I say it reluctantly because I'd rather not have to deal with this as the first priority—that when I become governor, the first priority for me will be to do everything we possibly can to bring down the grotesque crime rate. This is a pledge I made to my family and to myself as well as to you. Because crime has struck us the way it has struck everybody.

I'm a lieutenant governor. I have state troopers; I'm protected. I know every cop in New York City, I think—I taught a lot of them. I knew them when they were sergeants, and now they're inspectors. I even knew Sid Cooper, who is in charge of internal security for the New York City Police Department and became chief inspector.

I and my family should be safe in New York City, yet my daughter got attacked twice by the same guy down the block from our house at four-thirty in the afternoon, in broad daylight. We haven't caught him yet. We have his picture, or we think we have his picture—we have the police artist's rendition. We've got everybody looking for him, but we haven't caught him. At four-thirty in the afternoon both times, down the block from my house, in a "good" community—a beautiful girl, eighteen years old.

Now she'll never be the same, unless God is very, very good to us. And we're on our knees thanking God that she wasn't badly hurt; that she wasn't raped, that nothing worse happened to her, that she didn't get killed. So I feel it, and we feel it—the passion. If my son ever got his hands on this guy—forget my son, if I ever did, I cannot predict how I would behave. I'm not a saint, and I'm not God. And if you stood that person in front of me and said, "There he is," I don't know what I would do.

So I'm not shocked that a whole society that sees this day after day—that sees police mowed down, that sees nuns brutalized, that sees old women raped—should say, "My God, you've got to do something about this. And you've got to make the ultimate response, you've got to give us capital punishment. Give us something tough, if only because we must say to this world, 'We will not live this way any more!' " I understand that. I understand the feeling. People have had it for a long time in the history of civilization.

But I think we have to do something more basic about crime. I think one of the problems with that feeling is that politicians have used the death penalty to eclipse more important questions, more important things that need to be done.

I think basically what we have to do—and every penologist will tell you this, and everybody who ever wrote a book on criminology, and everybody who was ever on the street—is this: we've got to convince potential criminals that we're going to catch them, convict them, and can them. And that we're going to do it for sure. They've got to know they're going to pay a price.

The percentage of arrests for crimes committed is down. I don't care what the book says. You ask anybody who will tell you the truth in New York City or in Buffalo—for crimes committed, the percentage of arrests is way down. It has to be. There are a lot of crimes we don't even pursue anymore. Burglary in New York City: Who in the heck investigates a burglary in New York City? Who has the police? Who has the forces to investigate burglaries? If you're lucky and the car is going by and you see a guy coming through the window, then maybe you'll be able to make the arrest.

We have to catch them; they have to know they're going to be caught. We have to convict them; they have to know they are going to get convicted. And we have to can them; there has to be a place where they pay a price. It's not happening now. Now they know that the chances are we're not going to catch them. And if we do catch them, the chances are they won't get convicted. Twenty-six arrests and no trial—the death penalty is not going to frighten that kid because he knows nothing is going to happen to him.

I talked to an attorney yesterday from South Jamaica, my old community, who told me to bring these kids into the judge for sentencing and tell them, "Take the stuff out of your pockets. No hash, none of that stuff, because you may go to jail, and if you go to jail, they'll search you and find the stuff." But the kids bring it anyway. Why? Because they're not going to go to jail, and they know it. They go in with the stuff still in their pockets, and they come out of the damn place with the stuff still in their pockets. And you think you're going to change that by saying, "We're going to have the death penalty"?

If they do get convicted, we have a place to put them—a prison cell. We have to do something with them when we get them in Auburn for nine years. What do you do with them? Should we teach them some kind of skill, give them some kind of shot, do something about getting them a job when they get out?

Well, these are hard questions. We need more police, number one. And more state troopers. New York City is down about ten thousand police since 1972. Ten thousand fewer police than in 1972. Is the death penalty going to change that?

We need better prosecutorial capacity. We need more judges. We blew nineteen indictments in Brooklyn because there were no court clerks ready—the cop was ready, the witness was ready, the D.A. was ready, and the judge was on time, but they didn't have clerks.

We need prison cells—yet we lost the argument last year for the Prison Bond Issue. For all the people screaming for the death penalty and outraged at violence, when it came time to put some money up for the prisons, they wouldn't do it.

Will more police and judges and clerks and prison cells cost money? Of course, they will cost money. But what I'm saying to you is that everything worthwhile costs money, and this has to be the number one priority.

After you agree to spend the money, you have to learn to spend it more intelligently. You have to *manage* the system. You know what we don't have in this state? With all the police we have, local and state troopers, D.A.'s everywhere, prosecutors everywhere, an attorney general's office, the Feds you have to tie into, rehabilitation programs, parole, probation—we have no single place where all of that is coordinated statewide. Does that make sense? I don't think so. We coordinate everything else. We coordinate education. But there's no single place in state government where criminal justice is coordinated.

This year, for the first time, the governor, in response to that need, has asked Tom Coughlin of Corrections to put together a panel and at least start talking. But there has to be more than talk. There has to be a working, coordinative mechanism. We're just getting started in New York.

Now let me talk about my position on the death penalty. The truth is that I don't believe it works; that I remember this state when we had it; that I don't believe it deters; that I don't believe it protects my daughter or my mother. I believe it is a "copout," and I believe that the politicians have used it for years to keep from answering the real questions, the questions like these: how come we're short some ten thousand police? How come the state troopers are paid so little in this state, where they're supposed to be so important? How come we have run out of prison cells? How come probation and parole are not all that they should be? How did we get here? Politicians don't want to deal with those questions. So they deal with a nice, simple question—the electric chair—and that gets everybody off the hook.

Now, to those of you who want the death penalty, and I assume that's most of you, I want to say at least this: "Look, if you want the death penalty, at least don't let them con you. Insist on cops, insist on prosecutors. Insist! Don't let them buy you cheap." Hey, if I were a policemen, what I would want is a cop to my left and a cop to my right. You ask the fellows in New York City who are ten thousand short or the troopers upstate—in Herkimer County one night, there was one trooper on duty in all of Herkimer County—ask them what they'd like. I think "more police" is an answer they'd give you.

In the end, the people will decide for better or for worse what they want. I hope they will come to agree with me. I hope with all my heart that they will agree with me, because as much as I love and respect you, I think on this issue you're wrong, and I feel that deeply.

That's all that I feel on criminal justice that I can tell you in ten and a half minutes. If you have any questions, now or later, I'd be delighted to address them.

I'll add only this. I intend to stay in this race until the very end. I intend to be governor of this state. When I am, your concerns—what you need, what you are, what you represent—will be very, very important to me. There won't be anything more important. I pledge that to you. And I don't think you've ever heard anybody say about Cuomo that he didn't mean it when he said it—and he didn't live up to his word.

Thank you.

COMMENCEMENT SPEECH
VERNON E. JORDAN, JR.

A commencement calls for positive and uplifting remarks in a very brief speech. Sometimes, the speakers choose the opportunity to advance a political agenda. This brief (about 18 minutes) address by Vernon E. Jordan, Jr., to the graduating class of his alma mater *meets all the criteria for a good commencement address, and as well, advances a political idea. As you read the speech, try to imagine yourself in Jordan's audience. You can almost hear his voice.*

Thirty-six years ago, on a June day very much like this in Blackstock Stadium, my DePauw classmates and I sat where you sit anxiously, nervously waiting to be granted our hard-earned bachelors of arts degrees. Early in the program, as today, President Russell J. Humbert introduced the highly distinguished chairman and chief executive officer of a top-10 Fortune 500 company speaking on the subject "Conformity or Compromise." Our commencement speaker gave us a rather thoughtful, long, dull, boring speech of sound and fury signifying, we thought, absolutely nothing.

So as I rise to address you, I have great empathy for your situation. I sympathize with your anxiety. But believing as I do in equal opportunity, I plan to do to you what my commencement speaker did to me. (Laughter)

I came to DePauw University forty years ago from the South, from a segregated, ill-equipped, overcrowded, double-sessioned high school where I studied in 1951 from a plane geometry book that had been used by white students in Atlanta in 1935. In my hometown, Atlanta, public accommodations—libraries, parks, buses, water fountains and courtrooms—were all segregated.

When I traveled north to this campus, I found some similarities. I was the only black in my class. There were five blacks in the entire school body. The black barber in town would not cut my hair. I could not join a fraternity. Social mobility was limited. I couldn't get a beer at Moore's Bar, and the Greencastle theater was more welcoming if I sat upstairs.

Despite the sometimes inconvenient circumstances, I received an excellent education here. DePauw University expanded my mind, broadened my horizons, lifted my sights, and prepared me to serve and to lead. DePauw University nurtured my growth and maturity. I made lasting friendships here, and if I had my life to live over again, I would return to this place.

And I say to you as Daniel Webster said of another school in another time, "It is a small college, and yet there are those who love it." I too love DePauw and I thank you, President Bottoms, for this homecoming. And, sir, it is with honor and humility that I accept the John McNaughton Medal for public service.

I love DePauw more because of the way DePauw has changed. Today's DePauw is more diverse, more open, more in tune with what America is and what America can become. Like other colleges and universities, and indeed all American institutions, DePauw faces some big challenges in adapting to that diversity.

Diversity means a culture of inclusion, an environment that welcomes and values the differences among people of varied backgrounds; it recognizes that all people contribute to our society and that America's strength lies in the variety of its people's cultures and traditions. Diversity is a means to an end—the creation of an open, pluralistic, integrated society.

But since many people twist the meaning of diversity to fit their own agenda, let me say here what diversity is not. Diversity is not an excuse to substitute flattering myths for history, to distort the curriculum, or to excuse self-segregation and self-exclusion.

I am quite frankly disturbed that so many of this generation's beneficiaries of diversity refuse to embrace it and instead do to themselves what the segregationists did to those before them. Alumni and student associations organized along racial and ethnic lines are perfectly legitimate expressions of diversity, but insisting on single-race dormitories or racially exclusionary activities are not. Such practices subvert diversity, which values and respects all people and seeks to bring them together, not drive them further apart.

The introduction sets the tone, and also establishes Mr. Jordan as a warm human being.

Even while complimenting DePauw as a fine school, Jordan sets up his key idea— that Americans must adapt to change, to diversity—and that these graduates are responsible to see that it happens.

Study this impressive use of definition carefully. Notice how it leads up to and justifies the need case.

Creating diverse institutions is a difficult task because our history has emphasized separation and exclusion. Racism and prejudice have been negative forces throughout our history. We must overcome them if we are to prosper in the new century ahead. We need only look at places like Bosnia to see where the alternative leads.

All America, in my judgement, will have to pull together because the world is changing. This graduating class enters a world very different from the world of my class of 1957. When I left DePauw, the Cold War was at its height, America's economy was unchallenged, and its military might was contested only by the Soviet Union, and America was just beginning to deal with civil rights.

Thesis statement.

You now enter a world no longer threatened by superpower conflict and an America whose laws, if not its practices, recognize the rights of all its citizens. But technology and a new global marketplace have changed our economy beyond recognition. Your careers will depend, not only on the education you received at DePauw University and the lifelong learning that you will do, but also on obscure, little-understood developments.

Where and how you work over your lifetime will be influenced by the discoveries of scientists made in Silicon Valley, Tokyo, and Stuttgart. By policies that encourage economic growth and the revival of our cities by the terms of trade treaties negotiated at the Group of Seven summit meeting in Tokyo and by the passage of the North American Free Trade Agreement.

So if you want to exercise some control over your destiny, you will have to get involved in the world around you. Democracy is not a spectator sport, and you need to be participants in the political and policy decisions that will affect your lives.

As a lifelong Democrat, I'm not sure how hard to press that point. Because unless DePauw has changed a great deal more than I think it has, you graduates are probably the exception to the rule that youth and liberalism go together. In my days here, there were about six hundred young Republicans and six members of the Jackson Club. Bill Clinton may have changed that ratio a tad since you may have more in common with the saxophone player than the horseshoe pitcher.

But whatever your political affiliation, Republican, Democrat, or Independent, it is vital for you to be fully informed about the issues of our day and to participate in the public debate on those issues. The key word is *informed*. DePauw has prepared you to think critically and to rise above stereotyped opinions, whatever their source. Some crucial, difficult, almost insoluble policy issues are on the front burner of America today. We are indeed playing catch-up after a dozen years of national administrations that said government is the enemy.

The public recognized the need for change in America last November when it elected my friend and fellow southerner William Jefferson Clinton president of the United States. Bill Clinton won because more Americans believed that the Clinton program made more sense than the Draconian solutions offered by Ross Perot, or the failed solutions offered by George Bush.

And Bill Clinton did some amazing things for Democrats in that election. He won the active support of some very respected corporate leaders and former military leaders. He won the suburban vote and cracked the once-solid Republican South. He walked away with the once-Republican far-West. The Clinton-Gore ticket gave the baby boomers two of their own, and the long awaited generational shift in American politics finally took place.

Here the speech turns from a general argument about needed change toward support of the Clinton administration. Through the next ten paragraphs, the speech is almost an apologia—*a work written to explain or justify. But notice how the numbered arguments that the Clinton administration is "off to a good start" leads Jordan back to his central theme of diversity and change.*

I believe Bill Clinton brings a new spirit and a new hope to the American people, but it's been a short honeymoon. The administration has been criticized for not doing enough and for doing too much. Despite that, I believe the Clinton administration is off to a good start, problems notwithstanding.

First, it has set a new agenda for America. Whether you support the administration's positions on the issues or not, it is focusing on critical long-term issues like healthcare and economic renewal that have been neglected for too long.

Second, the Clinton administration is the first in memory to get serious about deficit reduction. Again, you may want more or less of it, you may prefer more of it come from spending cuts than taxes, but the essential point is that the president has put this issue on the table where it belongs, and a real debate on deficit reduction is taking place in America.

A third accomplishment is the administration's emphasis on renewing long-range prospects for our economy through concrete measures to improve the schools and the training available to our people and to help develop high-tech infrastructure. Some may believe that's not an appropriate role for the government, but Germany and Japan do and that's why they are such formidable competitors.

Fourth, the administration's proposal for a youth national service program and for financing college tuition are important steps that encourage social responsibility and create educational opportunity.

Finally, this administration has made a bold commitment to diversity. I know that the search for minorities and women to fill high cabinet posts gave some in the media and elsewhere a field day, but I say to you, it was the right thing to do.

It gave us an attorney general who is tough, well-respected, and decisive. It gave us an agriculture secretary who knows what it's like to till the soil. It gave us a commerce secretary who can face down the Japanese, an energy secretary who knows the industry inside-out, and a secretary of Housing and Urban Development who understands the needs and aspirations of urban Americans. More importantly, this administration showed that inclusion and diversity are important objectives that can be implemented without compromising competence.

And I believe these early months have been instructive, defining experiences in the education of a new president and a new administration. I believe this administration has learned some important lessons of governance, and we'll see a more focused, more disciplined approach, an approach that reaches out to the public, marshals grassroots support, makes the case for bipartisan cooperation, and thus assures a new consensus that transcends party and political boundaries.

The American public wants change. It voted 62 percent for change. The American public wants its leaders, public and private, Democratic and Republican, to address issues—issues basic to our future and our children's future.

I believe there is a growing consensus among the American people, a consensus that government can and should be a force for good; that fairness is the glue that holds our society together; that if some Americans are second-class citizens, then America will become a second-class country; that we are interdependent and can only be as strong as the weakest of the links that bind us together; and that our future depends on making the investments and sacrifices necessary to grow the economy.

That consensus is good for America. For whether the issue is debt reduction, health-care, education, economic stagnation, urban decline, crime or war, we are all in this together, and there is no hiding place down here. That consensus recognizes, too, that the democratic free-enterprise system will be in danger if America finds itself in economic decline with a diverse society torn by more living standards, racial, ethnic, and class divisions.

Graduates, wherever you go from this place and whatever you do, I say to you there is no hiding place down here. I would suggest that as you pursue your chosen professions, as your careers take hold, as you rear your families, as you plan your futures, that you become agents of change, that you play your part in building a better, more fair, more inclusive America. That you understand that every child that grows up hungry or homeless, every child that grows up uneducated, every young adult denied training and job opportunities represents precious human resources America cannot afford to lose.

It is written in Luke 19:26 "To whom much is given much is required." As witnessed here today, you have been given much, and you will get much more. But I have come simply to ask that in return you share, you care, you dare, and you lead. For you can help America change, change for the better. You can help America live up to its vast potential as a beacon of world freedoms and a land of plenty for all of its people.

The speech is now, clearly, a commencement address again. It builds from here to the charge Jordan gives the graduates in the last paragraph.

This commencement marks the beginning of your acceptance of what has been called the terrific responsibility to human life. You now share that responsibility fully: responsibility for shaping your own lives and your country's destiny. And as you do, hear the words of Herman Melville, who wrote, "We cannot live for ourselves alone. Our lives are connected by a thousand invisible threads, and along these sympathetic fibers our actions run as causes and return to us as a results."

Now as you go down from this place, as you take leave from these hallowed grounds, as you say farewell to your alma mater, as you accept the responsibilities and duties of citizenship, be steadfast, be strong, be of good cheer. And as you go, may your own dreams be your only boundaries henceforth, now and forever. Amen.

DePauw Magazine, Summer 1993, DePauw University, Greencastle, Indiana. Reprinted by permission.

Appendix B

How to Handle Nervousness

Every speech teacher and most speech students know that one of the first things they have to learn is how to manage nervousness.[1] Ask speech students on the first day of class, "Are you going to be nervous?" and they respond with nervous laughter and affirmative head-nodding that tells you that handling nervousness is one of their primary concerns. Some call these uncomfortable feelings of nervousness stage fright or apprehension or speech or communication anxiety. Whatever you call it, it involves feelings of uncertainty, agitation, and impending loss. Individuals worry that something bad is about to happen, that the world is out of control.[2] Anxiety is fear—fear of being hurt or fear of loss. And whether there is a real reason for fear, or merely an imagined one, the feelings are the same.

Fortunately, nervousness can be managed.[3] Better yet, it can be used to your advantage when you are speaking. But to learn to manage and handle nervousness, you must first understand it.

WHY NERVOUSNESS OCCURS

Perhaps our greatest anxiety is about losing our lives. We probably do not think about this directly—why would we? We live rather far removed from the food chain. Our instinctive need for self-preservation from aggressors has become confused and confusing. When humankind had a one-to-one relationship with each meal—when they had to go out into the woods and kill or gather their food, all the while being careful that they, themselves, did not become a meal for some other animal—things were quite different. Now the direct threat that we are hunted even while we hunt has been removed by our civilization. But the physical and psychological reactions to threat have not disappeared. Potential aggressors are less clearly defined. Still, we imagine them and continue to be influenced by the survival instinct. The aggressors we fear do not usually threaten our lives. Instead, they turn out to be arbitrary employers, overextended schedules, and the stresses and strains associated with organizational life. The most obvious example in the present context is listening audiences.

Six modern-day fears surround the public speaking experience for most people:

1. Fear of being in the spotlight
2. Fear of performing badly
3. Fear of the audience
4. Fear that your ideas are not good enough
5. Fear that you, personally, are not good enough
6. Fear of the unknown

All of these concerns are reasonable and understandable, but they do not have to paralyze you. Let us examine each of these six fears.

FEAR OF BEING IN THE SPOTLIGHT

In the one-to-many settings of a public speaking situation, the speaker is set apart from the group. The entire setting is designed to focus attention on the speaker. Some people are uncomfortable in the spotlight. They may wonder, what if I run out of things to say? What if I do or say something stupid? What if I embarrass myself? These are understandable and disconcerting questions. But they do not have to paralyze you. Notice how they focus attention on the speaker, rather than on the relationship between the speaker and listeners. They draw attention away from audience members' needs and interests.

Fear of being in the spotlight relates to audience feedback. As you speak to an audience, listeners begin to give you feedback. They see you and hear you. They nod, frown, smile and so on as evidence that you are the center of attention—that you are in the spotlight. In practical terms, their feedback *is* the spotlight and is what speakers experience as disconcerting.

It is often difficult, when you are a speaker, to know how well you are doing. Some speakers worry: "Are listeners following me? Am I missing any of the important feedback cues they are sending? Did that person who just left the room mean anything by it? What about those sudden noises? What does the silence mean?" Certainly, audience feedback is important. But you cannot truly know what is going on in listeners' minds from such cues.

People in theater say, "The show must go on." They know that they cannot truly read the nonverbal messages their audiences are sending them. They know, too, that one or two audience members cannot represent all the audience members. A small minority of the people in the audience may be uncomfortable, but others are undoubtedly enjoying themselves. And so, for the majority, the show must go on. Thus, even if one or two listeners are sending you negative messages, check the others. You will see that they are with you. Work with listeners.

FEAR OF PERFORMING BADLY

Many people believe that they are not capable of giving a speech. So they talk negatively to themselves, saying things like, "I just don't have what it takes. I'm not a born speaker." Fear of performing badly is one of the most common of the six fears. Intelligent, well-intended, competent people worry that their performance will be substandard. They think that they may embarrass themselves by misspeaking or by doing something dumb.

In reality, such occurrences are rare. If something unusual happens while you are giving a speech, you have only two choices for handling it: You can (1) decide that the event is horrible and then come unglued, or (2) decide to accept the unusual event and adapt to it. If you do, your audience will also. For example, a young man named Hank stood up to give his speech recently and then realized that his fly was unzipped. Hank could have decided that his unzipped fly was awful. Instead, he decided to play the situation as a mildly humorous but utterly understandable error. "Egads!" he said in mock horror. Then he turned his back to his audience, zipped his trousers closed, turned around again, and said, grinning: "It had to happen to someone. I wish it hadn't been me. But if you can forget it for the moment, I'd like to talk with you about . . ." In this way, Hank sensibly defused a potentially embarrassing problem.

FEAR OF THE AUDIENCE

Some people are afraid of their audiences. They say, "I don't know why, but there is something different about standing up to talk to an audience, even if the people out there are your friends." This kind of statement implies that an audience is somehow "out to get" the speaker.

To the contrary, however, audiences want speakers to succeed. You can verify this claim through your own experience as an audience member. As a listener, you want to turn yourself over for a while to the speaker. You want the speaker to take control of your thoughts and feelings—to inform you, to entertain you, or to call you to some action. And if, for example, the speaker forgets what he or she was going to say next, you, as a listener, would do almost anything to help the speaker get back on track. As a listener, you are pulling for the speaker.

As a speaker, you must know that audience members are pulling for you, too. You can—and should—use this fact. For example, a visiting minister speaking to a church full of people one evening apparently lost his train of thought. But, because he was an experienced speaker, he decided to use his audience. He said, in part, "I had three reasons why I wanted you to introduce an AIDS education program into your Sunday school curriculum. I've told you the first two, but, ladies and gentlemen, the third one completely slips my mind. Do you have any ideas?" The minister's candor resulted in warm laughter from the audience. Someone called out, "You don't need it. I'm already convinced." More laughter followed this remark. Thus, the minister used the glitch to strengthen his relationship with listeners. It was a wise strategy that you can use, too. The audience wants you to succeed.

FEAR THAT YOUR IDEAS ARE NOT GOOD ENOUGH

In some students' minds, fear that their ideas are not good enough is the most disturbing aspect of public speaking. But it is also the easiest to control. As a speaker, you are in charge of what you say. You are in charge of the quality of your ideas and of the skill with which you present them.

One simple fact may help: There are no uninteresting subjects. There are only disinterested people. Every idea, no matter how small, is worthy. Your ideas, therefore, are certainly good enough. The trick is to figure out how to tie your ideas to the needs or feelings of listeners. That, of course, is a big part of why you are taking this course.

FEAR THAT YOU, PERSONALLY, ARE NOT GOOD ENOUGH

Some students worry: "What if I do my best, prepare thoroughly, adapt ideas to the audience accurately and well, and the audience still rejects me and my ideas? What if I botch my speech? What if I mess up? What if the audience doesn't like me?" We often perceive ourselves as inadequate, and some people carry this sense of inadequacy to an extreme when they have to give a speech.

These questions, or questions like them, occur to many speakers, regardless of the extent of their speaking experience. The questions flow from an underlying fear that we are not good enough to give our speeches. The truth is, every famous speaker was, first of all, a real person, possessed of strengths and weaknesses. Each of us knows we are knowledgeable in some ways and ignorant in others.

You would not want to, and you would probably be unable to, pretend to be Dan Rather or Jane Pauley. You are going to look and sound just like you, and you are okay just the way you are.[4]

FEAR OF THE UNKNOWN

Almost everyone experiences some anxiety about the unknown, and this generalized fear has motivated a large and growing literature about communication anxiety. Charles R. Berger and James J. Bradac's influential book *Language and Social Knowledge: Uncertainty in Interpersonal Relations* argues that one of the most important uses of language is to absorb our uncertainty and to increase our ability to predict the unknown.[5]

Fortunately, planning and practice help to guarantee that some unknown does not occur while you are giving a speech. And as you gain experience in speaking, this fear tends to go away.

THE VALUE OF FEAR

One of the hardest lessons to teach—perhaps because the recommendation seems so far removed from students' sense of reality—is that the six fears just discussed have considerable value. Fear is a valuable emotion for several reasons. First, fear is the most obvious tool you have for protecting yourself. Second, fear energizes you. Physiologically, fear of speaking produces a primitive fight-or-flight response. Your endocrinal system pumps a variety of high-powered drugs into your system that make you physically strong. So you need your fear. It helps you to maintain your edge, to think fast, to speak up, to project yourself into the audience. It helps you to color and give force to your appeals.

WHAT TO DO ABOUT FEAR

You can work to control your nervous feelings and to use those feelings to improve your speech making. Here are a dozen suggestions that come from research and from the experiences of speech teachers and speakers:

1. **Keep your fear to yourself.** Nervousness does not usually show. The butterfly sensation you have in your stomach is rarely obvious to an audience. Moreover, although you may think and feel that your nervous shaking is going to make your hands fall off your arms, moderate trembling is almost invisible. You can make it worse by trying to overcome it. Good advice, then, is to not talk about your nervous feelings. Do not apologize for your feelings and do not try to force them to go away. Accept your fear as a normal and natural response. Then concentrate on helping listeners to get your ideas. Try not to think about your anxiety, but do try to channel the energy that it generates.

2. **Visualize yourself being successful.** Imagine yourself standing before a group of people who are enthralled with you and your ideas. Take time to engage in some positive self-talk. Positive imaging and positive self-talk help many nervous speakers to manage their feelings.[6]

   People have believed in the power of imaging for some sixty thousand years. Shamans and tribal witch doctors have used the technique in almost every primitive society known to anthropologists. Ancient Greek doctors—most notably the great physician Hippocrates—taught their patients to dream of being healed by a god. The ancient Chinese yoga masters also taught imaging.

   During the Middle Ages, the church taught that faith, alone, could cure all illnesses. Faith healing still occurs today. The idea was commonplace during the Renaissance. Indeed, it was not until the eighteenth century, sometimes called the Age of Reason, that the value of positive imaging fell into disrepute as Descartes and his contemporaries began to think of mind as separate from body.

   Even so, Mary Baker Eddy was enough convinced of the power of imaging that she founded Christian Science on the idea that the mind is responsible for both creation and cure of all human illness. People like Mesmer, Breuer, and Freud began, once again, to explore the value of positive self-imaging.

   By 1950, most of the ideas surrounding positive visualization had found support in research. The research continues, and with each year, the therapeutic value of positive visualization becomes more convincing.[7]

   So visualize yourself being relaxed and confident and successful as you present your speech to a group of spellbound listeners. Such imaging can often carry over into real life.

3. **Practice working with your body.** If you are like many nervous speakers, your heart may pound. Your hands and knees may tremble and shake. Your breathing may be rapid and shallow. Your face may become flushed and you may begin to perspire. Your throat may feel constricted, and your mouth may go to cotton. You may find

that your bladder seems full and that your stomach is churning. You may feel as though the hair on your neck and at the back of your arms is standing up. You may have any or all of these symptoms.

These physical symptoms of the fight-or-flight reaction can be distracting unless you begin to work on the symptoms wisely. Instead of deciding, "I'm going to die, and I can't go on," tell yourself something like, "This is a fairly normal, albeit unpleasant experience. But I can still get my point across." This will not take away the feelings or the symptoms, but it will channel your thinking into a positive course of action.

Try teaching yourself to relax. When you are relaxed, negative feelings are unlikely. Develop a systematic procedure for relaxing yourself and then learn to use it. First, identify your major muscle groups. A simple list includes:

Your feet and ankles
Your calves, knees, and thighs
Your pelvic girdle
The small of your back—the lumbar region
Your abdominal muscles
Your chest and upper back
Your shoulders, upper back, and the back of your neck
Your upper arms, elbows, and forearms
Your wrists and hands
Your neck muscles
The muscles of your face—around your mouth, cheeks and eyes, and the frown muscles of your forehead

Lie down or sit in a comfortable chair and then focus on these muscle groups, one by one. Tense the muscles in each group and then concentrate on relaxing them. Study the contrast between tension and relaxation. Let the tension flow away. Say to yourself: "I am able to relax. I can feel the tension going away. I am rested. I am calm. I am relaxed."

Combine this activity with deep breathing exercises. Draw in a deep breath, then exhale slowly and completely. Do this again and again.

If you practice deep breathing and relaxation exercises for about fifteen minutes once or twice each day, within a week or two, you will be able to achieve deep levels of relaxation quickly. You will know in which muscle groups you are most likely to carry tension and which ones are most likely to require some focus. You will be able to relax before a speech.

Have you ever wondered how a television set can control audience attention for so long? Primarily, viewer attention is held by image movement and change. The camera is continually zooming in and out, or panning back and forth. Someone constantly changes the image from one camera to another. People are moving. The result of all this movement is that viewers pay attention effortlessly.

You can use this information to help you overcome your fear. Move around during your speech. Walk toward the audience or toward your visual aids. Gesture.

Change from one position to another to signal that you are changing ideas. Allow yourself to relax. And remember, an audience that is hooked by your *ideas* is almost certainly not worrying about your physical delivery or bodily movement.

4. **Surround yourself with notes.** If you are sure that you will not forget what you were going to say, a lot of the unpleasantness surrounding the public speaking situation disappears. So surround yourself with notes, and do not try to hide them. Use a note card or two. Use some of your visual materials as notes. This ensures that you are not dependent on a single source of reference. No one cares if you use notes, as long as listeners believe that you are trying to make contact with them. But do not write out a manuscript, and do not memorize the speech.

This does not mean, however, that you should become dependent on your notes. Free yourself from your notes as much as possible so that you can focus on your relationship with listeners. Minimize the chances that you will get lost during your speech so that you have the maximum opportunity to work with your ideas and listeners.

5. **Know and understand your listeners.** Knowing and understanding listeners is your best means of overcoming any fear you may have of them. Analyze the audience carefully. Learn as much as you can about what audience members know of your subject and what they need to know. Try to identify with listeners. Think about your ideas and yourself from their point of view. The more you do these things, the less likely you are to experience an audience as something to fear.

Try not to look for problems that do not exist. The audience is not out to get you. Sometimes, audience members whisper to each other, stare at the ceiling, tweak their noses, shuffle their feet. These are not necessarily signs that they are restless and bored.

To illustrate, every teacher knows that there are at least three different kinds of students and that these people act differently during class. Some students are heavily dependent on the teacher. They come to class with pencils sharpened and poised over their notebooks, waiting to hear the headings and subheadings for the class notes. Other students are heavily dependent on their classmates. They talk a lot in class, asking, "What did he say?" "What does that mean?" A third group of students probably would not have to come to class at all. They sit in the back of the room, rarely take notes, sometimes stare at the ceiling, or sit quietly with their eyes closed. These behaviors do not mean that the students are not involved either with the ideas or the teacher. On the contrary, they usually mean that the students are enjoying the class, paying attention, and learning.

In the same way, audience members sometimes talk to each other, or take notes, or listen with their eyes closed. That does not mean that they are not listening to you or enjoying your speech.

6. **Check out all the arrangements carefully.** Go to the place where you will speak. Look it over. Make sure that any equipment you need is there and working. If you are going to use an overhead projector, for example, put one of your transparencies on the projector, turn it on and focus it. Make sure that there is a screen and that listeners will be able to see the screen and the visual materials you are projecting.

One speaker was invited to address some two hundred bank employees at a meeting held in the local Holiday Inn meeting room. He asked the hotel contact person, "Will there be an overhead projector?" "Yes," replied the contact person. The speaker assumed that there would also be a screen and did no further checking. When he arrived for his speech, he discovered that there was no screen and that the walls of the meeting room were covered with green and gold foil and flock wallpaper. It was too late to do anything about securing a screen, and the Holiday Inn people said that they did not have one available. The speaker solved the problem by tacking up four king-sized bed sheets on the wall and using them as a screen. But his experience would have been far less nerve wracking had he taken the time to check things out in advance.

You are more or less in charge of the space where you will speak. If you do not like something, you can usually arrange to get it changed, but only if you check out all arrangements in advance. Checking in advance also reduces a good deal of your uncertainty.

7. **Talk only about things you know and care about.** Remember that you are the expert on your subject matter. You know your speech better than anyone else in the room. You have prepared carefully. You have a point of view that is well taken and well directed. You know that your ideas are okay. So concentrate on communicating with listeners. After all, the purpose of your speech is to get *your* ideas across to listeners.

8. **Prepare carefully.** Polish your speech introduction. Most speakers have the greatest trouble at the beginning of the speech. All speakers need a few moments to "warm up" and get into their speeches. Those few moments are always at the beginning, during the introduction.

Practice. The greater your confidence that you know what you want to say and do, the less reason for you to experience some generalized fear of the unknown. This does not mean that you should commit your speech to memory. Rather, you should practice with the ideas, not a word-for-word progression.

If you ever took music lessons, you undoubtedly heard your teacher and parents tell you to practice a little every day. Your music teacher knew something that you can use to your advantage in struggling with your fears about public speaking. Distributed practice makes all the difference in the quality of the performance.

Practice the introduction. Practice the body. Practice the conclusion. Practice using the visual materials. Practice turning on and using the equipment. Practice.

9. **Remind yourself that nervousness is normal.** This may help you to accept nervous feelings and to direct and focus them. Pretend that you are confident, even if you are not. Imagine yourself being confident. Get an image in your mind of yourself doing a great job giving the speech. Tell yourself that you are confident, that your nervous feelings are normal and can be helpful. Act as though you feel confident. Before long, you will feel more confident because you look and act confident.

10. **Pause briefly before you start.** Pause for a few beats before you say anything. Take that opportunity to collect yourself. Look at the audience confidently. Give listeners a little time to adjust to the fact that you are standing there and that you have something to say. You are building your image and rapport with listeners when you do this. Then begin with a carefully planned introduction.

11. **Use your audience.** Establish eye contact as much as you can. Think about the audience. Decide to talk *with* the audience rather than at them or to them. Involve audience members early in the speech. Mention one or two of the listeners by name.

Include the audience with words like *you and I* and *we*. And remember—listeners want you to succeed. If you lose your place, or you are not sure about something, ask them. "Where was I, Bill?" will not offend Bill, and it will not offend anyone else in the audience either. And you can count on Bill, or someone in your audience, to help you find your place.

12. **Give yourself permission to make mistakes.** You are not perfect, and no one else is either. Audiences are always willing to give speakers some room for error. Why, then, are so many speakers unwilling to give themselves permission to make mistakes? Could it be that they have come to believe that others' acceptance of them depends on their perfection? Accept your imperfections and then tell yourself that you are okay just the way you are. Give yourself permission to make mistakes.

SUMMARY

People are sometimes nervous because they fear being in the spotlight or performing badly. They may be afraid of listeners. They may think their ideas are not good enough or that they, personally, are not good enough. People tend to be anxious about the unknown, and this fear may generate those feelings of nervousness that are common to us all.

Such fears can be valuable to a speaker who knows how to channel them constructively. Twelve suggestions for channeling any feelings of fear and nervousness that you might experience are:

1. Keep your fear to yourself.
2. Visualize yourself being successful.
3. Practice working with your body.
4. Surround yourself with notes.
5. Know and understand listeners.
6. Check out all the arrangements carefully.
7. Talk only about things you know and care about.
8. Prepare carefully.
9. Remind yourself that nervousness is normal.
10. Pause briefly before you start.
11. Use your audience.
12. Give yourself permission to make mistakes.

NOTES

1. Philip M. Ericson and John W. Gardner, "Two Longitudinal Studies of Communication Apprehension and Its Effects on College Students' Success," *Communication Quarterly* 40 (Spring 1992): 127.
2. David Viscott, *The Language of Feelings* (New York: Pocket Books, 1976), 61. See also, Kevin L. Hutchison and James W. Neuliep, "The Influence of Parent and Peer Modeling on the Development of Communication Apprehension in Elementary School Children," *Communication Quarterly* 41 (Winter 1993): 16.
3. See, for example, Lynne Kelly and James Keaten, "A Test of the Effectiveness of the Reticence Program at Pennsylvania State University," *Communication Education* 41 (October 1992): 361.
4. This idea was most clearly developed by Thomas A. Harris, *I'm OK—You're OK* (New York: Avon Books, 1969).

5. Charles R. Berger and James J. Bradac, *Language and Social Knowledge: Uncertainty in Interpersonal Relations* (London: Edward Arnold Publishers, 1982). See also, Lawrence R. Wheeless and Anna Maria Williamson, "State-Communication Apprehension and Uncertainty in Continuing Initial Interactions," *Southern Communication Journal* 57 (Summer 1992): 249.

6. A massive and growing literature supports this recommendation. You will find a little book by Matthew McKay and Patrick Fanning especially helpful. See *Self-Esteem: A Proven Program of Cognitive Techniques for Assessing, Improving, and Maintaining Your Self-Esteem* (Oakland, Calif.: New Harbinger Publications, 1987). See also, Joe Ayres and Theodore S. Hopf, "The Long-Term Effect of Visualization in the Classroom: A Brief Research Report," *Communication Education* 39 (January 1990): 75. Joe Ayres and Tim Hopf, "Visualization: Reducing Speech Anxiety and Enhancing Performance," *Communication Reports* 5 (Winter 1992): 1. And for an especially useful self-help book, see Patrick Fanning, *Visualization for Change: A Step-by-Step Guide to Using Your Powers of Imagination for Self-Improvement, Therapy, Healing, and Pain Control* (Oakland, Calif.: New Harbinger Publications, 1988).

7. Ayres and Hopf, "Visualization."

Appendix C

Troubleshooting Guide

Public speaking activity can continue throughout your lifetime. In school, at work, and in social, civic, and religious organizations, you will have many opportunities to give public speeches. Many people want a quick reference for refreshing their memory about public speaking or to give them new information about managing a public speaking situation. This book will serve as a helpful tool when those situations arise—helpful beyond the level provided by most public speaking textbooks.

At times, the typical book index, including the one in this book, is not a useful problem-solving tool because it is not problem oriented. To find solutions to your problems, you would ordinarily have to read through many sections of a book. This troubleshooting guide has been developed to provide something more. It is a problem-oriented index based on the kinds of problems that speakers most often confront when called on to give a speech. Make a habit of using this guide. You will find *Public Speaking for Personal Success* a helpful resource for many years to come.

HOW TO USE THIS TROUBLESHOOTING GUIDE

1. State the problem you are experiencing out loud or in writing.
2. Think of key words that describe the problem you have stated. Key words are listed alphabetically in the "Directory" that follows.
3. Locate those key words in the problem-solving index.
4. Find a question similar to yours and then turn to the referenced pages of the text for an answer.
5. If you do not find relevant key words for your problem in the "Directory," refer to the index at the back of this book to locate information related to your problem.

DIRECTORY

PROBLEM CATEGORY AND QUESTIONS

A

Anxiety

I am worried that I cannot succeed as a speaker. Is there any help or hope?
Chapter 2, 26–27; Appendix B, 423–427

I feel afraid even when I think about giving a speech. What can I do to prevent this feeling or at least deal with it? Chapter 2, 25; Appendix B, 419–427

Why am I afraid of giving a speech? Chapter 2, 26; Appendix B, 419–422

Is there anything wrong with me because I am fearful of giving a speech? Chapter 2, 26; Appendix B, 419

Argument (*See also* **Logic, Reasoning**)

I have to give a persuasive speech. What controls what a listener accepts and believes?
Chapter 6, 47–48; Chapter 15, 337–340

Where can I find an overview of how people reason? Chapter 6, 111–115

I want to use evidence wisely to make an argument. But where do I find evidence?
Chapters 6, 120–129; Chapter 7, 136

How can I judge the accuracy or value of evidence? Chapter 6, 129–130

What is the best way to use statistics in an argument? Chapter 6, 124–127

When I am giving a speech, what terms should I define, how, and why?
Chapter 11, 247–248, 254–255

Attending and Attention (*See also* **Listening**)

Sometimes when I am trying to listen, I cannot concentrate on what is being said. Is there anything I can do? Chapter 3, 51–53

Sometimes, I find myself drifting off instead of paying attention. Is there anything I can do to prevent this? Chapter 3, 54

How can I get attention from listeners when they are getting tired? Chapter 3, 46–48

What are the best ways to get the attention of my audience? Chapter 3, 54–55; Chapter 5, 92; Chapter 10, 221–229; Chapter 12, 261–262; Chapter 13, 292

Audience Adaptation

My listeners are relatively unsophisticated about my topic. What should I do? Chapter 3, 54–55

How can I know if my topic will be appropriate for my audience? Chapter 5, 96–105

I have a good idea, but I am not sure how to tie it into the interests of listeners. Chapter 5, 91, 100–105

I would like to know how listeners will respond to my speech. How can I predict their reactions? Chapter 5, 94–105

What can I do to get the audience to empathize with my position? Chapter 3, 57

Audience Analysis (*See also* **Demographics**)

I would like to develop a questionnaire to test the audience position on my topic, but I do not know how to begin. Any suggestions? Chapter 5, 97–98

Is there a way to analyze my class as though it were a real audience? Chapter 5, 96–99

I do not know anything about my audience. How do I begin an audience analysis? Chapter 5, 92–95

What affect does the place where I speak and the time when I talk have on my chances for success? Chapter 5, 92

What is inferential audience analysis? How does it work? Chapter 5, 99

I know that age, gender, socioeconomic status, and so on are important issues. What kinds of questions should I ask to find out about these characteristics of my audience? Chapter 5, 100–105

How do I actually perform an audience analysis? Chapter 5, 96–99

B

Brainstorm

How can I brainstorm for speech topics? Chapter 4, 66–69

C

Communication Anxiety (*See* **Anxiety**)

Communication Process

How does public speaking fit into the communication process? Chapter 1, 10–15

What is involved in the communication process? Chapter 1, 10–15

Comparison and Contrast (*See also* **Supporting Material**)

How do comparison and contrast work as supporting material for a speech?
   Chapter 11, 252–254; Chapter 14, 317

When should I use comparison and contrast as supporting material? Chapter 11, 252–254

Conclusion

When I come to the end of my speech, I have trouble finishing it. What should I do?
   Chapter 10, 230–233

Credibility

I want listeners to trust me and have confidence in me. What can I do to increase my
   credibility? Chapter 3, 55; Chapter 6, 115–116; Chapter 13, 303; Chapter 14,
   326–327; Chapter 15, 341–343

D

Definition of Terms (*See also* **Meaning Agreement**)

What should I define, and what can I leave undefined? Why? Chapter 11, 254–255

Delivery (*See also* **Visual Aids**)

Is it ever okay to read a speech from a manuscript? Chapter 13, 293

I am thinking about writing out my speech and memorizing it. Is this approach okay?
   Chapter 13, 294

Is there a style of delivery that is generally recommended? Chapter 13, 295–296

How do I actually give the speech? I am prepared, but what about delivery?
   Chapter 13, 292–293; 298–304

What is the best way to use visual materials when I am giving a speech?
   Chapter 12, 284–286

Are there any pointers about delivery? Chapter 13, 305–306

Demographics

I know that demographics are important to audience analysis and marketing research, but
   what should I look for? Chapter 5, 100–106

What should I do with the demographic information that I collect about an audience?
   Chapter 5, 100

E

Evidence (*See also* **Supporting Material**)

What is a good definition of evidence? Chapter 6, 121

What are the various kinds of evidence and their strengths and weaknesses?
   Chapter 6, 121–130

Where can I find evidence? Chapter 6, 121

How can I know if the evidence is any good? What tests can I apply? Chapter 6, 129–130

Eye Contact

How important is eye contact with my audience? Chapter 13, 303–304

G

Gestures

My gestures seem wooden and unnatural. What should I do? Chapter 13, 301–303

H

Humor
What kind of humor can I use to lighten the atmosphere? Chapter 10, 226–229

I

Inform
I am supposed to give a speech to inform. What techniques will help me?
Chapter 14, 323–328
What are the most common types of informative speech topics? Chapter 14, 316–322

L

Language
How can I use language more effectively? Chapter 11,246–255
What are the differences between written and oral language? Chapter 13, 297–298
What language techniques can I use to make my speech vivid and interesting
Chapter 11, 240–242, 251–254

Listening (*See also* **Attending and Attention**)
What are the key elements of listening that I must take into account as a speaker? Chapter 3, 53–57
What can I do to help audience members listen if they have difficulty seeing or hearing? Chapter 3, 53–54
People sometimes tell me I do not listen. I try to listen, but how can I improve my own listening skills? Chapter 3, 50–53
Can I help audience members to listen more effectively? Chapter 3, 53–57
I have been told that what I say is not always clear. What can I do to help listeners understand my ideas? Chapter 3, 54–57

Logic (*See also* **Argument, Reasoning**)
Something seems wrong with the logic of this speech, but I cannot figure it out. Any ideas? Chapter 6, 119–120
How can I strengthen the likelihood that listeners will accept the logic of my speech? Chapter 6, 115–116
What is the difference between beliefs and values? Chapter 15, 336–340

M

Meaning Agreement
Sometimes, listeners think I mean something quite different from what I intended. What is the problem? Is there a solution? Chapter 11, 245, 247–251
Sometimes, people misunderstand the words I use. What is the problem?
Chapter 11, 254–255

Motivation (*See also* **Persuasion**)
What motivates people to do what they do? Chapters 3,15, 355

N

Narrow and Focus

People tell me not to "bite off more than I can chew"—to narrow and focus my topic. How do I do that? Chapter 4, 73–83

Needs

I want to get people interested in my ideas. What are their basic needs? Chapters 14, 326

Notes

What is the best way to make and use notes? Chapters 7, 154–158

Can I use my outline for speaking notes? Chapters 9, 210–216

How can I use visual aids for notes? Chapter 12, 266–268

O

Organization of Ideas (*See also* **Outlining**)

Is there a surefire way to organize the ideas for my speech? Chapters 8, 174–187

What are the most commonly used ways of organizing speech ideas? Chapters 8, 174–187

I want to give a speech about a problem that needs to be solved. Is there a best way to organize such a speech? Chapter 8, 176–187

I want to talk about a topic that is really interesting to me, but I am not sure how to organize it. Chapter 8, 172–173

I want to talk about a problem and propose a solution. How should I organize my ideas? Chapters 8, 176–178

I have lots of evidence and examples that prove that my idea is right. What is the best way to organize this material? Chapter 8, 174–175

I want to propose some changes, even though there really is not anything wrong with what we are doing now. I just think my idea will make things better. How can I organize such a speech? Chapter 8, 179–187

I want to stimulate listeners to action. How should I organize this speech? Chapters 8, 182–187

Outlining

How do I make an outline for a speech? Chapter 9, 194–216

What is the difference between a planning outline and a speaking outline? Chapter 9, 194–195

Can I use an outline to plan a speech? Chapter 9, 210–211

P

Persuasion (*See also* **Organization of Ideas**)

How do I give a persuasive speech? Chapter 15, 340–355

Is it okay to tell listeners what I want from them? Chapter 15, 348

I want listeners to feel they need my proposal. How can I create such a need in them? Chapter 15, 338–340

Is there anything that affects the staying power of a persuasive message? I want listeners to be persuaded for a long time. Chapter 15, 347–354

What emotional appeals can I use to persuade listeners? Chapter 15, 349–354

Practice
What is the best way to practice a speech without memorizing it? Chapter 2, 37

R

Reasoning (*See also* **Argument, Logic**)
Someone said that all reasoning is reasoning from sign. What does that mean? Chapter 6, 113

How can I analyze a cause-effect relationship? Chapter 6, 113–114

Does it make sense to argue from example? Chapter 6, 127–129

What is the best way to test an argument from analogy? Chapter 6, 114–115

How can I judge the accuracy or value of evidence? Chapter 6, 129–130

What kinds of evidence are available, and how do I use them? Chapter 6, 120–130

Remembering
I am worried that I will forget what I want to say and lose my place in the speech. Chapters 13, 294–296

How can I help listeners to remember key ideas? Chapter 3, 56–57

S

Signposts
I do not understand the purpose of signposts. What are they supposed to do? Chapter 8, 188, 209

Specific Purpose
Why is it important to have a specific purpose for a speech? Chapter 4, 74–81; Chapter 9, 200

Speech Situations and Problems
I have to give a speech soon. Where can I find an overview of what I have to do? Chapter 2, 25–37

What should I do when I am called on for an impromptu speech? Chapter 13, 296–297

I am going to give the commencement address at my alma mater. What should I do? Chapter 16, 367–368

I will deliver the eulogy at a friend's funeral. How should I prepare for it? Chapter 16, 365–366

I must give a speech of introduction. What should I do? Chapter 16, 360–363

I have been asked to give the keynote speech at a conference. What goes into such a speech? Chapter 16, 369–370

I have been asked to make an award presentation. What should I do? Chapter 16, 363–364

I am supposed to give a speech to praise someone. I do not want to overdo it. What should I do? Chapter 16, 365–368

I have been asked to give an after-dinner speech. How do I prepare? Chapter 16, 371–373

Stage fright (*See also* **Anxiety**)

I think I am suffering from stage fright. What are the symptoms? Chapter 2, 26–27; Appendix B, 419–427

What can I do to handle my nervousness? Chapter 2, 26–27; Appendix B, 423–427

Supporting Material (*See also* **Evidence**)

Is there a way to tell if a statement needs support? Chapter 6, 110–111

How can I use comparison and contrast as supporting material for a speech? Chapter 11, 252–254

How can I differentiate between good and bad examples? Chapter 6, 127–129

How do I use examples wisely? Chapter 6, 129

Is there a set of do's and don'ts for using statistics as supporting material? Chapter 6, 124–127

How can I use quotations effectively? Chapter 6, 121–124

When is it appropriate to paraphrase a source? Chapter 6, 122

What are the most effective ways to use statistics? Chapter 6, 124–127

T

Testimony

How can I tell if the testimony I plan to use is believable? Chapter 6, 123–124

Is it more effective to use expert or lay testimony? Chapter 6, 121

Topic (*See also* **Narrow and Focus**)

I am supposed to give a speech, and I have no idea what I should discuss. Any suggestions? Chapters 2, 28–29; Chapter 4, 64–73; Appendix D

I am worried that my topic will not be interesting to listeners. What techniques can I use to hold their interest? Chapters 3, 54–55; Chapter 5, 92; Chapter 10, 221–279; Chapter 12, 261–262; Chapter 13, 292

How can I select a topic when I am out of ideas? Chapter 4, 66–69; Appendix D

Transition

What is a good transition? How can I develop it effectively? Chapter 8, 187–188

V

Visual Aids (*See also* **Delivery**)

What is a visual aid? Chapter 12, 260

When should I support my speech with visual materials? Chapter 12, 260–268

What should I support visually? Chapter 12, 268–270

How do I select the right visual medium? Chapter 12, 272–273

How do I judge the quality of a visual aid? Chapter 12, 273, 280–284

I want my visual to be well balanced. What criteria can I apply? Chapter 12, 277–279

How can I suggest action and tension with a visual aid? Chapter 12, 279

How can I suggest calm and peace with a visual aid? Chapter 12, 278

Appendix D

Possible Speech Topics

Selecting a topic for a speech is often a challenging task for beginning speakers. As explained in chapter 4, "Selecting and Narrowing Your Topic," an effective speech topic is one that you are knowledgeable about, that relates to your audience, that fits the occasion, and that can be discussed within the given time constraints.

This appendix lists titles from the Opposing Viewpoints ® Pamphlets Series of Greenhaven Press. The Opposing Viewpoints® Series is a collection of books that present both sides of current issues. Each Chapter of each Opposing Viewpoints® book is available in pamphlet form as a volume in the Opposing Viewpoints® Pamphlets Series. The pamphlet titles listed here may help you choose a speech topic. You may purchase Opposing Viewpoints® books ($9.95) or pamphlets ($3.50) by calling Greenhaven's toll-free number, 800 231 5163, or by writing to Greenhaven Press, Order Dept., PO Box 289009, San Diego, CA 92198–9009. Reprinted by permission.

AREA STUDIES

Africa

What Are the Causes of Africa's Problems?
How Can Famine in Africa Be Reduced?
How Will the Dismantling of Apartheid Affect South Africa's Future?

Central America

Why Is Central America a Conflict Area?
Is U.S. Involvement in Central America Justified?
What Policies Would Strengthen Central American Economies?
What Role Does Christianity Play in Central America?
Is Peace in Central America Possible?

China

Historical Debate: How Should China Modernize?
Are China's Economic Reforms Significant?
Does China Guarantee Human Rights?
Is China a World Power?

Eastern Europe

Historical Debate: What Led to the Division of Europe?
Do Eastern European Revolutions Signal the Demise of Communism?

What Economic Policies Should Eastern Europe Adopt?
How Will a United Germany Affect Europe?
Is European Unification Possible?

Israel

Historical Debate: Is a Homeland for the Jews Necessary?
Does Israel Treat the Palestinians Fairly?
Should the United States Support Israel?
What Is Israel's International Role?
What Is the Future of Israel?

Japan

Is Japan a World Power?
Are Japan's Economic Policies Fair?
Is Japan an Internally Troubled Society?
Should Japan Increase Its International Role?
Is Cooperation Between the United States and Japan Beneficial?

The Middle East

Why Is the Middle East a Conflict Area?
Are Palestinian Rights Being Ignored?
What Role Should the United States Play in the Middle East?
How Does Religion Affect the Middle East?
What Is the Future of the Middle East?

Third World

Why Is the Third World Poor?
Why Are Human Rights Threatened in the Third World?
Does U.S. Foreign Aid Benefit Third World? What Policies Would Promote Third World Development?
How Can Third World Debt Be Reduced?

CRIMINAL JUSTICE

America's Prisons

What Is the Purpose of Prisons?
How Do Prisons Affect Criminals?
How Can Prison Overcrowding Be Reduced?
Should Prisons Be Privatized?
What Are the Alternatives to Prisons?

Crime and Criminals

What Causes Crime?
How Should Criminals Be Treated?
How Can Crime Be Reduced?
How Should White-Collar Crime Be Controlled?
Would Gun Control Reduce Crime?

Criminal Justice

How Do Lawyers Affect the Criminal Justice System?
Should the Criminal Justice System Enforce Crime Victims' Rights?
What Reforms Would Improve the Criminal Justice System?
Do the Rights of the Accused Undermine the Criminal Justice System?
Do Police Abuse Their Authority?

The Death Penalty

Three Centuries of Debate on the Death Penalty
Is the Death Penalty Just?
Is the Death Penalty an Effective Punishment?
Does the Death Penalty Discriminate?
Do Certain Crimes Deserve the Death Penalty?

Violence in America

Is Violence in America a Serious Problem?
How Can Drug-Related Violence Be Reduced?
What Causes Family Violence?

What Causes Teen Violence?
What Motivates Serial Killers?
What Policies Would Reduce Violence?

ENVIRONMENT

The Environmental Crisis

Is There an Environmental Crisis?
How Should Pesticides Be Handled?
How Can the Garbage Problem Be Reduced?
How Should America Dispose of Toxic Waste?
How Serious Is Air and Water Pollution?
How Can the Environment Be Protected?
Global Resources
Are Global Resources Becoming More Scarce?
Is the Greenhouse Effect a Serious Threat?
Are Population Control Measures Needed to Protect Global Resources?
How Can Rain Forests Be Saved?
How Can Sustainable Agriculture Be Promoted?
What Policies Would Help Conserve Global Resources?

Water

How Should the Water Supply Be Managed?
How Can Water Pollution Be Reduced?
How Serious a Problem Is Acid Rain?
How Serious a Problem Is Ocean Pollution?

FOREIGN POLICY

American Foreign Policy

How Should the United States Deal with the Former Soviet Republics?
Is U.S. Intervention in Other Countries Justified?
How Should the United States Deal With Its Allies?
What Should be the Goal of U.S. Foreign Policy?
What Are the Effects of U.S. Foreign Aid?

America's Defense

What Role Should the United States Play in World Defense?
Should Women Serve in the U.S. Military?
Should Defense Spending Be Decreased?
What Weapons Would Strengthen America's Defense?

The Breakup of the Soviet Union

Why Did the Soviet Union Collapse?

How Will the Breakup of the Soviet Union Affect the World?

How Should the United States Respond to the Breakup of the Soviet Union?

What Policies Would Strengthen the Republics' Economies?

What Measures Would Reduce Ethnic Conflict in the Republics?

Latin America and U.S. Foreign Policy

Is U.S. Intervention the Cause of Latin America's Problems?

How Should the United States Deal with Latin American Human Rights Conditions?

What Form of Government Is Best for Latin America?

How Serious Is the Latin American Debt?

The New World Order

What Will the New World Order Be?

What Role Will the United States Play in the New World Order?

What Role Will Economics Play in the New World Order?

How Will the End of the Cold War Affect the World?

What Role Will International Organizations Play in the New World Order?

Nuclear Proliferation

How Serious a Problem Is Nuclear Proliferation?

Which Nations Contribute to Nuclear Proliferation?

How Can Nuclear Proliferation Be Prevented?

Terrorism

Is Terrorism Justified?

Do the Superpowers Sponsor Terrorism?

Can Terrorism Be Eliminated?

What Are the Causes of Terrorism?

The Vietnam War

Why Did the United States Become Involved in Vietnam?

Why Did U.S. Policy Fail in Vietnam?

What Are the Legacies of Vietnam?

How Has the Vietnam War Affected Veterans?

What Should U.S. Policy Be Toward Indochina?

War and Human Nature

Are Humans Aggressive by Nature?

GOVERNMENT AND ECONOMICS

American Government

What Is the Role of American Government?

Who Controls America?

Should the Constitution Be Revised?

How Can American Democracy Be Improved?

America's Elections

What Role Should the Media Play in U.S. Elections?

Censorship

Should There Be Limits to Free Speech?

Should the News Media Be Regulated?

Does National Security Justify Censorship?

Is School and Library Censorship Justified?

Should Pornography Be Censored?

Civil Liberties

How Should the Right to Privacy Be Defined?

Should Freedom of Expression Be Restricted?

Should Church and State Be Separate?

How Can Civil Liberties Be Protected?

Economics in America

What Is the State of America's Economy?

How Serious Is the Budget Deficit?

What Kind of Taxation Is Most Appropriate?

How Can America's Banking System Be Strengthened?

What Is the Future of American Labor?

Immigration

Historical Debate: Should Immigration Be Restricted?

How Do Immigrants Affect America?

How Should U.S. Immigration Policy Be Reformed?

What Policies Would Help Immigrants Adapt to the United States?

Politics in America

Does American Political Leadership Need Improvement?
Does the Two-Party System Effectively Represent
    Americans?

Space Exploration

What Should Be the Goal of Space Exploration?
Which Space Programs Should the United States Pursue?
Should NASA Be Eliminated?

Trade

Is Free Trade the Best Trading System?
Is the United States the Victim of Unfair Trade
    Practices?
Should Trade Be Restricted?
How Critical Is the U.S. Trade Deficit?
What Is the Future of the World Trading System?

HEALTH

AIDS

How Serious is AIDS?
Is AIDS a Moral Issue?
Is AIDS Testing Effective?
How Can the Spread of AIDS Be Prevented?

Biomedical Ethics

What Ethics Should Guide Biomedical Research?
What Ethics Should Guide Organ Transplants?
What Ethics Should Guide Fetal Tissue Research?
Are Reproductive Technologies Ethical?
Should Animals Be Used in Research?

Chemical Dependency

What Are the Causes of Chemical Dependency?
Is Smoking Harmful?
How Harmful Is Alcohol?
Should Drug Laws Be Reformed?
Should Pregnant Women Be Prosecuted for Drug Abuse?
How Can Chemical Dependency Be Reduced?

Death and Dying

What Is the Best Treatment for the Terminally Ill?

How Can Dying Patients Control the Decision to End
    Treatment?
How Should One Cope with Grief?
Is There Life After Death?

Drug Abuse

How Serious a Problem Is Drug Abuse?
How Should the War on Drugs Be Waged?
Should Drug Testing Be Used in the Workplace?
How Should Prescription Drugs Be Regulated?
How Can Drug Abuse Be Reduced?

Euthanasia

Is Euthanasia Ethical?
What Policy Should Guide Euthanasia?
What Criteria Should Influence Decisions?
Who Should Make the Euthanasia Decision?
Is Infant Euthanasia Ethical?

Genetic Engineering

Is Genetic Engineering Beneficial?
Can Genetic Engineering Improve Health?
Does Genetic Engineering Improve Agriculture?
Is Genetic Engineering Adequately Regulated?
Will Genetic Engineering Lead to a Biological Arms
    Race?

The Health Crisis

Are Health Care Costs Too High?
How Can Health Be Improved?

Suicide

Is Suicide an Individual Right?
Should Physicians Assist Terminally Ill Patients in
    Suicide?
What Are the Causes of Teen Suicide?
How Can Suicide Be Prevented?

SEXUALITY

Homosexuality

What Causes Homosexuality?
Should Society Encourage Increased Acceptance of
    Homosexuality?

Can Homosexuals Change Their Sexual Orientation?
Should Society Legally Sanction Gay Relationships?

Male/Female Roles

Have Women's Roles Changed for the Better?
How Does Work Affect the Family?

Sexual Values

Have Sexual Values Changed in America?
Is Pornography Harmful?
How Should Society Treat Homosexuality?
Is Sex Education Beneficial?

Teenage Sexuality

What Kind of Sex Education Is Appropriate for
 Teenagers?

SOCIAL ISSUES

Abortion

When Does Life Begin?
Should Abortion Remain a Personal Choice?
Is Abortion Immoral?
Can Abortion Be Justified?
Should Abortion Remain Legal?

America's Children

What Education Policies Would Help Children?
How Can Children Be Protected from Abuse?
What Government Policies Would Help America's Poor
 Children?
How Can the Health of America's Children Be
 Improved?
Are Working Parents Harming America's Children?

America's Cities

Why Are America's Cities in Decline?
How Can Urban Homelessness Be Reduced?
How Can Urban Conditions Be Improved?
How Can Urban Crime Be Reduced?
What Measures Would Improve Urban Housing?

America's Future

Is America in Decline?
What Is America's Economic Future?

Is America Falling Behind in Technology?
How Can American Education Be Improved?
What Lies Ahead for America?

Animal Rights

Do Animals Have Rights?
Is Animal Experimentation Justified?
Should Animals Be Used for Food?
Does Wildlife Need to Be Protected?
How Can the Animal Rights Movement Improve Animal
 Welfare?

Child Abuse

Is Child Abuse a Serious Problem?
What Causes Child Abuse?
How Widespread Is Child Sexual Abuse?
How Should the Legal System Respond to Child Abuse?
How Can Child Abuse Be Reduced?

Culture Wars

What Cultural Influence Should the United States
 Perpetuate?
Are Diverse Traditions Fairly Represented in American
 Education?
Is American Culture Decadent?
Should Government Enforce Cultural Values?

Education in America

How Can Public Education Be Improved?
How Can the Teaching Profession Be Improved?
Should Education for Minority Students Emphasize
 Ethnicity?
What Role Should Religion Play in Public Education?

The Elderly

How Does Society View the Elderly?
Are the Elderly Poor?
Is Social Security Necessary for the Elderly?
How Should Society Meet the Elderly's Health Care
 Needs?

The Family in America

What Is the Status of the Family?
How Does Divorce Affect the Family?
How Are Two-Career Parents Affecting the Family?

The Homeless

Is Homelessness a Serious Problem?
What Are the Causes of Homelessness?
Should the Government Help the Homeless?
Can Housing Policies Reduce Homelessness?

The Mass Media

Is Advertising Harmful to Society?

Poverty

What Are the Causes of Poverty?
Can Government Efforts Alleviate Poverty?
Why Does an American Underclass Exist?
Is Poverty a Serious Problem in the United States?
Why Does Poverty Disproportionately Affect Certain
    Groups?

Racism in America

How Serious Is the Problem of Racism in America?
Is Racism Responsible for Minority Poverty?
Does Affirmative Action Alleviate Discrimination?
Should Minorities Emphasize Their Ethnicity?
How Can Racism Be Stopped?

Social Justice

Is the United States a Just Nation?
Does America's Economy Promote Social Justice?
Does the United States Provide Equal Opportunities for
    Minorities?
What Policies Would Promote Social Justice for
    Women?
What Policies Can Promote Social Justice?

War on Drugs

Is the War on Drugs Necessary?
Can the United States Stop International Drug Cartels?

VALUES AND RELIGION

American Values

What Are America's Social Values?
What Are America's Economic Values?
What Are America's Religious Values?
What Does America Need?

Constructing a Life Philosophy

How Do Others Make Moral Decisions?
What Is Life's Meaning?
How Do Religions Give Life Meaning?
How Should One Live?

Paranormal Phenomena

Do Paranormal Phenomena Exist?
Are UFOs Real?
Does ESP Exist?
Can the Future Be Predicted?
Can Humans Interact with the Spirit World?

Religion in America

Is America a Religious Society?
Should Religious Values Guide Public Policy?
Does Religious Discrimination Exist in America?
What Is the Future of Religion in America?

Science and Religion

How Did Life Originate?
Great Historical Debates on Science and Religion

Notes

Chapter 1

1. The research literature about how self-esteem relates to personal success has become a virtual torrent since about 1970. If you are interested, start with a self-help book by Mathew McKay and Patrick Fanning, *Self-Esteem* (Oakland, Calif.: New Harbinger Publications, 1987). Then see Jeremiah Abrams, ed., *Reclaiming the Inner Child* (Los Angeles, Calif.: Jeremy P. Tarchen, 1990).

2. For a good overview and synthesis of research that supports this assertion, see Andrew King, *Power and Communication* (Prospect Heights, Ill.: Waveland Press, 1987). See also Hubert M. Blalock, Jr., *Power and Conflict: Toward a General Theory* (Newbury Park, Calif.: Sage Publications, 1989), especially chapters 2 and 3. For a classic work, and still the most complete, see Henry Mintzberg, *Power in and around Organizations* (Englewood Cliffs, N.J.: Prentice-Hall, 1983).

3. Virginia Silver, Personal letter, 5 November 1989. Printed by permission.

4. See Mintzberg, *Power in and around Organizations*, chapter 8, and King, *Power and Communication*, chapter 5.

5. Richard L. Johannesen, *Ethics in Communication*, 3d ed. (Prospect Heights, Ill.: Waveland Press, 1990), chapter 3.

6. See Robert A. Cocetti, "Understanding the Oral Mind: Implications for Speech Education" (Paper presented at the Annual Meeting of the Central States Communication Association, (Chicago, 11–14 April 1991).

Chapter 2

1. Communication apprehension, speech anxiety, stage fright, and the like have all been studied and researched a great deal. For a good source, see Michael R. Neer and W. Faye Kirchner, "Reducing Public Speaking Anxiety," in *Basic Communication Course Annual*, vol. 3, ed. Lawrence W. Hugenberg (Boston, Mass.: American Press, 1991).

Chapter 3

1. Abraham Maslow, *Motivation and Personality* (New York: Harper & Row, 1954).

2. Herman Ebbinghaus did basic research on the problem of forgetting in 1885. Scholars have been studying it ever since. Most recently, interest in this phenomenon has been tied to the so-called "split-brain research." See Herman Ebbinghaus, *Über das Gedachtnis: Üntersuchungen der experimentelen Psychologie* (Leipzig: Dancker & Humbolt, 1885).

3. Andrew Wolvin and Carolyn Gwynn Coakley, *Listening*, 4th ed. (Dubuque, Iowa: Brown & Benchmark Publishers, 1992), 226.

Chapter 4

1. Jess Stein, ed., *The Random House College Dictionary*, rev. ed. (New York: Random House, 1980), 641.

2. Deborah Tannen, *You Just Don't Understand: Women and Men in Conversation* (New York: William Morrow, 1990).

3. Some speeches seek changes in belief or attitude that cannot be observed. Nevertheless, for at least seventy-five years, speech teachers have encouraged their students to seek an action goal. In 1919, Charles H. Woolbert listed the possible action goals: observe, perceive clearly, think this over, accept a doctrine, renew faith, strengthen determination, change your mind, reverse your attitude, prepare for future action, ally yourself, take an active part, subscribe, join, buy, pay, vote, go, give, and die if need be. See Charles H. Woolbert, "Persuasion: Principles and Methods," *Quarterly Journal of Speech Education*, March 1919, 105.

Chapter 5

1. *Columbia Daily Tribune,* 21 February 1993, p. 3D.

Chapter 6

1. S. Morris Engel, *With Good Reason: An Introduction to Informal Fallacies* (New York: St. Martin's Press, 1986), 9.

2. *World Almanac and Book of Facts, 1993* (New York: World Almanac, 1993), 307.

3. Engel, *With Good Reason,* 27.

4. Engel, *With Good Reason,* 156.

5. Aristotle, *Rhetoric,* trans. W. Rhys Roberts (New York: Modern Library, 1954).

6. Daniel J. O'Keefe, *Persuasion: Theory and Research* (Newbury Park, Calif.: Sage, 1990), 167.

7. *World Almanac,* 675.

8. Sam Walton with John Huey, *Sam Walton: Made in America* (New York: Doubleday, 1992), 30.

9. Aristotle, *Rhetoric.*

10. Adapted from Charles U. Larson, *Persuasion: Reception and Responsibility,* 6th ed. (Belmont, Calif.: Wadsworth, 1992), 59–60.

11. J. W. Patterson and David Zarefsky, *Contemporary Debate* (Boston: Houghton Mifflin, 1983), 9.

12. Sharon D. Moshavi, "Advertisers Wary of New Syndicated Programing," *Broadcasting & Cable,* 15 March 1993, 55.

13. "Government Reform," *United We Stand America,* March 1993, 1.

14. Miranda Rich, "Reducing Your Car Insurance," *Smart Money,* April 1993, 61.

15. "Global Entertainment," *Wall Street Journal,* 26 March 1993, R6.

16. *World Almanac,* 169.

17. *World Almanac,* 389.

18. Adapted from "On the Road," *Smart Money,* February 1993, 59.

19. Paul Harvey, Jr., ed., *Paul Harvey's For What It's Worth,* (New York: Bantam Books, 1992), 98. (Reprinted with permission.)

20. David Donald, "The Folklore Lincoln," in *Myth and the American Experience,* ed. Nicholas Cords and Patrick Gerster (Beverly Hills, Calif.: Glencoe Press, 1973), 45.

21. Kathleen Hall Jamieson, *Dirty Politics* (New York: Oxford University Press, 1992), 46.

Chapter 7

1. Gerald L. Wilson and H. Lloyd Goodall, Jr., *Interviewing in Context* (New York: McGraw-Hill, 1991), 17.

2. Jerry Pournelle and Michael Banks, *Pournelle's PC Communications Bible: The Ultimate Guide to Productivity with a Modem* (Redmond, WA: Microsoft Press, 1992).

3. This figure for the basic service was "good" in April 1993. If you want more current information, call them at (800) 848–8990.

Chapter 8

1. See Margaret Fitch Hauser, "Message Structure, Inference Making, and Recall," in *Communication Yearbook 8,* ed. Robert N. Bostrom and Bruce Westley (Beverly Hills, Calif.: Sage, 1984), 278–92; Tom D. Daniels and R. Samuel Mehrley, "The Effects of Message Introduction, Message Structure, and Verbal Organizing Ability upon Learning of Message Information," *Human Communication Research* 7 (1981): 147–60.

2. Alan H. Monroe, *Principles and Types of Speech* (Chicago: Scott, Foresman, 1935).

Chapter 9

1. Alan H. Monroe, *Principles and Types of Speech* (Chicago: Scott, Foresman, 1935).

2. The most commonly used styles are: APA style, specified by the American Psychological Association; Chicago style, specified by the Chicago University Press; JACS style, prescribed by the *Journal of the American Chemical Society;* MLA style, prescribed by the Modern Language Association; MLA note style, used when references appear in footnotes or endnotes; and Science style, specified by *Science Magazine.*

Chapter 10

1. Mario M. Cuomo, *Diaries of Mario M. Cuomo: The Campaign for Governor* (New York: Random House, 1984), 432.

2. Jay Leno, "Laughing at Our Fears," *USA Weekend,* March 22–24, 1991.

3. Paul Harvey, Jr., ed., *Paul Harvey's for What It's Worth* (New York: Bantam Books, 1991), 87.

4. Chuck Sheperd, "News of the Weird," *Columbia Daily Tribune,* 2 April 1992, 10A.

5. Charles Goldsmith, "Look See! Anyone Do Read This And It Will Make You Laughable," *Wall Street Journal.* 19 November 1992, B1.

6. *London Times,* 14 March 1991.

7. Paul Dickson, *The Official Explanations* (New York: Delacorte Press, 1980), 141.

Chapter 11

1. See Paul Watzlawick, *How Real is Real? Confusion, Disinformation, Communication—An Anecdotal Introduction to Communications Theory* (New York: Random House/Vantage Books, 1976) for a fascinating look at this question.

2. An enormous literature exists that describes the central role language plays in human communication. If you wish to read further, two good sources are: Charles R. Berger and James J. Bradac, *Language and Social Knowledge: Uncertainty in Interpersonal Relations* (London: Edward Arnold Limited, 1982), and Howard Giles and Nikolas Coupland, *Language: Contexts and Consequences* (Pacific Grove, Calif.: Brooks/Cole, 1991).

3. Dean E. Hewes and Sally Planalp, "The Individual's Place in Communication Science," in *Handbook of Communication Science,* ed. C. R. Berger and S. H. Chaffee (Newbury Park, Calif.: Sage, 1987), 146–83. See, also, Sally Planalp and Dean E. Hewes, "A Cognitive Approach to Communication Theory" in *Communication Yearbook 5,* ed. M. Burgoon (New Brunswick, N.J.: Transaction, 1982), 49–78.

4. Charles E. Osgood, "The Nature and Measurement of Meaning," *Psychological Bulletin, Vol* 49 (1952): 197–237. See, also, Charles E. Osgood, "An Exploration of Semantic Space," in *The Science of Human Communication,* ed. Wilber Schramm (New York: Basic Books, 1963), 28–40. The fullest description of this classic work is Charles F. Osgood, George Suci, and Percy Tannenbaum, The Measurement of Meaning (Urbana, Ill.: University of Illinois Press, 1957).

5. Lillian R. Jackson, "Made My Day," *Mobile Register,* 25 April 1985, 4A.

Chapter 12

1. International Communications Industries Association, 3150 Sprint Street, Fairfax, VA 22031.

2. To illustrate the magnitude of OHP usage, see *Multimedia Source Guide, a Supplement to THE (Technological Horizons in Education) Journal, 1992–93* (Tustin, Calif.: THE Journal).

3. A liquid crystal display (LCD) is a screen for showing text and graphics based on a technology called "liquid crystal," in which very small currents change the reflectiveness or transparency of a screen. The advantages of LCD are very low power consumption and low price of mass production. Disadvantages include a narrow viewing angle, slow response, invisibility in the dark (unless the display is backlighted), and poor color reproduction.

Chapter 13

1. See, for example, J. A. Graham and S. Heywood, "The Effects of the Elimination of Hand Gestures and of Verbal Codability on Speech Performance," *European Journal of Social Psychology* 5 (1976): 189–95; W. G. Woodall and J. P. Folger, "Encoding Specificity and Nonverbal Cue Content: An Expansion of Episodic Memory Research," *Communication Monographs* 48 (1981): 39–53.

2. Mark L. Knapp and Judith A. Hall, *Nonverbal Communication in Human Interaction,* 3d ed. (Orlando, Fla.: Harcourt Brace Jovanovich, 1992), 199, 203.

Chapter 14

1. These two terms are used synonymously here. We pay attention to the things that interest us. We get interested in the things that draw our attention. For practical purposes, then, attention and interest are the same.

Chapter 15

1. Kathleen Kelley Reardon, *Persuasion in Practice* (Newbury Park, Calif.: Sage, 1991), 3.

2. Hugh Rank, "Teaching about Public Persuasion," in *Teaching about Doublespeak,* ed. Daniel Dieterich (Urbana, Ill.: National Council of Teachers of English, 1976), chapter 1.

3. See Charles U. Larson, *Persuasion: Reception and Responsibility,* 7th ed. (Belmont, Calif.: Wadsworth, 1995) for a comprehensive and lively discussion of these and other aspects of persuasion.

4. Tony Schwartz, *The Responsive Chord* (Garden City, N.Y.: Anchor Press/Doubleday, 1973); Tony Schwartz, *Media: The Second God* (New York: Random House, 1981).

5. Ward Gardner, *The Shattered Mind* (New York: Vintage Press, 1975); J. P. Henry and P. M. Stevens, *Stress, Health and the Social Environment* (New York: Springer-Verlag, 1977); Melvin Konner, *The Tangled Wing: Biological Constraints on the Human Spirit* (New York: Holt, Rinehart and Winston, 1982); Barbara Lex, "Neurobiology of Ritual Trance," in *The Spectrum of Ritual,* eds. E d'aquili et al. (New York: Columbia University Press, 1979), 117–51.

6. R. A. Jones and J. W. Brehm, "Persuasiveness of One- and Two-Sided Communications as a Function of Awareness: There Are Two Sides," *Journal of Experimental Social Psychology* 6 (1970): 47–56.

7. Daniel J. O'Keefe, *Persuasion: Theory and Research* (Newbury Park, Calif.: Sage, 1990), 166.

8. O'Keefe, *Persuasion,* 160.

9. Vance Packard, *The Hidden Persuaders* (New York: Pocket Books, 1964).

10. O'Keefe, *Persuasion,* 166.

11. F. J. Boster and P. Mongeau, "Fear-Arousing Persuasive Messages," in *Communication Yearbook 8,* ed. Robert N. Bostrom (Beverly Hills, Calif.: Sage, 1984), 330–75.

Glossary

A

Abstract
Brief summary of the contents of an essay or article.

Acceptance speech
Brief talk that thanks a presenter and the organization that publicly gives a gift or award.

Accessibility
Criterion for making a two-dimensional visual aid. The requirement that an audience must be able to understand the visual material.

Activity dimension of language
Movement dimension of connotation that relates to a word's dynamics—to what a word does.

Affect
Combination of physical experience plus the language we use, either consciously or unconsciously, to describe the physical experience.

After-dinner speech
Brief speech following a meal. Usually designed to entertain.

Analogy
The explanation of a particular subject by pointing out its similarities to another subject, usually one that is better known or more easily understood.

Antonym
Word that has the opposite meaning of another word.

Argument
Reasoning in which one or more statements are offered as support for some other statement.

Argument from analogy
Argument that what is true of something known is also true of something unknown compared to it.

Argument from cause
Argument based on the assumption that something happened because of an earlier event.

Argument from sign
Assertion that certain characteristic features or symptoms suggest a state of affairs.

Artistic proofs
Three kinds of appeals described by Aristotle: ethos, logos, and pathos.

Attending
The process of selecting and focusing on certain stimuli.

Audience
Collection of unique human beings, each of whom has particular characteristics and makes his or her own decisions.

Audience analysis
Process by which a speaker tries to identify and understand the major characteristics of a group of listeners.

Audience setting
The speaking environment.

B

Because test
Technique for identifying that all of your main ideas support your thesis and all your subpoints support the main ideas.

Belief
A statement that something _is_.

Body of the speech
Major portion of a speech, in which are developed the main ideas and arguments.

Brainstorming
Timed procedure for generating a large number of ideas quickly.

C

Card catalog
Holdings catalog printed on cards and stored in a cabinet of file drawers.

Causal order organizational pattern
Pattern for organizing ideas that relies on either cause-to-effect or effect-to-cause reasoning.

Cause-to-effect arguments
Reasoning pattern that argues that a particular effect was caused by a prior event or preexisting condition.

Cause-to-effect organizational pattern
Organizational pattern that flows from the causal fabric to its effect. Pattern for organizing ideas that

help an audience to see that one set of conditions is responsible for a result.

Channels
Means of transmission. The vehicles through which messages are sent.

Code
Systems of signs and symbols used to transmit messages.

Cognition
The act, power, or faculty of apprehending, knowing, or perceiving.

Cognitive process
Mechanism used to handle information in the mind.

Commencement speech
Address given during graduation ceremonies.

Communication apprehension
Specific type of anxiety characterized by distress, worry, nervousness, and fear in a communication situation.

Communication power
Degree of potency and memorability of visual or other symbolic material.

Comparison and contrast
Form of support in which two things are compared for some informative or persuasive purpose. May be used to develop a definition.

Conclusion
The end of a speech that focuses listeners' thoughts and feelings on the speech's main ideas. The unifying element for the ideas or tone you develop in the speech body.

Concretion
Act or process of using language to make something real, tangible, or particular.

Connotation
The affective value or meaning of a word.

Context
Physical, social, psychological, and temporal environment in which communication takes place.

Credibility
Degree to which a receiver believes in something. In speech, the listener's belief in the speaker or the speech content.

D

Decoder/receiver
Another term for *listener*.

Decoding
Process of drawing information from communication channels and then interpreting it.

Deductive argument
Opposite of inductive argument. Works from a general conclusion to specific instances that establish the conclusion.

Definition and explanation
Type of evidence that can be used to support arguments. Is particularly useful for clarifying ideas.

Definition speech
Informative speech in which you try to teach listeners what something means.

Delivery
Verbal and nonverbal expression of ideas, feelings, and impressions.

Demographic analysis
Facet of audience analysis in which the vital characteristics of a population are used to make educated predictions about responses of listeners in that population.

Demographic profile
The description of an audience that results from analysis of statistical data that describe audience members' vital and social features, such as age, gender, and socioeconomic status.

Demonstration speech
Informative speech that describes, explains, or illustrates by examples, specimens, experiments, and the like.

Denotation
Meanings of language that are shared by a speech community. The so-called "dictionary definitions" of words. The features of a word that native speakers of a language usually accept.

Derived beliefs
From Milton Rokeach's model, beliefs that are formed (derived) from other beliefs.

Derived interest
Interest that flows from associating a new subject with something listeners already care about.

Descriptive speech
Informative speech that uses concrete and colorful language to picture some object, phenomenon, or event.

Differentiation
Method of definition that involves separating or distinguishing something from other members of its class.

Direct-access audience analysis
Gathering information about an audience by asking questions, listening to discussions, conducting interviews, and asking audience members to fill out questionnaires.

Direct quotation
Exact replication of an original written or spoken statement.

E

Effect-to-cause argument
Reasoning pattern that stresses the consequence first and the causes second.

Effect-to-cause organizational pattern
Pattern for organizing ideas in which you deal with the consequence first and then proceed to the cause.

Emotional context
The social and psychological portion of the communication event.

Empathy
Identification with another person, coupled with a response the other person experiences as appropriate.

Enthymeme
A syllogism based on probability that is usually truncated.

Ethics
Study of moral value, of rightness or wrongness.

Ethos
Perception of a person's character. A listener's perception that a speaker is honest, knowledgeable, and of good will and intention. One of Aristotle's artistic proofs, referring to the kind of person you are, including your education, honesty, reputation, and skill in delivering a speech.

Etymology
Study of the history of change in the meaning of a word.

Eulogy
Speech of praise.

Evaluative dimension of language
Overall positive and negative determinations stimulated by a word.

Evidence
Facts, objects, or testimony used as proof to support knowledge claims or to draw inferences.

Evoked recall appeals
Needs that drive humans to believe or act.

Evoked recall model of persuasion
Model of the persuasion process in which the appeals are designed to stimulate identification by appealing to a set of memories, experiences, attitudes, and opinions that people already hold.

Exaggeration
Blowing things up beyond the limits of truth. To increase or enlarge abnormally.

Example
An instance used as an illustration. A form of support that uses one of a number of things to show characteristics of the whole number.

Expert testimony
Definition to come.

Explanation speech
Informative speech that describes or interprets how something works, how to evaluate it, or why it occurred.

Explicit conclusion
Message strategy characterized by telling listeners precisely what you want them to do or believe.

Extemporaneous delivery
Style of delivery that uses careful preparation but minimal notes—not memorized or read from a manuscript.

F

Fear appeal
Message strategy that involves using evidence or argument designed to induce fear in listeners as a means of motivating them to some decision or action.

Feedback
Messages that listeners send to speakers that allow people to correct and control errors in how they understand and interpret each other.

G

General purpose
The broad intention that motivates the speech: to inform, to persuade, or to entertain.

H

Holdings catalog
Index of the materials in a given library or collection.

I

Identification
The process of responding to incoming messages with attitudes, values, and beliefs we hold now, or once held, in situations or contexts similar to those presented by the persuader.

Immediate audiences
Those groups that a speaker can contact directly for audience analysis.

Impromptu delivery
Style of delivery that involves speaking without preparation or advance planning.

Index
Any alphabetized listing of names or topics.

Inductive argument
Argument that works from a series of individual cases to a conclusion. Opposite of deductive argument.

Inferential audience analysis
Method of audience analysis when you do not have direct access to

listeners. Involves educated guesses based on what is already known about the audience.

Inflection
Short-term change up or down in pitch of voice.

Information-gathering interview
Interview designed to acquire information about a subject, process, or person.

Information structure
How information is organized in your cognitive system.

Informative speech
Speech in which the speaker seeks to add to the general storehouse of knowledge that an audience already possesses. *To inform* is one of the three general purposes of speech. Others are *to entertain* and *to persuade*.

Intensification/downplay model of persuasion
Model of the persuasion process in which persuaders play up their own strong points and their opponents' weak points, or play down their own weak points and their opponents' strong points.

Internal summaries
Mini-summary used at the conclusion of a major point to remind listeners of the ideas just discussed.

Introduction
The beginning part of a speech, the purpose of which is to get attention, state the speaker's thesis, and prepare listeners for what is coming.

Introductory speech
Brief speech in which you present another speaker to an audience.

Irony
Saying one thing but meaning the opposite.

K

Keynote speech
Speech given at the beginning of social or business functions that sets the tone of the meeting.

L

Language
System of signs and symbols used by a speech community to share meaning and experience.

Lay testimony
Definition to come.

Logical completeness
Feature of a message that exists to the extent that listeners think a statement is warranted by the evidence and arguments presented.

Logos
One of Aristotle's artistic proofs, consisting of appeals to the rational intellect.

M

Manuscript delivery
Style of delivery in which the speaker reads from a written document.

Matters of taste
In Milton Rokeach's hierarchy of beliefs, peripheral, arbitrary, and rather insignificant beliefs about the world.

Memorized delivery
Style of delivery in which the speaker commits the speech to memory and delivers a word-for-word progression of ideas.

Messages
Information a speaker sends through channels.

Metaphor
Implied comparison between two unlike things that is used to show some unexpected likeness between the two.

Model
Physical representation of an object or process.

Motivated sequence
A pattern for organizing persuasive speeches that consists of five steps: attention, need, satisfaction, visualization, and action.

N

Noise
Anything that interferes with the fidelity of message exchange between two people.

O

Observable behavior
Any behavior that you can see or hear.

Occasion
The context component in the communication process model. The particular time, place, and purpose of a speaking event.

One-point after-dinner speech
An after-dinner speech that states a central thought and then wraps stories, anecdotes, quotations, and the like around that central thought.

Online catalog
Holdings catalog stored as a computer database.

Operational definition
Defining something by describing what it does.

Oral style
Style of language usage characterized by short words, repetition of ideas, use of contractions. Spoken language as opposed to written language.

Organizational links
Transitions, signposts, and internal summaries that tie a speech together and keep listeners headed in the right direction.

Outline
Framework for structuring ideas that consists of written phrases or sentences that show the structure or arrangement and relationships among ideas.

Overhead projector (OHP)
A machine that projects light through a transparent image onto a screen.

P

Paraphrase
Summary in your own words of an original written or spoken statement.

Parody
Imitation for the sake of humor.

Pathos
One of Aristotle's artistic proofs, consisting of appeals to the passion or to the will. The so-called emotional proofs.

Persuasion
The activity of attempting to change the behavior of at least one person through symbolic interaction.

Persuasive speech
Speech that seeks to change attitudes, beliefs, or behaviors. *To persuade* is one of the three general purposes of speech. Others are *to inform* and *to entertain*.

Physical context
Physical and temporal surroundings in which a communication event occurs.

Physical noise
Noise that occurs in the channels—for example, static in the telephone line.

Pitch
Level of the vocal sound at which your voice mechanism works with maximum efficiency and ease.

Plagiarism
Taking another person's ideas or language and claiming them as your own.

Planning outline
Working document in which you develop the structure and relationships among your ideas and the evidence that supports them.

Pleasantry speech
After-dinner speech that gently pokes fun but is not satirical.

Potency dimension of language
Power dimension of connotation involving such judgments as *strong-weak, hard-soft* and *heavy-light*.

Presentation speech
Brief talk given when a person receives an award or gift in public.

Primitive beliefs
From Milton Rokeach's model, central beliefs that we have about ourselves, about existence, and about our personal identities.

Problem-to-solution organizational pattern
Pattern for organizing ideas that identifies a difficulty and then presents a solution that solves the elements of the problem.

Process model
Model of communication showing dynamic, interactive process.

Proofs
Logical and emotional supporting materials. Statements made to support arguments.

Proposition
Assertion of a speaker's position on some subject.

Proposition of fact
Argument, knowledge claim, statement that something *is*.

Proposition of policy
Argument that some action should be taken.

Proposition of value
Argument, statement that attempts to establish that something is good, bad, valuable, worthless, right, or wrong, and so on.

Psychological noise
Noise that occurs inside people.

R

Rate
Speed at which a person speaks.

Receiver
Person or thing that takes in messages.

Relational meaning
The part of language, usually nonverbal, that tells people how speakers define their relationships with listeners.

Remembering
Bringing back to consciousness those things that are stored in the mind.

Reversal of values
Technique in which a speaker makes something significant out of the trivial, or something trivial out of the important.

Roast
Special occasion that involves numerous speakers who aim exaggerated insults at a person as a means of having fun and of honoring the person.

Rule of thirds
Principle of design for two-dimensional visual aids in which the visual plane is divided into thirds, both horizontally and vertically, and the major design components are located at the intersections of the dividing lines.

S

Satire
Use of ridicule to expose, denounce, or deride.

Selective perception
Choosing to focus on one idea or one person to the exclusion of others.

Sensing
Receiving stimuli through the senses.

Shared beliefs
From Milton Rokeach's model, beliefs that result from experiences we are willing to discuss with others.

Shared meaning
Similar perceptions of a word, person, place, or thing in the minds of speaker and listener.

Signposts
Unit of speech that announces or points to some new or important idea.

Simplicity
In reference to a visual aid, plain, immediately obvious, easy to see from a distance, unmistakable even to a person who is not familiar with the subject.

Source
Location of an idea or the originator of a message.

Source-encoder
Another word for *speaker*.

Space pattern of organization
Pattern for organizing ideas that relies on geographical relationships.

Speaking outline
Brief outline of the topics you will discuss. Provides you with notes to refer to as you speak.

Specific purpose
The particular action goal of a speech. What you want from the audience as a result of your speech.

Speech community
All of those who use the same language system.

Speech to entertain
A speech that seeks to hold audience attention agreeably, to divert, or amuse. *To entertain* is one of the three general purposes of speech. Others are *to inform* and *to persuade*.

Statistics
Numerical facts or data used as supporting materials.

Supporting material
Any verbal or nonverbal material used to develop credibility or to win acceptance for a speech.

Syllogism
Formal argument having three parts: a general case, a specific case, and a conclusion.

Synonym
A word that has the same, or nearly the same, meaning as another word.

T

Testimony
A statement used as proof or evidence in support of an argument or knowledge claim. Involves using the words of another person as evidence for an argument.

Thesis statement
Statement in the introduction of a speech that gives the most important point or purpose of the speech.

Time pattern of organization
Pattern for organizing ideas based on some sequence of events.

Topical divisions organizational pattern
Pattern for organizing ideas according to the natural divisions of a topic.

Transitions
Verbal bridges designed to move listeners from consideration of one idea to consideration of the next.

U

Understanding
Interpreting and evaluating what comes in through our senses.

V

Value
Statement containing the words *should* or *ought*, or such subjective terms as *good, beautiful, correct*, or *important*.

Visual aid
Any object, photograph, chart, graph, sketch, or lettered poster that supports a speech or the speaker.

Volume
With regard to voice, loudness.

W

Welcoming speech
Speech of greeting. Usually given when groups visit organizations and local businesses.

Written style
Style of language usage that may be fairly complex, rather abstract, and formal in expression. Written language as opposed to spoken language.

Index

Abstractions, visual aids to help, 262–65
Abstracts (in library), 154
Absurdities, in humor, 226–27
Acceptance speeches, 365
Accessibility, in two-dimensional visual aids, 273, 276
Action
  call for, in conclusions, 232
  interest generated by, 324
  language of, 251–52
  in motivation sequence organization, 184, 186–87
Activity dimension, of semantic space, 244
Address to the Democratic National Convention, July 1992 (Glaser), 390–92
Affect, language and, 242
After-dinner speeches, 371–73, 374
Analogy
  supporting ideas with, 114–15
  use of, 252–54
Antonyms, in definition speeches, 317
Anxiety
  communication apprehension and, 22, 26–27
  management of, 27, 258, 304, 419–28
    fear of the audience, 421
    fear of being inadequate, 422
    fear of being in the spotlight, 420
    fear of inadequate ideas, 421
    fear of performing badly, 420–21
    fear of the unknown, 422
  in public speaking, 15
  value of, 422
Appeals
  to courage, 118
  evoked recall model of persuasion, 336
    creative outlets, 352
    ego gratification, 351–52
    emotional security, 349–51
    fear, 349–50
    immortality, 354
    love objects, 352–53
    reassurance of worth, 351
    roots, 353–54
    sense of power, 353

    to fear, 117–18, 349–50
    to pity, concern, 118
    to pride, 118
Appearance. *See* Personal appearance
Argument, 110–11
  from analogy, 114–15
  from cause, 113–14
  deductive argument, 112
  inductive argument, 111
  one vs. two-sided, 347–48
  from sign, 113
  See also Persuasive speaking
Aristotle, 4, 115, 117, 119, 335
Artistic proofs
  ethos, 115–16, 335, 350
  logos, 119–20, 335
  pathos, 117–18, 335, 350
Ashe, Arthur, 315
Association of derived interest, to maintain interest, 325
Attending
  developing skill of, 50
  explanation of, 45
  problems with, 54–55
    interfering attitudes, needs, 47–48
    low message intensity, 48
    poor attention habits, 47
    selective perception, 46–47
  visual aids to help, 261–62
Attention
  methods to gain, 323–25
  in motivation sequence organization, 182, 184
Attitudes, as listening problem, 47–48, 55
Audience
  class as, 96
  eye contact with, 303–4
  fear of, 421
  focusing on desired listener behavior of, 32
  goal statement, adapting to, 74–80
  identification with, 343
  as individuals, 91
  perceptions, expectations of, 94–95, 316, 319
  problems of

    with attending, 54–55
    with comprehension, 55
    with empathy, 47
    with remembering, 56–57
    with sensing, 53–54
  self-interests of, 325, 326
  topic selection and, 69–70
  visual aids to help, 261–62
  See also Audience analysis; Informative speaking, guidelines for
Audience analysis, 90–91
  comprehension and, 55–56
  demographic profile and, 90–91, 100–105
  fear management and, 425
  methods of
    direct-access method, 96–98
    inferential method, 99
  reason for, 54, 57
  setting and, 91–93, 95
  topic selection and, 69–70

Because test, in outline, 200–201
Behavior
  contextual environment and, 10–11
  observable vs. unobservable, 75, 77
  in speech delivery, 304
  See also Appeals, evoked recall model of persuasion; Persuasive speaking
Beliefs
  appealing to, 340
  changing beliefs, 338–39
  persuasive speaking and, 336
  types of
    derived beliefs, 337, 338
    matters of taste, 337, 338
    primitive beliefs, 337
    shared beliefs, 337–38
Bibliographies
  development of working, 158–61
  note-taking for, 154–55
  periodical indexes and, 154
Body
  anxiety management and, 423–25
  in planning outlines, 194, 197

of speech, 32–33
Books in Print, 147
Brainstorming, 66–67
Burning Money: The Waste of Your Tax Dollars
(Grace), 399–405

Card catalog, of library, 147, 148–51
Cause, supporting ideas with, 113–14
Cause-to-effect
arguments in, 114
speech organization by, 179–80
CD-ROM library collections, 146–47
Ceremonial speeches. *See* Special occasion
speeches
Chamber of commerce, information source of,
137–38
Channels, 12
Chesterton, G. K., 231
Chronological speech organization, 174–76
of acceptance speeches, 365
of eulogy speeches, 364
in planning outline, 202, 203
of presentation speeches, 363
of welcoming speeches, 37
Circulation department, of library, 143
Cizik, Robert, *Will California be Invited to the
Next Industrial Revolution?,*
392–99
Clarity, of language, 247, 250–51
Clinton, Bill, 15, 51, 56
Closing, in conclusion, 198
Cognition, language and, 241–42
Cole, Johnetta, 221
Combinations, of methods in conclusions,
233
Commencement Speech (Jordan), 413–17
Commencement speeches, 367–68, 413–17
Communication
apprehension. *See* Anxiety
library resources on, 144
public speaking as, 13–15
visual aids and, 273
See also Language; Messages
Communication process
channels in, 12
context in, 10–11
decoder/receiver in, 12
feedback in, 13
messages in, 12
noise in, 13
source/encoder in, 12
See also Language

Comparison, contrast
informative speeches and, 317
of language, 252–54
Comprehension
explanation of, 45
misunderstandings and, 48–49
problems with, 55–56
Computer database, network services, 139–41
Concentration. *See* Attending
Conclusions
explicit vs. implicit, 348–49
in planning outlines, 198
purpose of, 230
of speech, 33
strategies for
call for action, 232
combinations, 233
introduction reference, 232
quotation, 231
summary, 230–31
Concretion, interest generated by, 323
Conflict, interest generated by, 324
Confusion, in humor, 227–28
Congressional Record, 137
Connotation, 243–44
Context, 10–11, 44
Courageous appeals, 118
Creative outlet, persuasive speaking appeal to,
352
Credibility
attending to message and, 55, 57
explanation of, 115
informative speaking and, 326–27
in public speaking, 7–8
of speaker
audience identification with, 343
knowledge of, 341–42
physical appearance of, 342–43
trust in, 341
of supporting material, 158–59, 160
Cuomo, Mario, 225, 246
*Speech to the Police Conference of the State of
New York,* 410–13
Current Index to Journals in Education, 147

Database services, networks, 139–41
library searching department of, 146–47
Decoder/receiver, 12
See also Audience
Decoding, 12
Deductive argument, 112
Definitions
as informative speeches, 316–18
to support ideas, 124

Delivery
choosing a method of, 292–93
extemporaneous delivery, 295–96, 297
impromptu delivery, 296–97
manuscript delivery, 293
memorized delivery, 294, 295
definition of, 292
nonverbal messages in
eye contact, 303–4
gestures, 301–3
personal appearance, behavior, 304
practicing, 305–6
speaking voice in, 298–99
pitch, 300–301
rate, 299–300
volume, 301
written vs. oral style of, 297–98
Demographic profile of audience, 90–91
age, 100, 102
educational level, 102
gender, 100
occupation, 104–5
organizational memberships, 105
political affiliation, 102
race, 104
religious affiliation, 104
socioeconomic status, 102–3
Demonstrative speeches
chronological organization and, 176
as informative speeches, 318–19
Denotation, 243
Derived beliefs, 337, 338
Derived interest, to maintain interest, 325
Descriptive informative speeches, 320–21
Dewey decimal system, 150
Diaries of Mario Cuomo (Cuomo), 246
Differentiation, definition speeches and,
317–18
Direct quotations, 122–23, 156, 157–58
Direct-access audience analysis method,
96–98
*Directory of Video, Computer & Audio-Visual
Products,* 273
Dirksen, Everett, 362
Downplay model, of persuasion, 335–36

Educational Resources Information Center
(ERIC), 147
Effect-to-cause
arguments of, 113
in planning outline, 203, 206
speech organization, 180–81
Ego gratification, persuasive speaking appeal
to, 351–52

Nonverbal messages, 12, 13
Noonan, Peggy, 171
Notes
    extemporaneous speech delivery and,
        295–96
    fear management by, 425
    listening aids, 52
    meta-notes, 295, 296
    note-taking, how to, 154–58

Objectivity, of listener, 51–52
Observable behavior, 75
Offensive language, 246–47
Olson, Amy, untitled speech, 384–86
One-point after-dinner speech, 372
Online catalog, of library, 152–53
Openings
    in outlines, 195
    See also Introductions
Operational definition, 318
Opposing Viewpoints Series (Greenhaven
        Press), 437–42
Oral, vs. written delivery, 297–98
Organization
    of body of speech
        cause-to-effect, 179–80
        chronological, 174–76, 202–3
        effect-to-cause, 180–81, 206
        motivated sequence, 182–87, 206,
            207–8
        problem-to-solution, 176–78, 203, 205
        spatial relationship, 176, 177, 203, 204
        topical division, 181–82, 183
    characteristics of
        clarity, simplicity, 172
        limited main points, 172–73
        local development, 173–74
    of first speech
        idea organization, 32–36
        idea support, 36
        practice, 37
        purpose selection, 30–32
        sample speech, 38–39
        topic selection, 28–30
    importance of, 170–72
    links of
        internal summaries, 188
        signposts, 188
        transitions, 187–88
    visual aids and, 261, 266–68
Osgood, Charles, 244
Our Attitude About Women (Shaw), 405–9
Outlines
    planning of
        label parts, 195–98

standard format, 199
general purpose, specific purpose,
    thesis statement, 200
thesis support, 200–201
follow organization pattern, 201–8
complete, simple entries, 208
organizational links, 209, 210
supporting evidence, documentation,
    209–10
checklist, examples, 210, 211, 212–14
speaking outline, 210
    follow planning outline, 211, 212–14
    be brief, 211
    a working tool, 211
    example of, 214, 215–16
types of, 194–95
Overhead projectors, 273, 276, 285–86

Paraphrases
    in note-taking, 156, 157–58
    speaker feedback and, 51
    in testimony, 122
Parody, in humor, 373
Pathos, 117–18, 335, 350
Periodicals, serials department, of library, 146
Perot, Ross, 121
Personal appearance
    speaker credibility and, 116, 342–43
    in speech delivery, 304
Personal testimony, 122–23
Persuasive speaking, 24–25, 73–74, 340–41
    ethical considerations of, 334–35
    vs. informative speeches, 312, 314, 315–16
    message credibility and, 344–45
        propositions of fact, 345–46
        propositions of policy, 346–47
        propositions of value, 346
    message strategies and
        evoked recall appeals, 349–54
        explicit vs. implicit conclusions,
            348–49
        motivated sequence organization,
            182–87, 355
        one vs. two-sided arguments, 347–48
    organization techniques for
        causal order, 180
        motivated sequence, 182–87, 355
        problem-to-solution, 177
    samples of, 384–86, 387–90, 392–99
    speaker credibility and
        audience identification, 343
        knowledge, 341–42
        physical appearance, 342–43
        trust, 341
    theories of

Aristotle and artistic proofs, 335
    beliefs and values, 336–40
    evoked recall model of, 336
    intensification/downplay model of,
        335–36
Physical context, 11
Physical noise, 13
Pitch, of voice, 300–301
Piteous appeals, 118
Plagiarism, 136, 156, 157–58
Planalp, Sally, 241
Planning outlines
    labelling of parts, 195–98
    standard outline format, 199
    general purpose, specific purpose, thesis
        statement, 200
    thesis statement support, 200–201
    organizational pattern of, 201–8
    complete, simple entries, 208
    organizational links, 209
    supporting evidence, documentation,
        209–10
    checklist, example of, 210, 211, 212–14
Plato, 4
Playful ridicule, in humor, 227, 228
Pleasantry speech, 372
Policy, propositions of, 346–47
Potency dimension, of semantic space, 244
Powell, Colin, 33
Power appeals, of persuasive speaking, 353
Practice
    extemporaneous speech delivery and,
        295–96
    fear management by, 426
    importance of, 37
    of manuscript delivery, 293
    of speech delivery, 305–6
    with visual aids, 271, 305
Praise and tribute speeches
    acceptance speeches, 365
    eulogies, 365–67
    introductory speeches, 360–63
    presentation speeches, 363–64
Presentation speeches, 363–64
Preview, in planning outlines, 195
Pride appeals, 119
Primary source materials, 160
Primitive beliefs, 337
Problem-solving index, 429–36
Problem-to-solution speech organization,
        176–78
    in planning outline, 203, 205
Procrastination, 158
Proofs, argument supported by, 110–11